The Home Plot

The University of Massachusetts Press

Amherst

The Home Plot

Women, Writing & Domestic Ritual

Ann Romines

Copyright © 1992 by
The University of Massachusetts Press
All rights reserved
Printed in the United States of America
LC 91–34053
ISBN 0–87023–783–7 (cloth); 794–2 (pbk.)
Designed by Edith Kearney
Set in Adobe Caslon by Keystone Typesetting, Inc.
Printed and bound by Thomson-Shore, Inc.

Library of Congress Cataloging-in-Publication Data

Romines, Ann, 1942–
    The home plot : women, writing, and domestic ritual / Ann Romines.
        p.   cm.
    Includes bibliographical references and index.
    ISBN 0–87023–783–7
    1. Domestic fiction, American—History and criticism.   2. American
fiction—Women authors—History and criticism.   3. Women and
literature—United States.   4. Home economics in literature.
5. Ritual in literature.   6. Home in literature.   I. Title.
PS374.D57R66   1992
810.9'355—dc20   91–34053
                                                                               CIP
British Library Cataloguing in Publication data are available.
Acknowledgments for permission to reprint material under copyright
appear on the last printed page of this book.

This book is for all the housekeepers of my family,

with admiration and with love

I stack the dishes and I wring the dish-cloth,

like mum says; I clean the sink with Rinso,
not too much; I shake the mat before the door,

I water the geranium—is this being good?
mum says, "good girl": I do this not for mum

or anyone: I do it for myself; if I go on,
I make a sort of track, I can't say what,

it's pebbles and hard stones, it's something in a story,
I can't say where it goes—

H.D.
from "Sagesse"

Acknowledgments

*F*OR AS LONG as I can remember, my women relatives and friends have been helping me to understand what a rich, complicated, and artful story housekeeping has been for American women. This book began with my own domestic education, at the hands of my mother and grandmothers. Since then, many others have become parts of the process of thinking and writing *The Home Plot*. A very different version of this project was my doctoral dissertation. George McCandlish served as my first dissertation director; it was he who informed me, to my amazement, that the phenomenon I was finding in women's texts had a name: "domestic ritual." After Professor McCandlish's death, my friend and colleague Robert Ganz provided direction and encouragement.

At George Washington University, my past and present English Department chairpersons, Christopher Sten and Judith Plotz, have been especially helpful as readers and advocates, as have Faye Moskowitz and my fellow housework scholar, Phyllis Palmer of the Department of Women's Studies. I am grateful to the George Washington University Committee on Research and to the Department of English for supporting funds and to the Gelman Library for an undomestic space in which to write. My work has also been sparked and challenged by the responses of my graduate and undergraduate students of the past ten years.

Colleagues at other universities have heard, read, and responded usefully to portions of this book in earlier versions. I am especially endebted to Ann Fisher-Wirth, Josephine Donovan, and Susan Rosowski. At the University of Massachusetts Press, my manuscript found sympathetic and scrupulous editors in Pam Wilkinson and Bruce Wilcox.

Special thanks to my parents, Ruth Rogers Romines and Elmer Romines, for their many years of loving support, and to my astute and generous sister, Marilyn Romines, who patiently listened to this book taking shape over many long dinners at her table and mine. I also owe much to the advice and enthusiasm of my dear friend Astere Claeyssens, who helped me submit this book for publication during the last weeks of his life. To everyone who is mentioned here and to many who are not, my thanks and praise.

31 August 1991

Contents

The Home Plot

Introduction

"CIRCE" is Eudora Welty's luminous retelling of Odysseus' encounter with the island witch. In this 1955 version, *she* is the center of attention. This Circe is both charmed and repelled by the mortal men, "beautiful strangers" with grimy fingernails, who flock to the promises of her well-run household and eagerly drink the savory, swine-making broth.

Odysseus, himself protected with his own magic, will not be transformed by domestic sorcery. To learn his secret and gain his love, Circe must undo her magic and retransform his men (improving them, while she is about it). But, although the men enjoy her housekeeping and love for a year, hostess and guests never really understand each other. For Circe cannot live by the time of mortal men. She thinks, "There exists a mortal mystery that, if I knew where it was, I could crush like an island grape. Only frailty, it seems, can divine it—and I was not endowed with that property. They live by frailty! By the moment" (*CS* 533). When the men seize the moment and leave Circe, they bear her gifts, "all unappreciated, unappraised" (536). She is pregnant with a son, who will not stay with her, and can speak her mind only to her fixed, female companions in the sky: Cassiopeia and the rising moon. Circe longs for grief, like that the men expressed and expelled for a dead companion. But grief must be a stranger to her imperishable, perfectly ordered life. "Grief," says Circe, "couldn't hear me—grief that cannot be round or plain or solid-bright or running on its track. . . . I cannot find the dusty mouth of grief" (537). And there Eudora Welty leaves her Circe, weighted with feelings she can never put behind her: a goddess who is defined, exalted, and imprisoned by her powers of housekeeping.

"Circe" is like nothing else Eudora Welty has written. And yet, with its palpable tension between the wanderer and the housebound witch, it is also her quintessential story. With its classical Greek antecedents, it is hardly an American regional story of the sort for which Welty is (perhaps erroneously) known. And yet again, it is in many ways a quintessential story by an American woman, toward which much of the previous hundred years' worth of fiction by American women had been pointing. This fiction is animated by the question that Circe, in her frustration at Odysseus' departure, directs to the "old moon, still at work" in the sky above her. "Why keep it up, old woman?" she whispers.

Circe asserts her will through domestic ritual: a perfected round of household tasks, as regulated as the moon's appearances. With these rituals—with her magical wand that is also a broom—she has conquered time (she is immortal) and the vicissitudes of mortal men, who come and go unpredictably. But she can also love one of those men and will bear his child. While that boy is still in her womb, she *knows* "the story" of his future, but she cannot intercede in its unwinding. Circe is both powerful and powerless. Both qualities are rooted in her gender. And both make her uncomfortable and uncontainable within a male story, bearing a man's name; what Welty tells of her, we could not have learned from Homer's *Odyssey*.[1]

One of Circe's quarrels with Odysseus is about storytelling. Welty has written her tale in Circe's voice; it counterpoints Odysseus' version of the Circe episode, also related in the first person, at a king's feast. Odysseus' tale is a self-contained incident in an ordered narration. Welty's story begins in mid-act, with a patriarchal interruption of female housekeeping: "Needle in air, I stopped what I was making" (531). It ends with Odysseus' departure and Circe's acknowledgment of her pregnancy; for Circe, everything is still both foreordained and up in the air. Odysseus' boastful tales have bored her: "I had heard it all before. . . . I didn't want his story" (533). Circe knows the ends to all the stories, which keep repeating, just as her wine making is repeated, year after year, again and again: "I must consider how my time is endless, how I shall need wine endlessly" (535). In her privileged immortality, she lacks the clear satisfactions of closure. Although her foresight is infallible, she mourns, in her oracular language: "foreknowledge is not the same as the last word" (536). Circe's lament at the story's end is terrible—all the more so because there is nowhere (not even death) where she can go. She is "tied to [her] island, as Cassiopeia must be to the sticks and stars of her chair" (537).

In the language of nineteenth-century American housekeepers, Circe has "faculty"; she is a housekeeper of exemplary competence. According to Harriet Beecher Stowe, faculty is high art, and she describes it in wittily ponderous biblical cadences:

To her who has faculty nothing shall be impossible. She shall scrub floors, wash, wring, bake, brew, and yet her hands shall be small and white; she shall have no perceptible income, yet always be handsomely dressed; she shall not have a servant in her house,—with a dairy to manage, hired men to feed, a boarder or two to care for, unheard-of pickling and preserving to do,—and yet you commonly see her every afternoon sitting at her parlor-window behind the lilacs, cool and easy, hemming muslin cap-strings, or reading the last new book. She who hath faculty is never in a hurry, never behind-hand. She can always step over to distressed Mrs. Smith, whose jelly won't come,—and stop to show Mrs. Jones how she makes her pickles so green,—and be ready to watch with poor old Mrs. Simpkins, who is down with the rheumatism. (*Minister's Wooing* 2–3)

This description both valorizes faculty and gently mocks the ideal of domestic competence it embodies. The very idea of one woman who can effortlessly manage (servantless) the endless round of cooking, cleaning, sewing, "pickling and preserving," and other self-perpetuating chores is both familiar and preposterous. And note that this woman has a literary context as well. She supports literary production, "reading the last new book."

The ideal of such a capacious female life, centered in housekeeping, was an insistent presence in nineteenth-century American culture. Thus all Stowe's New England novels contain portraits of women who have achieved faculty. In *The Pearl of Orr's Island*, for instance, the memorable seamstress, Aunt Roxy Toothacre, is an exemplum: brisk, capable, with superior powers of foreknowledge. When she must be first to diagnose the tuberculosis of the novel's young heroine, she is uncharacteristically unstrung, and the girl is "confounded. This implacably withered, sensible, dry woman, beneficently impassive in sickness and sorrow, weeping!—it was awful, as if one of the Fates had laid down her fatal distaff to weep" (342). The distaff, which often still denotes both "women's work" and the whole female sex, is a practical appurtenance of a domestic task, a rod used in spinning thread. It is also an emblem of the Fates, who control human destiny by spinning, measuring, and cutting the thread of life. Thus at the most basic level of metaphor, the practice of housekeeping is problematically associated with women's work and with female power. Stowe's telling passage implies the difficulties of this complex heritage; even for the most sympathetic observer, it is almost impossible to perceive a woman such as Aunt Roxy as a distinguishable individual. The culture has a vested interest in the suppression of Aunt Roxy's personality. Her blank impassivity is *"beneficent,"* and any lapse into personal expression is a story too "awful" to read. Although she inhabits a realistic novel, Roxy Toothacre shares Circe's predicament. By her prowess at domestic ritual, each woman has made herself a goddess, exalted for extraordinary powers and placed above the realm of commonplace human feeling. But at the same time she is a woman—capable of pregnancy, frustration, tears—stingingly aware of the finite limits of her faculty.

Aunt Roxy's and Circe's ways of life are very much like the "housework as ritual enactment" described by theologian Kathryn Allen Rabuzzi. Such housekeeping, weighted with significance for the woman who performs it, "makes the individual a player in a scene far older and larger than her individual self. No longer does she participate in profane historical time; instead, she is participating in mythic time" (96). The time that this woman spends at her household tasks is "typically characterized by amorphousness or circularity or both, and a content frequently imperceptible within the structures of dominant male culture" (146). Such activity, opposed to sequential, progressive time, becomes the kind of ritual that most cultures have found necessary to their survival. In such rites, according to Mircea Eliade, the ideal life of the tribe's ancestors is "ritually made present." The ritual maintains a continuity of belief and knowledge from one generation to the next (88, passim).

For most men and some women, such ritual occasions, important as they may be, are infrequent high holy days, like the festivals Eliade discusses, on which accustomed work may be set aside. But for many traditional women, who have invested much of their selfhood in housekeeping, ritual is domestic, and it is a constant of everyday life. Their ritualized housekeeping may be a sacramental activity that provides essential cultural continuity. But it is also their daily work. Yet this work commands low wages, or none, and is often considered trivial or demeaning, "shitwork." What these women do is essential yet impermanent and invisible; according to Stowe, one sign of an accomplished housekeeper is that she is never caught in the act. The culture consumes the products of the housekeeper's labor; the fact and the process of that labor are suppressed.

The new book to which Stowe's woman of faculty directs her attention may well be a book by a woman; female authorship burgeoned in nineteenth-century America. And it may be—like one of Stowe's own books—a text that takes domestic ritual as its shape and/or subject. Judith Fetterley writes of fiction by nineteenth-century American women that "much of the *pleasure* that the contemporary reader takes in this literature stems from its ratification of women as significant subjects" (*Provisions* 8). But if a woman writer takes on women's lives as "significant subjects," and especially if she has chosen to write of traditional women who have been deeply involved with housework, she is beset by special problems. One problem is that, as

Rabuzzi says, the quest-pattern that has dominated Western literature "may not be formally appropriate to express traditional female experience" (153). So we see such feats of adaptation as in "Circe," where Welty remakes an episode from the *Odyssey* in order to find a voice for Circe and a shape for her tale. If we look again at *The Pearl of Orr's Island* (1861), we see that Stowe is, in some ways, still writing what Nancy K. Miller has called "the heroine's text," which dominated novels about women in the eighteenth century. Such a text, assuming that a woman's life has a single (often sexual) "determining event," is characterized by "linear continuity" and a "persistent sense of sexual consequence" (ix–x). But Stowe has begun to reshape that text to accommodate a heroine, Mara Lincoln, for whom spiritual experience is at least as important as sexual-romantic experience. The novel's plot sets the brief trajectory of Mara's maturing, courtship, and death against the regular, ritualized occurrences of domestic life and the women of faculty, such as Aunt Roxy, who survive.

Josephine Donovan proposes, and I agree, that the post–1850 women local colorists, of whom Stowe was one of the first and best, launched a form of "woman-identified realism" that was the "first women's literary tradition which moved beyond a negative critique of reified male-identified customs and attitudes" (*New England* 3). Such a project was very different from that of the earlier "sentimental" women novelists who dominated the popular-fiction market in mid-century America. Nina Baym describes the prototypical plot of a "sentimental" novel as the story of a heroine "who is deprived of the supports she had rightly or wrongly depended on to sustain her throughout life and is faced with the necessity of winning her own way in the world" (*Woman's Fiction* 11). These heroines are domestic outsiders by definition; often, too, they are at odds with the rituals of the households in which they find themselves. Sentimental novels typically culminate with their female protagonists' marriages but leave undepicted their subsequent incorporation into the realm of housekeeping. Such climactic marriages, according to Baym, "are symbols of successful accomplishment of the required task and resolution of the basic problems raised in the story, which is in most primitive terms the story of the formation and assertion of a female ego" (12).

If we compare a prototypical sentimental novel, Susan Warner's *The Wide, Wide World*, with a male-centered novel also vastly popular with Americans in the 1850s, such as Charles Dickens's *David Copperfield*, we find that the differences between them have little to do with the dynamics of their plotting. Both are voluminously episodic; both have as their central subject the ego-formation of their protagonists from childhood to young adulthood. Both plots are facilitated by the dying of a mother. But if we compare two of the most striking, important, and experimental works of fiction published by Americans in the 1890s, forty years later—William Dean Howells's *A Hazard of New Fortunes* (1890) and Sarah Orne Jewett's *The Country of the Pointed Firs* (1896)—we find pronounced and typical differences in their *shaping*. Howells's voluminous book, with its polyglot urban setting, is aggressively undomestic; its central couple, based on Howells and his wife, have just moved from a settled house into an apartment in an unfamiliar city. They take meals in restaurants and spend time on the streets and streetcars of New York, observing. The unifying devices of the novel come from business or politics. Jewett's book is a fourth the size of Howells's; it is elliptical and concentrated where his is profuse. Its central consciousness is also an autobiographical figure, an unnamed writer. But she is placed against and drawn into the woman-made domestic life of a village where a smashed teacup or an afternoon's visit can have as much significance as the strike that centers Howells's novel. Jewett's reader is drawn into—and out of—these domestic rhythms, just as decisively as Howells's reader is forced to encounter urban and moral flux.

Like other readers, I have no doubts about calling *A Hazard of New Fortunes* a *novel;* surely it is one of the best examples of the "loose baggy monster" that nineteenth-century American literature has to offer. And the earlier sentimental fictions by American women, however otherwise denigrated, were clearly recognized as *novels* and labeled thus. But controversy continues about *The Country of the Pointed Firs:* is it short stories, sketches (autobiographical or not?), or, indeed, novel? Critics cannot agree. Jewett herself wrote equivocally of "the Pointed Firs papers" (Cary, "Jewett to Dresel" 45).

For when a writer turned to domestic life and its recurring rhythm as a primary subject, placing her central characters inside, not outside, this world, she found herself in a literary and psychic realm with few precedents and little terminology, a domestic realm that traditionally privileged privacy and unwritten texts. Until recently, a woman writing fiction about housekeeping was likely to find her choice of subject matter excused as a cautious, diversionary "politico-economic strategy," as Annis Pratt in 1971 imagined the motivation of Jewett and Mary Wilkins Freeman ("New Feminist Criticism" 874). Or she might find the domestic aspects of her work separated from the rest and labeled as relatively trivial, as in Joyce Carol Oates's 1969 description of Eudora Welty's fiction as a "bizarre combination of a seemingly boundless admiration for feminine nonsense—family life, food, relatives, conversations, eccentric old people—and a sharp, penetrating eye for the seams of the world, through which a murderous light shines" (54). Worst, she might find some of her deepest concerns and best work dismissed as boring, as in Ernest Earnest's 1974 characterization of Jewett's and Freeman's domestic fiction as "minor tragicomedies. . . . nice safe subjects" (261).

Feminist scholarship of the last twenty years, work in history, anthropology, sociology, psychology, and women's studies, as well as the literary "gynocritics" which is "concerned with *woman as writer . . .* producer of textual meaning" (Showalter, "Toward" 128), has begun to provide the tools we need to read women's writings about housekeeping not as safely minor diversions but as central, powerful, and potentially explosive documents of women's culture. This book is built on this important new tradition of scholarship. I argue that, about the time of the Civil War, perhaps influenced by the climate of American realism and by local color's new interest in the particularities of regional life, American women began to write about housekeeping in a new way, not as the unarticulated denouement of every female story but as subject and ongoing substance, in itself. I will argue that some of the best fiction by American women writers is dominated and shaped by the rhythms and stresses of domestic ritual, by the complex of domestic-literary concerns I have called the home plot. Books such as *The Country of the Pointed Firs,* Willa Cather's *Shadows on the Rock,* Eudora Welty's *Losing Battles,* and Mary Wilkins Freeman's *A New England Nun and Other Stories* have often seemed anomalies to critics who tried to fit them into various versions of "the" American tradition. But when one looks at them as works that probe a complex human activity by which many women have shaped their lives and within which they have discovered their powers, limits, restrictions, and connections as female and human creatures, the importance, daring, and necessity of such fiction become apparent—as does a tradition of the depiction of domestic ritual by American women writers.

Within that tradition, domestic ritual is not always celebrated. Welty's Circe, for example, is the islanded prisoner of her own faculty. The skills that give her immortal power are also malign; they make men swine. (Circe says, with the asperity of a confident housekeeper, "In the end, it takes phenomenal neatness of housekeeping to put it through the heads of men that they are swine" [531].) At their best, the writers discussed in this study are trying to shape a fiction that tells complex truths about the satisfactions *and* dangers that domestic ritual has meant in female lives. Despite the indifference or sometime hostility of a patriarchal literary establishment, they took housekeeping and the women who did it seriously, seriously enough to subject them to close interrogation. Again and again, they pose the question that Circe addressed to the archetypal moon: "Why keep it up, old woman?"

It was virtually impossible for a woman to come to thinking, feeling maturity in nineteenth- or early twentieth-century America without asking Circe's question. Encouraged by the cult of the home to idealize domestic life as the arena in which she wielded her influence and established her moral superiority, she was nevertheless expected to deal with the insistent realities of daily domestic labor, as cataloged by Susan Strasser in her history of American housework: "tainted water supplies, rancid food, soot and skin burns from open fires, and full chamber pots" (9). To create domestic order in such circumstances could be a task doomed to failure or despair, or it could be a source of deep gratification and self-esteem. Housekeeping manuals and magazines proliferated in nineteenth-century America and, according to Laura Shapiro, the women who consulted them were beset by a sense of "hurry, confusion, disorganization—a domestic chaos always just out of sight. This image of barely averted chaos did more than lend a moral urgency to the drama of housekeeping; it called for women to seize control of their surroundings, perhaps for the first time in their lives" (85). This call must have been especially compelling to a woman who had experienced a typical nineteenth-century girl's education in passivity, as described by historian Barbara Welter: "The major events of a girl's life were to be products of arrangement and fate, not of intellect and will, and she was expected to passively await them" (17).

A woman who achieved faculty and made effective ritual of her house-keeping was taking on godlike status, as she pushed back confusion daily, to create her own domestic sphere. Establishing an awareness of the ever-lurking threat of chaos, should a housekeeper let down her guard, seems to have been an essential part of a girl's education. For example, in a chapter of Louisa May Alcott's *Little Women* entitled "Experiments," Marmee leaves her recalcitrant adolescent daughters alone for a week, to exercise the housekeeping skills they are confident they possess. The results of their lackadaisical efforts and omissions are a topsy-turvy dinner table with salt in the sugar bowl, sour cream in the pitcher, "a very young lobster, some very old asparagus, and two boxes of acid strawberries" (17). This is a comic, if cautionary, version of domestic chaos, with a pathetic reminder of the irrevocable consequences of omissions in Beth's canary, found dead from neglect. The scene is replayed, with progressively graver implications, by Meg, the first of the girls to marry, as she tries to juggle jelly-making, unexpected dinner guests, household accounts, and, eventually, child care, without help from mother and sisters.

However crucial such matters might have been in American women's lives, nineteenth-century literature by men had given them almost no serious consideration. Housekeeping and female housekeepers are not entirely absent from these men's work. But they are likely to be approached as objects of humor and/or nostalgia (as in Irving and Cooper) or made into transcendental metaphor (as in *Walden*). Or women may be banished from the processes and authority of housekeeping, in order to make domestic ritual, transplanted outside the house, a safe medium of male communion, as in *Moby-Dick* and *The Adventures of Huckleberry Finn*. Huck is typical of many nineteenth-century males in his assumption that an ordered domestic life, like that in the Widow Douglas's house, means being under a woman's thumb. When he retreats to the all-male world of Pap's cabin, he experiences the absolute and terrifying chaos of an undomesticated life. Much of the utopian satisfaction of Huck's "free and easy" river interval with Jim has to do with the fact that it combines domestic felicity (good cooking and a flexible routine) with an inversion of Saint Petersburg order (Huck and Jim sleep by day, travel by night). Quintessentially boyish as he has been considered, Huck is very much interested in what it might be like to be a girl, as his disguises and investigations suggest. And his domestic experiments and rebellions would surely have been attractive to many nineteenth-century girls—Alcott's Jo March, for one. Yet neither Mark Twain nor any of the other canonical nineteenth-century male writers whom I have just mentioned indicates any interest in what domestic ritual might fully mean to a woman.

As Nina Baym has emphasized in an influential essay, "we never read American literature directly or freely, but always through the perspective allowed by theories" ("Melodramas" 63). The theories that have determined the American literary canon have taken little notice of texts by women that focus on women's domestic lives. For example, in a much-cited and promisingly titled 1979 study, *Home as Found: Authority and Genealogy in Nineteenth-Century American Literature*, Eric Sundquist considers issues that are relevant to domestic life and writers who explore it. He sees American Romantic writers (Cooper, Thoreau, Hawthorne, and Melville) as torn by a double desire to return to "those forms of practical and ceremonial behavior in which are dramatized the sacraments of a culture" *and* to "place in their stead others that are yet more potent and binding" (xi). This anxious tension between "keeping up" the sacramental forms of the past and inventing new ones informs the work of Alcott, Freeman, Cather, and Chopin, for examples, as well as the male subjects Sundquist has chosen. But the theoretical basis of Sundquist's study is Freudian, particularly Freud's account of the totem meal, a myth about male rivalry and desire. Women figure in the myth only as disputed property, objectified as they have been by many of the most popular and influential theories of American literature.

Most nineteenth-century American women lived within what Carroll Smith-Rosenberg has described in a famous and important essay, "The Female World of Love and Ritual." So it is not surprising that, when the "woman-identified realism" discussed by Donovan began to flourish, many writers turned to that world of "female support, intimacy and ritual" (Smith-Rosenberg 28) in which most American women had been reared and educated, for the substance and shape of their fiction. Yet this literature and tradition of domestic ritual has been so little acknowledged that Rabuzzi, for example, understandably assumes that it does not exist; she noted, in 1982, a "paucity of stories" about Hestia and housekeeping (95). Josephine Donovan, one of the most assiduous scholars and theorists of American women's writing in the second half of the nineteenth century, offered, in 1984, a more informed and imperative view: "We already have stories of Hestia, but we have yet to identify their formal patterns; we have yet to establish their poetics" ("Toward" 105). In this book, I have begun work on the project Donovan describes: a study of Hestia's tales and of the poetics of domestic ritual.

Domestic ritual offers a writer a wide range of possibilities. When I use the term in this study, I simply mean rituals performed in a house, a constructed shelter, which derive meaning from the protection and confinement a house can provide. They possess most of the qualities that, according to Orrin E. Klapp, are common to all rituals: regular recurrence, symbolic value, emotional meaning and (usually) a "dramatic" group-making quality (10–11). Thus a domestic ritual can be a large, important household occasion, such as a family reunion or a home wedding, or it can be an ordinary household task such as serving a meal or sewing a seam. All such rituals help to preserve the shelter.

The tendency of human-made shelters is to accede to nature and thus to decay and to change. Ritual opposes that tendency. "The whole idea of ritual," says Ernest Becker, is "the manmade forms of things prevailing over the natural order and taming it, transforming it, and making it safe" (238). Thus a woman who is committed to domestic ritual is participating in an enterprise connected with the continuity of a common culture and the triumph of human values over natural process. A housekeeper, whether

Circe or Aunt Roxy Toothacre, beats back chaos every day with her broom. Doing so, she is victor and victim—for in beating back nature, she is also subduing an aspect of herself. This may be an especially fraught situation for women, who have so often been encouraged to identify with nature. Sherry B. Ortner's early feminist essay, "Is Female to Male as Nature Is to Culture?", discusses some of the complications of this identification. Ortner, an anthropologist, defines ritual as "the purposive manipulation of given forms toward regulating and sustaining order." That order is evidence of culture's distinctive achievement: "its ability to transform—to 'socialize' and 'culturize'—nature." Ortner emphasizes that domestic life, controlled by women, is "one of culture's crucial agencies for the conversion of nature into culture" (10, 21).

At the same time, as critics have often noted,[2] American literature is full of images of women that signify nature. No one who reads Archibald MacLeish's poem "Landscape as a Nude," for example, is surprised to discover that the nude is female. Some of the most striking work of recent French theorists speculates that women's writing that truly reflected women's experience would celebrate the singular *natural* world of the female body, learning to inscribe it and to "defend their desire notably by their speech" (Irigaray, "This Sex" 106). But Ortner urges that women should become more fully identified with *culture*, especially "projects of creativity and transcendence." She apparently does not consider that domestic life offers full opportunities for such projects (28). Whether it does or not is an urgent question for the women writers in this study, who return again and again to questions of nature and culture, female body, female achievement, and female tradition as they have been inscribed and circumscribed by domestic ritual. By attending to these questions, framed in domestic language that may seem recessive and unimportant to readers who have not learned to read it, this book proposes to address central issues of American women's history and culture in the years since 1870.

In much male literature of the nineteenth century, domestic ritual is presented as a paradigm of triviality and limitation, the oppressively "sivilized" alternative to the wide expanses of the "territory." But several other studies of ritual also stress its liberating capacities to generate play, invention, and art, especially in the "liminal" stage.[3] Victor Turner argues for this view; to him,

> ritual is a transformative performance. . . . It is not, in essence, as is commonly supposed in Western culture, a prop for social conservatism whose symbols merely condense cherished cultural values, though it may, under certain condi-

tions, take on this role. Rather does it hold the generative source of culture and structure. (77)

Such views suggest that ritual is culture at its most volatile. Viewed thus, housekeeping is not only the unspoken, unvalued routine by which a patriarchal regime is maintained. It is also the center and vehicle of a culture invented by women, a complex and continuing process of female, domestic art.

The literary representation of domestic ritual allows writers to scrutinize their characters in the most social *and* the most inward and private of moments, which sometimes occur simultaneously. According to Monica Wilson, ritual is inherently social; through it, "the values of a group (as opposed to those of individuals) are revealed" (8). But when housekeeping, a series of daily acts often performed in solitude, becomes ritual, it may also be valued highly as an act of private meditation and as a medium of individual expression. The ideal of the masterful self-made person is one of the largest and most problematic legacies of nineteenth-century American democracy. And while domestic ritual may express group values, it has also often been the medium in which women worked to distinguish themselves as distinctively gifted housekeepers, as artists. Looking at the literature of domestic ritual, we see the idea of the individual, which American culture has privileged, being tested in the context of an ongoing traditional culture, that of housekeeping. The woman who chooses to *write* domestic ritual is also enacting these tests and conflicts in the medium of her own life; thus the figure of the domestic artist is a persistent, problematic presence in much of the fiction I will discuss.

Quilts, which were central texts of women's culture in the nineteenth century, illustrate this doubleness in domestic ritual. Highly valued as evidence of their makers' capacity to follow the rules of fine sewing, they were equally prized for originality of design and execution within the conventionalized limits of the craft. They were usually pieced together by one woman, often in private; the piecing was fitted into the rhythms of her everyday life. But quilting—the assembling and decorative stitching of the layers—was usually a communal project, center of an often-storied ritual occasion. The finished quilt, expressing the controlling vision of one woman given depth and elaboration by the stitches of many others, might be praised in its maker's name and treasured throughout and beyond her lifetime. But it was seldom signed; of the thousands of nineteenth-century quilts that survive, most must now be considered anonymous creations. Almost every quilt is a fabric of contingency and choice, individual will and communal support, representing many hours of repetitive work. As such, it is both a product and an emblem of domestic ritual.

In much of Western civilization, domestic ritual, like the quilts, has traditionally been the province of women. In their 1950 book, *Ritual in Family Living: A Contemporary Study*, James H. S. Bossard and Eleanor S. Boll claimed that domestic ritual still exerted undiminished power among Americans. In many of the prototypical families they interviewed, ritual was preserved by women. One young woman, Janet, speculated about her small children's future: "When he marries, Tommy will probably come into a new set of rituals (his wife's). . . . but Catherine must and will transmit them intact, to a daughter of her own. . . . Janet remarks that it would be a tragedy in her family not to have a daughter" (181–82). The powerful imperatives—"*must*" and "*will*"—that Janet uses to describe her young daughter's obligation to domestic ritual (and by implication her own obligation to prevent the "tragedy" of its disappearance) indicate the weight and pressure that the very subject of domestic ritual has exerted for many women.

My own conscious interest in the subject of this book began when, as a graduate student preparing for an exam, I happened upon Jewett's *The Country of the Pointed Firs*. The woman-centered world, with its subtle recurrences, its deepening discovery of a ritual rhythm, struck chords in my own life that had never been sounded before by my adult reading. I fumbled through my memory for analogues: The Alcott books I had read again and again as a child? My grandmother's turn-of-the-century photographs of family reunions and of herself, playing dolls with her sisters? Eudora Welty's *Losing Battles*, which I had found a dense and perplexing and yet unforgettable text?

My initial efforts to locate a tradition of writing about domestic ritual were fueled and extended by my teaching and by the burgeoning resources of feminist scholarship. For when other women readers first encountered the books I was writing about, their responses were as intense and uneasy as my own. Here were fictional women spilling soup, piecing quilts, frosting cakes, scrubbing floors, digging herbs, serving supper—engaged in these and other literarily unmentionable acts, acts that our mothers and grandmothers had almost certainly committed, acts that we might ourselves continue. Traditionally, housekeeping has been an essential rhythm of most women's lives. When readers encounter a literature that acknowledges that rhythm and its complex traditions and imperatives, they find themselves drawing from their own lives and histories in unaccustomed ways. No longer must women follow Judith Fetterley's admonition to be "resisting readers" of American literature, "consciously exorcising the male mind that has been implanted in us" (*Resisting Reader* xxii). In the work of Jewett, Welty, and others, they may encounter, perhaps for the first time, traditional female experience taken fully seriously as the material of American art.

Yet this art provokes other kinds of resistance. For in its very successes, it forces readers to experience stresses and cycles that have limited, silenced, and killed some women. In the American masterpieces of domestic ritual, a woman reader encounters herself, or a self she might well have been, staring back from a dangerous, complex female past which has become, by art, profoundly felt life. What to do with the newness, the rawness, and the haunting familiarity of that life—how to respond as woman, reader, critic— these have been the problems I have discovered, as an American woman writing this book.

I have chosen five writers: Sarah Orne Jewett, Mary Wilkins Freeman, Willa Cather, Eudora Welty, and (for briefer discussion) Harriet Beecher Stowe. Dozens of other writers might be included as well; I was tempted by Rose Terry Cooke, Katherine Anne Porter, Ellen Glasgow, Gertrude Stein, Jean Stafford, and Louisa May Alcott, to mention only a few, and I hope that this study will, by implication and extension, illuminate their careers as well. I finally chose these particular five writers because they all produced a substantial body of domestic fiction, throughout their careers, because they represent a suggestive sampling of American regions, and most important, because I consider them great American writers, who offer capacious and problematic oeuvres. I chose them, too, because of their canonical status, which seems to have been achieved almost *in spite of* their domestic concerns. This book proposes that these five writers are linchpins in another American canon, which both perpetuates and questions the ongoing practice of domestic culture.

In the United States, that culture has been associated with the largely white middle class. As historian Glenna Matthews has observed, "the ideology of domesticity arose in the middle class and may well have been one of the principal means by which the middle class assumed a self-conscious identity in the antebellum period. Much more research must be done before we know the extent to which working-class families subscribed to the ideology" (xvi). For African-American women, housekeeping has yet another distinctive history, bound up with the institution of slavery. So this book views housekeeping largely through the eyes of white American women of the middle class (including myself) who have been influenced by a coherent, continuing domestic tradition. However, the texts I discuss are often themselves aware of other domestic traditions and probe the connections among them—as in Willa Cather's immigrant hired girls in *My Ántonia* or the central alliance, in *Sapphira and the Slave Girl,* between the daughter of a slave housekeeper and the daughter of a plantation mistress. Although all these texts are touched by the myth of the self-sufficient, servantless housekeeper that Stowe presents in her description of faculty, relations between middle-class women and the servants who share their housekeeping surface frequently in this fiction, suggesting how housekeeping has served as both instrument and foe of oppressive institutions of class and caste.

The texts I discuss, although they honor women's culture with attention, are not the "often naively essentialist" "celebratory" art which "often revives traditional female crafts," as described by Janet Wolff (82).[4] Instead, looking at housekeeping, they all evoke on some level the largest and most troubling questions of human rights, especially in women's lives. Of such questions, Matthews writes, "Because the reconciliation of domesticity with justice for women requires so much imagination and intelligence, we still lack all the answers to how this may be accomplished. Indeed this reconciliation, which also involves the relationship between personal life and social obligations in a complex, technologically sophisticated society, will require the best efforts of our best brains. It is regrettable that there was a large gap in American history between the 1870s and the 1970s, when almost no one gave the issue any thought" (143).

This book aims to show that, between the 1870s and 1970s, a body of American women *were* thinking about these very questions, which were situated at the centers of their histories and lives. One important form their thought took was that of *writing domestic ritual.* I argue that the story of housekeeping, the "home plot" of domestic ritual, has generated forms and continuities very different from those of the patriarchal American canon and pushes readers to attend to texts that are not inscribed in conventionally literary language. Domestic language often seems invisible to those who have not learned to read it. Thus, for example, in the large body of criticism of Eudora Welty's work, there is no discussion, until this one, of Circe as a housekeeper, even though the domestic staples of soup, herbs, broom, kitchen, and pigsty signify powerfully throughout the story. Odysseus himself was the first to misread Circe's tale, ignoring her housekeeping. In other cases, people (usually women) who know housekeeping well may not grasp its importance on the page. At lunch recently, a woman friend carefully explained to me the kitchen procedures for making a complicated dessert. Then, when the talk turned to Willa Cather, whose fiction she reads with skill and enthusiasm, she said, "Oh, does Cather write about cooking? I never noticed. . . ." This woman, an elegant housekeeper, is a fine teacher and a trained reader with a graduate degree in literature. But no one has taught her to read the literature of domestic ritual, as Cather and others have inscribed it. Thus she devalues her own domestic life as too trivial to notice on the page.

In this book, I have tried to take notice. By attending to the lessons in domestic ritual offered by American women's fiction, I hope to show how domestic prerogatives shaped five important careers and an enduring, ambivalent tradition in women's art. For most of us, the home plot is still very close to home, as it is in the fiction I discuss in this book. Only if housekeeping is made visible and acknowledged as a telling, pervasive language can we ask the questions that are still at the heart of women's history and of many women's lives. Unless we acknowledge and study the pervasive powers of the home plot, we cannot fully know what it has meant to be a woman and an artist in America.

1

False Starts and False Endings

Stowe, Jewett, Realism, and Housekeeping

ONE OF THE most exciting and gratifying turns in recent criticism of nineteenth-century American fiction is the renewed interest in *Uncle Tom's Cabin* as a landmark in literary history and as a literary achievement. *Uncle Tom's Cabin* is probably the most comprehensively influential novel ever published in the United States; much of its power comes from its brilliant weighting of domestic metaphors. In this book, as Gillian Brown says, housekeeping becomes "a political mode." The very title of Brown's important 1984 essay, "Getting in the Kitchen with Dinah: Domestic Politics in *Uncle Tom's Cabin*," indicates the direction of a substantial body of criticism now regarding domestic life with the full seriousness that Stowe brought to it in her first novel. Clearly Dinah, cook and slave to Augustine Saint Clare, is doomed to kitchen chaos that resists her sporadic efforts to "clar up" because she is a slave and therefore unfree to govern her own considerable talents and will (Brown 504). Thus disciplined, humane housekeeping becomes a metaphor for the well-governed life, as lived by a woman who possesses and exercises free will.

But *Uncle Tom's Cabin* is not a novel of domestic ritual.[1] Instead, it chronicles the repeated *violation* of domestic ritual occasioned by slavery. Again and again, patriarchy interrupts housekeeping. For example, because of her husband's patriarchal control of property, Mrs. Shelby must profane her generous hospitality by extending it to the trader who buys Uncle Tom. Uncle Tom and Aunt Chloe's cabin is violated and abandoned because of slavery's disregard for the sanctity of family housekeeping. The book achieves its extraordinary coherence through fugal repetition of these domestic violations.

Later, when Stowe does write fiction dominated by the rhythms of functioning domestic life, that fiction is almost invariably set in a New England past—either that of her own childhood, beautifully elegized in *Poganuc People,* or that of an earlier historical past, such as that of *The Minister's Wooing,* in which Aaron Burr figures as a major character. Josephine Donovan sees Stowe's important contribution to "woman-identified realism" in such novels, with their powerful version of a "female Arcadia," sustained by "many original and strong women characters" (*New England* 56, 67). In this fiction, mostly written in mid-career, Stowe experimented with ways of shaping her novels that would more fully reflect the rhythms of housekeeping and would provide a more sustained antidote to patriarchal interruption. *The Minister's Wooing,* for example, by its title would seem to offer a doubly conventional plot of male and ecclesiastical volition and action. On one level, that is an accurate assumption; courtship is the conventional shaping device in this 1859 novel. But on another level, the title becomes ironic, given the importance of female response and of the powers of female faculty to direct, deflect, and counter male action.

Three years later, in *The Pearl of Orr's Island* (1862), Stowe chose a title that more clearly pointed to the centrality of a female character, Mara Lincoln (the pearl). In this novel, the parallel maturing of a girl and a boy orphan, in the same household, provides one important plot strand; just as important is a series of spotlighted domestic rituals and a constant commentary on them. Despite the intermittent incisiveness of this novel, probably the most interesting and ambitious of Stowe's New England books, there is something inchoate about it. The often-frenetic plotting seems antithetical to the delicate progress of Mara's spiritual awakening and to the sustaining recurrences of domestic ritual. Sarah Orne Jewett, in an often-quoted letter to Annie Fields,[2] commented on this quality:

> I have been reading the beginning of "The Pearl of Orr's Island" and finding it just as clear and perfectly original and strong as it seemed to me in my thirteenth or fourteenth year, when I read it first. I never shall forget the exquisite flavor and reality of delight that it gave me. . . . It is classical—historical—anything you like to say, if you can give it high praise enough. . . . Alas, that she couldn't finish it in the same noble key of simplicity and harmony; but a poor writer is at the mercy of much unconscious opposition. You must throw everything and everybody aside at times, but a woman made like Mrs. Stowe cannot bring herself to that cold selfishness of the moment for one work's sake, and the recompense for her loss is a divine touch here and there in an incomplete piece of work. (*Letters* 46–47)

The sense of "incompleteness" that Jewett regretted in her mentor's novel—for no American novel more obviously influenced *The Country of the*

Pointed Firs than *The Pearl of Orr's Island*—is shared by most readers. Drawing from her earlier successes, Stowe makes gestures toward conventional closure with a final funeral and a projected wedding, and she also tries to create a sense of cyclical continuance, as the "mantle" of domestic faculty passes from old Roxy Toothacre to young Sally Kittridge. Yet these gestures now seem both excessive and inappropriate. In this novel, Stowe attempted a more complex portrayal of women's culture than in *Uncle Tom's Cabin*. The vocabulary of plot and of moral-political exhortation, which served her so well in her first novel, hinders this new commitment.

In the 1870s, Stowe attempted to combat the "unconscious opposition" that may have beseiged her in *Pearl* by turning to other kinds of fiction, which would allow her to approach contemporary, urban domestic life for the first time. This is the work for which Stowe has been most universally chided; it has frequently been considered a regressive betrayal of the earlier, vigorous female characters and interests.[3] These novels of the early seventies, *My Wife and I* (1871) and *We and Our Neighbors* (1873), are set in modern New York.[4] The first novel is narrated by a young male New Englander, Harry Henderson, a fledgling journalist newly arrived in New York, who recounts his childhood, his education, and his courtship of a New York society belle, Eva Van Arsdel, whom he marries and with whom he settles into early, intense domestic bliss.

In some ways, it is difficult to imagine a novel more predictably conventional than this. For example, many of the chapter titles play with conventions of the male bildungsroman—such as "I Am Introduced into Society." But as the plot gets fully underway, and as female machinations and the domestic rituals that prepare for the wedding become increasingly important, we find Stowe chafing at the restrictions of her male protagonist and point of view.[5] Increasingly, she bombards us with letters, usually from and to women and sometimes chapter-long, giving access to Eva's and other points of view. One chapter is actually framed as a playlet; it begins, "SCENE.—Ida's study—Ida busy making notes from a book. Eva sitting by, embroidering." Harry is not a member of the cast and presumably not author of this playlet; it dramatizes a colloquy of sisters from which he would have been excluded. Eva's first speech begins, "Heigho! how stupid things are. I am tired of everything. I am tired of shopping—tired of parties—tired of New York—where the same thing keeps happening over and over. I wish I was a man. I'd just take my carpet-bag and go to Europe" (332).

Here Stowe gives voice to the complaint of a modern woman who is dissatisfied with social life and with the cycles of traditional women's culture, where things "happen over and over." Momentarily, Eva fantasizes a male life of linear destination, traveling fast and light. But, in the context of this book, what Eva, whose "femininity" is constantly emphasized, is missing is not really such a "man's" life. Nor is it an unconventional woman's life, like that of her sister Ida, a medical student. (Eva's deficiencies for such a life become apparent as the chapter proceeds and she tries to read her sister's Darwin.) This novel would have us believe that what Eva misses is a sustaining domestic rhythm, notably lacking in the gadabout round of shopping and parties that New York offers to a woman of her class and that she professes to disdain (although at the playlet's end her interest is piqued by the arrival of a fresh invitation). Subsequently, her father loses the family fortune and Eva marries fortuneless Harry Henderson, both apparent regressions that deny the imperative "rise" that was a central principle of male-dominated plot in popular nineteenth-century fiction. Now Eva cannot be validated by the patriarchal fortune of either father or husband. Instead, she bids for the female riches of the home plot and finds her sphere, a domestic stronghold in a modern city.

Another of this novel's formal distinctions is that it does not end with a wedding, as most of the domestic "sentimental" novels did.[6] Instead, Stowe adds a honeymoon visit to Harry's mother and returns her newlyweds to New York, where they purchase a modest house with Eva's female inheritance, a small legacy from her grandmother. Then Stowe stages the true climax of her novel, the setting up of Harry and Eva's housekeeping, with much detail of stove, drapery, and wallpaper. Only through such matters of housekeeping is Eva's selfhood confirmed and made concrete. Harry says, "Our house formed itself around my wife like the pearly shell around the nautilus. My home was Eva,—she the scheming, the busy, the creative, was the life, soul, and spirit of all that was there" (478). By this infatuation, expressible only when Eva has become a *housewife*, Harry is finally transformed into a feasible narrator for a domestic novel. The last chapter is a paean to the new little house, "The House-Warming," in which Harry has been instructed to observe every detail of household arrangement, from the placement of bibelots to the composition of the flower arrangements to the serving of "transcendental coffee" (437).

Thus, at the end of *My Wife and I* Stowe is finally in position to write a novel of domestic ritual. Her male narrator, under female tutelage, has learned to acknowledge the nuances and priorities of domestic language. The setting is a modern, urban present. The heroine, Eva, has ostensibly turned her back on fashionable New York "society" life, which Stowe sees as a violation of true domestic life, just as slavery was in *Uncle Tom's Cabin*. Courtship and the premarital formation of a female ego are behind her, as primary plot conventions, for Harry and Eva's marriage is accomplished, and Eva has apparently located her self, which is coexistent with her home. *My Wife and I* ends with the apotheosis of a house that is inseparable from a living female occupant, Eva; it is "an expression of [her] personality, a thing wrought out of her being" (478). Although her novel had grown to 499 pages, Stowe had only just located her subject. And she did not let it go. Instead she concluded the book with a postscript promising and advertising a sequel—her first.

That sequel, *We and Our Neighbors*, is the most interesting of Stowe's New York fictions. John Adams noted in 1974 that the structure of these later novels "has never been studied carefully . . . though they are not rewarding aesthetically, I suspect that they reflect the decades around 1870 rather well . . . for Mrs. Stowe was always observant and intelligent, and sometimes predictive" (53–54). *We and Our Neighbors* reflects many of the structural experiments associated with American realism; the American novel it most resembles is William Dean Howells's most ambitious and experimental novel, in many ways the prototypical text of critical realism: *A Hazard of New Fortunes*, published seventeen years later.

Like Howells, Stowe puts a marriage at the center of her book; husband is New York journalist and wife is housekeeper. Both books are voluminous and episodic. Stowe has abandoned the constraining convention of Harry as male narrator for a chatty, omniscient, and apparently female third person, quite as forthcoming as Howells's male narration could be with observations on a wide range of subjects—often to the apparent detriment of what Stowe called "the story."[7] But "in our modern days," she asserted, "it is not so much the story as the things it gives the author a chance to say" (*My Wife* xii). Here Stowe attempts to put "story" at the service of housekeeping, as it had served the abolitionist cause in *Uncle Tom's Cabin*. Thus *We and Our Neighbors* is a grab bag of contemporary women's issues. Entangled in its loose plot and addressed by its narration are alcoholism and its relation to marriage, women's suffrage, professions for women, church ritual, consumerism, prostitution, servant-employer relations, and other domestic matters. Stowe also includes hints on cookery, houseplants, and domestic hygiene, which suggest the book's kinship with contemporary housekeeping manuals.

Furthermore, *We and Our Neighbors* retains the epistolary chapters Stowe occasionally resorted to in *My Wife and I*. The most frequent correspondents are Eva and her mother-in-law, still a rural New Englander. Mrs. Henderson is Eva's connection (however tenuous) with the world of domestic faculty; her wedding gift to the couple is homespun linen, generations old, which evokes a skill, weaving, long linked to women's culture. For Harry and Eva, such handmade things are venerated icons, not objects for everyday use; they are "relics of [female] ascended saints" (453). Mrs. Henderson is the closest Eva can come to such a tradition of sustaining domestic work. She also presents Eva with the emblematic gift of a handwritten receipt book, passed down by generations of Henderson women, and Eva aspires to preserve the priorities of the old book by inscribing her own receipt book and private domestic text.

Although Harry is an aspiring writer, he cannot insert such an intimately evocative text in the print culture valorized by his work as journalist. As I have noted, by the end of *My Wife and I,* Harry's narration is much marked by his education in the domestic lore of his foremothers and wife. But, when Harry sees Eva's feats of wallpapering, he typically exclaims, "You are a witch. . . . You certainly can't paper walls." Eva retorts, "Can't I! Haven't I as many fingers as your mother? and she has done it time and again" (477). Here and elsewhere, while becoming increasingly attentive to domestic skill, Harry clearly sees it as the product of a female tradition (like witchcraft) that he cannot join, although it links his wife and mother. Thus the novel reinforces the doctrine of separate spheres, as indicated by the newlyweds' decisive distinctions between the world of Harry's office and that of their home. The fiction of Harry's narration establishes that a man can be schooled to produce a domestic text, yet the powerful gender dualism that the Hendersons observe simultaneously disqualifies Harry to write a book with the intimate authority of a *housekeeper's* book of housekeeping.

Thus it is not surprising that Harry's narrative voice is overridden in the sequel by an omnivorously female one. Stowe, who had recently collaborated with her sister Catharine Beecher on a new housekeeping manual,[8] tries in *We and Our Neighbors* to show how capacious a contemporary housekeeping text might be. Her heroine, Eva, makes no antiquarian efforts at spinning and weaving linen. Instead, her early domestic resolve, even before she has a house, is to make a book. Through her mother-in-law's initiation and continuing epistolary tutelage (and with occasional reinforcement from other traditional women, such as a Quaker neighbor), Eva is placed in the continuing, sustaining text of domestic life and begins to regard "herself as a past mistress." Assuming this traditional role, the bride claims a female past as well as a future; Harry notes that, as Eva begins her receipt book, "she began to be my little mother as well as my wife" (*My Wife* 454).

Eva also turns to her mother-in-law (whom she immediately addresses as "Mother") because she feels, as Stowe did, that, for women, domestic life is inextricably bound with family. Eva's most frequent visitors and confidantes are her younger sisters, whose mentor she becomes. The sisters' mother is domestically ineffectual; she always defers to *her* formidable elder sister, widowed "Aunt Maria" Wouvermans. Aunt Maria is as domestically ubiquitous as Aunt Roxy Toothacre; a cabbage leaf cannot fall in a cellar without her ferreting it out and warning that whole families have been killed by the "poisonous exhalations" of such waste (48). But unlike Aunt Roxy, who was essential to the life of her community, urban Aunt Maria is a woman without occupation—so she expends her enormous energies on petty bigotry, meddling, harassing servants, and shopping. When Eva wishes to divert her aunt from these malicious occupations, she asks her to judge two samples of commercially manufactured linen, suggesting that judicious purchasing is the only field left for her aunt's faculty. Only an extraordinary domestic occasion can make Aunt Maria useful, as she finally is, supervising the double wedding of Eva's sisters. "It opened a field to her that everyone was more than thankful to have her occupy" (444). But they cannot hope for double weddings to fill every day of Aunt Maria's life. Eva's neighbors, last survivors of an old New York family, also echo Stowe's Toothacre sisters. They too, like Aunt Maria, are ineffectual and without occupation. The sisters' housekeeping authority has been preempted by a proprietary black woman servant, and their affections are centered on a pampered pet dog. Through such characters, Stowe tries to investigate what has become of domestic ritual in contemporary New York.

In a confessional letter to Mrs. Henderson, Eva establishes the largeness of her own contemporary domestic ambitions: "Not that I am satisfied with a mere culinary or housekeeping excellence, or even an artistic and poetic skill in making home lovely; I do want a sense of something noble and sacred in life—something to satisfy a certain feeling of the heroic that always made me unhappy or disgusted with my aimless fashionable girl career" (37). As Eva sets up housekeeping—arranging furniture, training houseplants, cooking, and entertaining—the rhythm of the book is established and she learns to use her housekeeping as an instrument of her will. The marriages of Eva's sisters to her minister and her husband's colleague are "made" at Eva's hearth, and when the new couples plan to begin housekeeping in the neighborhood, Eva claims that her ambitions are fulfilled. She writes to her mother-in-law again: "Mother, does n't it seem as if our bright, cosy, happy, free-and-easy home was throwing out as many side-shoots as a lilac bush? . . . We shall be a guild of householders, who hold the same traditions, walk by the same rule and mind the same things. Won't it be lovely? . . . I think the making of bright, happy homes is the best way of helping on the world that has been discovered yet" (441–42).

Ann Douglas has commented acerbically on Eva's letters to Mrs. Henderson, suggesting that they are nothing more than self-congratulation, a way, through "the narcissistic process on which the book operates structurally as well as thematically, to re-reflect, to gloat" (305). The repetitions and the close identification of Eva and her house, which Douglas reads as narcissism, are in this novel a structural expression of housekeeping, a set of infinitely repetitive tasks which can induce an almost trancelike state of meditation ("re-reflection")[9] and which some housekeeping manuals, including those by Stowe and her sister, encouraged women to regard as artful expression. The mythos of housekeeping justified Eva's self-absorption, and in her letters she solicits necessary confirmation from an older woman, secure in her domestic status. The passages I have quoted thus reflect something beyond narcissism. Eva strains toward a spiritual fulfillment that she cannot quite even name and that she knows her neighborhood church cannot supply. What she wants is extraordinary, beyond excellence or patriarchally sanctioned "artistic and poetic skill"; it is "something noble and sacred" and "heroic." Her ambitions are as large as those of John Marcher in "The Beast in the Jungle," who also yearned for an archaically heroic plot of significance and immediacy which seemed to be precluded by the ordinary terms of daily life in a modern city. But, unlike Marcher, Eva does not await a coup of the extraordinary. Instead, she proposes to realize her ambitions through the most ordinary of female occupations—housekeeping. Eva is planted in the city that epitomized late nineteenth-century modernity, New York, and she speaks the brightly spurious language of "progress" that characterized postwar America, trying to devise a way "of helping on the world." Yet the language in which she describes her aspirations is anything but modern. The "guild of householders" is medieval, perhaps in the spirit of the contemporary revival of medievalism.[10] And the lilac bush image evokes the remotely rural New England of Stowe's "female Arcadia," where Eva will never live. It suggests that a traditional household can be transplanted to flourish in New York City.

Eva is Stowe's second character to bear that prototypical female name. Both are presented with admiration and affection, and both aspire to change the world radically. The first Eva, the saintly white child of *Uncle Tom's Cabin,* died hoping to reinstate a Christian Eden. The second Eva survives to preside over a snakeless Eden, with its center her own hospitable house. *We and Our Neighbors* embodies Stowe's search for a self-perpetuating domestic order in modern urban life, in a novel that takes advantage of the formal possibilities of the new American critical realism. Eva's "sacred," "heroic" text would bring the intimacy of the domestic receipt book to contemporary urban-literary life.

Henry James's comments in a review of *We and Our Neighbors* are telling. He complains of numerous characters "who never do anything but talk—and that chiefly about plumbing, carpet-laying, and other cognate topics. . . . the reader remains in an atmosphere of dense back-stairs detail which makes him feel as if he were reading an interminable file of tradesmen's bills. There is in particular a Mrs. Wouvermans . . . who pervades the volume like a keeper of an intelligence office, or a female canvasser for sewing machines" (211). James's disdainful comments indicate the odds stacked against *We and Our Neighbors* in the American literary establishment of the 1870s; they betray an innate hostility to housekeeping as a legitimate fictional subject. Even in the more sympathetic climate of current feminist scholarship, this novel has yet to find admiring readers. *We and Our Neighbors* is Stowe's final attempt to valorize the moral force of good housekeeping in a contemporary setting. Thus it is obviously comparable to Stowe's first novel. *Uncle Tom's Cabin* was powerfully horrific because it dramatized a world in which the nurturing order of domestic ritual, as created by women, could not be sustained. Slavery was identified as cause and abolition as remedy for such violation. But, for most readers, *We and Our Neighbors* has remained a jumble of detail, without the moral and aesthetic coherence of *Uncle Tom's Cabin* or the sense of sustaining private order suggested by the Henderson receipt book. *Uncle Tom's Cabin* claimed the domestic sphere as a large public concern by linking it to a great public issue. *We and Our Neighbors* attempts similar claims, as in the numerous contemporary concerns it addresses. But in her first novel, Stowe had the narrative advantage of a plot propelled by slavery, which repeatedly forced women characters to leave home and interrupt their housekeeping. With Eva Henderson at the center of *We and Our Neighbors*, Stowe is committed to the fictional obstacle of a woman who insists on *staying home;* in this novel, unlike *Uncle Tom's Cabin*, Stowe attempts a contemporary home plot.

Most readers have found the attempt only partially successful—if at all. It is difficult not to agree with the suavely authoritative voice of Henry James, who finds the novel's female characters either trivial or ridiculous. For James, Aunt Maria becomes a canvasser for sewing machines—a saleswoman for domestic machinery.[11] Again and again, the exhorting voice of Stowe's prodomestic narration may seem just such a saleswoman's voice, hawking a dubious product. This importantly problematic novel indicates the difficulty of publicly inscribing a housekeeper's text in a newly modern and capitalistic climate. Is *We and Our Neighbors* a failure of Stowe's feminism, as some critics have suggested?[12] Is it a failure of postwar urban America? Is it a failure of readership? Or is it a failure of realism—is domestic ritual a subject and a concern that literary realism somehow refuses to sustain?

Alfred Habegger, in *Gender, Fantasy and Realism in American Literature,* hypothesizes that the American realist novel grew out of the "sentimental" women's best-sellers of the 1850s. These novels were not really domestic fiction, Habegger claims; instead they were a "daydream" literature which allowed women to fantasize fulfillment and "embodied this fantasy in homely detail," making marriage its most common goal.[13] To move beyond this fantasy required, in Habegger's view, a writer who could eschew it, and thus "our first great realists *had to be men,* and the reason why they had to be is precisely that the noble and maternal ideal was all wrong." Habegger sees the origins of realism's greatness in "two sissies," James and Howells, male writers who were able to take on women characters and women's concerns, presumably without ties to a domestic aesthetic. "Women's fiction led to James' and Howells' realism (and in another direction, to the triumphs of local color. . . .)" (65).

What is interesting, for my study, in Habegger's debatable hypotheses is that he sees women's fiction as pointing to realism, and then preventing it, for women, and that he uses "local color" as a conveniently parenthetical territory in which to colonize the successful American women writers who were contemporaries of James and Howells. Donovan's study of several such women writers calls them local color writers *and* practitioners of "woman-identified realism."[14] In Donovan's view, Stowe could (in her New England novels) be simultaneously local colorist, realist, and creator of a utopian "female Arcadia."

This confusion and conjunction of terms suggest the complications that historians of nineteenth-century American literature have encountered when they have tried to contemplate women writers' relation to realism. With the best of such writers—Stowe, Jewett, Chopin, Freeman—domesticity has been at the center of this confusion. All of these women, when they attempted "the objective representation of contemporary social reality" (Réné Wellek, quoted in Habegger 103), turned to the housekeeping that was central to most nineteenth-century female lives. At the same time, that housekeeping was often made the substance of a fantastic female Arcadia or a horrific trap—sometimes both, and sometimes in the same text. *We and Our Neighbors* is a significant experiment because in it we see Stowe alluding to utopian domestic rituals, through Mrs. Henderson and the rural relics she preserves, cautioning against abuses and atrophy of domestic ritual through Aunt Maria's malicious and ultimately pointless machinations, and simultaneously, through Eva's fledgling household, making an evangelistic attempt to present benign domestic ritual as contemporary social reality. *We and Our Neighbors* is quite as ambitious as *Uncle Tom's Cabin* or *A Hazard of New Fortunes*. Even Stowe's choice of the unexceptional Eva as vehicle for her contemporary domestic vision suggests a prototypically realist commitment to the artistic possibilities of the ordinary.

Architectural historian Witold Rybcyzynski has recently traced the development of domesticity from seventeenth-century Holland, where specialized, solitary housework first became an important occupation for bourgeois women. Then, Rybcyzynski says, domesticity provided ordinary people with a new setting and rationale for privacy and intimacy. In such a setting arose what historian John Lukacs has called "the most precious heritage of the Western civilization of the last five hundred years": the concept of interior life, "the deepening human recognition that the sense of reality exists within" (629–30). Thus, Rybcyzynski concludes, the "feminine achievement" of traditional, ritualized domestic life was inextricably linked with "the development of a rich interior awareness . . . that was the result of the woman's role in the home" (70–75). Lukacs and Rybcyzynski would encourage us to consider the connection between inner life and indoor, household life. That equation is central to the idea of domestic ritual. *Ritual* implies repetition because the repeated act has or creates meaning, which becomes tradition through its continuance. *Domestic* implies an enclosure, somehow sacralized, which is both the house and the perceiving self.

To convey something of this rich sense of the perceiving self is one of the goals of American realist fiction at its best—as in *The Portrait of a Lady* and *A Hazard of New Fortunes*. Stowe made a significant early effort at such a project in *We and Our Neighbors*. Her most successful heirs and successors, Sarah Orne Jewett and Mary Wilkins Freeman, took on a project unrealized by their male colleagues: to write a contemporary American realist fiction that took domestic ritual as its shape and subject. With cues from Stowe, they inscribed home plots.

Harriet Beecher Stowe ended her career as a writer of novels with an autobiographical return to the New England of her childhood, in *Poganuc People* (1878). That novel begins, "The scene is a large, roomy, clean New England kitchen of some sixty years ago" (7). As the paragraph proceeds, the kitchen is furnished, with plentiful evidence of faculty, and populated, with one young woman, kneading bread dough. By the time Stowe has completed her first paragraph, she has evoked a domestic world with more solidity than the five hundred pages of *We and Our Neighbors* ever managed to create. This novel follows the maturation of a girl, Dolly Cushing, through a series of ritualized occasions—Christmas festivities, election day, apple bee, and so on. These occasions often begin and end in the kitchen, the capacious, confirming domestic space. Stowe's first paragraph establishes this harmonious relation between domesticity and the world outside: "There was the tall black clock in the corner ticking in response to the chirp of the crickets around the broad, flat stone hearth. . . . the scoured tin and pewter on the dresser caught flickering gleams of brightness from the western sunbeams" (7). Now Stowe is writing idyll, with a calm certainty of tone that she never located in her New York fiction. Here the clock, keeping human time, is placed in the kitchen, and it ticks in concert with the voice of the crickets, comfortably ensconced at their traditional home, the hearth.

Poganuc People ends as Dolly plans marriage to a Bostonian and is thus "to be no longer one of the good people of Poganuc." The narration then concludes with a catalog of the deaths of the novel's characters, who now inhabit the graveyard's "village of white stones." The tone is elegiac, far from the exhorting cheer that ends *We and Our Neighbors* and *My Wife and I,* but it is not melancholy. The narrator reminds us that the natural and domestic beauties of Poganuc still survive. "As other daisies have sprung in the meadows . . . so other men and women have replaced those here written of, and the story of life still goes on from day to day among the POGANUC PEOPLE" (373–75).

In this last novel Stowe regains her assurance, her domestic "perfect pitch," plus a formal felicity and a final sense that the perfect symbiosis of outside and inside worlds which was initially established in the Cushing kitchen continues still, as other lives proceed "day to day" on established and beautiful paths. The tone of *Poganuc People* is a genuine achievement, and to retain it, Stowe declined to follow Dolly, her lively protagonist, into the problematic urban housekeeping essayed by Eva Henderson. Stowe also turned her back, here, on the concerns and methods of American realism, which she had tried out in the New York novels.

Sarah Orne Jewett was born three years before *Uncle Tom's Cabin* was published, in 1849. She grew up in South Berwick, Maine, reading Stowe intently, in her girlhood. As Stowe's career ended in 1878 with *Poganuc People,* Jewett's began with a first book, *Deephaven,* published in the previous year. Recent criticism has tended to see Stowe and Jewett as representatives of two distinct generations of American women writers; Elaine Showalter, for example, writes of Jewett and her postbellum contemporaries as "a new generation of American women writers writing to assert themselves as artists . . . and looking towards both native and foreign models of narrative design" ("Piecing" 238).[15] Yet a comparison of the two writers is a more complex project than chronology can entirely support. Stowe essayed an early realist project in *We and Our Neighbors,* when she tried to put some of the narrative strategies associated with American realism at the service of domestic ritual. *Poganuc People* seems a decisive return to prerealism method and manner—or perhaps another excursion into the catchall territory of local color? Yet its emphasis of ritual over plot, its amalgam of autobiography and fiction, link the novel to other realist projects.

Jewett's first book, with its contemporary urban-rural setting, its elusive, antisequential narrative form, and its often-recessive observing first-person narration, is a quintessentially realist and almost self-consciously literary project. Yet it yearns toward the same idyll embodied in Stowe's New England kitchen, where clock and crickets keep simultaneous, perfect time. In a preface for an 1893 edition of *Deephaven,* Jewett noted that the book was written in response to urban change in New England, where city dwellers, "feeling the new discomforts of overcrowding caused by the steady flow of immigration . . . set countryward in summer." This new current of tourism "meant something more than the instinct for green fields and hills and the seashore; crowded towns and the open country were to be brought together in new association with each other." "The young writer of these Deephaven sketches," as Jewett characterized herself sixteen years later, "was possessed by a dark fear that townspeople and country people would never understand one another, or learn to profit by their new relationship" (1–3).

So Jewett began her career with a project that responded to some of the social conditions that are generally held to have generated American literary realism—a response fueled by "dark fear" of division, conflict, and loss. She wrote of her family house as if it were a bulwark against such loss: "I was born here and I hope to die here, leaving the lilac bushes still green and growing, and all the chairs in their places" (*Letters* 125). The best hope she could articulate is expressed by stable housekeeping, furniture in place. In fact, South Berwick was obviously in the grip of historical change during all the years of Jewett's life; its economy had been radically altered by the 1807 embargo, which crippled Maine's shipping industry. Although she and her siblings were financially cushioned by a well-invested family fortune, they could not ignore the decline and fall of industry in New England and the inroads of the Civil War and the new tourist industry. In 1892, when a developer approached the Jewetts with a plan (which they refused) for "cutting up" the local riverbank and selling it in lots, Sarah Jewett's response was, "Sometimes I get such a hunted feeling like the last wild thing that is left in the fields" (*Letters* 98). As her writing career burgeoned, she did not choose to live exclusively in South Berwick; she divided her time between the Jewett house, shared with her mother and later with a sister, and the Boston house of her companion and closest friend, Annie Fields, with whom she shared a Boston marriage.[16] Annie Fields, widow of publisher James Fields, had been a friend of Emerson, Arnold, Whittier, Hawthorne, Rebecca Harding Davis, Henry James, and others; she was Stowe's biographer. Her house was a sort of literary time capsule; according to Willa Cather, an enchanted guest, there even "an American of the Apache period could come to inherit a Colonial past" (*Not Under* 57).

Deephaven opens in a genteel Boston neighborhood very like Fields's, although Jewett had not yet come to live there. Two independent young upper-middle-class Boston women are deciding how to spend a summer. The narrator, Helen Denis, begins, "It happened that the morning when this story begins I had waked up feeling sorry, and as if something dreadful were going to happen. . . . I have never known any explanation for that depression of my spirits, and I hope that the good luck which followed will help some reader to lose fear, and to smile at such shadows if any chance to come" (9–10). Here Helen already reveals the fertility, acuity, and evasiveness of her sensibility. That morning, her friend Kate Lancaster will invite her to spend the summer "housekeeping" in a mansion inherited by Kate's mother, in a declining port town, Deephaven. That summer will be the substance of the book.

Helen and Kate are genteelly unoccupied, hovering at the edge of an adulthood they are not eager to claim. Both girls (as they call themselves) are attracted to the continuities of ritual, and a Deephaven summer offers an opportunity to tap into ritual as adult women most commonly do: as housekeepers. They are delighted to order supplies and to confer with servants about summer preparations; with a new sense of importance, they feel themselves "housekeepers in earnest" (16). Yet the summer also promises *child*like delights, "for two little girls who were fond of each other and could play in the boats and build houses in the sea sand . . . and carry their dolls wherever they went" (12). The Deephaven summer is a retreat from the exigencies of coming of age in a postwar city, back into girlhood and an apparently less complex rural past. But it is also an advancement into the womanly authority conferred by housekeeping. Even at the beginning, there is a suggestion, which will intensify, that this enterprise is both temporary and futile; the houses these girls build are made of sand. Yet Helen clings throughout to her notion of the Deephaven summer as a sunny, lucky interlude. Richard Cary describes *Deephaven* as an "inchoate work" ("Introduction" 18). But, in a sense, an inchoate state is Jewett's *subject* here. As well as its specifically autobiographical implications for Jewett, the book suggests the ambivalence of a generation of women artists caught between their ties to traditional female culture and an urban, partriarchal literary establishment.[17] For the young Jewett, the quintessential expression of such ambivalence was domestic: two younger women contemplating a house, an old woman's bequest.

William Dean Howells, one of *Deephaven*'s first reviewers, found in it qualities that were, for him, among the best hallmarks of realism: lack of exaggeration, delight in "the very tint and form of reality," a "sense of conscientious fidelity," and "a sympathy as tender as it is intelligent" (25). Jewett had begun writing *Deephaven* when she was about twenty; large portions of it were published in *Atlantic Monthly* between 1873 and 1876. In the course of putting the book together, over a period of about eight years, Jewett came of age, as writer and woman. Her narrator, Helen, is sometimes maddeningly jejune, as in her early praise of Kate, with whom she is obviously infatuated.[18] Yet Helen also conveys the scrupulous mix of intelligence and sympathy that Howells admired. In fact, though it was published eighteen years earlier, *Deephaven* is as much a realist examination of a self-conscious young person's grappling with adulthood and its gendered emblems as is such a canonical text as *The Red Badge of Courage*, and Jewett's conclusion is quite as subtle and equivocal as Crane's.

Deephaven's first and last chapters establish a chronological framework; the first transports them to Deephaven and the last returns them to Boston, in autumn. Within that framework, the chapters range about in time, loosely organized about a theme, an episode, a character, or some combination of these. Perhaps this is why early readers—and Jewett herself— referred to them as sketches. Howells, for example, ended his review with hope that Jewett would soon turn her "powers of observation and characterization to the advantage of us all in fiction" (26). Yet *Deephaven* itself today seems clearly to be a work of formally experimental fiction. For Jewett's organization, despite its fidelity to a block of time (one summer), refuses to allow a pattern to emerge—either a rhythm of dailiness or a plotted sequence. Instead, the book reflects Kate's and Helen's double attraction to and revulsion from the ritualized life they find in *Deephaven*.

The first three chapters are entirely dominated by female characters; no man has a speaking part. These women are grouped around the two dwellings that dominate the girls' Deephaven summer: "The Brandon House and the Lighthouse" (title of chapter two). The aristocratic Brandon house, in which all Deephaven takes communal pride, belonged to Kate's recently dead aunt, Katharine Brandon; it represents a female heritage. Throughout the summer, the girls piece together a portrait of the aunt, last single survivor of a large, fragmented family. Helen describes her house minutely, and she fantasizes about the house as permanent dwelling; it has "great possibilities" and "might easily be made charming" (25).

In their domestic investigations and speculations, the girls stumble on fragments of a narrative, secreted in the things Miss Brandon ordered and preserved. Each of these material texts demands a reading, and housekeeping becomes a complex project of intertextuality, which the girls read always in the looming context of their own problematic lives. They even make a lighthearted attempt to insert themselves in the past, jointly writing "a tragic 'journal'" on old paper and hiding it in a desk; "we . . . flatter ourselves that it will be regarded with great interest some time or other" (26). Kate and Helen can never quite admit to themselves the concern which is so apparent to us: how are their lives inscribed in this house's story?

Thus their responses are skittish and erratic. When they discover a packet of love letters from a lost sailor, which may explain Miss Brandon's singleness, they elect not to read them, spurning a possible tale of heterosexual romance. Instead they turn to letters from young Miss Brandon's "dearest" female friend—and discover that they also end abruptly; the girl died at eighteen. And when they find yet another packet of papers, concerning an estranged brother, Kate tells Helen that her aunt longed vainly for his return, all the rest of her life. At this point, Helen makes the most rawly abrupt transition in her narrative. She abandons the subject of the Brandon house and never returns to her catalog of its charms. For the girls' playful housework is turning up a complex human narrative, a problematic story that could well become their own. (In fact, Kate is her aunt's namesake and the heir of her treasured china.) Soon a neighbor adds another fact about Miss Brandon, which the girls never discuss: this proud, generous, elegant, affectionate, and independent woman died mad.

The other Deephaven beacon, to which Helen's narration turns when the Brandon story becomes too threatening to read or write, is the actual lighthouse, dominated by Mrs. Kew, whom the girls met on the stage ride to Deephaven. A "wise" and engaging countrywoman, Mrs. Kew is the only female character in this book who presently has a working marriage. The marriage is built on mutual compromise. Mrs. Kew, Vermont-born, finds the sea disquieting. Yet she married a seaman, who agreed to stay ashore if she would move with him to the isolated Deephaven lighthouse, at land's end. In this book, even the most successful housekeeping is executed on the edge of extremity. Mrs. Kew's life has real satisfactions, but its stringencies and deprivations are obvious, as indicated by her earnest farewell to the girls at summer's end: "She told us that she loved us as if we belonged to her, and begged us not to forget her." The girls are amazed; "we had no idea until then how much she cared for us" (19–20). Again, their amazement is symptomatic of their unwillingness fully to imagine another woman's story and their links to it.

Complexities multiply when the girls meet their nearest neighbor, Widow Jim Patton, who was Katharine Brandon's longtime housekeeper and friend. Their friendship, even with its restrictions of class, suggests the female alliances in Deephaven that informed Miss Brandon's life. Now, Widow Jim is the surviving woman of faculty, the domestic arbiter, in this book: "There must be her counterpart in all old New England villages. She sewed, and she made elaborate rugs . . . and she went to the Carews' and the Lorimers' [local aristocrats] at housecleaning or in seasons of great festivity. She had no equal in sickness, and knew how to brew every old-fashioned dose . . . and when her nursing was put to an end by the patient's death, she was commander-in-chief at the funeral . . . she sometimes even had the immense responsibility of making out the order of the procession, since she had all genealogy and relationship at her tongue's end" (63–64).

Such a character seems a remnant from the historical fiction of Stowe, a last survivor of the female Arcadia. Her bustling, ordering domesticity is the strongest force in Deephaven. In her snug parlor, she offers the girls ceremonial gossip and well-preserved plumcake. Widow Jim was left "destitute" by an abusive alcoholic husband; her security is insured by a legacy from Katharine Brandon. She is the only female character who ever mentions the possibility that Kate and Helen might marry, and she advises against it: "Don't you run no risks, you're better off as you be, dears" (67). She personifies the best of domestic ritual and the ongoing support of women's culture. But Widow Jim also reminds the girls that *breakdown* is the traditional and inevitable foe of housekeeping—as suggested by the violent husband, the moths and mice that beseige the Brandon house, and the mental illness of Katharine Brandon's last years. It is Widow Jim who tells Helen of this madness; despite the girls' intimacy, Kate did not. Typically, Helen does not comment; she only records the widow's words. *Deephaven* often bears out the premonition of "something dreadful" that Helen felt on the day Kate unfolded her plan. But the most typical response of Helen's narrative is *no comment,* as here.

In Katharine Brandon, Widow Jim, and Mrs. Kew, Kate and Helen scrutinize three very different versions of Deephaven womanhood. The older women share a dilemma: they are aging housekeepers without daughters. If the circuit of domestic ritual is to continue, their faculty and their tasks must be taken up by younger women. The only such potential successors this book presents are Kate and Helen themselves. Thus these early chapters replicate the girls' Deephaven housekeeping and suggest pervasive rhythms of women's culture. They are much concerned with finding and placing things, learning their uses and their stories—as with the numerous teacups, which hint that "the lives of [Kate's] grandmothers must have been spent in giving tea parties" (33). Such telling things now belong to Kate and her mother, Miss Brandon's heirs.

As the book proceeds, the girls recoil from the intense possibilities for domestic identification and confrontation that the early women-chapters present. None of the later chapters will spend so much time at home and indoors; in none of them will Helen indicate again how she and Kate kept house in Deephaven. (They have brought servants from Boston, so the responsibilities of cooking and cleaning do not fall fully upon them.) Instead this new chapter trains a wider lens on Deephaven; Helen assumes the self-conscious gaze of an affectionate amateur anthropologist. Deephaven appears arrested, petrefied as Pompeii: "It seemed as if all the clocks in Deephaven . . . had stopped years ago, and the people had been doing over and over what they had been busy about during the last week of their unambitious progress" (87). Facetiously, Kate and Helen try out local rites; after tea with one local family, they join the evening ritual of family prayers. Afterward, "we told each other, as we went home in the moonlight down the quiet street, how much we had enjoyed the evening, for somehow the house and the people had nothing to do with the present, or the hurry of modern life. I have never heard that psalm since without its bringing back that summer night in Deephaven, and the beautiful quaint old room, and Kate and I feeling so young and worldly, by contrast, the flickering shaded light of the candles, the old book, and the voices that said Amen" (102). Here ritual is approached as spectator sport, with a kind of sympathetic voyeurism. In the "old room," where tea is elegantly served and an ancient text intoned, domestic ritual provides a memorable *frisson*. But the *frisson*'s source is the young women's dissociation. Back on the street, they resume their voluble "modern" commentary and their volition. They imagine themselves free, "worldly," and "young"—able to walk into and out of whatever rituals they choose.

Next, they exercise that volition by visiting the world of Deephaven men. The equivocal nature of Deephaven tranquility is especially evident in these male characters. Having sailed around the world, most of them now hang around the deserted warehouses and fish for a modest living, suffering from the decline of their industry and their aging bodies. Their main recreation seems to be the telling and retelling of tales, and they welcome a new audience in Kate and Helen, who listen with voracious curiosity. They almost never see these men in the company of other women. Even when old Captain Lant entertains the girls at home, he breaks off his tale in midsentence when his "women-folks" return. By seeking out the old sailors and their stories, Kate and Helen reach beyond female domestic limitations. But for every tale of light-hearted male adventure Helen records, there are two contrasting tales of loss, of abrupt and violent death, of life without the cushioning compensations of housekeeping. Women, with ritual domesticity, may have learned to wrest some satisfaction and meaning from a landlocked life; men cannot.

In her first chapters, then, Jewett establishes the female and male worlds of Deephaven. Kate and Helen appear to have safe passage in both worlds; they take tea with Widow Jim and fish alongside Captain Sands. Yet the men's chapters are less fraught with unnamed danger for them. In the second half of the book, instead of returning to the obviously problematic texts of the village households, Kate and Helen strike *out* again, restlessly and nervously. Before her conclusion, Helen recounts five excursions, both exploratory and escapist, into the countryside around Deephaven.

In Denby, a nearby village, they attend a circus in the company of Mrs. Kew, who deeply enjoys a day out of the lighthouse. Obviously, a delicate balance of hermetic housekeeping and such communal occasions makes her domestic life possible. Pressing questions of balance and proportion in women's lives are raised by the day's most memorable and troubling encounter, with a sideshow fat woman, who turns out to be Mrs. Kew's old neighbor, Marilly, who "used to be spare." Marilly explains:

"Father, he run through with every cent he had before he died, and 'he' [her husband] took to drink and it killed after awhile, and then I began to grow worse and worse, till I couldn't do nothing to earn a dollar, and everybody was a-coming to see me, till at last I used to ask 'em ten cents apiece, and I scratched along somehow till this man come around and heard of me, and he offered me my keep and good pay to go along with him. . . . [her son's] wife don't want me. I don't know's I blame her either. It would be something like if I had a daughter. . . . I believe I'd rather die than grow any bigger. I do lose heart sometimes, and wish I was a smart woman and could keep house. I'd be smarter than ever I was when I had the chance, I tell you that!" (170)

Helpless Marilly has become a pawn in an antidomestic patriarchal institution, the traveling sideshow, in which her value is exclusively her body, over which she has no control. She comes from a life in which male obsession and addiction have cut her off from all possible resources of work, money, and will. To her, *housekeeping* seems the only remedy for her condition—the recourse of a "smart woman." And the only imaginable rescuer is female—a nonexistent daughter. Even the competent Mrs. Kew is powerless now to do anything for her old friend. She considers inviting her for a visit, but "she'd sink the dory in a minute" (174). The hard-won domestic equilibrium of the lighthouse is not accessible to such a giantess; distorted and daughterless, she has no entrée to the supportive world of women's culture. Obviously, the figure of Marilly explicates much of the animus of the temperance movement, in which women organized to secure their lives and their housekeeping against domestic violations and neglect caused by addiction. (Male alcoholism is a recurrent motif in this book.) Through Marilly, the lighthearted circus expedition becomes a female horror show, in which Kate and Helen are forced to contemplate a woman who has become entirely a body without will, and thus is bereft of the empowering traditions of housekeeping.

No wonder that Helen begins her next chapter, "Cunner Fishing," by insisting that she and Kate are among the "smart women," for one of their "chief pleasures in Deephaven" is "housekeeping" (181). But their housekeeping is very partial; it is usually limited to marketing, at their servants' instruction. Most frequently, they are sent forth to acquire the main course for their dinner—which often propels them into the world of men. This chapter begins with a day spent fishing for dinner, with Captain Sands. As usual, the captain is full of tales and lore; for example, he declares that the sunshine after rain indicates that "the Devil is beating his wife" (204). Everywhere Kate and Helen turn, male and female worlds seem somehow at odds. Yet the captain's most fascinating speculations, for the girls, are about a mysterious supernatural link between him and his wife. In the boat, he receives her signal, from land, that an unseen storm is approaching. The girls, who share the nineteenth-century mania for the occult, are drawn to such accounts of inexplicable links between gendered worlds that appear to be separate.

Back at the Brandon house, that night, the girls drift into "a long talk about the Captain's stories and those mysterious powers of which we know so little." In Deephaven, certainties and boundaries seem to blur: between fact and mystery, men and women, "the simple country people" of Deephaven and their supposedly more cultivated selves. Musing, Kate turns to mythology, for a goddess who seems the antithesis of the disturbing Marilly:

"Do you remember, in the old myth of Demeter and Persephone, where Demeter takes care of the child and gives it ambrosia and hides it in fire, because she loves it and wishes to make it immortal and to give it eternal youth; and then the mother finds it out and cries in terror to hinder her, and the goddess angrily throws the child down and rushes away? And he had to share the common destiny of mankind, though he always had some wonderful inscrutable grace and wisdom, because a goddess had loved him and held him in her arms. I always thought that part of the story beautiful where Demeter throws off her disguise and is no longer an old woman, and the great house is filled with brightness like lightning, and she rushes out through the halls with her yellow hair waving over her shoulders, and the people would give anything to bring her back again, and to undo their mistake. I knew it almost by heart once . . . and I am always finding a new meaning in it." (222–23)

Current criticism has been much interested in reading Demeter's story in nineteenth-century American women's culture. Donovan traces a concern with this crucial myth of the separation and union of earthbound mother and journeying daughter in Jewett's generation and then follows the myth's transformation in the next generation of American women writers, in *After the Fall.* Sarah Way Sherman's recent critical biography of Jewett views her as Demeter's daughter. Sherman provides an extended and useful reading of this scene in *Deephaven,* indicating the various classical nuances and nineteenth-century variations of the myth (most notably, Walter Pater's essays and Annie Fields's poems about Demeter) which Jewett wove into Kate's enormously suggestive speculations (Sherman 95–108).

For my study, it is especially significant that Kate is drawn to meditate on a traditional housekeeper, tending a hearth fire and a child. The housekeepers Kate and Helen have met in Deephaven, even the imperious Miss Brandon, have been subject to change, abuse, decay, and death. But Demeter, like Welty's Circe, is an *immortal* housekeeper. In the portion of the myth that Kate recites and Helen transcribes, Demeter tries to use her powers to confer her immortality on a beloved mortal child. Her medium is the hearth fire itself, into which she thrusts the baby. The child's mother intervenes and snatches him away; she wishes to preserve his human, linear, end-stopped life. And Demeter storms away in anger which shows her full beauty, size, and power; the fireside crone is revealed as a beautiful, striding woman.

This version of the tale suggests Kate's present absorption in questions of time, gender, and housekeeping. She conjures up a housekeeper whose power can both preserve and transform. As practiced by Demeter, housekeeping is anything but trivial. Her domestic rituals can confer immortality, but only through enormous risks to the individual, who must be immersed in transforming fire. Sherman makes the important point that Demeter proposes to "cook" the child, following Lévi-Strauss's "symbolic logic of cooking," by which "raw, unformed nature" is transformed "first into physically human forms, then into cultural forms, then into spiritual forms" (100). Cooking, of course, is one of the central tasks of housework. And one of the central dilemmas of a domestic life, for women who have lived it in nineteenth- and twentieth-century America, is that it *can* confer a kind of immortality, as one's life becomes devoted to perpetuation of very old and very basic acts and forms, reconstituting the lives and values of ancestors in the ways that Eliade describes. The cost of that immortality is risk and perhaps death to the mortal individual and to the myth of the self-made person so prized by patriarchal American culture.

It is significant that Kate chooses to meditate on Demeter's appropriation of a *male* child. She and Helen have been noting ways in which male and female culture are both discrete and interpermeable. Demeter's act is revisionary and utopian because it tries to make immortality, mythic time, and the transforming powers of the hearth accessible to female *and* male. But Kate's choice is evasive too; the most pressing question on her and Helen's minds has to do with the *daughter* at the hearth, for they are potentially such daughters to the Deephaven housekeepers. Persephone does not appear in this portion of the myth (these events presumably occur during her months underground, acting out her adult, heterosexual life with Hades) but she must be in and on Kate Lancaster's mind; anyone who knows this rather obscure elaboration of Demeter's story is bound to know its more celebrated mother-daughter plot.

In no scene of *Deephaven* does Jewett attempt to tap deeper levels of Kate's and Helen's consciousness; it is appropriate that "fishing" is the taking-off point of this speculative chapter, in which Jewett uses myth to suggest concerns that underlie the book. Kate and Helen sit up late, in a room lit only by the fire they have kindled on the domestic hearth. Kate goes on to say, "I was just thinking that it may be that we all have given to us more or less of another nature, as the child had whom Demeter wished to make like the gods. I believe old Captain Sands is right, and we have these instincts which defy all our wisdom and for which we never can frame any laws" (223). Such musings suggest a rich and capacious vision of human consciousness, in which the mortal and the immortal, the linear and the cyclical, the explicit code and the unregulated intuition coexist. With such a consciousness, one need not choose between modern and archaic, masculine and feminine.

Yet the minute Kate voices such a vision, the girls begin to back away from it. Helen suggests that such belief in "dreams . . . and supernatural causes" is "a kind of fetichism" typical of "simple country people" (223), which they of course are not. Both girls seem eager for trite resolutions to the mysteries they have been approaching, and they finally choose one that features a *male* God expressed through *female* Nature.[19] This version puts them in the accustomed and utterly conventional position of unresisting readers of male-written texts; "We may read the thoughts that He writes for us in the book of Nature" (225). It is a silencing conclusion, perhaps particularly daunting for Helen, who is beginning to perceive herself as a writer, a producer of texts. The female texts of *Deephaven* are almost all discovered and deciphered indoors, in the recesses of the Brandon house or at the hearths or tea tables of other women; even Demeter is depicted in a house. The outdoor "book of Nature," however valorized by transcendentalist American Romanticism, is not a sufficient text for the study of housekeeping and female culture. Dimly, Kate and Helen acknowledge this; while their last *words* are of a male God's book, they stay up after these words are spoken, silently and mutually watching the fire on the hearth, "until there were only a few sparks left in the ashes. The stars faded away, and the moon came up out of the sea, and we barred the great hall door and went upstairs to bed" (225). As Demeter's fire dies down, they wait for another great female light, the archetypal moon. Only then do they rise to complete the day's housekeeping, barring the doors and locking themselves in the house.

This subtle and powerful scene shows Kate's and Helen's profound and ambivalent attraction to a continuous tradition of female power and their groping efforts to *express* that attraction, in syllables of myth, archetype, and symbol much larger than the trite formulations of the great male book, of which their culture has taught them to prattle with ease. The complicating truths of "Cunner Fishing" seem to propel the final expeditions of the book, which range farther into the surrounding countryside. While earlier chapters tend to ignore chronology, these three have an urgent sense of time; in late summer the girls must acknowledge the coming exigencies of New England winter. Each of these last visits poses a sharp challenge to their self-possession.

First, they encounter widowed Mrs. Bonny, whose isolated, cluttered upcountry house has no clear boundary between inside and out—chickens amble into her kitchen. Mrs. Bonny is not confined by her housekeeping; she has a close and comprehensive knowledge of nature, like "a good-natured Indian," and an "amazing store of tradition and superstition." In her down-to-earth way, Mrs. Bonny lives by the revisionary mix of nature and hearth fire which Demeter suggested: her kitchen cabinets yield up an assortment of dried herbs, newspapers, turkey wings, and a "mixture of old buttons and squash-seeds" (241). The name "Bonny" indicates the positive implications of her life. However, although the girls find her an amusing and instructive outdoor companion, they will not partake of Mrs. Bonny's housekeeping. Warned by the village women against the products of her unhygienic kitchen, they refuse to eat her cooking or to drink spring water from her dusty tumbler. Mrs. Bonny suggests a "wild and unconventional" reinvention of a female life, and Kate and Helen are too timid and squeamish to entertain her vigorous model and her hospitality; they share the inhibiting, exclusive scruples of the Deephaven housekeepers. Instead of a safely hypothetical goddess, Mrs. Bonny is a problematically actual native American countrywoman.

Next, Kate and Helen make a return visit to a farm family and find that both parents have died; first the mother, of fever, and then the father, of the drinking to which he turned, in grief. Kate and Helen arrive on his funeral day, to be confronted by the shocking, suggestive spectacle of dispersed family and abandoned house. Kate says, "What a pitiful ending. . . . Do you realize that the family is broken up, and the children are to be half strangers to each others?" (269). Although they do not say so, the situation of this family resembles both their own. This scene of mortal domestic *breakdown* obviates their pose as amused voyeurs, and it is indelibly printed on Helen's consciousness. Back in Boston, she cannot shake the memory, and writes, "I think today of that fireless, empty, forsaken house . . . the snow has sifted in at every crack; outside it is untrodden by any living creature's footstep. The wind blows and rushes and shakes the loose window sashes . . . the padlock knocks—knocks against the door" (266). The desolation of this house without hearth fire followed inevitably from the death of a housekeeping woman. Without the domestic ritual imposed by a woman's shaping will, the house is besieged by accelerating decay. Helen's most terrible memories of Deephaven are of this deadly decline of housekeeping.

A final visit repeats, once more and most powerfully, the image of the decaying house. Miss Chauncey, an ancient aristocrat, greets the girls in a falling-down mansion. Indoor chickens solemnly welcome her guests; cobwebs "festoon" the elegant woodwork, mocking a domestic past of ceremony and civility. Nevertheless, Miss Chauncey considers herself the compleat housekeeper; in her wrecked house without comforts or provisions, she offers the most exquisite hospitality. Her housekeeping can respond to change and natural process only by denial, denial of death. Reminded that her old friend Katharine Brandon has died, Miss Chauncey replies, "Ah, they say that about every one nowadays. I do not comprehend the strange idea!" (278). Huddled in one room which is furnished with remnants of antique furniture, she keeps house at the expense of sequence, of narrative, and of reality. However much her actual house may decay, in Miss Chauncey's mind, time stands shockingly still. She reads from her Bible to the girls: "In my father's house are many mansions; if it were not so, I would have told you" (286).

Kate and Helen immediately recognize the "insane" Miss Chauncey as a kinswoman, and the recognition is mutual; Miss Chauncey sees in Kate Lancaster a resemblance to her dead mother. As Kate and the old woman exchange a long gaze, Helen is moved to tears and confirms Miss Chauncey's intuition: "There was a kinship, it seemed to me, not of blood, only that they were of the same stamp and rank" (279). It is a dangerous kinship, which disqualifies Kate and Helen as sane, vigorous housekeepers in the present and ties them to a romantic patriarchal heritage. By contrast, class and squeamishness kept them from a full alliance with sane Mrs. Bonny, who also became racially "other" when framed as an Indian. Mrs. Bonny's and Miss Chauncey's houses are both invaded by the outdoor world. Mrs. Bonny thrives on the mix, but Miss Chauncey's housekeeping denies and defies it; she subsists within the ruin of patriarchy, in her dead father's house. Her holy text locates richness and possibility within domestic mansions, but it does not indicate that the time is the present, the house is crumbling, and its legal owner is not her father but herself. The language of Miss Chauncey's female inheritance is not written; she can only glimpse it in hints of fugitive resemblance, as when she sees her mother in young Kate's face.

Kate, like her Aunt Katharine, is yet another single woman confronted by an inherited house. And with each of the final *Deephaven* visits, the troubling, compelling nature of that inheritance becomes clearer. Back in Boston, the decaying houses fill Helen's mind. The only Deephaven story that she continues beyond the summer's boundaries is Miss Chauncey's. She died of exposure, when she insisted on returning, ill, to her chilly, derelict home. Miss Chauncey insisted fatally on inhabiting an untenable house. Kate and Helen came to Deephaven in a similar spirit, imagining they could again be "two little girls" building houses of sand.

After Miss Chauncey's unforgettable tale, Helen launches into her conclusion, "Last Days in Deephaven." Cold weather decisively ends the summer interlude; in late, chilly October, the girls must "admit that . . . it was almost time for sealskin jackets" (303). But Helen cannot end her narrative with similar dispatch. "It is bewildering to know that this is the last chapter, and that it must not be long" (295), she says. Inchoate bewilderment and a sense of unnamed outside forces determining the shape of her fragile female narrative ("it must not be long") pervade her ending. The girls try to persuade themselves of the success of their summer's endeavor: "we said over and over how happy we had been" (290). In a final round of goodbye calls, they pretend they will return next year. But they know they will not.

To the end, they are perplexed by their own relation with Deephaven. Kate thinks of the village in specifically female terms: "Dear old Deephaven! . . . It makes me think of one of its own old ladies, with her clinging to the old fashions. . . . I don't dispute the usefulness of a new bustling, manufacturing town with its progressive ideas; but there is a simple dignity in a town like Deephaven, as if it tried to be loyal to the traditions of its ancestors" (292). Leaving Deephaven, the girls align themselves with urban modernity. But the daughterly piety which has been such a compelling subtext of the summer for them is expressed in Kate's respect and tenderness for the ancestral traditions embodied by the town. Most pervasive and problematic of such traditions, of course, has been domestic ritual. Kate makes a token stab at perpetuating those traditions in her own Boston housekeeping; an appealing portrait of a young woman is rescued and rehung in her city bedroom, and bunches of Deephaven cattails are arranged there.

Although Jewett does not elaborate the differences between the two young women, they are considerable and are very apparent in the book's ending. Kate's view is the more straightforward. She makes external adjustments, slightly changing her Boston decor, and her sympathy is for *old* women, clearly moribund or dead "old ladies." It is she who has the more demanding city life, and they leave Deephaven because Kate must "take up" that life again. They return to separate houses. Helen's life, with a Boston aunt, is more shadowy and uncommitted. We know only that, on her return to the city, she writes and thinks obsessively of Deephaven. Helen identifies not with the "old ladies" there, but with the young daughters, who are implicitly responsible for perpetuating Deephaven life. She tells Kate, "I was thinking today how many girls must have grown up in this house, and that their places have been ours; we have inherited their pleasures, and perhaps have carried on work which they began" (293). Literally, the work the girls have "carried on" has been their dilatory summer housekeeping, and as the writer Helen broaches these questions of domestic continuity, she touches on subjects that will become much more explicitly the concern of *The Country of the Pointed Firs*, with its woman writer-protagonist. Can domestic ritual be inscribed? Is writing a way of carrying it on? Ultimately

Helen is unable to sustain the question of how a woman writer "carries on" in the last quarter of the nineteenth century in America. In the words that end the book, she imagines a return to Deephaven in a distant future, when the "old gentlefolks" will be dead.

> I should like to walk along the beach at sunset and watch the color of the marshes and the sea change as the light of the sky goes out. It would make the old days come back vividly. We should see the roofs and the black chimneys of the village, and the great Chantrey elms look black against the sky. A little later the marsh fog would show faintly white, and we should feel it deliciously cold and wet against our hands and faces; when we looked up there would be a star; the crickets would chirp loudly; perhaps some late sea-birds would fly inland. Turning, we should see the lighthouse lamp shine out over the water, and the great sea should move and speak to us lazily in its idle, high-tide sleep. (304–05)

This final fantasy of the future is of Helen's sole imagining. In it, she moves toward the largest and most anonymously capacious symbol earth has to offer: the sea. Her vision is elegiac in tone—but the very lives that presumably are being elegized are refined away. In this unspecified future, the reader may be the only companion that Helen can command. While she speculates a future in which she will fondly contemplate the past, Helen evades a problematic present (as indicated by the complicated future-conditional tenses of her last paragraph). Deephaven has become a series of oblique runes for her; trees, lighthouse, and townhouses are dark, iconic shapes against the sky, enigmatic as Stonehenge. These last images evoke once again the questions about the relation of houses and nature that have pervaded the book. Helen, however deeply felt and imagined her education in Deephaven housekeeping may have been, cannot invent and inscribe a narrative that addresses these questions. Her last image of her future self is as a woman at the edge of the sea, walking by.

This final paragraph is as much a denial of present reality as the fantasy of "soft and eternal peace" into which Henry Fleming retreats from battlefield actuality at the end of *The Red Badge of Courage*.[20] Helen and Kate, despite their glimmers of insight, finally turn their backs on the education Deephaven offers. What they have learned about being a woman or a man in Deephaven cannot be assimilated into the rhythm of urban, "modern" lives. In her last paragraph, Helen resembles Miss Chauncey. She too prefers to live in memory and fantasy. The energy of Demeter, powerful enough to flood a great house with light, is nowhere to be found.

Thus the form of *Deephaven* is significantly appropriate. The girls note ritualized patterns in their own lives and others', but they refuse fully to acknowledge or to enact them. The narrative, with its discrete yet related chapters and groupings, its recurrent images and patterns, and its abrupt contrasts, does likewise. The novel alludes to rhythms which are then suppressed. That is perhaps why Kate and Helen's Deephaven friends are so constantly a surprise to them; they have not really entered the ritualized rhythm of their lives. In Helen's final description, the lighthouse is a symbolic shape on the horizon. But if the implications of this book were fully acknowledged, the lighthouse would inevitably evoke Mrs. Kew and the complex life she shaped there. Our knowledge of Mrs. Kew is acquired through the medium of Helen, as narrator, yet Helen will not accept the weight of its implication. The novel ends in a peace that seems spurious because it is a triumph of repression. And what Helen is repressing most is a full acknowledgment of what a *woman's* life must mean. That meaning has been suggested in the lives of Miss Brandon, Widow Jim, Mrs. Kew, Mrs. Bonny, Miss Chauncey, even Demeter herself. Episodic and evasive, *Deephaven* protects itself against the powers and precedents of such housekeeping lives.

Thus the unity of Jewett's first book comes from its pervasive subject, failure. The failure is Helen's; although she hungers dimly for wholeness, authority, communion—for a sustaining life as an adult woman—she cannot grasp such a life. In Helen, Jewett found a character whose personal situation mirrored the rapid social change in the New England of the 1870s; she was able to employ the methods and matter of American realism to inscribe that situation. Despite the girls' antiquarian leanings, there is a peculiar modernity about Helen. She is not unlike J. Alfred Prufrock in his seaside musings; it is as if Jewett's narrator has leapt a generation forward, into the discontinuities of patriarchal modernism. Helen too lacks "the strength to force the moment to a crisis." To force a crisis would be to intervene in plot, to impose shape on experience. Helen is too timid to do that; ultimately, she cannot be a housekeeper. For she will not take responsibility for plot and for time; she eschews a continuous female culture. For example, the two most independently successful women in *Deephaven* are Mrs. Bonny and Mrs. Kew. Both are unorthodox housekeepers who altered the domestic plot to accommodate contingencies of their own lives. These energetic, inventive women triumph because they manage to keep house *and* to keep themselves. It is a mark of Helen's uncertainty, as fledgling woman artist, that, although she has rendered both women vividly, her conclusion seems to forget the possibilities they represent. At the end, she thinks only of Deephaven's "gentlefolk"; her prejudices and timidities cut her off from the most life-giving mothers Deephaven has to offer.

Deephaven deserves to be read and valued today for the acuity with which it captures Kate and Helen's inchoate situation, for its affinities with other works of American realism, and for the distinctively female version of stasis and evasion that it conveys. Like the end of Stowe's auspicious career, the beginning of Jewett's dramatizes the difficulties of writing fiction that does full and complex justice to domestic life, as experienced by women, within the climate created and chronicled by American realism. But the project that Jewett launched with *Deephaven* would eventually provide impetus for a new cycle of richly innovative domestic fiction that reclaims the ambivalent heritage of the home plot for American women writers. Jewett's great book, *The Country of the Pointed Firs*, would become the central text of that cycle.

2

The Country of the Pointed Firs

Claiming the Sibyl's Text

THE YEARS after *Deephaven* were productive ones for Jewett: several volumes of short fiction and of sketches, a vigorous feminist novel, *The Country Doctor* (1884), as well as fiction for children. Most of the best stories are linked to the domestic concerns of *Deephaven*, and most are written in third-person narrative, without the distracting medium of a Helen Denis. In Jewett's sketches, often splendidly innovative, the first person is used unaffectedly to evoke her rambles, physical and mental, through the town and country Maine life of her own past and present. These sketches often memorialize the traces that housekeeping has left on the countryside—a child's grave near the ruins of an old cellar, a series of white rosebushes, passed from neighbor to neighbor; an abandoned house where Jewett takes shelter and kindles what she fears will be the last hearth fire.

After such work, when Jewett reread *Deephaven* at the time of its 1893 reissue, she wrote to a friend that she felt very far removed from it, but still related by (female) blood, "as if I had come to be the author's grandmother." She found its enduring distinction in the conjunction of the narrator's immaturity and a particular historical moment. "It is the girlishness that gives it value. . . . It is curious to find how certain conditions under which I wrote it are already outgrown" (Cary, "Jewett to Dresel" 25). Three years later, Jewett published her finest work, *The Country of the Pointed Firs*, the American ur-text of domestic ritual. This book brings together, refined and distilled, the first-person medium of the sketches, the sharply observant characterization of the stories, and the visitor framework of *Deephaven*.

While *The Country of the Pointed Firs* was appearing in four substantial installments in the 1896 *Atlantic Monthly*, Jewett wrote to the same friend, "I am hurried very much with getting an end written to the Pointed Firs papers, which are to make a little book of themselves this autumn. I shall do very little to the sketches as they stand but speak of my getting away and add some brief chapters" (Cary, "Jewett to Dresel" 45). This revealing letter emphasizes Jewett's strong autobiographical link with this narrator; she refers to her as "I." It also establishes that Jewett herself shares in the controversy about how to designate the form of her new work; she calls it "sketches," "papers." This controversy still continues: Is this important book a novel, short stories, autobiography, or some other form of narrative?[1] Although typically understated, the letter emphasizes that Jewett thought of *The Country of the Pointed Firs* as a shaped whole, as do the slight but telling changes she made in the brief, hurried interval between *Atlantic Monthly* and book publication.

Joanna Frye, in an important recent book, notes that women characters in the contemporary English and American novel "lack autonomy because an autonomous woman is an apparent contradiction in cultural terms" (5). Frye projects a "feminist poetics of the novel," the major effort of which is "to enable women to claim the explanatory possibilities of narrative" (31). In such a poetics, plot becomes "a possible interpretive schema for lived experience rather than the entrapment of a falsifying code" (40). Although Frye is writing about contemporary, living novelists, much of what she says applies strikingly to Jewett's prescient narrative experiments. For Frye, as in Jewett, the major instrument by which women have begun to redefine plot and to grasp "the explanatory possibilities of narrative" is the first person. A female narrating "I" redefines plot: now it is "overtly a function of an individual human consciousness; as an openly subjective act, it necessarily loses some of its iconic force and can be presented as hypothesis rather than truth" (56). We may view Helen's *Deephaven* narration thus; her youthful fallibility and enthusiasm are always apparent, and her local explorations are means of trying out a series of hypotheses, particularly about the shapes of male and female lives.

Frye concludes that first-person narration is a crucial instrument of much fiction by women, because "through the heightened consciousness and the narrative implementation of choice, the female narrator is redefining our conventional expectations for female characters and, through them, for women's lives" (70). *The Country of the Pointed Firs* is narrated by a single woman writer, traveling alone; she does indeed redefine gender expectations. In the course of the book, this narrator confronts some of the most conventional expectations for women's lives: various versions of housekeeping. In the space of a single charged summer, she must work through her own relation to such domestic paradigms. The scattered and sometimes condescending excursions that characterized much of the "local color" writing that flourished in the eighties and nineties become, with this unassuming narrator, a meditation on the enduring cultural heritage with which women endow one another. Jewett's choice of female first-person narration, as opposed to the authoritative third person favored by Stowe, indicates the problematic, speculative, and autobiographical nature of her enterprise.

The Country of the Pointed Firs opens as the narrator returns for a summer visit to a place where domestic ritual is taken seriously—Dunnet Landing, a Maine coastal village. The first chapter's title, "The Return," resonates with suggestions that this woman is approaching something more portentous than a favored vacation spot. The very idea of *beginning* with *return* subverts linear plot, suggesting a cyclical pattern. The first group of chapters, originally published in *Atlantic Monthly*, is dominated by the tensions of a narrator who has been drawn to this village by obscure need, yet finds that the domestic rhythms of village life threaten to deconstruct her persona as contemporary professional woman. Her uneasiness is indicated by the fact that the first brief chapter is framed in the third person (she calls herself "a single passenger. . . . a lover of Dunnet Landing" [2]); then, at the beginning of the second chapter, she resorts to a second person "you," before claiming her first-person voice. She does not do this until she is established in the house of her landlady, with a domestic locus in Dunnet Landing; then she refers to "my hostess and I."

We never know the plot of the narrator's life outside this summer. While *Deephaven* is littered with details of Helen's and Kate's Boston lives, this narrator is stripped to the essentials of character that emerge in the course of a summer visit. But, recessive and reticent as she may attempt to be, as the visitor takes up residence in an older woman's house, she finds that she is writing her own story and discovers a new plot that will both transform and confirm her female selfhood.

The agent of that discovery is her herbalist landlady, Almira Todd, whose powerful female faculty is linked to this writer's voice. Mrs. Todd, a childless widow of sixty-eight, has lived in the village since her marriage. Her small house provides excellent comfort and cuisine, with the felicitous symbiosis of faculty and nature that Stowe elegized in *Poganuc People*. Yet Mrs. Todd's house and person encompass something darker and more complex than the soothing rural domestic vision of Stowe's last book. The narrator intuits this as she observes the care with which her landlady dispenses herbal remedies to customers: "it seemed sometimes as if love and hate and jealousy and adverse winds at sea might also find their proper remedies among the curious wild-looking plants in Mrs. Todd's garden" (4). She describes this as a textual problem: the "queer" and "puzzling" garden is a "rustic phar-macopoeia," which she cannot read. From the beginning, the narrator feels, warily, that there is an organic connection between what Mrs. Todd grows in her garden and prepares in her kitchen and the deepest, most rending human feelings. At first she sees Mrs. Todd's domestic art as representing the decline of great mysteries: "some strange and pungent odors . . . roused a dim sense and remembrance of something in the forgotten past. Some of these might once have belonged to sacred and mystic rites . . . but now they pertained only to humble compounds brewed at intervals with molasses or vinegar or spirits in a small cauldron on Mrs. Todd's kitchen stove" (3–4). The narrator's whimsical modernity[2] seems a cautious defense against the profound and undiminished meaning of Mrs. Todd's female life, a text that is both frightening and compelling.

The figure of Mrs. Todd calls up one of the essential parables of the nineteenth-century woman writer, as suggested by Mary Shelley in 1826 and elaborated by Sandra M. Gilbert and Susan Gubar: the parable of the Sibyl's cave. "This . . . is the story of the woman artist who enters the cavern of her own mind and finds there the scattered leaves not only of her own power but of the traditions which might have generated that power. The body of her precursor's art, and thus the body of her own art, lies in pieces [Sibyl's leaves] around her, dismembered, dis-remembered, disintegrated. How can she remember it and become a member of it, join it and rejoin it, integrate it and in doing so achieve her own integrity, her own selfhood? Surrounded by the ruins of her own tradition, the leavings and unleavings of her spiritual mother's art, she feels . . . like someone suffering from amnesia" (*Mad-woman* 98).

As a professional writer, the narrator lives by written, printed texts. In Mrs. Todd she finds a woman of depth and passion whom she cannot explain or dismiss, a woman who reads nature and people so well that she is a skilled cook, diagnostician, herbalist, mentor, and friend. But Mrs. Todd's texts are not inscribed. When she sells her herbal medicines, she speaks the accompanying text to her customers; "she *muttered* long *chapters* of direc-tions" (4, emphasis mine). And some of her traditional practices are entirely wordless, to her curious lodger's chagrin: there is one plant in her garden "whose use she could never be betrayed into telling me, though I saw her cutting the tops by moonlight once, as if it were a charm" (14). To the narrator, the words ("telling") by which she lives seem a "betrayal" of deepest mysteries—a betrayal that she compulsively pursues.

In a pertinent essay, "Sibyls in Welty's Stories," Peter Schmidt sketches the importance of the sibyl in American women's fiction of the nineteenth

and twentieth centuries. He reminds us that "sibylline powers are traditionally associated not only with the recovery of memory but with oral
rather than written authority" (87). Housekeeping has its own tradition of
unwritten authority; survivals of that tradition still exist, for example, in the
legendary women cooks who refuse to use written recipes. Eudora Welty
describes her mother as such a cook, who scorned written directions,
claiming that "cooking was a matter of born sense, ordinary good judgment,
enough experience . . . and tasting." Mrs. Welty's authorities were tradition
and experience, as expressed in "taste" and "sense," Eudora Welty, the
quintessential daughter-writer, adds, "I had to sit on a stool and take down
what I saw like a reporter, to get her [spoonbread] recipe" (*Eye* 325).

The Weltys exemplify an important development in nineteenth-century
American housekeeping, as middle-class women's domestic work became
professionalized. Inscription was a major strategy of professionalization; the
burgeoning literature of housekeeping, particularly women's magazines, was
a nineteenth-century publishing phenomenon. As Gilbert and Gubar emphasize, sibylline texts by women present the possibility of reconnecting
with the sibyl's original wisdom. But *not* by the written word. Aunt Roxy of
The Pearl of Orr's Island is sibylline in just this sense; her housekeeping is
medium for her profound comprehension of death, loss, and endurance,
which she communicates to the two young women in the course of her
careful nursing and household tasks, teaching Mara how to die and Sally
how to live. Aunt Roxy and her sister speak of the "mantle" of their wise
faculty falling upon the surviving Sally. The very idea of writing this
transmission would undermine its effectiveness as domestic ritual, destroy-
ing intimacy, immediacy, and physical authority. Also, the nonwritten nature of traditional domestic instruction makes it accessible to women of
every level of education and linguistic condition, including women who
have been excluded from written discourse by illiteracy or by more subtle
patriarchal taboos. Rabuzzi observes that housekeeping is the only form of
work in which neophytes are still widely instructed by parents or other
elders. "To do a task precisely as you observed or were taught by your
mother or grandmother is to experience a portion of what they each once
did. . . . The ritual enactment of housework thus helps provide continuity
from one generation of women to another. . . . Homemakers in general are
the largest group still to connect back in this particular fashion to their
forebears. . . . It is one of the major ways that women (whose lives have
typically been isolated from the public sphere dominated by men) have been
able to share in the entire community of women" (102–03).

A woman *writer*, whether her texts are novels or recipes, has an ambivalent relation to that whole past of instructing mothers and sibylline housekeepers. Traditional ritualistic housekeeping emphasized connections, continuity, and a community where an old woman's domestic "mantle" inevitably fell to a young girl. It naturally opposed the domestic science movement, which came to dominate popular ideas about housekeeping in the late nineteenth century and which emphasized individual achievement and invention, as in traditional American men's culture. Laura Shapiro, who provides one of the best accounts of the domestic science movement, cites Anna Barrows, a professional home economist writing in 1898. Barrows concentrated on such issues of textuality, complaining that women "were not accustomed to thinking for themselves and had not been educated to understand the value of new ideas." To Barrows, most housekeepers were "servile imitators," particularly in their cooking. "The devotion to family recipes for foods is amazing when we compare it with our custom regarding clothing. . . . Few of us would care to cut our garments by the patterns our grandmothers used" (174). This passage shows the enormous threat that traditional housekeeping, especially the unwritten "family recipes" and practices passed from female generation to generation, posed for any "modern" woman who had made a commitment to print culture.

All these issues are included in the baggage Jewett's narrator brings to Mrs. Todd's house. And Mrs. Todd is sibylline in yet another traditional way; as an herbalist, she reads leaves and transforms them into the nonverbal media that express her power and understanding: medicines, sirups, spruce beer. Early in *The Country of the Pointed Firs*, the narrator jokes about such remedies, which "may endanger the life and usefulness of country neighbors" (4), and sides with the village's modern man of science, the doctor, Mrs. Todd's friendly professional rival. When Mrs. Todd confides that she still feels an early, enduring love for a man she could not marry, the narrator does not offer any revelations of her own in response. She is "only too glad to listen," silently. Thus she is exercising her initial skill as a writer, observation, the skill that Jewett says she herself learned from her father in young girlhood.[3] Observation is the first skill that a scientist (and a doctor, as Jewett's father was) must cultivate; it is also one of the qualities most prized by contemporary male theorists of American realism, such as Howells. It requires distance and objectivity. The narrator's gifts as observer are evident in her first extended description of Mrs. Todd: "She stood in the center of a braided rug, and its rings of black and gray seemed to circle about her feet in the dim light. Her height and massiveness in the low room gave her the look of a huge sibyl, while the strange fragrance of the mysterious herb blew in from the little garden" (8).

This description conveys much of the power, attraction, and danger that Mrs. Todd initially exerts for the narrator. Her largeness—in body, spirit, and importance—is projected, as is the narrator's sense of her friend's confinement by the house's dimensions—she is *too* massive for this "low room." A sibyl is a woman of extraordinary size and power, and every act of Mrs. Todd's here exerts unusual resonance. For example, the most compelling visual component of this description is the braided rug. Mrs. Todd almost certainly made it; Dunnet women commonly braid rugs, fulfilling domestic custom and necessity. Much of Mrs. Todd's import may be read in the multiple suggestions of this common household thing. Her centrality is traced by its encircling rings, like a mandala or a full moon. Do they radiate from her, or do they close in, to confine and constrict? The gray and black tones of the rug set a further seal of solemnity and ambiguity on the picture. The "strange fragrance" from the herb garden outside offers no respite from the mystery of Mrs. Todd; instead it is a further reminder of her large, unclassifiable implications. All these suggestions demand that the narrator go beyond careful realist observation to eventual leaps of meditation, speculation, and imagination. Already, in this richly suggestive passage, she is indicating the limits of what she can now write of her landlady. The sense of smell is perhaps the most profoundly and indescribably evocative sensory trigger of early memory. Here the "strange fragrance" of Mrs. Todd's sibylline leaves tantalizes the narrator, making her aware of some obscure amnesia in herself.

As in the homemade rugs, the essence of Mrs. Todd's character is interwoven with the domestic rituals of her life. And the narrator, although middle-aged herself, runs through a series of abrupt responses to those rituals, which suggest the experimental fits and starts of adolescence. First, like Mrs. Todd's dutiful daughter, she becomes caught up in the household industry, the herb business, staying home to attend to customers while her landlady makes seasonal gathering forays. Mrs. Todd praises her aptitude as apprentice herbwoman: "I have never had nobody I could so trust," she says (7). But the narrator must withdraw; she recalls the professional identity that she has come near to abandoning. She is a writer, with an overdue assignment to complete. So she hires the empty schoolhouse for a solitary workplace. Ensconced there, fortified by the lunches Mrs. Todd packs for her, she tries out a life pattern more commonly enacted by men. But in the schoolhouse she feels bereft, locked away from the heart of village life and from herself.

The rest of the book addresses this problem of separation. Like Kate and Helen in their Deephaven housekeeping, the narrator essays a project in intertextuality, by which Mrs. Todd's sibylline leaves and her own pages are bound together, to form the single text that is *The Country of the Pointed Firs*. As opposed to the jittery, evasive first person of *Deephaven*, this book's narration has rare, calm authority. Yet the narrator lacks such assurance in these first chapters, where she switches from third to second to first person and skips from whimsy to practicality to awe, as skittishly as Helen Denis did. By the plot that she discovers in the remainder of the summer, she achieves integrity, a wholeness of book and self. The means by which she achieves it, often under Mrs. Todd's direction, is a series of visits, each an intense encounter with priorities of domestic ritual.

This series is launched on a day when Mrs. Todd has lost one of her closest women friends. The narrator, trying halfway measures, attends the funeral but then retreats to the schoolhouse to work, abandoning the funeral procession. Back at her desk, she feels her work an insufficient support. Uncertainty marks her prose, and she even relapses briefly into third person:

> Now and then a bee blundered in and took me for an enemy, but there was a useful stick upon the teacher's desk and I rapped to call the bees to order as if they were unruly scholars, or waved them away from their riots over the ink, which I had bought at the Landing store, and discovered too late to be scented with bergamot, as if to refresh the labors of anxious scribes. One anxious scribe felt very dull that day; a sheep-bell tinkled near by, and called her wandering wits after it. The sentences failed to catch these lovely summer cadences. For the first time I began to wish for a companion and for news from the outer world, which had been, half unconsciously, forgotten. Watching the funeral gave one a sort of pain. I began to wonder if I ought not to have walked with the rest. . . . Perhaps the Sunday gown I had put on for the occasion was making this disastrous change of feeling, but I had now made myself and my friends remember that I did not really belong to Dunnet Landing.
>
> I sighed, and turned to the half-written page again. (14–15)

Here, the narrator begins to apprehend that her dualistic plan for splitting her summer's life, between schoolhouse and Todd house, between ritual and writing, cannot satisfy her. This is the only passage in the book where she expresses loneliness for the "outer world" and its resources. And her writing, for the sake of which she has supposedly implemented this plan, is the worse for it; her sentences do not "catch these lovely summer cadences" and suffer from uncharacteristic imprecision. It becomes apparent that one of the submerged subjects of this book is a realist writer's relation to her materials, as artist and woman. If local weather were all she wanted to write about, the schoolhouse would be an ideal observation post. But "summer cadences" are rhythmic patterns that come from human temporality and are often reinforced by ritual. It is significant that the narrator casts herself in the role of cultural arbiter (the teacher, "that great authority") and foe of bees, who live an orderly, female-centered life, ruled by queens. The bees have a taste for the local ink, with its strong, leafy, herbal scent. But the narrator is stymied; what can she write with such ink, which is a faint reminder of a sibyl's text?

Thus she welcomes the interruption of her first visitor, Captain Littlepage; he is a potential ally. The old captain, a retired bachelor, is a proper nineteenth-century businessman, who believes in progress and sees it confounded in the local decline of the shipping industry. He says, "The worst have got to be best and rule everything; we're all turned upside down and going back year by year" (21). Well read in a patriarchal canon, Captain Littlepage captures the narrator's interest and provokes her to unwonted literary allusions (significantly, one is to Darwin). The captain's views have made him an outsider in his own village. He finds Dunnet Landing, largely inhabited by women, to be small-minded and limiting—a "handful of houses" where "they fancy that they comprehend the universe" (18).

Townswomen are skeptical of the story he tells the narrator, of a voyage north of Hudson's Bay, where he met a dying explorer who entrusted him with a tale of an unmapped city of "fog-shaped men," speechless specters who finally drove the explorers back south, to sea. "Those folks or whatever they were, come about 'em like bats; all at once they raised incessant armies, and come as if to drive 'em back. . . . Sometimes a standing fight, then soaring on main wing tormented all the air. . . . Say what you might, they all believed 'twas a kind of waiting-place between this world an' the next" (26). Captain Littlepage is now the only survivor entrusted with this story— or mirage—of a world without substance, between worlds. He wants to legitimize it, by inscribing it in "official" (male) culture, and has written the Geographical Society and "done all I could" (27). But none of the officials will accommodate him, and in the schoolhouse, he finally sits and stares in bewildered silence at a recent map of North America: it does not confirm his vision.

Captain Littlepage insists on the power of words—he wants his vision written somewhere, on a page. Memorized poetry sustained him when he was stranded at the North Pole; although he loves the "loftiness" of Milton, "up there it did seem . . . as if Shakespeare was the king" (24). For the captain, the worlds of literature, patriarchal prerogative (kingship), and printed texts are inseparable. The narrator shares his love for literature; this very afternoon, she is anxiously trying to fulfill her commitment to the "half-written page" before her, which may also commit her to patriarchal, institutional values. The captain tells her, of the North Pole, that "there was nothing beautiful to me in that place but the stars above and those passages of verse" (240). Such a statement denies much of the mediating human worth the narrator will discover in the unpublished village of Dunnet Landing. And the name *Littlepage* itself suggests the limited dimensions of written culture.

Another feature of the captain's world of extremity is its lack of women and the civilizing supports of domesticity: "We lived like dogs in a kennel" (23), he says. Again and again, Captain Littlepage evokes a modernist desert, a place where "things fall apart," populated by fog-shaped hollow men. His haunting tale is an unconscious critique of the male culture he supposedly supports. It evokes a world of warlike, bestial, insubstantial men: a psychic wasteland that patriarchy must suppress and deny.

Mrs. Todd finds much that is convincing in Captain Littlepage's nightmare vision. Only when she sees that the narrator shares her respect for the old man's tales does she begin to reveal an alternative vision, starting with the disclosure that her aged mother is still alive. This revelation is sealed by a ceremonial draught of spruce beer, spiked with an unknown herb. The narrator feels "as if it were part of a spell and incantation" (31), for now Mrs. Todd begins to induct her lodger into another enduring model of gendered culture, a world of domestic ritual, ordered by women. Tiny Green Island, where Mrs. Todd's mother and brother live, is probably also invisible on the schoolroom map. However, it is no wasteland, but a place that sustains rich life.

The chapters in which Mrs. Todd takes the narrator to a visit to Green Island were published as the second *Atlantic Monthly* installment of *The Country of the Pointed Firs*. The narrator undertakes this visit with enthusiasm that suggests a new phase in her personal plot. It suggests, in fact, that her days in Dunnet Landing are becoming text, that she is receiving instruction in the domestic language of that text's inscription, and that she will ultimately achieve a relation to that text that is both receptively *readerly* and actively *writerly*.[4] As she and Mrs. Todd make their way, by boat, to the isolated island, Mrs. Todd anticipates her mother's domestic needs—she has brought an onion and picks out a haddock for a company chowder—and when the Blackett house comes into view, "standing high like a beacon" (34), she reads the signs of her mother's reaction to the prospect of visitors: "There, look! There she is: mother sees us; she's waving somethin' out o' the fore door! . . . Look at the chimney now; she's gone right in an' brightened up the fire" (35).[5] Obviously, a shared knowledge of housekeeping makes for a sustaining telepathy between daughter and mother. Mrs. Todd's instructional tone indicates that she is passing that knowledge to the narrator. And the narrator's close observation of the domestic order shows that she is an apt pupil. For example, when Mrs. Todd congratulates her eighty-six-year-old mother on having managed to turn the parlor carpet without another woman's help, the narrator comprehends the old woman's pride in her housekeeping resourcefulness and understands that this is, seriously indeed, a "great moment."

The narrator immediately loves Mrs. Blackett; to her, she offers none of the resistance with which she initially protected herself from Mrs. Todd. Mrs. Blackett confounds linear time; she is an "old woman" who can assume "a sudden look of youth . . . as if she promised a great future" (40). In her life, the narrator reads none of the conflict between priorities of selfhood and housekeeping by which she is herself beset. Instead, the older woman's housekeeping and hospitality express "the gift which so many women lack, of being able to make themselves and their houses belong entirely to a guest's pleasure . . . so that they make a part of one's own life that can never be forgotten" (46). Mrs. Blackett perpetuates a domestic idyll by inscribing it in memory. When she shows her "best things," glassware and china, to the narrator, it is not an expression of a consumer's or an antiquarian's pride. Instead they are the tools with which she creates a supportive rhythm that includes variation and release from routine, even on this tiny island, populated only by her son and herself. She says, "These I call my best things, dear. . . . You'd laugh to see how we enjoy 'em Sunday nights in winter: we have a real company tea instead of livin' right along just the same, an' I make somethin' good for a s'prise an' put on some o' my preserves, an' we get a'talking' together an' have real pleasant times" (51).

The best Mrs. Blackett can offer her guests is to include them in her idyllic housekeeping. She beckons the narrator into her most private spot, her bedroom, and says, "I want you to set down in my old quilted rockin' chair there by the window; you'll say it's the prettiest view in the house." As the narrator complies, she thinks, "Here was the real home, the heart of the old house on Green Island!" (54). Mrs. Blackett's chair, where she reads and sews, is a literary domestic icon. It recalls a passage that Jewett surely knew well, Stowe's paean in *Uncle Tom's Cabin* to Rachel Halliday's quilted rocking chair, which enthroned the Quaker matriarch who embodied a nurturing, coherent domestic alternative to a patriarchal world spoiled by slavery. By the grace of Mrs. Blackett's similarly generous hospitality, the narrator can sit in the emblematic chair. Momentarily, at least, she is mentally and physically *inside* the female sphere of nineteenth-century housekeeping. The quilted rocking chair is the focal point that gives Green Island its beautiful sustaining order.

Although the narrator would happily remain indoors with Mrs. Blackett, Mrs. Todd insists that she explore farther reaches of Green Island. Together, they hike to a hidden field where choice pennyroyal grows. The spot is "sainted" to Mrs. Todd; she and her dead husband courted there and she has shared it with only two women: the narrator and her mother. It is a grassy extremity, beyond which "rocky cliffs" fall to turbulent sea. For Mrs. Todd it is associated with emotional extremity, as well; the very scent of pennyroyal reminds her of the dear husband she could not love, and the unattainable "other one" to whom she had given her heart.

Yet again, the leaves that Mrs. Todd gathers seem to speak. Elizabeth Ammons observes that pennyroyal, Mrs. Todd's favorite herb, is traditionally associated with women's sexual lives.[6] The pennyroyal landscape recalls the metaphoric female landscapes that Ellen Moers began to explicate in *Literary Women*. It combines typical fertile grassland and precipitous depth (382–481). By taking the narrator there, Mrs. Todd seems to extend an invitation into deeper intimacy, as friend, sister, daughter, and/or lover. Powerful emotion, spirituality, and physicality are all suggested by the resonance of the outdoor imagery.

In the scene at the pennyroyal spot, the narrator does not speak, beyond expressing initial enthusiasm for the herb. At last Mrs. Todd leaves her alone:

> She . . . presently rose and went on by herself. There was something lonely and solitary about her great determined shape. She might have been Antigone alone on the Theban plain. It is not often given in a noisy world to come upon the places of great grief and silence. An absolute, archaic grief possessed this countrywoman; she seemed like a renewal of some historic soul, with her sorrows and the remoteness of a daily life busied with rustic simplicities and the scents of primeval herbs.
>
> I was not incompetent at herb-gathering, and after a while . . . I gathered some bunches, as I was bound to do, and at last we met again higher up the shore. (49)

Up until this point, the narrator has been describing Mrs. Todd as sibyl, as supporting "*caryatide,*" as "a large figure of Victory." Now, as Antigone, she is associated with a human protagonist, in whom power and presence are tempered by mortal vulnerability; thus the archetypal "great determined shape" is marked by individual need, "something lonely and solitary." This passage emphasizes the *human* continuity of Mrs. Todd's complexity, as expressed in her domesticity and "primeval herbs." Mrs. Todd's intense communication with the narrator is completed by silence, not speech; to comprehend her, the narrator must renounce the buzzing languages of the contemporary "noisy world."

Although the narrator responds to the power of Mrs. Todd's feeling, her description also offers defensive resistance to it. Mrs. Todd's powerful grief seems "archaic," her life, "remote" and "rustic." The narrator admits her link to Mrs. Todd's occupation in hedged language—"I was not incompetent at herb-gathering"—and tells us that she practices that occupation with a verb suggesting compulsion, not volition: "I gathered some bunches, as I was *bound to do.*" In the course of this domestic visit to Green Island, the narrator begins, uneasily, to apprehend that she is not simply on a voluntary exursion; she herself, with her talent for herbs, may be part of a compelling continuity of female tradition, "a renewal of some historic soul." Earlier, she used similar language, referring to a "piece of writing . . . I was *bound to do*" (6, emphasis mine). Such repetition suggests that her compulsions as writer and herbwoman are linked and are similarly problematic to her sense of contemporary female selfhood.

Mrs. Todd's younger brother, William Blackett, provides another model of selfhood for the narrator to meditate on. Gentle, dignified, and pathologically shy, William loves his life with his mother on Green Island, and he understands its rhythms as deeply as his sister does. When she brings a fish for the chowder, he invisibly intervenes and places it "all cleaned and ready in an earthen crock on the table." "Son an' daughter both" (41) to his mother, William is a model of androgyny and has escaped much of the confinement of gender stereotypes—although obviously at much expense in wider human communion. The narrator's sense of kinship with William is intensified by his silence, which expresses intensity rather than absence of meaning. Such signification has special meaning for a writer—indeed one of the largest distinctions of *The Country of the Pointed Firs* comes from its power to suggest levels of meaning through observation, intuition, and silence. The narrator herself is learning to respect unwritten texts. Thus she is much moved by William when, during their stroll in the woods he knows intimately, "he picked a few sprigs of late-blooming linnaea . . . and gave them to me without speaking, but he knew as well as I that one could not say half he wished about linnaea" (45). William expresses by his silence the narrator's own growing sense of the insufficiency of words. He is androgynous, too, in that he here appropriates the sibyl's medium; *leaves,* as in the sprig of linnaea, become his text.

To end the rich day at Green Island, William and Mrs. Blackett sing for their guests, beginning with William's "touchingly" serious rendition of "Home, Sweet Home." Both visitors are moved to tears by William's "true and sweet" singing (52–53). This signals the narrator's growing involvement in complex questions of gender, text, and voice. William gives voice to a classic Victorian text, extolling woman's home "sphere" in words he did not himself write. Although the narrator has observed some of William's other means of communication, at this point she considers his singing supreme, his "real and only" communication. His sister and mother are permitted a wider range of languages. In fact, William himself has a keen awareness of how domestic things can speak; when Mrs. Blackett shows her "best things" to the narrator, it is at his empathetic suggestion: "William thought you'd like to see this, when he was settin' the table" (51). If language is a more multiple project than the narrator had realized on her arrival at Dunnet Landing, and *if* the female traditions of the herbwoman-housekeeper-sibyl are central to that project, how can a man relate to the project, except through the oppressive traditions of patriarchy that William eschews?

The narrator has already touched on such questions with antidomestic Captain Littlepage, who seems cruelly isolated in his masculine, literary preoccupations. An alcoholic male Bowden cousin, with unrealized military ambitions, suffers from similar limitations. William, on isolated but fertile Green Island, has contrived a mutlilingual life in which he practices tradi-tional male occupations (farmer, fisherman) without being excluded from domestic discourse. But the costs of this achievement have been high. Like his mother and sister, William is apparently celibate. In addition, unlike them, he is a social anomaly, frightened of meeting his neighbors on the village street and mocked by his loving sister, Mrs. Todd, whose own lan-guages are a gendered inheritance which she employs with unfettered ease.

According to Paul John Eakin, the scene in which William and his mother sing "is unrivaled in American literature as a picture of absolute goodness, with the possible exception of little Eva on her deathbed" (528). The two scenes make an interesting and pertinent comparison. Both Wil-liam and Eva suggest possibilities of utopian lives that strain the limits of gendered stereotypes. Eva wanted to extend her Christian love beyond the limits of a young girl's power; her character could not survive in a world flawed by slavery. Stowe cannot bear to expose Eva's "absolute goodness" to the contingencies of the marriage market, on which she would become a commodity if she survived to womanhood. William (whom the narrator repeatedly calls a "boy," although he is over sixty) has achieved his version by remaining celibate and cloistered with his sympathetic mother. Unlike the moribund Eva, the Blacketts have managed to maintain an earthly home that is truly sweet. The nearly (but finally not) cloying sense of "absolute goodness" that Eakin notes comes from the smitten narrator, who has fallen in love with the Blackett domestic idyll. She says, "It was impossible not to wish to stay forever at Green Island" (52).

Mrs. Todd could live on Green Island too, if she wished. But she did not wish, and her mother understands, saying that Almira "wanted more scope . . . an' to live in a larger place, where more things grew" (52). By her revelations at the pennyroyal field, Mrs. Todd has intimated something of the multiple needs that drew her away from the island hermitage, much as she values it. Mrs. Todd has internalized the rhythms of her mother's household; she can read from afar the waxing and waning of the Blackett hearth fire. But it was necessary for her to establish an independent household and womanhood, on the shore. For the narrator, these new revelations about her landlady are the most disquieting aspects of her day on Green Island.

Despite their mutual love and understanding, in many ways Mrs. Todd is *not* her delightful mother's daughter. (It is William who resembles Mrs. Blackett, physically and otherwise, not Almira.) "Like mother, like daughter" is not the guiding principle of *The Country of the Pointed Firs*. Mrs. Blackett is not herself an herbwoman, for example; the mother depends on her daughter for diagnoses and restorative doses, claiming that "Almiry's got an herb for everything" (52). In this book, questions of female inheritance are more complicated than simple genealogy; Mrs. Todd has located her profession, in unspecified ways, by acknowledging her own nature and by appropriating a body of female tradition, herbal medicine and perhaps witchcraft, which was not taught by her mother. By contrast, lovable Mrs. Blackett presents no problems of obscurity, distance, or complexity. In other words, she is not sibylline, as is her daughter, and she does not speak to the most troubling questions of the narrator's life as woman writer, as does Mrs. Todd. Thus the closing of the Green Island day must be "the *end* of a great pleasure," for the narrator's place in this plot has become more apparent. She has been visitor for a day, but now she must return to what she newly calls "home"—Mrs. Todd's house.

Enchanted by the Blacketts' housekeeping, the narrator returns to shore with a fond tendency to idealize and oversimplify domestic life. At this point she veers toward an essentialist and escapist view of women's culture, settling back into Mrs. Todd's womblike house "with as much comfort and unconsciousness as if it were a larger body, or double shell, in whose simple convolutions Mrs. Todd and I had secreted ourselves" (55). *The Country of the Pointed Firs,* although it honors domestic ritual, does not allow such oversimplification. So the narrator must be roused to difficult complexities. The next chapters, in which this occurs, are the heart of Jewett's book.

Mrs. Fosdick, a widow of Mrs. Todd's age, is a welcome visitor, reputed "the best hand in the world to make a visit—as if to visit were the highest of occupations" (58). As Carroll Smith-Rosenberg has observed, such "endless trooping of women to each other's houses" was a centrally important domestic institution for nineteenth-century women (10). Since the domestic visit has become the narrator's sole apparent summer occupation, she is now put on her mettle; in cheerful, self-possessed Mrs. Fosdick she has a new rival and a new instructor. Positions in the household shift; some part of the burden of housekeeping becomes the narrator's own, as Mrs. Todd sends her to the kitchen to tend the stove. Performing housekeeping tasks for the first time under Mrs. Todd's roof, she finds her sense of proportion and proprieties altered: "there were so few emergencies of any sort at Dunnet Landing that this one appeared overwhelming" (50). As the visit proceeds, with much of tea, knitting, and conversation, the anxious, jealous narrator comes to value it as much as the older women do. One stormy evening, she assumes some of the domestic prerogatives of a hostess, kindling her first fire in her room and inviting her "housemates" to be her guests at the hearth. The house is filled with the strong scent of the cough sirup Mrs. Todd is preparing—reminder of a change of season, for "the time of gathering herbs was nearly over, but the time of sirups and cordials had begun" (62). In other words, in the narration as well as the season, we have come to a moment of distilled, concentrated, and perhaps therapeutic meaning.

When conversation begins and Mrs. Fosdick brings up the name of a Joanna Todd, Mrs. Todd is unwontedly skittish and reticent. "I never want to hear Joanna laughed at" (65), she remonstrates, setting an almost sacramental tone. A story's rudiments begin to emerge. Joanna Todd, a cousin to Mrs. Todd's husband, was jilted by her fiancé. Distraught, she signed away her shore property and moved to small, barren Shell-heap Island, to live out her life alone. Soon the two women are trading facts and speculations about Joanna, in response to the narrator's discreetly neutral questions. Joanna's history, as it emerges, is encrusted with their memories, responses, changed views, and reports or surmises of the responses of others and is interspersed with the narrator's own responses, mostly unspoken.

Mrs. Fosdick supposes that Joanna's withdrawal was the natural result of losing the domestic life she had planned: "she acted just like a bird when its nest is spoilt" (65–66). Some of the older women's keenest questions, still fresh after more than thirty years, are about Joanna's solitary housekeeping:

"Almiry, what did she do for clothin' when she needed to replenish, or risin' for her bread, or the piece-bag that no woman can live long without?"

"Or company," suggested Mrs. Todd. . . . "There must have been a terrible sight o' long winter evenin's that first year." (58)

The narrator has been indulging in gently supercilious reflections on village life, which confirm her status as a sophisticated foreigner in Dunnet Landing. Now her silent thoughts of Joanna are far more self-consciously lofty than the older women's homely questions; she meditates "upon a state of society which admitted such personal freedom and a voluntary hermitage. There was something mediaeval in the behavior of poor Joanna Todd" (69).

As Mrs. Todd launches into an account of her one visit to Joanna on the island, the narrator falls silent and the two older women seem "quite unconscious of a listener" (69). Suddenly, Mrs. Todd's narrative is interrupted by a knock at the door, someone wanting a remedy for a sick child. The women, who have been absorbed in the tale, are pitched into multiple awareness: their domestic circle, centered by the bright stove, must contend with dark rain and waves outdoors and with the present urgent needs of another household. Now the narrator does not frame lofty historical abstractions; instead she empathetically imagines Joanna's feelings: "what separation from humankind she must have felt, what terror and sadness, even in a summer storm like this!" When Mrs. Todd reenters the room, she brings outer weather inside their warm circle; there is "a mist about her from standing long in the wet doorway, and the sudden draught of her coming beat out the smoke and flame from the Franklin stove" (73). Memory, weather, and circumstance combine to show how equivocal this shelter is, how easily its comfortable present inhabitants might find themselves outside, elsewhere. Mrs. Todd's commanding presence evokes again the mixture of inner and outer worlds in her life: garden and stove, outdoor weather and indoor life. With the mist swirling about her, she seems a large figure of mysterious, perhaps supernatural, powers.

Yet, when she resumes the tale of her visit to Joanna's island, in a voice which sometimes trembles with emotion, Mrs. Todd is very humanly empathetic. The visit was obviously a crucial scene of instruction for her. Newly married to Nathan Todd, she had become Joanna's kinswoman and was greeted thus. To her eager listeners, Mrs. Todd repeats Joanna's own explanation of her retreat: she had "committed the unpardonable sin" by the "wickedness" of her thoughts toward God in her disappointment, and thus hadn't "got no right to live with folks no more. . . . tell them I want to be alone." Joanna had begun to resemble her mother, who "had the grim streak" (74–76). The narrator falls silent for the rest of the evening as the others continue. Mrs. Fosdick, whose cheerful modernity is a foil for Mrs. Todd's more profound and cyclical views, urges that a case like Joanna's must be a thing of the past; "the world's bigger and freer than it used to be." But Mrs. Todd disagrees, and her fatalism and stalwart respect for Joanna's unknowable self end the night's talk: "No, Joanna was Joanna, and there she lays on her island" (78).

Apparently, Joanna had set her heart on a domestic, conjugal life, and when her fiancé destroyed that prospect, she turned away from all shore comforts, punishing herself in the cruelest way she knew. And yet—there is some suggestion that, like her mother before her, Joanna desired this separation; she said, "I *want* to be alone." Mrs. Todd describes Joanna's island housekeeping, with braided rush mats and sandals, flowers "in shells fixed to the walls . . . so it did look sort of home-like." Alone, she wore a pretty dress; "she must have kept it nice for best in the afternoons" (68). This is ritualistic housekeeping performed for its own sake: Is Joanna's life a rejection or an apotheosis of domesticity? Following the example of her father, who brought her to camp on Shell-heap Island when she was a child, Joanna has devised a female life that is impervious to patriarchal interruption. The very title of this chapter, "The Hermitage," insinuates questions. Does it refer to the hermit Joanna's house or to Mrs. Todd's, where these three single women are sheltering now? Or to both? Is a hermitage anti-domestic or quintessentially domestic?

For local people, Joanna Todd became an object not only of curiosity but of real concern, and perhaps of quiet identification; a path is beaten to her grave. Although the narrator receded into silence as Joanna's tale emerged, she becomes principal actor of a final chapter on Joanna, in which she too makes a solitary pilgrimage to Joanna's grave and attests to her own kinship. No longer is Joanna's retreat "something mediaeval"; instead, she concludes, "we understand our fellows of the cell to whatever age of history they may belong" (82). The chapter ends as the narrator hears distant laughter from a pleasure boat. "I knew, as if she had told me, that poor Joanna must have heard the like on many and many a summer afternoon, and must have welcomed the good cheer in spite of hopelessness and winter weather, and all the sorrow and disppointment in the world" (82). Here the narrator has completed an almost absolute identification with Joanna—but with a transformed Joanna, her maternal "grim streak" subdued, who could take pleasure from distant laughter.

Through Joanna's story, the narrator begins to move beyond her oversimplification of domestic life. These chapters take deep advantage of the possibilities of domestic life and literature. In Mrs. Todd's shell-like house, intimacy and privacy flourish simultaneously, as the women excavate and invent Joanna's story. At first the narrator seems as silently passive as the shell on the mantelpiece, with which she compares herself, as she hears the tale emerge. But her absorption of the tale empowers her to become an active pursuer of Joanna's legend, in her own pilgrimage, and finally even to become, like the other storytellers, an *inventor* of Joanna. She too appropriates Joanna as text. In the course of these four chapters the narrator is hostess and guest, insider and outsider, housekeeper and hermit. Joanna's tale pushes her to meditate on the dangers and necessities of housekeeping as that woman felt them and as she must confront them herself.

The most pressing questions that emerge from this meditation are about the relation of domesticity and solitude. Such questions were implied in *Deephaven,* but Jewett did not pursue them as she does in this mature book. For example, Mrs. Blackett, who has never lived long alone, is perplexed by "how Joanna lived without having nobody to do for, getting her own meals and tending her own poor self day in and day out" (69). For the three single women gathered in Mrs. Todd's house, such questions have more immediacy and application. Mrs. Fosdick, gregarious and domestically adaptable, invents solutions out of her own nature, assuming that Joanna must have assuaged loneliness by "making folks" out of her only livestock, her hens. The narrator follows Mrs. Fosdick's example when she asserts her "knowledge" that Joanna heard and "welcomed the good cheer" of laughter from pleasure boats. For herself, the narrator is discovering in Dunnet Landing how to balance private experience with a communal, domestic life. Sociably, intrusively, she assumes such a solution for Joanna too.

Mrs. Fosdick's model is easier to follow than Mrs. Todd's (although the narrator has moved toward Mrs. Todd's cyclical views in her conclusion that Joanna is not a "mediaeval" phenomenon, but a person with relevance to any historical period). As a young wife, Mrs. Todd "entreated" Joanna to come ashore with her and join her household. But now she knows what Mrs. Fosdick has not realized and the narrator is loath to learn: that Joanna Todd, as a historic individual, will remain impervious to efforts at understanding or appropriation. As Mrs. Todd concludes, "Joanna was Joanna, and there she lays." What Mrs. Todd has gained from her meditations on Joanna is *self*-knowledge—and wisdom.

Such wisdom keeps Mrs. Todd's housekeeping from rigidity or self-importance and makes her house a hermitage where one may live both as reflective hermit and sociable woman. It is significant that the Joanna Todd story is the only one in this book that is told under Mrs. Todd's own roof.

Through Joanna's story, the narrator joins a community of meditative women that extends beyond Mrs. Todd's hearth. This episode provokes the gravest, most intense, most active and revisionist responses to date from the narrator. It raises the stakes of housekeeping far above matters of cosiness and caretaking, acknowledging the rich communion of domestic culture while admitting the distances that that culture cannot go. Here too Jewett interrogates the problematic nineteenth-century American valorization of the free-standing individual. In Joanna Todd's solitary housekeeping, questions broached by Hawthorne, Mark Twain and others are reframed in the context of women's culture.

Newly enlightened and newly vulnerable, the narrator is ready next to move outward into the crowning ritual of the Bowden family reunion. Mrs. Blackett was born a Bowden; the reunion is a celebration of the female line. As the narrator sets out with Mrs. Todd and her mother for this great annual occasion, she sees William Blackett "escaping" in his boat, and Captain Littlepage, at his window, "watching for someone who never came. . . . with whom to speak his own language" (88). It is from women that she must learn the lessons of this great day (although plenty of Bowden men will be in attendance). The reunion is a ritual written larger than the daily rites in Mrs. Todd's house. It affirms, on one day of the year, that her house is *not* a solitary hermitage but a strong link in "a golden chain of love and dependence" (90). Mrs. Todd and Mrs. Blackett are not only mother and daughter, joined by domestic telepathy; they are also members of a larger family.

As they journey upcountry, images of unseen connections, nourishing underground tributaries, predominate. These profound connections find expression in the smallest acts of housework—when a woman at a wayside house hospitably offers them doughnuts, Mrs. Todd says, appreciatively, "We've observed there was doughnuts all the way along; if one house is frying all the rest is; 'tis so with a great many things" (191). Mrs. Todd has not entered any of these houses; how has she been able to "observe" the signs of doughnuts frying? Again, her sibylline wisdom is rooted in her domestic acuity.

The expansiveness of the reunion allows the narrator to think of many matters in a larger cultural context; Mrs. Blackett is not just a singular phenomenon of hospitality, charm, and endurance, but the "queen" of a large hospitable family. And Mrs. Todd, whom the narrator has sometimes thought "limited," is newly vivacious. The reunion is held outdoors, overlooking the sea and the comfortable old Bowden house—a suitably expansive setting. Here, Mrs. Todd seems for once "the picture of content" (100).

The family's procession into the grove where they hold their feast (a

homely potluck picnic) has grave dignity and beauty unsurpassed by anything in this book. The classical Greek imagery recurs for a last time,
embracing not only Mrs. Todd but her entire extended family, transformed
by ritual into proper company for this extraordinary woman. The narrator,
feeling "like an adopted Bowden" (99), marches with the rest; her usual
reticent "I" becomes "we": "We might have been a company of ancient
Greeks going to celebrate a victory, or to worship the god of harvests. . . . It
was strangely moving to see this and to make part of it. . . . We were no
more a New England family celebrating its own existence and simple
progress; we carried the tokens and inheritance of all such households from
which this had descended, and were only the latest of our line" (100). The
reunion is housekeeping written on a very large scale; it is an extension of
that most ordinary of domestic events, the family dinner. Such expanded
housekeeping is not limiting or "heavily domestic," as the narrator has
feared Mrs. Todd's life to be. Instead, it implies that the sibylline text has
been reconstituted and that the narrator, no longer amnesiac, is joined with
the family of her earliest ancestors. For once she is not torn between
observing (as realist writer must) and participating. The experience is
"*strangely* moving" because it is so rare for her simultaneously to "see this
and make part of it." The reunion posits a new and beautiful wholeness.
One aspect of this beauty is a celebratory combination of domesticity and art
that breaks down the accustomed barriers between the two, which the
narrator observed when she separated her work as a writer from Mrs. Todd's
house.

Other women artists take part in the feast. One is a poet, with a "long
faded garland of verses." Her verbal text is excessive and prepossessing; even
the "generous" Mrs. Todd says that "she harps too much" (109). It is the
domestic artists whose work is the heart of this occasion. The narrator
celebrates that work in the language of a discerning critic; for example, she
expresses her delight in "the elegant ingenuity displayed in the form of pies"
(108). Despite the copiousness of the feast, no one complains of *culinary*
excess. The artist with whom the narrator is most sympathetic is a cook, the
baker of a gingerbread representation of the old Bowden house. This
woman has "the gleaming eye of an enthusiast . . . a look of high ideals,"
and a realist's concern with verisimilitude. She says, "The old house, as you
observe, was never painted, and I concluded that plain gingerbread would
represent it best. It wasn't all I expected it would be," she said sadly, as many
an artist has said before her of his work" (108–09).

The narrator is newly attuned to connections between domesticity and
art; with the baker, she feels rueful empathy. It is the cooks who provide the

most capacious symbols of communion at the feast. Language itself is edible; they share an inscribed apple pie. The way Mrs. Todd cuts the pie, keeping words intact, indicates that she regards it as text as well as dessert; she "helped me generously to the whole word *Bowden* and consumed *Reunion* herself." The gingerbread house too is consumed by the company, not preserved as an artifact. If it is ephemeral, its meaning is not: "it was shared by a great part of the assembly, not without seriousness, as if it were a pledge and token of loyalty" (108). According to Jane Marcus and others, such "ephemerality" is characteristic of the domestic art traditionally created by women. "The *boeuf en daube* or the embroidered robe is not produced to survive eternally. It is eaten; it is worn; culture consists in passing on the technique of its making" ("Still Practice" 85).

In Marcus's terms, the reunion is a triumph of a functioning culture, effected by women artists who are housekeepers. As such, it is an irresistible magnet, especially for women, for it both supplements and validates their everyday, isolated domestic lives and allows them to see those lives as a sustaining part of a pattern that will survive them. In lives that feel the constant press of daily tasks—frying doughnuts, gathering herbs—the reunion affirms a further future and a cyclical calendar. At the day's end, the narrator "heard the words 'next summer' repeated many times, though summer was still ours and the leaves were green" (110).

On the way back home, she observes how her two companions begin to incorporate the reunion, now becoming past, back into the pattern of their everyday lives. Mrs. Todd's mind turns back to the mullein leaves she left drying, and she steals an anxious glance at her mother, betraying for the first and only time her anxiety about Mrs. Blackett's advanced age and impending death—for the reunion has heightened her awareness of the passage of time. As Mrs. Todd explains, the day is not really complete until the celebrants are back where they started: "Those that enjoyed it best'll want to get right home so's to think it over" (111). The reunion confirms again those qualities that Rybcyzynski says have been associated with housework since the seventeenth century: enforced privacy, intimacy, and a rich, reflective interior life. Appropriately, this episode ends where it began—back at Mrs. Todd's kitchen table, as the women begin the long process of thinking and talking over their "happy day." Through the Bowden reunion, the narrator's summer education moves beyond the study of compelling village individuals, such as Mrs. Todd, William, or Joanna. Now she comprehends the cultural context that joins them, enforcing, sanctioning, and problematizing the practice of domestic ritual.

The reunion chapters are the last segment of *The Country of the Pointed*

Firs published in the *Atlantic Monthly*. To complete the book, Jewett wrote two additional chapters, one describing a final visit and the last indicating the narrator's departure from Dunnet Landing. The last visit is with a local fisherman, Elijah Tilley. The narrator has "wondered a great deal about the inner life of these self-contained old fishermen; their minds seemed to be fixed upon nature and the elements rather than upon any contrivances of man, like politics or theology" (115). She already knows something of Captain Littlepage's exclusion from domesticity and William Blackett's use of domestic retreat as a bulwark against complications of human intercourse. Wondering about men's "inner life," the narrator begins to question the relationship between gender and the rhythms of daily life. In Tilley, she contemplates a male housekeeper.

Elijah Tilley tends a domestic shrine: the house his wife left behind when she died, eight years ago. Everything is dustless and shining, in the places she chose. In his touching, crippling devotion, Tilley denies his own creative power to shape and to change; his obsessive, static housekeeping rejects the process-oriented fluidity of female culture as described by Marcus. Tilley cleans and cooks well and knits proficiently by the patterns his mother taught him. But his skills seem to enslave him; he can take no pride in the fact that he does, in fact, have faculty. "I can't master none o' them womanish tricks" (126), he says. The juxtaposition of the words *master* and *womanish tricks* indicates some of the gender trauma endured by a housekeeping man. Because he cannot believe in his "mastery" of the rhythm of his own home life or perceive himself as a fully fledged participant in domestic culture, cyclical time is a trap for Elijah Tilley. He can find no respite from his constant grief for an absent woman; he tells the narrator, "Folks all kep' repeatin' that time would ease me, but I can't find it does. No, I miss her just the same every day" (121).

At Tilley's house, a parlor tour ends inevitably with the display of the dead wife's tea service, brought by her husband from Bordeaux, which is kept in a locked cabinet. Both delighted in the china's perfect preservation. But when she died, a broken cup was discovered. "Poor dear!" Elijah Tilley says. "I knowed in one minute how 'twas. We'd got so used to sayin' 'twas all there just's I fetched it home, an' so when she broke that cup somehow or 'nother she couldn't frame no words to come an' tell me. . . . I guess there wa'n't no other secret ever lay between us" (124–25). In the static Tilley household, housekeeping was a language so heavily freighted that it could not be spoken; Sara Tilley "couldn't frame no words" for a tale of a teacup. In such straits, domestic things have signifying power that can be terrible. For Tilley, things exert such pressure that he cannot fully comprehend the distinction between a human life and a household object. He tells the narrator, "There's that little rockin' chair o' her'n, I set an' notice it an' think how strange 'tis a creatur' like her should be gone an' that chair be right here in its old place" (122). The narrator says of the local fishermen that although they have "houses and lands . . . their true dwelling places were the sea" (115). A domestic man like Tilley presents a puzzle the narrator cannot quite solve; he reads both the language of the sea (where he acknowledges change and cyclical recurrence) and the language of his house (where change is death). If he could let his outdoor wisdom into the house, as do Mrs. Todd and Mrs. Bonny, it might assuage his compulsive grief. But when grief assails him most intensely, Elijah Tilley cannot tolerate the very shelter he tends so carefully; he says, "I get feelin' so sometimes I have to lay everything by an' go out door" (122). Everything about Tilley's housekeeping turns inward on him, making his cherished house and housework an embodiment of pain. This last excursion takes the narrator inside a house where domestic ritual has become a controlling obsession.

Elijah Tilley is an admirer of Mrs. Todd; twice he says, "Almiry's got the best of mothers" (127). No man honors the matriarchy of Dunnet Landing more than he. Yet Mrs. Todd thinks less of him than she does of addled Captain Littlepage; she says, "'Lijah's worthy enough; I do esteem 'Lijah, but he's a ploddin' man" (128). Mrs. Todd's situation is very much like Tilley's; she too lives alone in a dead spouse's house. But she has created a more complex mix of ritual and spontaneity in her life; she is *not* a "ploddin'" woman. Mrs. Todd says scornfully, "I must say I like variety myself; some folks washes Monday an' irons Tuesday the whole year round, even if the circus is goin' by" (34). It is significant that this defiance of monotony is a spirited repudiation of household gospel, the ritualistic prescription of work order ("Wash on Monday, / Iron on Tuesday, / Mend on Wednesday . . .") that was long traditional among American housekeepers.[7] Mrs. Todd would never confuse a woman and a thing; skilled housekeeper that she is, she guards against the plodding, obsessive routine that housekeeping threatens.

As the narrator surveys the Tilley parlor, she acknowledges that she has become proficient in the language of female housekeeping. She says, "I looked at the unworn carpet, the glass vases on the mantelpiece with their prim bunches of bleached swamp grass and dusty marsh rosemary, and I could read the history of Mrs. Tilley's best room from its very beginning" (124). Such reading confirms that her summer's education has been accomplished. In the last chapter, it is summer's end; the narrator must leave Dunnet Landing. This book has never denied or scrambled time, as *Deephaven* did; the chapters have been arranged chronologically, and each episode has begun with a cue to calendar time. The narrator's growing wisdom and equilibrium are signaled by her changing sense of time. In the first weeks of the summer, Dunnet time seemed a phenomenon of nature; "nothing happened except the growth of herbs and the course of the sun." But now, in her last Dunnet days, "there were many delightful things to be done and done again, as if I were in London. I felt hurried and full of pleasant engagements" (128–29). Time has been domesticated, socialized, ritualized, and made human; now Dunnet Landing seems as rich as London, the city that epitomizes densely civilized life. An important feature of such a life is the value it places on the repetition ("delightful things to be done and done again") which characterizes domestic life.

Departure from such a place, to return to what *seemed* civilization when she left it, is unnerving, and that fact is reflected in the narrator's prose: "At last I had to say good-by to all my Dunnet Landing friends, and my homelike place in the little house, and return to the world in which I feared to find myself a foreigner. There may be restrictions to such a summer's happiness, but the ease that belongs to simplicity is charming enough to make up for whatever a simple life may lack, and the gifts of peace are not for those who live in the thick of battle" (129). This passage is thick with implied questions. Why does the narrator "have to" say goodbye? Why is her place in the Todd house "home*like*" instead of "home," as it was in July? Why would her Dunnet summer transform her into a "foreigner" in the place she left behind? If she does not really belong *here* and fears to be a foreigner *there*, does the narrator really belong anywhere? In the second half of the passage, perhaps retreating from such questions, she sets up a smoke screen of "fine writing"; the language resembles that of her first chapter. Words such as "charming" and "simple life" condescend to the complexities she has witnessed in Dunnet Landing, and the arrogant notion that "the thick of battle" is somewhere far from Dunnet's restricted "peace" is an insult to such lives as those of Mrs. Todd, Captain Littlepage, Joanna Todd, and Elijah Tilley, in whose village existences there is much of intense and constant battle. In this disturbing paragraph, the narrator seems as obtuse as Kate and Helen sometimes did in *Deephaven*.

But she is not allowed to remain in that uncharacteristic state, for Mrs. Todd has final lessons for her. On her departure day, the narrator is puzzled by her friend's brusque, "almost disapproving" manner; Mrs. Todd bids her lodger a businesslike farewell and sets forth on a call. But her face betrays a depth of feeling beyond words: "I glanced at my friend's face and saw a look that touched me to the heart. I had been sorry enough before to go away" (130). Mrs. Todd's look returns the narrator to honest style and honest feeling. For the rich communion these women have shared, verbal forms are insufficient. Mrs. Todd turns her back and walks silently out of the house, away—exactly as Joanna walked away from Mrs. Todd herself, the day of their visit on Shell-heap Island. Even a woman as socially and domestically accomplished as Mrs. Todd has a kinship with the hermit, Joanna. Now the narrator sees her friend's large outlines: "her distant figure looked mateless and appealing . . . strangely self-possessed and mysterious" (131). Mrs. Todd remains singularly "mysterious." However well one may know her house and her routine, this large woman can never be exhaustively read. Observing her friend, the narrator reassumes the realist writer's observing posture, but with an awareness of the *limits* of literary language.

Although the relationship of the two women is finally beyond words, it is not beyond language. When the narrator goes back into the empty house, she is able to decipher the domestic meanings that her landlady has taught her, throughout the summer. Her empty room tells how she will be missed: "My room looked as empty as the day I came. I and all my belongings had died out of it, and I knew how it would seem when Mrs. Todd came back and found her lodger gone. So we die before our own eyes; so we see some chapters of our lives come to their natural end" (130–31). In this spare language, weighted with feeling, the narrator has fused her writer's vision with domestic vision: now a *room* is a *chapter* in her *life*. She has learned to inscribe domestic ritual.

Mrs. Todd's scorn for official, patriarchal language has often been expressed, throughout the summer. For example, she says disparagingly of an insensitive minister, "he seemed to know no remedies, but he had a great use of words" (77). Her gifts for her friend, left wordlessly on the kitchen table, speak the herbwoman's silent, effective language of remedies. In domestic code, they offer a reprise of the summer. "There was a quaint West Indian basket which I knew its owner had valued . . . there was an affecting provision laid beside it for my seafaring supper, with a neatly tied bunch of southernwood and a twig of bay, and a little old leather box which held the coral pin that Nathan Todd brought home to give to poor Joanna" (131).

These gifts combine indoors and out, past and present, communion and solitude. Each one signifies. Mrs. Todd's herbs are practical signs of her housekeeping faculty, but they also express her enduring friendship. Southernwood is a moth repellent, which staves off deterioration and decay. Bay was the classical tribute for heroes and poets; it is also an essential culinary herb and, in the Victorian language of flowers, meant "I change but in death" (Burke, unpaged). The twig of bay eloquently links language, housekeeping, and endurance. The basket and pin are heirlooms, objects that would more logically be passed on to a descendant. Joanna's pin, which Sharon O'Brien calls "a visible sign of female inheritance and attachment" (415), tells the narrator that Joanna's legacy of female isolation has, through Mrs. Todd, come down to her. None of these meaningful things can be left behind. Such gifts express powerful cultural connections and obligations. As Marcel Mauss has established, they are both necessary and "dangerous to accept. The gift itself constitutes an irrevocable link" (44, 58). By accepting Mrs. Todd's gifts, which would be meaningless things unless the narrator had mastered the language in which they signify, she must admit important, dangerous, and "irrevocable" links to an ongoing culture.

Mrs. Todd does not present the narrator with a single text to wrap up her summer's instruction. Instead, her gifts are a model of intertextual multiplicity, a collection of sibylline leaves. Unlike the amnesiac nineteenth-century writer of Gilbert and Gubar's parable, the narrator is learning to read those leaves. Through her education in the medium of domestic ritual, she has apprehended that a book about Dunnet Landing must be multiform; it must find ways to inscribe silence, absence, monotony, cycles, and human mystery. It is these qualities that infuse the summer's epiphanies of communion and understanding. The form of *The Country of the Pointed Firs* indicates a woman artist's decisions about how to make the leaves of a housekeeper-sibyl into a book that spells out a female aesthetic.

Recent appraisals of Jewett have emphasized her major status and her importance for American women's literature. Much of this criticism has concentrated on *The Country of the Pointed Firs,* generally considered Jewett's finest work, and has speculated about its structural principle. Most agree that the book is somehow "structurally innovative" (Donovan, *Jewett* 99).[8] The book is episodic; each episode has a certain narrative coherence. But connections among episodes, continuities of character, place, relationship, and—most notably—the narrator's developing sensibility give the book the self-possessed unity we may associate with a novel. Yet it lacks the pattern of complication and climax, the sense of accomplished external action, which we are accustomed to finding in nineteenth-century novels. The events of this book occur again and again, as domestic tasks do. Mrs. Todd has visited her mother many times; the Bowden reunion is held annually; Mrs. Todd and Mrs. Fosdick have discussed "poor Joanna" again and again, over the years. But repetition does not mute the importance of the visit and the reunion, or the urgency of the story. In lives as circumscribed as those of the residents of Dunnet Landing, validity and meaning are found not by striking out, but by going in deeper, through the apparent boredom and triviality of repetition, toward the hidden understanding that must be approached cyclically.[9] Mrs. Todd, whose life is intensely domestic and physically confined, understands this cyclical quality and she, like Jewett, sees it as a distinctively female way of feeling. She tells the narrator that her male lover "has forgot our youthful feelin's, I expect, but a woman's heart is different; them feelin's comes back when you think you've done with 'em, as sure as spring comes with the year" (8).

Our increasing regard for Jewett would have come as no surprise to Willa Cather, who predicted it in 1925. She wrote, "I like to think with what . . . a sense of rich discovery the young student of American literature in far distant years to come will take up this book and say, 'A masterpiece!' as proudly as if he himself had made it. It will be a message to the future, a message in a universal language" (Preface, unpaged). Cather's conventional male pronouns and the word "masterpiece" seem especially ironic here, for the "message" that Jewett's book conveys to many of its current readers locates validity and endurance in a network of (largely) female lives. If *The Country of the Pointed Firs* is, as Cather says, "a message in a universal language," that language is the domestic code that Mrs. Todd taught the narrator to read.

Early in the book, the narrator despaired of catching the "cadences" of a Maine day on her page. This implies that she is trying to transmute her summer into literature. The book's existence is evidence that she finally succeeds. The life she conveys is finely cadenced, and subtle, ordinary domestic signs are translated, by the narrator's acuity, into a widely accessible language. Many of Jewett's innovative decisions about the shaping of this book have the effect of emphasizing its domestic cadences. *Deephaven* had thirteen chapters, each a thematically complete unit that could have been published separately. *The Country of the Pointed Firs*, although much briefer, has twenty-one chapters, which fall into six or seven episodes. Chapters range in length from one to fourteen pages; each is titled.

These frequent breaks help Jewett to replicate domestic rhythms. For example, the single evening in which the narrator hears the story of Joanna Todd is broken into three chapters. The first, "Poor Joanna," emphasizes the pitiful, archaic qualities of her retreat, ending just as Mrs. Todd reaches a dramatic moment in her account of her visit to the island house: "All of a sudden Joanna come right to the fore door and stood there, not sayin' a word" (72). It is as if the powerful silent figure defies the epithet, and the chapter, which would oversimplify and diminish her. The next chapter begins with the interruption by Mrs. Todd's customer, which allows the narrator and Mrs. Fosdick an interval for silent meditation. When Mrs. Todd returns, the story's view of Joanna grows more archetypal and more profound, as reflected in the title, "The Hermitage." Then the sequence concludes in a third chapter, "On Shell-heap Island," as the narrator acknowledges her kinship with Joanna by traveling to her island. The solitary pilgrimage follows naturally from the deepening reflections that began in a domestic ritual, the fireside telling of Joanna's tale. The combination of these small units, with titles pointing as signposts to meanings as they emerge, consolidate, and accrue, creates a stop-and-start rhythm that replicates, on yet another level, the interruptible, repetitive, yet cumulative qualities of domestic life. Thus Jewett suggests cadences within as well as between domestic occasions. For example, the rich expanse for reunion, reflection, solitude, and indoor and outdoor exploration that was offered by a day's visit at Green Island is indicated by presenting that episode in four chapters. Jewett's acute awareness of the importance of such matters is shown by the fact that one of the few changes she made in *The Country of the Pointed Firs* between *Atlantic Monthly* and book publication was to consolidate two chapters in the family reunion sequence.

By bequeathing to the narrator some of her most valuable possessions—stories, wisdom, herbs, language, and coral pin—Mrs. Todd establishes that the *breakdown* that Donovan, Gail Parker, and others have seen in late nineteenth-century American women's culture need not be inevitable. To transmit her sibylline female heritage, this daughterless, nieceless woman must find female heirs to whom she is related by affinity, not genealogy. It is crucial that a *writer* is her chosen heir, for the narrator can mediate between the sibyl's uninscribed tradition and the written texts sanctioned by patriarchal culture, as she also mediates between declining village and ascendant city. Jewett's subtle adjustments in her written text, attuning it to domestic rhythms, express the very continuity of female culture that is her subject.

On her writing desk, Jewett had pinned a maxim from Flaubert: "Écrire la vie ordinaire comme on écrit l'histoire" (*Jewett Letters* 16). History, of course, validates what it records. And in *The Country of the Pointed Firs*, one of Jewett's largest accomplishments is the validation of ordinary life. In the first book on Jewett, F. O. Matthiessen concluded that "Miss Jewett does not generally deal with the central facts of existence" (149). Another early critic, Paul Elmer More, regretted Jewett's "inability to make passion or action real and vital" ("A Writer" 42). Such misapprehensions occur when Jewett's readers do not share her respect for "*la vie ordinaire.*" The ritualized rhythm of dailiness is a central fact of existence and a medium for or solace from some of the most powerful passions we feel. For women, as I have said, that rhythm has often been domestic. *The Country of the Pointed Firs* is an enormously innovative narrative because of the ways it observes and reflects such rhythms. In a culture oriented to progress and to a male-dominated idea of plot as instrument of quest, conflict, and completion, the circularity of female lives such as those of Mrs. Todd and Mrs. Blackett was sometimes difficult to recognize and to acknowledge, as it was for these early male critics. In such situations, according to Rabuzzi, female culture may go underground, becoming secret and hidden—as with witchcraft, to which Jewett sometimes alludes. It may seem that "women's culture is a kind of gnosis, a special knowledge, even a heresy, with explicit rites and rituals of its own" (21). Yet, read closely, *The Country of the Pointed Firs* is a kind of primer, instructing its readers, syllable by syllable, in the language by which some of the deepest meanings of ordinary life are explicated, spoken, and written—and thus validated as central to a common culture. It is worth remembering that, while *The Country of the Pointed Firs* has sometimes suffered from disparaging literary assessments ("slight," "minor," or "peripheral"), it has always been a popular book, finding readers who have valued it for what it has to teach.

After *The Country of the Pointed Firs* was published, Jewett discouraged her readers from thinking of the book as a finished artifact and a completed plot. In the five years that remained in her writing life, she returned to Dunnet Landing and her visitor-narrator in four major stories. Three of these stories ("The Queen's Twin," "A Dunnet Shepherdess," and "The Foreigner") seem to reenter the time frame of the book, the months of the narrator's summer visit; the fourth ("William's Wedding") is set in the spring following the narrator's autumn departure, at the end of *The Country of the Pointed Firs*. Thus she suggests that, within the continuum of a cycle, one can move backward and forward in time, reentering a domestic life that offers unique insights and satisfactions.

The later stories all return to concerns already introduced, deepening and extending their implications. Two focus on relations among women. "The Queen's Twin" (1899) takes the narrator on her hardest journey with Mrs. Todd, a long hike upcountry to visit Abby Martin, an old widow who was born on the same day as Queen Victoria and whose solitary life is dominated by an obsession with her royal "twin." The route to Mrs. Martin's "inland" farm is a model of obscurity, "so overgrown . . . that you keep losin' the path in the bushes" (191). Alone, with only very occasional visits from the few (such as Mrs. Todd) who sympathize with her, she lives a life that seems almost entirely unacknowledged by culture, effaced and unwritten. In this story Jewett frames questions about privacy and publicity in the lives of nineteenth-century women; subtly but persuasively, the story links Abby

Martin's domestic situation to the great questions of abolition and suffrage that dominated nineteenth-century politics. Describing her friend's hard-working life, unsatisfactory husband, and inattentive children, Mrs. Todd says, "Yes, you might say that Abby'd been a slave, but there ain't any slave but has some freedom" (200). Abby Martin freed herself from the potential slavery of her domestic obscurity by linking herself with the most famous public woman of her time, Queen Victoria. She says, "There is something between us, being born just the same time; 'tis what they call a birthright. . . . She's been everything to me" (207). Abby has domesticated her images of the distant sister-queen, claiming Victoria's public life as a precious part of her privacy. Constructing frames for the queen's newspaper portraits, placing flowers at her shrine, and even assigning her a special teacup, she makes the queen her sister by including her in the language of her housekeeping. Abby is certain that this domestic language is mutual, a link between women of different nationalities and stations: "I expect she's a beautiful housekeeper . . . and she's been as good a mother as she's been a queen" (204).

This connection has become a sustaining force in Abby's life because of *publicity*—newspapers, contemporary history books, and most especially Victoria's own writing. Thanks to Mrs. Todd, who again serves as mediator between a writer and Dunnet Landing, Mrs. Martin says, "I've got her [Victoria's] beautiful book about the Highlands . . . it's been a treasure to my heart. . . . Before that I used to have to imagine a good deal, but when I come to read her book [*Leaves from the Journal of Our Life in the Highlands*], I knew what I expected was all true. We do think alike about so many things" (206). *Writing* makes Victoria a palpable presence to Abby Martin. *Leaves from the Journal of Our Life in the Highlands* records family travels and local visits; Victoria at first resisted its publication, saying, as her editor, Arthur Helps, recorded, "that she had no skill whatever in authorship; that these were, for the most part, mere homely accounts of excursions near home." It was this very "homeliness" that made the book so valuable to Abby Martin; it validated her dream of a common language and a mutual birthright. These links elaborate Jewett's concerns with continuities of women's lives and culture and with how they might be facilitated by women's writing. The conclusions of Jane Marcus, examining late nineteenth- and early twentieth-century autobiographical writing by women, suggest that Victoria's strategy of publishing her life in "homely" terms that contrasted with the diplomatic language of her official life was typical. Marcus concludes, "what seems significant is not the female struggle to enter male public discourse, which feminist scholars have documented, but the recognition of the inability of that discourse to include their voices in history, the necessity of the return to the personal" ("Invincible Mediocrity" 115).

Victoria's book, read by Abby Martin, suggests a female discourse that can be articulated in both writing and housekeeping and can confirm a sisterhood beyond genetic kinship, which may be a model for Jewett's autobiographical writer-narrator. Mrs. Martin, warmed by the sympathy of her visitors and her intuition that they, too, are fluent in that discourse, tells them for the first time a parablelike tale from her solitary life:

> One day I got to thinkin' so about my dear Queen . . . an livin' so in my thoughts, that I went to work an' got all ready for her just as if she was really comin'. I never told this to a livin' soul before, but I feel you'll understand. I put my best fine sheets and blankets I spun an' wove myself on the bed, and I picked some pretty flowers and put 'em all round the house, an' I worked as hard an' happy as I could all day, and had as nice a supper ready as I could get, sort of telling myself a story all the time. She was comin' an' I was goin' to see her again, an' I kep' it up until nightfall; an' it came to me I was all alone, the dream left me, an' I sat down on the doorstep an' felt all foolish an' tired. An' if you'll believe it, I heard steps comin', an' an old cousin of mine come wanderin' along, one I was apt to be shy of. She wasn't all there . . . but harmless enough and a kind of poor old talking body. And . . . we sat down to supper together; 'twas a supper I should have had no heart to eat alone. (207–08)

The prospect of communion with her exalted public "twin" gave new meaning and value to all Abby Martin's prototypical housekeeping tasks, from weaving to cooking. The power of this "dream" and the intensity of her need allowed Abby to recognize her actual kinswoman, whatever her deficiencies, in the wandering cousin, with whom she shared communion at the suppertable. When she articulates this story to her friends for the first time, she extends communion and sisterhood to them. Mrs. Todd, deeply moved, claims Abby's parable for herself and other women; she says, " 'I guess you wa'n't the first one who's got supper that way, Abby,' and then for a moment she could say no more" (208). Here Victoria's writing, Abby's housekeeping and storytelling, and her friends' empathetic response create a continuum of supportive female culture that nourishes everyone from a wandering pauper to a distant queen.

"The Foreigner" (1900)[10] follows these continuities of female culture even further, to the edge of the supernatural. Like Joanna Todd's story, it is told in the narrator's room in Mrs. Todd's house, as if it, too, has special import for the relation between these two women. And it poses crucial questions about how to tell an obscure woman's story. On a frighteningly stormy night, when she is worried about her mother on Green Island, Mrs.

Todd tells of Mrs. Tolland, a long-dead Frenchwoman who settled in Dunnet Landing after marrying a local captain. Not long after his death, she died too, apparently of grief and her own "foreignness."

At first, the woman of the title seems almost effaced. Her original name is forgotten; she bears only her last husband's name and rank, "Mrs. Captain Tolland." Mrs. Todd recounts the tale as she heard it from her father; with three other voyaging Dunnet captains, he met the Frenchwoman in Jamaica, where she was singing and dancing for her keep, having lost husband, children, friends, money, and destination in a yellow fever epidemic. Her history suggests a horrifying sequence of near obliteration. She appealed to the Dunnet captains for help and Captain Blackett's story frames this woman as a problem for men. They cast lots and bargained for her and Captain Tolland agreed to take her on his ship, to escape. At the voyage's end, sailing into a Maine port, "they stepped right afore a justice of the peace" (165), and Captain Tolland brought his new wife home to Dunnet Landing. The men's legalistic version presents the Frenchwoman as a problematic piece of property.

Mrs. Todd's mother offers another way to view the foreigner. Young Almira, newly widowed herself, at first shared the town's narrow disapproval of the Frenchwoman. In many ways this story explicates the dark underside of local color, showing how cruelly insular a village such as Dunnet can be. Mrs. Tolland's gay and demonstrative ways violated local custom, something even Mrs. Todd found hard to forgive. But Mrs. Blackett at once extended her generous friendship. When she came late to the "nice supper" her daughter had prepared, because she was comforting the foreigner, Mrs. Todd resented the interference with her ordered housekeeping. Mrs. Blackett firmly instructed her daughter in domestic priorities, placing the obligation to offer communion to a neighbor far above the need for a prompt supper:

> "I want you to neighbor with that poor lonesome creatur'," says Mother to me, lookin' reproachful. "She's a stranger in a strange land." . . .
>
> "What consequence is my supper?" she says to me; Mother can be very stern,—"or your comfort and mine, besides letting a foreign person an' a stranger feel so desolate. . . . think if 't was you in a foreign land!" (169)

Mrs. Todd, in the forty years since the Frenchwoman's arrival, is still mediating between her parents' versions of Mrs. Tolland's story—one emphasizing law, difference, and loss of identity; the other suggesting sympathy and identification. As the tale emerges, Mrs. Todd indicates her own changes in attitude, through years of meditation on the foreigner. As her mother did, she calls Mrs. Tolland a "poor creatur'," and says, "it all seems so different to me now" (166). She tells the woman's story through to its end, four times. Each time, something crucial is omitted, and Mrs. Todd retells the tale. It emerges that she, who eventually befriended and nursed the woman, was her heir; an income from the small inheritance has been Mrs. Todd's mainstay over the years and has allowed her to live independently.

Mrs. Todd's uncle, Captain Bowden, was one of the four men who discovered the Frenchwoman in Jamaica. For him, as executor of her will, the woman remained to the last a problem in property; after her death, he maintained that money was hidden in her house, and eventually burned it down in one of his obsessive searches. To Mrs. Todd, such an obsession is "childish" as well as destructive. For her, the problem is finding some way to express, in the syllables offered by culture, the connection between herself and a woman who remained, however pleasant a companion, obdurately "foreign." Learning of her inheritance, Mrs. Todd mourned the solidity of this barrier: " 'I begun to cry,' said Mrs. Todd; 'I couldn't help it. I wished I had her back again to do somethin' for, and to make her know I felt sisterly to her more'n I'd ever showed" (179–80).

Mrs. Todd's parents and her village propose conflicting ways of dealing with the Frenchwoman. More than anything else, housekeeping provided a common language; Mrs. Todd's responses to the problem of a *foreigner* as *kinswoman*, someone to whom she feels "sisterly," are worked through in the vocabularies she knows best: storytelling and domestic ritual. Mrs. Tolland, too, was an exemplary solitary housekeeper. A "beautiful cook," she taught Mrs. Todd French cuisine and shared her regard for herbal cookery and medicine: "she taught me a sight o' things about herbs. . . . she went right down on her knees in my garden when she saw I had my different officious herbs" (170). Although she could not find peace in the village church, Mrs. Tolland knelt in obeisance to the continuity of women's culture when she discovered the plants she knew in her neighbor's garden. As Mrs. Todd evokes her, she resembles the narrator's description of Mrs. Todd, early in *The Country of the Pointed Firs;* Mrs. Tolland would "act awful secret about somethings too, an' used to work charms for herself sometimes" (170).

Telling the foreigner's story to another woman, herself a storyteller, Mrs. Todd replicates the story the narrator writes of herself and Mrs. Todd. They too are foreigners to each other, who find a common language in Mrs. Todd's house but retain their separateness to the end, and beyond it. They are also each other's heirs; Mrs. Todd finds the narrator worthy to inherit the story of her inner life, as well as household treasures, and she is memorialized as the narrator inscribes her in these stories. Similarly, the foreigner was naturalized, posthumously, as her recipes, herbal lore, and household treasures were incorporated into Mrs. Todd's housekeeping.

Having told the foreigner's story through for a third time, Mrs. Todd takes it up once more, with an air of special import: "'I ain't told you all,' she continued; 'no, I ain't spoken of all to but very few.' . . . The cat [on Mrs. Todd's lap] suddenly lifted her head with quick excitement and gleaming eyes, and her mistress was leaning forward toward the fire . . . as if they were consulting the glowing coals for some augury. Mrs. Todd looked like an old prophetess . . . she was posed for some great painter. The woman with the cat was as unconscious and mysterious as any sibyl of the Sistine Chapel" (182–83). Here Jewett returns to the suggestive sibylline imagery of *The Country of the Pointed Firs*, spelling it out more explicitly than ever before. Accompanied by her female listener and the cat, a female familiar, Mrs. Todd looks for her truths in the domestic hearth fire, and the narrator sees her as a subject worthy of the greatest art. She resembles one of Michelangelo's powerful sibyls, repositories of primal wisdom. Peter Schmidt suggests that "when sibylline women appear in women's literature, they stage scenes of instruction that teach their initiates to identify, question, and alter the cultural texts . . . that define what a woman's identity may be" (88). Mrs. Todd's tale is the center of such a scene.

For Mrs. Tolland in Dunnet Landing, "foreignness" was the only possible role. But now Mrs. Todd makes another revelation: as she sat watching with the dying woman, she saw the apparition of Mrs. Tolland's mother come to claim her. Mrs. Todd and Mrs. Tolland are linked by this vision; it dissipated the boundaries of "foreignness" as established by the village culture. Dying, the Frenchwoman again asked, "You saw her, didn't you?" needing to the end the confirmation of a sympathetic living woman. Mrs. Todd bravely replied, *"Yes dear, I did; you ain't never goin' to feel strange and lonesome no more"* (186). Performing one of the oldest domestic rituals, "watching" at a deathbed, Mrs. Todd glimpsed a supernatural truth so profound that it altered her very idea of rationality: "I never called it beyond reason I should see the other watcher. I saw plain enough there was somebody with me in the room" (186). She sees a continuity of care among women, powerful enough to abrogate the line between life and death.

With this last revelation, Mrs. Todd has at last accomplished her tale. Its telling has taken the repetitive form of domestic ritual, with its returns to a recurrent subject, and with the assumption that meaning inheres in such repetition. She has moved from her father's initial pragmatic, patriarchal narrative through successive versions to the final sibylline tale. None of these versions cancels out the others. As she tells it, Mrs. Todd's tale embodies intertextuality. But on this stormy evening, when Mrs. Todd is especially anxious about her aged mother, the last twist of the tale is a necessary completion. By it, the links to sibylline wisdom and tradition are reaffirmed and the unseen woman, "the other watcher," finds her place in the tale and, through the narrator, *on the page*. The narrator's own sympathy has allowed Mrs. Todd to speak a story that most listeners would find "beyond reason." And housekeeping, the warm fire, and the snug room provide the necessary medium in which women can express the deepest continuities of gendered culture. It is not insignificant that Mrs. Todd's knitting continues throughout the tale.

A modern, urban woman in a male-dominated profession, the narrator has felt and feared the curse of foreignness herself. In "The Foreigner," the last of these stories completed and published during her lifetime, Jewett found a way to affirm the links between women without denying the stringencies of their lives or the potential conflict of women's culture and local culture. The calm of the story's last paragraph is conveyed by the narrator's style; it contrasts with the agitated anxiety with which the story began and indicates that Mrs. Todd has been successful in locating her resolution and sharing it with the narrator, who at last says, "We sat together in the warm little room . . . the high wind had done blowing." Mrs. Todd pronounces final words: "the storm's all over" (187). Knowing of Mrs. Tolland, the narrator can read the meanings of Mrs. Todd's housekeeping still more fully; she now knows the source of her French omelets and her French prints and sees the Todd household as a medium shaped by many women, named and nameless. She has also discovered the (partial) antidote for her own foreignness. Just as Joanna's isolated hermitage is part of every woman's heritage, so is the communion that these two women feel in the "warm little room." The mother-daughter bond may symbolize such communion, but it is not solely a genetic connection. Through ritual and attention, it is accessible to any woman, and it passes from Mrs. Todd to her lodger—the narrator—and on to us.

The other two additional Pointed Firs stories both return to the enigmatic figure of William Blackett, his sister's quiet counterpart, an androgynous man with powerful domestic sympathies, who can make silence speak. For Jewett and her autobiographical narrator, there is much to be learned from such a figure. In "A Dunnet Shepherdess" (1899), the narrator spends an upcountry day with him, fishing and accompanying him on his annual visit to his longtime sweetheart, Esther Hight, who tends a large flock of sheep and an embattled, paralyzed old mother. When William comes to the schoolhouse with his invitation for this day's excursion, he rescues the eager narrator from the day's stint of writing. Departing with him, she says, "I saw a flutter of white go past the window as I left the schoolhouse and my morning's work to their neglected fate" (139). William's tutelage, like his sister's, will help this writer expand the narrow confines of her text; in fact, her voyages into the "happy world" literally give that text wings, as the narrator glimpses her pages fluttering in the breeze.

William is an apt model for a writer, because of his capacity to inscribe and read enduring meaning in the smallest phenomena. Even Mrs. Todd notes this sensitivity to language; she says, "I don't know sometimes but William's kind of poetical. . . . You'd think if anything could cure him of it, 'twould be the fish business" (137). In William's hands, the humble dried fish he presents to his lover are a jewellike tribute, "each one chosen with perfect care" (155), and although he sees his beloved for an afternoon of conversation only once a year, he takes sustaining satisfaction in the view of her pasture from his island. Such feats of sympathetic reading have been the lovers' sustenance for forty years.

This story provides a balance to the near-matriolatry of "The Foreigner." Mrs. Hight, despite the severity of her handicap and her "noble courage and persistence" (155), is a bossy old dictator. Esther has chosen a career that has allowed her to tend to business *and* to tend her demanding mother. Although "well able to hire somebody," she often "stays out all night," watching her sheep (150). After a long visit with the old woman, the narrator divines that such nights out must have been a solace; "I had seen enough of old Mrs. Hight to know that nothing a sheep might do could vex a person who was accustomed to the uncertainties and severities of her companionship" (154). Such a willful mother and the demands of maintaining her housekeeping threaten the dearest wishes and deepest needs of her child. And Jewett implies that Mrs. Hight is not the only such mother. Mrs. Blackett, however charming and wise, is one as well. The lovers have always lived apart; "William had his mother, and Esther had hers" (155).

William himself has been in danger of effacement by the two master housekeepers, his mother and sister. Significantly, the story begins with Mrs. Todd's insistence that William, before setting off to see Esther, be anointed with a dark ointment of pennyroyal, to keep off mosquitoes. The remedy, made from Mrs. Todd's favorite herb with its female associations, obscures William's face with the mask of his sister's powerful faculty; he goes to Esther with his ties to his mother and sister written all over his face. The story ends with the narrator's reference to this; "We had seen a solitary mosquito, but there was a dark stripe across his mild face, which might have been an old scar worn long ago in battle" (156). Beneath the gentle and romantic surface of this story is the intimation of the battle for self waged against a trio of powerful housekeeping women—a battle that has left even William with ancient scars. The narrator's comprehension of such battles is implied in her description of the compelling Esther: "Then she smiled at me, a smile of noble patience, of uncomprehended sacrifice which I can never forget. There was all the remembrance of disappointed hopes, the hardships of winter, the loneliness of single-handedness in her look, but I understood, and I love to remember her worn face and her young blue eyes" (155). No character of the Pointed Firs fiction is romanticized more than Esther, the dutiful daughter; she is an iconic figure who speaks fewer than a dozen words in the two stories in which she appears, but whom the narrator "understands" with immediate telepathy.

"William's Wedding," the last Pointed Firs story, was left unrevised when Jewett died, in 1909. In it, the narrator returns, in the spring following her departure at the book's end, for a brief visit with Mrs. Todd, to find that Mrs. Hight has died and William and Esther are to be married. After a private ceremony, they visit Mrs. Todd's house and then set out for Green Island, where Mrs. Blackett awaits them.

Here the narrator's problems as woman writer and daughter of the nineteenth century converge. In its unrevised state, the story at first seems to project an uncharacteristic near-clean sweep of resolutions. Mrs. Blackett, the more benevolent of the two powerful old mothers, has managed to outlive the termagant Mrs. Hight and, by marriage, Esther becomes Mrs. Blackett's daughter and joins her household. William can now act out his love for the first time, and his language is accordingly expanded. He greets the congratulating neighbors with quiet "heartiness," as if acknowledging that the great events of his life are communal rituals, meant to be shared. The ceremony itself, at the minister's house, is unseen; Mrs. Todd and the narrator wait, Mrs. Todd in tears.[11] The language in which the import of this marriage may be expressed is the highest refinement of Mrs. Todd's housekeeping; under the privacy of her roof, she embraces the couple in an unwontedly open display of feeling and then sets forth cake from her "best receipt" and a carefully preserved bottle of rare wine. "We took the cake and wine of the marriage feast together, always in silence, like a true sacrament" (224). Words are inadequate to the meaning of this occasion; to read its full, sacramental implications, one must be fluent in a vocabulary of gesture and housekeeping, which the narrator has acquired in Dunnet Landing. Much of Mrs. Todd's day, before the bride and groom arrive, is spent in fending off the inquiries of curious neighbors; proudly taciturn, she "routs" them all. From the moment of the bride and groom's arrival, there is no word of dialogue; the most meaningful messages are exchanged in other ways, such as "a happy glance of comprehension" (224) between Esther and the narrator, William's tender care in pinning Esther's shawl, and his last sign to the narrator: he "looked me full in the face to be sure I understood how happy he was" (226).

Quiet Esther has disposed of her property and left her flocks behind (except for one orphan lamb), exchanging outdoor independence for a place in the most idyllic household of the Pointed Firs fiction, as daughter-in-law and wife. She remains an archetypal shape, "like a figure of Millet's" (147). On Green Island, Esther will join the myth of domestic accord that the narrator loved on her own visit there. That myth is a powerful part of Jewett's story, a compelling presence in the nineteenth century's depiction of women's culture. Every woman who lives on Green Island becomes an icon, beautiful and problematic in her absolute wisdom and goodness.

Mrs. Todd, as we have seen, was the daughter who could not stay on Green Island. With her, the narrator has experienced another version of housekeeping, a domestic life that is a constant process of shifts, adjustments, nuances, stories, solitudes, and rituals. In this narrative, if Mrs. Blackett embodies domestic myth, Mrs. Todd enacts domestic experience. It is not for nothing that the two are mother and daughter, for myth and experience were closely and problematically related in the late nineteenth century. Mrs. Todd, as we have seen, has monumental qualities, and in "William's Wedding" she is once again described as sibylline, beckoning the narrator "as if she were a sibyl" (219), and as a repository of primal female wisdom. But she is also a needful mortal woman. The narrator feels some anxiety and guilt on this return visit (which will be short, for she is spending the summer in France). Subtly, Mrs. Todd lets her know that she has been missed and that distant loyalties and written texts are not necessarily the equivalent of her constant collaborating presence in the house. When a sickly little girl is brought by for Mrs. Todd's diagnosis and dosing, the herbwoman is "very indignant and very wistful. . . . 'I wish they'd let me keep her,' she said" (221). Obviously the writer's friendship, allegiance, and occasional domestic presence have not obviated Mrs. Todd's need for a *present* female heir.

Coming back to Dunnet Landing, the narrator must realize that she is returning to a world of needs as present and pressing as her own. The women's reunion is charged with feeling: "Then on my homesick heart fell the voice of Mrs. Todd. She stopped, through what I knew to be excess of feeling, to rebuke Johnny for bringing in so much mud, and I dallied without for one moment during the ceremony; then we met again face to face" (215). It is Mrs. Todd for whom the narrator has been "homesick"; now she reads the import of her ritual domestic rebuke to a muddy boy, and, unlike her eagerly verbal self of the previous summer, she herself "dallies" for a silent moment. At this point, the story's first chapter ends; the next chapter resumes with Mrs. Todd's question about bonnet styles in the city, delivered "as soon as she could say anything" (215). The narrator is shaping her text to accommodate the meaningful domestic code of silence she has learned from her friend. Back in this longed-for place, she feels at first uneasy, "a little unsupported" (217). She is supported only when she begins again to feel herself a part of the domestic rhythm of the house; "on the second morning I woke with the familiar feeling of interest and ease . . . I could hear Mrs. Todd's heavy footsteps pounding about in the other part of the house" (217), as if the older woman is laying down that rhythm with her body, as she goes about her morning housekeeping.

This morning is the wedding day. And when Mrs. Todd has readied her house for the feast, the two women share what Rabuzzi calls the "traditional mode of being" for housekeeping women: "waiting" (141). In a charged atmosphere, attending the bride and groom, they sit "in different rooms. . . . She was knitting, I believe, and as for me I dallied with a book" (219). The little house is now a model of women's culture as Jewett projects it: it accommodates, under one roof but in separate rooms, a knitting woman, plying the traditional domestic web, and a woman occupied with words.[12] Although an idealized marriage is ostensibly the subject of this last tale, the story finally values relations among women as highly as any male/female union, as is apparent in its last words. As Mrs. Todd and the narrator watch William and Esther sailing to Green Island, Mrs. Todd says:

> "Mother'll be watching for them. . . . Yes, mother'll be watching all day, and waiting. She'll be so happy to have Esther come."
> We went home together up the hill, and Mrs. Todd said nothing more; but we held each other's hands all the way. (226)

Now Mrs. Todd retells the story Jewett has titled "William's Wedding" in terms of her mother's vigil, reminding us of the story of the housebound woman, "watching . . . and waiting," as she and the narrator have also done. Her story maintains the myth of perfect domestic peace and accord on Green Island, asserting her mother's joy in Esther's arrival. The story of a marriage is thus retold as the tale of two women in a house.

As Mrs. Todd and the narrator return to Mrs. Todd's house, they return to another such story, of themselves as two women in a house. This story is not spoken—even Mrs. Todd has no more words—instead it is told by gesture, silence, and a mutual sense of "home." In this last ambitious tale, drawing from the capacious Pointed Firs vocabulary of speech, silence, and housekeeping, Jewett found ways to indicate domestic myth, heterosexual romance, and the subtle communion shared by the two women in Mrs. Todd's house, where a sibylline housekeeper and a modern woman writer may find a mutual home.

The Country of the Pointed Firs, as I have said, is Jewett's mature reworking of *Deephaven.* And in these four last stories, we can see Jewett continuing to rework the second book. As the last chapter of *The Country of the Pointed Firs* indicates, the narrator has acknowledged domestic ritual as a central subject and medium of her narrative. But her problematic leavetaking from Mrs. Todd shows that she is still deeply uncertain about how her life and her language are linked to Dunnet housekeeping. Thus she returns in "William's Wedding" to questions with special significance for her generation of American women. The concerns of these four late stories would also be the starting point for a next generation of women writers, most notably Willa Cather and Ellen Glasgow. In "The Queen's Twin" and "The Foreigner," issues of obscurity, publicity, isolation, and gender are highlighted, and the possibility of housekeeping as the common language of female culture is reemphasized. As the most obvious emblem of such commonality, the mother-daughter bond is scrutinized, both in the idealized form of Mrs. Tolland's supernatural mother and through the various difficulties and imperatives of mother-daughter relations between Mrs. Blackett and Mrs. Todd, Mrs. Hight and Esther, Abby Martin and her absent daughters, and finally projected in the future proximity of Esther and Mrs. Blackett. The last stories offer a far more complex sense of mother-daughter relations.[13]

William Blackett also obviously continued to tease Jewett's imagination. A silent "poet" of the ordinary, he offers a model of an artist who has managed to survive even within a stronghold of idealized domesticity and to make the most hackneyed domestic cliches (dried fish or "Home, Sweet Home") richly expressive. Jewett does not deny the cost of William's and Esther's loyalties to their powerful mothers; most obvious of these costs (especially in fiction of the Darwinian nineties, when reproduction was a crucial marker of a character's power and success) is the fact that they are too old to have children. The narrator is clearly established as Mrs. Todd's heir at the end of *The Country of the Pointed Firs;* at the end of "William's Wedding," it is apparent that she is, to some degree, William's heir as well. Despite his shyness and dislike of the direct gaze, William looks straight at his writer-friend, "to be sure I understood how happy he was" (226), insuring that his own obscure joy will be memorialized in her written text. William's androgyny also indicates that Jewett is thinking about ways of expanding the exclusivity of traditionally domestic women's culture. Significantly, Esther and William's union is the marriage of a domestically sensitive man and a woman who has succeeded in the traditionally male sheep business; Sherman notes that both have "traits . . . usually associated with the opposite gender" (264).

Returning to these persistent questions after the publication of *The Country of the Pointed Firs* in 1896, Jewett did not reinvent another narrator and another village as she had when *Deephaven* was completed. As I have said earlier, she had discovered, in the text of *The Country of the Pointed Firs*, formal strategies of repetition and return, which allowed her to suggest meaning as it has often accrued in the lives of traditional women, within the structure of domestic ritual.[14] "William's Wedding" is a uniquely important component of this project, for it tackles the problem that Helen Denis alluded to only in the unpeopled fantasy that ends *Deephaven:* the problem of the narrator's return to the ongoing community of domestic culture.

The story begins with a scene of travel: "The hurry of life in a large town, the constant putting aside of preference to yield to a most unsatisfactory activity, began to vex me, and one day I took the train, and only left it for the east-ward bound boat" (213). This reads like a more assured revision of the first chapter of *The Country of the Pointed Firs*, which depicted the same journey. For this narrator, contemporary urban life imposes a rhythm that is alien to her truest self, forcing her to suppress "preference" for activity that cannot satisfy. Setting forth, she thinks of a male model, a writer valorized by the nineteenth century: "Carlyle says somewhere that the only happiness a man ought to ask for is happiness enough to get his work done; and against this the complexity and futile ingenuity of social life seems a conspiracy. But the first salt wind from the east, the first sight of a lighthouse . . . the flash of a gull, the waiting procession of seaward-bound firs . . . made me feel solid and definite again, instead of a poor, incoherent being. Life was resumed, and anxious living blew away as if it had not been. . . . It was a return to happiness" (213).

To Carlyle, a writer's "work" is clearly top priority and highest happiness; "social life" is the enemy of work. At the beginning of *The Country of the Pointed Firs* the narrator agreed with Carlyle; thus she felt compelled to hire the schoolhouse as her workplace. But now she separates her own situation from the male writer's with a firm *But.* Returning to Dunnet Landing, her sense of true selfhood is restored, and it is not "poor" and "incoherent" but has the qualities of her best writing: "solid and definite." The signs she observes—gull, lighthouse, firs—are silent characters in a code taught by William Blackett and Almira Todd, a common language that affirms the continuities of "life," not the restless and temporary individual imperatives of "anxious living." Such a language and such continuity must necessarily be social; this story confirms that fact by making the reluctant William, most retiring of men, the public hero of a marriage, who must share the great moment of his life with the townspeople who celebrate his wedding. The narrator's (and Jewett's) art is grounded in such communion. Her art extends communion to her readers and is inherently social, for it assumes that Dunnet Landing can be *shared*. Speaking of her powerful emotions on William's wedding day, the narrator says, "I felt something take possession of me which ought to communicate itself to the least sympathetic reader of this cold page. It is written for those who have a Dunnet Landing of their own: who either kindly share this with the writer, or possess another" (217).

Such passages reveal that Jewett's concerns with domestic ritual and with a writer's relation to her materials are not two discrete themes of the book and later stories, as it may at first appear. Instead, they are parts of the same process. By discovering domestic cadences in the only possible way—by *sharing* them—the narrator has achieved Jewett's goal, to write "la vie ordinaire" with the authority of "histoire." By this process, Jewett subverts the limited dimensions of the "cold page," the little page of patriarchy to which the old captain confined himself. Instead, her pages become a living, livable text, inhabited by women and men who are fluent in domestic culture.

Stowe's New York novels failed fully to confirm housekeeping as a telling medium for complex truths of women's experience. Helen Denis, although she is drawn to the implications of such a domestic language, as glimpsed in Deephaven, finally cannot read those implications as a coherent present text. But *The Country of the Pointed Firs* and the four additional stories are the great domestic text of American realism. It excavates, teaches, validates, and preserves the language of domestic culture, inscribing it in a multiform text that is both contingent and provisional, as in the peripatetic narrator, and rooted, as in the sibyl's garden. Realist concerns with social contexts and psychological complexities facilitated such a project. And because Jewett felt free to loosen boundaries of plot, sequence, and time, altering and restitching her narrative with the insertions and additions of her later stories, she also deconstructs her own text. Its greatness is not as a final, accomplished product, but, like housekeeping itself, as a richly ambiguous process of repetitive, continuing work, spelled out in women's changing lives.

3

Freeman's Repetitions

The Housekeeper and Her Plot

ALTHOUGH her subjects often resemble Jewett's, Mary Wilkins Freeman's local color stories are domestic fictions of a very different sort.[1] Her narration is invariably executed by a commanding third-person voice. And with that voice comes an insistent sense of plottedness. In the hundreds of stories she wrote between 1882 and her death in 1932, and most especially in the 1887–1900 short fiction generally considered her best work, the jaws of plot snap with steely efficiency. Read en masse, the stories at first seem formulaic because their plots move so inevitably through the stages of conflict and climax and because their elements repeat, again and again.

Critics have long commented on these repetitions. In 1909, Paul Elmer More considered her the heir of a New England tradition that extended from Cotton Mather to Nathaniel Hawthorne; her characters act out the same plotted patterns Hawthorne's did, More said, but sans significance. What were "telling matters of will and morality" in the early writers are in Freeman only a "sad" matter of "palsied nerves" (*Shelburne* 184). In 1917, F. L. Pattee claimed that the "key" to Freeman's best work "is the word *repression*" and he saw her plots culminating in "climactic episodes . . . when the repression gives away" (237). Other readers have described important Freeman stories in terms of genres that might imply more clarity and certainty of plotted meaning: as parable or folk tale.

Recent criticism has begun to reclaim Freeman from such simplistic, androcentric views. Donovan's discussion of her in *New England Local Color Literature*, for example, views her fiction as a response to the closing of the "woman-centered" Arcadia of Stowe's New England fiction; now "the mothers are taking a last stand, going down to apparently inevitable defeat." To Donovan, Freeman displays a near-modernist sensibility; she has "distilled the local color topos down to its essence. . . . a script of gestures reduced to mechanical repetition" (119). And Elizabeth A. Meese, in a recent reading of Freeman, uses the methodology of deconstruction, pointing to a complex multiplicty in Freeman's stories that would seem to be at odds with the arbitrary, insistent gestures of plot that readers of all persuasions have noted in her work.

Housekeeping is a constant of Freeman's stories. Most of her characters are New England village women of limited means whose lives have been significantly shaped by the facts and requirements of domestic rituals. As we have observed, domestic life, with its recurrent rhythms, opposes sequential plot. Peter Brooks argues that plot has been, for the past two centuries in the Western world, a persistent habit of human thought. In many ways this concept of plot has served as another means to foreground the prerogatives of patriarchal culture. Brooks claims that it was born with the idea of "modern man" which displaced a myth-centered, ritualistic world view (xii). In some ways, a housekeeping woman still inhabits that earlier world view. As Rabuzzi writes, the housekeeping of traditional women's culture "depends heavily on the amorphousness and circularity of mythic time." Most domestic tasks "are so obviously circular that their completion can scarcely be experienced" (49).

So what can *plot* do and be, for a woman whose life is shaped by domestic rhythms? As character and as reader, how can she employ plot as an instrument for thought? The career of Mary Wilkins Freeman provides a wealth of responses to these questions, which were obviously and pressingly on Freeman's mind. Plotting has a powerful attraction for many of Freeman's women, who have enduring allegiances to housekeeping but who also need the freedom of movement and freedom of thought that were far more obviously available to nineteenth-century men. Freeman was very much a part of the realist project to render consciousness and social context with as much complexity and fidelity as possible, and for a late nineteenth-century woman and writer, that often meant repeated efforts to explicate the relationship between the rhythms and demands of housekeeping and the shaping, controlling interventions of Aristotelean plot.

Unlike Jewett, Freeman was compelled to support herself by her writing, which was first published in magazines. Restrictions of space, the local color conventions that were already established when she began to publish, and even seasonal requirements[2] were matters she had to consider, as she began a remarkably successful career of marketing her work.[3] A typically shrewd and apparently straightforward example of a Freeman plot is provided by "A Tardy Thanksgiving," a holiday story collected in her first volume.

Jane Muzzy, mourning her husband and her two children, recently dead, refuses to celebrate Thanksgiving in the way her village prescribes, by attending a church service and then eating dinner with her sister's family. Instead, she decides to be true to her feelings and to continue with her everyday housework. For her, she says, celebration would be hypocrisy. So, on Thanksgiving morning, she is doing her "pigwork," with the help of her jilted niece, also in no mood for celebration. But the niece is rescued by her repentant lover and goes off happily to dine with his family. When she is left alone, Jane Muzzy's faculty fails her, and she drops a kettle of boiling lard on her foot. When her sister, Hannah, comes by, she finds Mrs. Muzzy marooned on the kitchen floor, enduring severe pain. Before she will allow her foot to be treated, Jane Muzzy determinedly eats the turkey and plum pudding her sister has brought, acknowledging that she was wrong to refuse to "keep Thanksgiving" (*Humble Romance* 59).

The plot, it would seem, turns on an error about housekeeping. This is not the proper day for pigwork—and only by eating the proper fare, in company, can Mrs. Muzzy reclaim her rightful place in her community. She had thought she could retreat into a domestic world that she could govern by her own skill, without appalling "accidents" like those that killed her family. "It had always been her boast that she wasn't one of the kind of women who are forever dropping things, and getting burned and scalded, and cutting their fingers. She thought there was no kind of need of it, if anybody had her wits about her, and didn't fly about like a hen with her head cut off" (57). Such decisiveness and surehandedness are marks of Mrs. Muzzy's faculty. Yet she sacrifices those qualities, and her own vision of her controlling selfhood, to perform a prescribed ritual on a day that sanctions the expression of certain feelings ("thanksgiving") and proscribes others. Eating on the kitchen floor, surrounded by disarray and congealing lard, racked with pain, Mrs. Muzzy reverses her former refusal: "I said I wouldn't, but the Lord got ahead of me, and I'm glad he has" (59). Thus she offers her version of the day's plot. The conflict was between herself and the highest authority of her community, God *him*self. He won the contest, "getting ahead" of her, and she gives thanks for the defeat of her own will.

The injury's cause is presented with careful nonspecificity: "how she did it she never knew, whether the sudden weakening of a muscle or the slipping of a finger occasioned it—" (57). Mrs. Muzzy could easily have concluded that her injury is yet another of the accidents her family has suffered. Why does she instead choose the Thanksgiving plot as her way of thinking about her mishap in terms of causation and meaning? What has she to gain from that plot? Most readers conclude that she gains community and communion. Mrs. Muzzy is no longer at odds with the other women in the story. As she eats, her sister keeps her company, and they talk about the niece, whose day of defiance also ended in a Thanksgiving dinner.

As she made her Thanksgiving plans, Mrs. Muzzy knew that she was plotting a revolutionary act. Her community had a plan for her, a sequence of actions it considered meaningful and appropriate. In the story's first sentence, that plot is spelled out by a visiting neighbor woman: "I s'pose you air goin' down to Hannah's to spend Thanksgivin', Mis' Muzzy?" (49). Jane Muzzy rejects this scenario while she executes a domestic task with decisive skill: "No; I ain't goin' a step," she replies. "The words shot out of Mrs. Muzzy's mouth as if each one had had a charge of powder in its rear, and the speaker went on jerking the stout thread viciously through the seam she was sewing" (49).

Her defiance of the expected plot is simultaneously a confirmation of her own housekeeping, and the language of the passage above combines traditionally female sewing with dangerous aggression more usually associated with male power (gunpowder). The story would seem to sanction Mrs. Muzzy's later reversal, in which she becomes an acquiescent celebrant at the communal feast. Yet the first time that standard plot is proposed, in the opening sentence, it comes from a "weak natured" woman clearly inferior to Mrs. Muzzy. The spiritless niece, Lizzie, is also "unresisting, hopeless," in contrast with her aunt, whose "passionate, defiant nature" (54) is apparent. Lizzie's one visible spirited decision is to join her aunt in holiday pigwork. When Mrs. Muzzy acquires an ally, her situation is complicated by doubt. "She took the responsibility for herself with sullen defiance. It was another thing, however, to be responsible for a similar state in another. Lizzie, standing there, with her dull, hopeless face, indefatigably cutting pork, seemed to her like the visible fruit of her own rebellious nature" (55). As "visible fruit," the niece becomes a spiritual daughter, and Mrs. Muzzy is faced with the additional problem of transmitting her alienation to Lizzie through her housekeeping. Furthermore, over the pigwork the two women admit taboo feelings: estranging envy for other women who have not lost their lovers or children. The narration signals the danger of such frank communion: "It was as if their two natures were growing more and more into an evil accord" (55).

In her kitchen, Jane Muzzy is grappling with many of the largest issues of nineteenth-century fiction—the relation of shaping self to the forces of God, accident, and communal life. She and her neighbors postulate plots that reflect their thoughts about these issues. And childless Mrs. Muzzy's thinking is complicated when an additional preoccupation of nineteenth-century fictional plots is added to her story: the relation of the generations and "the transmission of wisdom" (Brooks 63). The scene with aunt and niece might signify the female Arcadia at its most beneficent: an older generation passing a domestic skill and an attitude of competence and self-respect to a younger woman. But here the scene is grimly flawed; Lizzie seems a will-less doll, and the women's mutual grief encourages festering, isolating resentment of other women. Housekeeping has a double aspect here, represented by the two sisters' choices of how to spend Thanksgiving. One uses her domestic skills to facilitate the community plot and to do homage to the patriarchal god; Hannah cooks the prescribed menu and serves it to her family. The other sister, Jane, employs her faculty in a gesture of individual assertion, refusing to let her housekeeping serve the Thanksgiving plot, and thus estranging herself from more acquiescent domestic women. The two sisters, both committed to housekeeping, embody important nineteenth-century debates about the uses of domestic culture and its relation to patriarchy.

The daughter-niece, their female heir, becomes a pawn in their disagreement, and she is as valuable and significant as a commodity as she is pallid as an individual. Significantly, the one direct male intervention in this story is that of the fiancé, who wrests Lizzie away from her dangerous aunt. When the doorbell rings, Lizzie "obediently" answers, talks in another room with the unseen caller, and returns to her aunt, physically transformed by ecstasy, to announce her defection. "I'm going," she says. "He's come for me" (56). George, her lover, is an off-stage deus ex machina; everything about his minimal presentation encourages us to read him as pure force. Mrs. Muzzy scorns his proposed plot; she tells Lizzie, "I wouldn't play second fiddle for any feller" (56). By acquiescing to George's plot, Lizzie refuses the more complex plot of transmission and definition suggested by her aunt, and she also refuses self-determination.

The accident, which soon follows, is clearly Mrs. Muzzy's conscious or unconscious doing. Wounding herself, she puts herself at the mercy of *accident*, then places the responsibility for ensuing events on God, who forced her to change plots. Her last words in the story, addressed to her sister while she is eating her ritual Thanksgiving meal, are about Lizzie: she is now "glad" that the girl has accepted George's invitation, just as she was "glad" that God forced her to recant. Mrs. Muzzy's sister has the last, maternal word, about Lizzie: "'You would be [glad] ef you was her mother,' said her sister, simply" (59).

Hannah sees her daughter's and her sister's happiness in their acquiescence to the communal, patriarchal plot for this day. Jane Muzzy, the defiant rebel, is doing what the story's first sentence said she would: having Thanksgiving dinner with her sister. As childless widow, she inhabits a domestic stronghold largely populated by women. (Only women come to visit her; no man has a speaking part in the story.) Yet she has acceded to the unseen, shaping force of male power. Celebrating Thanksgiving, Mrs. Muzzy acknowledges her own history as a New England woman. The holiday alludes to the Puritan past. It is a paradigm of accommodation: native Americans accommodating Puritan settlers; private domestic life (cooking, feasting) accommodating public diplomacy. In this spare story, Mary Wilkins Freeman utilizes her vocabulary of gesture and symbol to suggest the still-compelling force of such accommodation in Mrs. Muzzy's life. She eats at the end, not from hunger but to signal her move from isolation to communion. And yet the honestly rebellious spirit in Jane Muzzy, who valued her own feelings enough to act them out, through the medium of her housekeeping, has not entirely subsided.

The conflict on which plot classically turns has here been a conflict of alternative plots. Jane Muzzy postulated a plot; the community postulated a plot. The latter "won." Yet the supposedly defeated and suppressed alternative plot leaves behind disturbing, interrogative echoes, which counterpoint the "harmony" of the story's conclusion. The stronghold of housekeeping is finally violated by a mess of flour and lard. And Mrs. Muzzy, who earlier said that the deaths of her children alienated her from other mothers, ends by maternally discussing Lizzie's welfare with her mother. She takes the same attitude to the outcome of Lizzie's plot and her own; in both cases she describes herself as "glad" for the patriarchal victory. Still, her style is anything but acquiescent—she remains decisive, giving her sister orders. And although she smiles at Hannah, her forehead is "wrinkled with pain."

This story's plot suggests the lucidity of fable: pride goes before a fall; Mrs. Muzzy (fortunately) falls. With the turkey and plum pudding, she also eats her own words—and her own will. Yet Freeman's narrative also clearly suggests the difficult and problematic nature of that meal. Mrs. Muzzy's forehead wrinkles with the pain of her burn, but also with the effort of thought. Plot has been a way to externalize and to articulate her thoughts about her situation. Thought continues; pain continues. Mrs. Muzzy's housekeeping is a medium for that thought, no escape from it.

Reading "A Tardy Thanksgiving" with the other stories in Freeman's first collection, I was initially struck by the apparent constriction and merciless monotony of this fictional world. But, reading again, I also began to notice the considerable vocabulary of variations that Freeman achieved within the restrictions of her domestic plots. Although plot may indeed be economic formula for her, it also becomes a language in which she instructs her continuing readers, no less than Mrs. Todd taught her guest a similar (although possibly more benign) language. It is not surprising that the short story is the medium for Freeman's most telling domestic fiction. As John Gerlach says, "for all its diversity, the [American] short story is a surprisingly coherent genre, one whose brevity demands special attention to formal concerns. As Poe maintained, we can sense, can feel narrative structure in the short story with an intensity the novel rarely permits" (161).

This intensity is obvious in another brief story from Freeman's first volume, "An Honest Soul." Martha Patch, single and old, sews for a meager living. She sits at her work all day, without the relief of a view of the passing village traffic, for her father, long-dead, was unable to afford window glass for the tiny house. Short of money and supplies, Martha sets to work patching quilts for two neighbor women. But she confuses the scrap bags and has to rip up her work and begin again. Otherwise, she thinks, "it won't be doin' the squar' thing. . . ." (82). When the repiecing is finished, she discovers another error and must repiece yet *again*. Although Martha works longer hours, this labor, replayed three times, consumes weeks; her food and money run out, and she has only the scant diversions that she can see from her small side window. The smallest variations of detail become weighted with meaning; she speculates endlessly about whether a slightly brighter patch of grass "is greener than the rest because the sun shines brightly thar, or because something's buried thar" (82).

The problem of this story is not that Martha Patch despises housework. In fact, ritualized housekeeping is "one of the comforts of Martha's life. Putting and keeping things in order was one of the interests which enlivened her dullness and made the world attractive to her" (86). It is the *control* of housekeeping that appeals to Martha, "putting and keeping things in order." But as she works interminably on the quilts, she thinks despairingly of this task as something she is compelled to do; all control is gone. "Lordy Massy," she thinks, "*hev* I got to rip them two quilts to pieces agin an' sew 'em over?" (83).

Martha's two customers contributed different collections of scrap materials for their quilts, and Martha expresses her taste by choosing and arranging these scraps in her designs. Otherwise, the quilts are projects of endless replication.[4] They are alike in design; both are made up of duplicate units assembled with tiny "methodical" running stitches, which must be as nearly identical as possible. It is Martha's attempts to do justice to the individual differences of the scrap collections, and thus to make her domestic work *art*, that get her in trouble and make her feel obligated to reassemble the quilts repeatedly, even though the scrambling of the materials probably would not matter much to her customers. The repetitious nature of the task takes over, again and again. When Martha thinks she is finally finished, she permits herself signals of closure and personal control. "With a sigh of relief and a sense of virtuous triumph," she sets the quilts aside. " 'I'll sort over the pieces that's left in the bags,' said she, 'and then I'll take 'em over an' git my pay' " (83).

But in her sorting she discovers an error which necessitates repiecing the quilts yet again, and the decisive, controlling Martha Patch disintegrates into despair; she is "helpless," "bewildered," "her poor old eyes . . . dim and weak with tears" (83). Her plot cannot terminate. Again and again the reader is alerted to the approach of closure. John Gerlach maintains that "anticipation of the ending" is often "used to structure the whole" (3) in American short stories by both men and women. This apparently simple tale exerts several of the traditional closure signals Gerlach cites. Most obvious of these is "natural termination. . . . certain activities, once begun, imply natural ends" (9). If one starts to piece a quilt top, one finishes the task—especially if one is doing the job for needed pay. But again and again, Martha Patch's apparently finished task must be repeated. The plot's drive toward its "natural termination" clashes with the repetitive, circular nature of domestic work (Rabuzzi 149). And Martha's entrapment, triggered by her own unconscious errors, becomes a paradigm of the most horrifying aspects of housework. It is a nightmare of compulsive repetition, impervious to closure.

Finally, Martha manages to finish the two quilts correctly:

> She set the last stitch . . . then she spread the quilts out and surveyed them.
> "Thar they air now, all right," said she . . . "I've airned my money. I'll take 'em hum in the mornin', an' then I'll buy somethin' to eat." (87)

But the next morning she collapses, weakened by hunger, on her kitchen floor. She is unable to deliver the quilts. Although she has completed her tasks, Martha cannot regain control of her life, her household, and her art. Her helplessness seems unbearable, a destruction of her sanity. " 'Lor sakes!' she snapped out at length, 'how long *hev* I got to lay here? I'm mad!' " (87)

Like Jane Muzzy, Martha Patch finds herself incapacitated on the kitchen floor, deposed in the midst of her domestic stronghold. And like Mrs. Muzzy, she is "rescued" by another woman; her neighbor, Mrs. Peters, climbs in the kitchen window, puts Martha to bed, and feeds her. Martha consents at last to consume "borryed" food. When she has done so, she revives enough to enact the closure of her plot; she marches off to deliver her quilts to her gratified customers and to collect her pay. She can achieve that completion only by opening her house to another woman and allowing that woman to assume the most basic of domestic responsibilities, feeding her. Martha is over seventy; her parents are long dead. Alone, she has struggled to support herself honestly by completing a series of finite domestic tasks and by maintaining her tiny household. The exigencies of these commitments, their jarring rhythms—the competing pressures to repeat and to complete—have broken her, made her "mad." Although domestic ritual is a form of caretaking, Martha, determined to preserve her fierce independence, cannot care for herself. Thus she acts out a central dilemma for many housekeeping women, as described by Rabuzzi. She must find a way "to circumvent the emptiness at the center of her housebound experience and keep it from engulfing her demonically instead of enlarging her divinely." One way out of this dilemma, Rabuzzi says, is through "close female companionship," which allows one woman to experience another woman's domestic care (135–37).

Finally, the intervention of Mrs. Peters enlarges the story and Martha's inner and outer vision. For the story's climax is not, as we had been expecting, the completion and delivery of the quilts. Instead, it is Mrs. Peters's announcement that her husband, who has free time and scrap materials, will install a front window in Martha's house, broadening her view and extending her life. The window is a "great thing" to Martha, she says; "it kinder makes me feel younger" (91). The window enlarges Martha's vision, adding new dimensions of thought and imagination to her life. Although Mrs. Peters provides the initiative for the window, her husband must provide labor and materials, and the lack of windows is presented as the fault of Martha's impoverished father. Thus, in another story without a single appearance by a male character, Freeman indicates the relation of women's domestic lives to men's support. At Mrs. Peters's prompting, Mr. Peters will finally execute some amends for the deficiencies of the house Simon Patch left to his daughter.

Martha Patch is certainly not liberated from domesticity. She will pay for her window and her keep by more commissions for laborious, repetitive sewing—but with a change of form and a new view. Now the spot on the lawn seems to her not an anonymous grave but a bed of new life, with "lots of dandelions blowed out on it, an' some clover." In the story's last words, she shares with Mrs. Peters a hint of the constraints she has suffered and hitherto concealed, admitting that she is glad her next job will be rugs, for she is "kinder sick of bed-quilts somehow" (91).

This story's ending offers a sharp, definitive sense of finality, on several levels. The quilts are completed; Martha is paid and fed, her reason restored. The windowless walls of her house, and of her life, are pierced to admit new light. Not only can she see out, but others can see in. Martha's exchange with the other women of the town has moved beyond a simple financial transaction (she sews, they pay) to a more nourishing kind of barter, in which the caretaker is cared for, without sacrificing her self-possession and her self-respect. At the story's end, little has changed externally. But the adjustment of Martha's inner vision has made a definitive difference, so that the spot of bright grass blooms for her with new possibility. In many ways, Martha Patch represents a domestic life reduced to its lowest common denominator of anxious drudgery. Even her name suggests this; like the biblical *Martha*, she would first seem to shut out rich spiritual possibilities by a neurotic attachment to housekeeping. And her last name denotes a frugal domestic object and occupation. Her name signifies obsessive domesticity and is a command to do what she does: Martha, patch. But within the confines of Martha's life, Freeman manages to suggest, through the subtleties of her plotting, a life of multiple complexities, where every aspect of an order signifies. The gradations of green on a lawn, the placement of a square of calico patchwork: Freeman has evoked a fictional world where such matters bear the weight of life, death, and art.

Most of the stories in Freeman's first two collections are centered by housekeeping women as unexceptional as Martha Patch. Their houses and routines establish a pattern as insistently repetitive as the blocks of a grid quilt, a staple of nineteenth-century Euro-American women's culture.[5] Yet, from block to block and from quilt to quilt, the possibilities of variation within this strict grid are infinite, as any practiced reader of quilts discerns. In many ways, Martha Patch's occupation is an analogue for Freeman's, plot after plot; quilter and writer both work within a constraining frame of domestic repetitions. Freeman's efforts in her later stories and novels to expand the matter and concerns of her fictions and to essay other kinds of plots suggest that, like Martha, she grew "kinder sick of bed-quilts," although they may be emblematic of her own best work.

Like "A Tardy Thanksgiving," "An Honest Soul" touches on a concern that recurs in Mary Wilkins Freeman's domestic fiction, one that characterized much local color writing by women: how will the domestic rhythms the story reflects be continued in the lives of younger women?[6] This concern occurs to Martha at one of her lowest moments of despair, as she watches neighbor children passing: "'Thar's the Mosely children comin',' she said; 'happy little gals, laughin' and hollerin', goin' home to their mother to git a good dinner. Me a'settin' here's a lesson they ain't larned in their books yit;

hope they won't ever hev to piece quilts fur a livin', without any front winder to set to'" (83). In this passage, Martha's images of felicity and of doom are both domestic: the "good dinner" prepared by a mother, the windowless drudgery. How can a woman inherit the felicity without the doom?

Freeman's life echoed these concerns. It was women who provided much of her support during the years when she established herself as a writer, after first her mother and then her father had died, in poverty. She lived in Randolph, Massachusetts, with the family of a nurturing single woman friend, Mary John Wales, for nearly two decades. When Hamlin Garland visited her there, he commented admiringly on the cooking and the hospitality and noted that Mary Wilkins was "almost as much a guest as myself" (127–28). Despite the writer's apparent detachment, the housekeeping lives of neighboring women were constantly on her mind. In 1885, when she was writing the first stories that would be collected in *A Humble Romance*, she wrote to an editor of being exhausted from a round of nursing a neighbor and lamented, "The poor thing [the ill woman] has probably overworked, and overworked, when she was far from well. No body knows how some of these country women, with large families, and small purses do work. O they are the ones I would help, if I were rich. Nothing, hardly, touches me so much" (*Infant Sphinx* 62). Again and again, her letters return to a wish to do something, to rescue women whom she sees as imprisoned in restrictive lives. In 1893 she wrote to an old friend with "a frantic desire to write something to amuse you after your letter. My dear, I wish you could go to Chicago [presumably to see the Columbian Exposition]. . . . You've got your own true individual shine. That you needn't lose, dear" (*Infant Sphinx* 145–46). In the next-to-last of her extant letters, written a few weeks before her death in 1930, Freeman speaks of the Christmas boxes she is dispatching to friends in the Brattleboro Home for the Aged—including the woman to whom she had written in the 1893 letter above. Throughout her working life, she thought about ways in which she might intervene in the lives of women she knew, to advance or alter a stultifying plot. The stories were ways to work out some of these same problems, as well as the central problems of her own life, one of which was, as with Martha Patch, earning a living. The danger and necessity of the repetitions through which she approached these problems were apparent to Freeman herself; early in her career she wrote to the editor of *Harper's Bazar,* "I am on another story with an old woman in it; I only hope people wont tire of my old women" (*Infant Sphinx* 61).

The old women continue in Freeman's second collection, *A New England Nun and Other Stories* (1891). Many of the quintessential plots of this book have to do with women who pit the requirements of their selfhood—their "true individual shine," as Freeman put it—against their culture's muffling formulations of them. Again and again, the central issue is accommodation: how can the community accommodate a woman whose life does not fit prevailing ideas of what the shape of a woman's life should be? The woman's weapon, by which she attempts self-preservation, is plot, as defined by Peter Brooks: "a principle of interconnectedness and intention" (5). Such plotting is a resolute effort of will, "the product of our refusal to allow temporality to be meaningless, our stubborn insistence on making meaning in the world and in our lives" (323). Plot, then, is a way by which women may affirm the value of female selfhood. Such women may use plot not as an alternative to domestic ritual but as a means of defending their versions of housekeeping and the prerogatives of women's culture. Thus Freeman's village women express emerging issues associated with contemporary women. Joan I. Roberts observes that "the age-old bonds among women, quietly expressed in the confines of home, family and neighborhood . . . are now stretched tight and taut with overt demands for full, public personhood. . . . In the emerging women's culture, the old concern for cooperation now mingles with a new respect for strong individuality" (14).

"A Church Mouse" is Freeman's clearest example of the triumph of such a female agenda. Susan Allen Toth has described this story in terms that emphasize the logic of its plotting, as "a parable of the feminine will to survive even in the harshest of male worlds" (87). The story's protagonist is a woman in her seventies who has lived out her life as a domestic servant, compensated only with room and board. When her employer dies, Hetty's "disposal" becomes a "problem" for her community. Although she is still well able to work for her keep, "people were afraid to take her into their families; she had the reputation of always taking her own way and never heeding the voice of authority" (*Nun* 416). Dispossessed, Hetty conceives a plot: she will assume the position of sexton in the local church and set up housekeeping in the sanctuary. The selectmen, pillars of the local male power structure, are nonplussed. When Hetty confronts their chairman, Deacon Gale, in his hayfield and demands the church keys, he says, "I never heard of a woman's bein' saxton," and he catechizes Hetty, confronting her with every possible objection, all of which she counters decisively. Standing in the middle of the hayfield, Hetty seems a defiant fact and force of nature, "like a May-weed that had gathered a slender toughness" (408). And as such, she is at odds with patriarchal culture; Deacon Gale with his scythe, like Father Time, is armed to cut down the likes of Hetty.

But when the only alternative solution to the problem of Hetty's disposal seems to be to take her into his own household, Gale relents and gives Hetty permission to sleep for a few nights in the meetinghouse. Commandeering a neighbor boy, she moves in: cookstove, bedstead, quilts, needlework, and all, overriding the men's objections. And for three months, "Hetty sailed in her own course" (413). Having implemented her plot, she is described as exerting the controlling surety of a navigator. Her personal domestic relics and rhythms are established under the sheltering roof of the meetinghouse, central institution of this community. As she sails her course, she is now an executor of culture, navigating her own way through the natural world. As Sherry B. Ortner has argued, most cultures have valued women less than men and nature (with which women are identified) less than culture. This is indicated by women's frequent "exclusion from the most sacred rite and the highest political council" (6–10). Becoming sexton, Hetty overturns that traditional exclusion, claiming a place in the sanctuary for herself and for the traditional concerns of women's culture.

Eventually, Hetty's housekeeping precipitates a capsizing storm. The parishioners are satisfied with the shining order Hetty maintains in the meetinghouse; they admire the woolwork flowers, wax cross, and embroidered mottoes with which she adorns the sanctuary. But one Saturday she forgets "the limitations of her housekeeping" and prepares a boiled dinner. On the next Sunday morning, the smell of cabbage is still faintly in the air, "superseding the legitimate savor of the sanctuary" (418–19). The community is offended; housekeeping has violated their sanctuary. The selectmen resume the prerogatives of plotting; Deacon Gale announces, "Well Hetty . . . we've found a nice comfortable place for you [with a woman Hetty dislikes], an' I guess you'd better pack up your things, an' I'll carry you right over there" (419).

Now Hetty, "small and trembling and helpless before them," is once again cast as a creature of nature, this time "a little animal driven from its shelter, for whom there is nothing left but desperate warfare and death" (419). But at the same time, language identifies her with audacious feats of cultural control. Now the meetinghouse is "*her* tabernacle" (418, emphasis mine), and when, by a clever thrust of strategy, she locks herself inside, she makes "her sacred castle impregnable except to violence" (422). Without a key, the men propose to break down the door, in a rapelike act of violation that would also be grossly self-destructive, for the building is *their* spiritual sanctuary too. Although the townswomen have not been Hetty's allies up to this point, they now change their tune. Mrs. Gale says of the attacking men, "They are a parcel of fools to do such a thing. Spoil that good door!" (423).

Just as the violating crowbar is set against the church door, Hetty appears at a window and speaks. Formerly, her mien was sternly self-possessed. Now "all her coolness was gone" and she speaks in self-revelatory supplication: "I jest want to say a word. . . . Can't I stay here, nohow? . . . I'll keep the meetin'-house jest as clean as I know how. An' I'll make some more of them wool flowers. I'll make a wreath to go the whole length of the gallery, if I can git wool 'nough. Won't you let me stay? I ain't complainin', but I've always had a dretful hard time; seems as if now I might take a little comfort the last of it, if I could stay here" (424). Henceforth, this story supports Roberts's assertion that "cooperation among women is the force that sustains civilization" (14). When the women in the crowd listen to Hetty, they are stung, by sympathy, into alliance and action, by which they preserve the sanctuary for all the villagers. Mrs. Gale calls to Hetty, "'Of course you can stay in the meetin'-house . . . I should laugh if you couldn't'. . . . Mrs. Gale stood majestically, and looked defiantly around; tears were in her eyes" (424). The women conspire to place Hetty securely; she is established in a small anteroom, displacing the minister's hat. The language emphasizes power ("majestic") and military strategy; the women are executing a triumph of culture. The male "beseigers" dispersed, "the feeble garrison was left triumphant" (425).

Edwin Ardener diagrams male and female cultures as two overlapping circles. The male circle is superimposed over the "muted" female one; in the large area where the two overlap, male influence is still dominant, as indicated here by the fact that the select*men* make decisions for all the church members, male and female. The area of the female circle that does not overlap with the male circle represents female culture that men do not share; to men, this area, if they perceive it at all, is both muted and "wild," outside their concept of civilization (22–24). It is significant that the selectmen did not smell Hetty's dinner in the meetinghouse; it was their wives who were alert to the smell and to the revolutionary implications of Hetty's incursion. With her quilts and her cabbage, she has executed an act of profound cultural revision, moving from an unacknowledged periphery to the center of communal life.

This story is unusual among Freeman's fictions in the degree to which it views its characters from outside. Hetty's private thoughts and feelings are unplumbed; the reader sees her only as a member of "this little settlement of narrow-minded, prosperous farmers" (415) could. The only consciousness that the narration explores in some detail is that of the community as a whole, as it confronts the "problem" propounded by Hetty. This externalized emphasis on the dynamics of collective life is one reason why "A Church Mouse" has the near-didactic clarity of a parable. The plot, too, has remarkable lucidity. An *outsider,* Hetty, gets *inside* the meetinghouse sanctuary, by executing her own canny plot. But the community turns against her because it cannot tolerate the idea of an individual woman living a private domestic life within their tabernacle, which has become "her tabernacle," her home. Hetty can secure her place and complete her plot only by turning herself inside out to her fellow townspeople, framing her life in words, at last. When she does so, the townswomen realize that their sanctuary is meaningless unless it can acknowledge and shelter, at its heart, a housekeeping woman. During the three months of her first, provisional residency, Hetty was "watchful," defensive, and taciturn. Now she has publicly admitted her private need. The other women have admitted and acted upon their commonality with Hetty, and the men have acknowledged that a woman sexton is a central figure in their community life, not a weed or a trapped animal to be cut down by patriarchal culture. With Hetty's bed and stove in the former place of the minister's hat, a more equitable disposition of space and support has been accomplished.

This remarkable feat of multiple admission and accommodation has been achieved through women's support of a woman. Now Hetty is fixed within the world of common culture; "established in that small, lofty room, with her bed and her stove, with gifts of a rocking-chair and table, and a goodly store of food, with no one to molest or disturb her, she had nothing to wish for on earth" (425). Finally the story is free to explore Hetty's inner life, which is no longer at odds with the community's will. At the story's conclusion, it is Christmas Day, and Mrs. Gale has promised to share her holiday dinner with Hetty. The old woman is "radiant" with "delight": "'I'm goin' to have turkey an' plum puddin' today,' said she; 'it's Christmas,' Suddenly she started, and went into the meeting house, straight up the gallery stairs. There in a clear space hung the bell-rope. Hetty grasped it. Never before had a Christmas bell been rung in this village; Hetty had probably never heard of Christmas bells. She was prompted by pure artless enthusiasm and grateful happiness. Her old arms pulled on the rope with a will, the bell sounded peal on peal. Down in the village, curtains rolled up, letting in the morning light; happy faces looked out of the windows. Hetty had awakened the whole village to Christmas Day" (426). Ringing the festive bells, Hetty has her place at the center of the local life, and she can express her deepest inner impulses for all to hear. She has become the community timekeeper, a fixture of culture. The "happy faces" which respond to the bells are not designated by gender; Hetty no longer speaks pleas to women or men. Instead, her bells have become the voice of a common culture. No other character in Freeman's fiction so successfully makes *fact* of Adrienne Rich's persistent, problematic "dream of a common language."[7]

Like "A Tardy Thanksgiving," this is a holiday story, first printed in a December magazine. The final sentence anchors it perfectly as such; obviously Hetty has "awakened" her village on more than one level. Essentially, she has aroused her neighbors to her own value and legitimacy, as expressed in the rhythms and products of her domestic life. The tribute she offers her community is a product of that life, the projected wreath of wool flowers, domestic art made visible. As Hetty makes her public declaration, adolescent girls watch intently, drawing "close to each other" (422). It is these girls whom Hetty will teach her "art" of making wool flowers—and of self-preservation. From her, they learn commitments and continuities of women's culture.

J. Hillis Miller writes that one of the essential questions about narrative is *"Why do we need the 'same' story over and over?"* and concludes that we "need" such repetition "as one of the most powerful, perhaps *the* most powerful, of ways to assert the basic ideology of our culture" (70–72). In "A Church Mouse," it is especially apparent that Freeman uses the powerful cultural impetus of her repetitive plots to inscribe and to legitimize the strengths and problems of women's culture. In fact, the three stories I have been discussing have essentially the same plot: an older woman tries to maintain herself as an independent housekeeper but encounters a situation in which she cannot survive alone. She shares her distress with another woman (or women) who offers support which alters the protagonist's view of the world. In each case, the protagonist's household is brought closer to community life, so that her housekeeping is less an act of isolation, more an act of communion: Jane Muzzy celebrates Thanksgiving, Martha Patch sees her townspeople from her new window, Hetty Fifield rings the bells. Yet the effects of the three stories are different, illustrating Thomas M. Leitch's assertion that "our appetite for what we usually consider different versions of the same story is based on the expectation that each version will display not simply a given situation or plot or state of affairs but different aspects or implications of that situation" (28). Freeman's housekeeping plots, as suggested by this sampling of stories, start from the archetype of housekeeping as a repetitive, essential, yet submerged, relatively undifferentiated and unstoried act. They bring the reflective, resolving work of plot to bear on that archetype, as these "old women" struggle to live out the possibilities of their selfhood within the space defined by domestic ritual. Freeman manages to suggest both the pervasiveness of their situations (again and again, other women recognize their community with these housekeeping protagonists) and the infinite, telling range of variations on this plot and theme. Freeman's capacity to replay, with deepening suggestivity, this vocabulary of repetition is probably her greatest contribution to local color realist writing.

Rabuzzi reminds us that the archetypal representation of housekeeping woman in Western culture is Hestia, the hearth goddess, "oldest of the twelve great Olympians" and central "to the household and its cult." However, few myths and stories about her have been canonized. Virginal "Hestia, unlike other members of the Greek pantheon, remains chained to the hearth; she is never seen in other locations." Rabuzzi equates Hestia's situation with that of "traditional women. . . . For her . . . home will actually be a workplace, the domestic sphere. . . . Functioning as a priestess who performs for others, she typically has no one but herself to perform those rites for her" (94–95). Freeman devised ways to tell Hestia's stories, and she uses plot both as a medium for those stories, as they are generated by domestic life, and as an instrument for critique of them.

Fiction was only one way to invent a literature for Hestia. In nineteenth-century America, another form of housekeeping literature existed in the form of the "professional" guides and manuals for housekeepers that continued to proliferate.[8] In postbellum America, they took advantage both of increasing literacy and of the increasing isolation of women, who found that trusted female elders were not so likely to be available to answer questions and to impart their expertise to neophyte housekeepers. Such literature offers the illusion, at least, of completion (a recipe, followed step by step, will produce a predictable result) and control. For example, the chapter on cookery in *The American Woman's Home*, the manual that Stowe wrote with her sister Catharine E. Beecher, begins with extravagant claims for the competent housekeeper's capacity to control the vicissitudes of health, through cooking: "The person who decides what shall be the food and drink of a family, and the modes of its preparation, is the one who decides, to a greater or less extent, what shall be the health of that family" (119). Postbellum manuals solicit greater respect for housekeeping as profession, craft, and art. Beecher and Stowe begin by stating this sweeping defense: "It is the aim of this volume to elevate both the honor and the remuneration of all employments that sustain the many and varied duties of the family state, and thus to render each department of woman's profession as much desired and respected as are the most honored professions of men" (17).

Jewett suggests such concerns in *The Country of the Pointed Firs* when she celebrates the near-magical competence of Mrs. Todd and presents the baker of the reunion's gingerbread house as an artist. But those women are presented through the medium of the narrator's editing consciousness and are never viewed from within. Freeman's approach to domestic art is more richly detailed and more problematic. The perfected order of Jane Muzzy's house is typically described as "exquisitely neat," executed with "religious exactitude" (51), emphasizing the heavy cultural legacy borne by this woman's housekeeping. In "A Church Mouse," Hetty's final incorporation into the community is facilitated by shared aesthetic values. The townspeople admire her domestic art: needlework, housecleaning, and "her chiefest treasure of art: a white wax cross." When this art is brought into the meetinghouse, "the neatness and the garniture went far to quiet the dissatisfaction of the people. They had a crude taste" (416).

Both Jewett and Freeman are writing in a period of rapid transitions in domestic decoration. As Bonnie Loyd writes, "in the first days of American settlement, folk arts were the most popular way to embellish the home. Housewives served as both patrons . . . [of] local craftspeople, and as artists themselves. . . . They learned sewing, crocheting, quilting, knitting, weaving, dying, and needlework" (185), producing useful artifacts such as Mrs. Todd's braided rug. With the industrial revolution, the institutionalization of women's domestic sphere, and the proliferation of housekeeping magazines and manuals, priorities changed, and the arrangement of mass-produced items or the replication of the latest published craft fad took precedence for many middle-class women. Hetty Fifield's treasures indicate that she and her community are on the cusp of this change. Her "blazing sunflower" quilt represents the older tradition of women's folk art rooted in economy and utility. But the decorative wax cross, a patriarchal emblem embellished with "silver frost work," a craft fad promoted in magazines, expresses very different priorities. The two objects indicate Freeman's sensitivity to changes in women's domestic lives. The relations of domestic art, "taste," and popular culture are probed in a group of stories that inscribe another quintessential Freeman plot. In that plot, a woman is living an intensely aesthetic life, her art the center of her domestic world. Then she must face an antithetical public, patriarchal world and devise means to preserve her art against its incursions.

This is the situation of Freeman's best-known and most frequently discussed story, "A New England Nun." Louisa Ellis enacted the most common female plot, courtship, fourteen years ago, when she was courted by her "first lover," Joe Dagget, and, on her mother's "wise" advice, accepted his proposal. Then Joe went away to "make his fortune" in Australia. While he was absent, Louisa's mother and brother died, and she lived on alone in an apotheosis of perfect domestic order, which became her greatest pleasure.

It is this order that the story first presents, and within it, Louisa seems perfectly attuned: culture is in harmony with nature. As evening approaches,

> There seemed to be a gentle stir arising over everything for the mere sake of subsidence—a very premonition of rest and hush and night.
> This soft diurnal commotion was over Louisa Ellis also. She had been peacefully sewing at her sitting-room window all the afternoon. Now she quilted her needle carefully into her work, which she folded precisely, and laid in a basket with her thimble and thread and scissors. Louisa Ellis could not remember that ever in her life she had mislaid one of these little feminine appurtenances, which had become from long use and constant association a very part of her personality. (*Nun* 1)

Louisa's personality itself is inseparable from the "appurtenances" of her housekeeping, in a union of form and self, inner life and outer expression, which is quintessentially artful and is expressed through traditional tools of domesticity, contained in her sewing basket. Louisa's housekeeping is expressly presented in terms of art: she has "almost the enthusiasm of an artist over the mere order and cleanliness of her solitary home." Her windows shine "like jewels"; her laundry is "exquisitely folded"; she has created a "delicate harmony" (9–10). And this art is frequently executed for art's sake alone: "more than once she had ripped a seam for the mere delight of sewing it together again" (9). Louisa has discovered in her housekeeping the perfect medium of self-expression.

Marjorie Pryse has commented astutely on the historical context of this story: "The very chaos which the challenge of the frontier for American men brought to the lives of American women also paradoxically led the women, in nineteenth-century New England, to make their own worlds and to find them in many ways, as Louisa Ellis does, better than the one the men had left. . . . [Louisa] defends her power to ward off chaos just as strongly as nineteenth-century men defended their own desires to light out for the territories" ("Uncloistered" 295). Nineteenth-century precedent encouraged men to live out a double plot, as Joe Dagget does. Having secured a future domestic life by extracting a promise from Louisa, he lights out for an open-ended adventure in fortune-hunting. "He had gone to make his fortune . . . he stayed until he made it. He would have stayed fifty years if it had taken so long, and come home feeble and tottering, or never come home at all, to marry Louisa" (6).

Meanwhile Louisa was expected to wait, like Sleeping Beauty, with few letters and no visits from her lover. Obediently, she "always looked forward to his return and their marriage as the inevitable conclusion of things" (7)—

as if her only possible plot must be completed by Joe. But in his absence, Louisa discovered in domestic ritual a cyclical, compelling plot of her own. When Joe returns, this home plot is threatened. Married to Joe, she would be obliged to leave her house, expand her routine, endure the rips that well-meaning Joe would make in the "fairy web" of her housekeeping, and suffer the household authority of another woman, Joe's "domineering" mother. Although Louisa's faint passion for Joe has abated, she continues to prepare for her wedding, acting out her commitment to the engagement plot: "It was not for her to prove untrue and break his heart" (12). Within her household, Louisa has an artist's surety. But her idea of being "true" comes from external convention and requires her to act out prerogatives that are no longer her own.

Louisa is saved when an alternative plot materializes. A week before the wedding, she overhears a conversation between Joe and another woman, Lily Dyer, in which it becomes apparent that the two are in love. Joe makes it clear that he will not break his engagement to Louisa—"Of course I can't do anything different," he says—and Lily agrees that that is unthinkable: "Honor's honor, and right's right" (14), she says. All three are committed to a marriage that none of them wants; they are locked into a received vocabulary of contradiction and tautology which cannot express their deepest needs. But now Louisa has a vision of multiple possibilities which allows her to break out of the tautology. She realizes that the engagement plot can be completed by another "willing" woman, and Louisa can thus maintain her domestic life. So she ends her engagement, in a triumph of delicate diplomacy. After a few hours of dim, reflexive regret, Louisa wakes feeling "like a queen who, after fearing lest her domain be wrested away from her, sees it firmly insured in her possession" (16).

This story was traditionally read as a triumph of repression. In one of the best of such readings, David Hirsch describes Louisa as "almost a case study of an obsessive neurosis . . . a neurotic disorder in which there are repetitive impulses to perform certain acts" (125). Yet the language of the story does not emphasize Louisa's anxiety, obsession, or neurotic qualities; instead, it underlines her calm, surety, deliberation, and self-possession. The rhythms of her chosen life, which may indeed seem "a neurotic disorder" in one context, may appear both artful and benign when viewed in the traditional context of women's culture, domestic life. The story's title, which even a receptive critic like Elizabeth Meese finds "superficially pejorative" (27), legitimizes Louisa's decision by connecting it to an old and respected women's tradition, the choice of a celibate nun's life of retreat, order, and meditation.

Louisa does not speak to another woman in the course of the story; she communicates only with Joe. And yet she acts on behalf of other female lives when she chooses her plot. Timid and conventional as she has been, Louisa discovers that more than one plot is available and legitimate for a woman's conscious choice. It is significant that both Louisa and Lily Dyer are described in regal language; in this story, there is more than one way to be a queen.

The story's last paragraph is one of the most complex Freeman ever wrote. It ends:

> If Louisa Ellis had sold her birthright she did not know it, the taste of the pottage was so delicious, and had been her sole satisfaction for so long. Serenity and placid narrowness had become to her as the birthright itself. She gazed ahead through a long reach of future days strung together like pearls in a rosary, every one like the others, and all smooth and flawless and innocent, and her heart went up in thankfulness. Outside was the fervid summer afternoon; the air was filled with the sounds of the busy harvest of men and birds and bees; there were halloos, metallic clatterings, sweet calls, and long hummings. Louisa sat, prayerfully numbering her days, like an uncloistered nun. (17)

The emblem of Louisa's plot is the rosary, an endless circle of pearls, products of nature ordered into art. The beads tellingly link language, repetition, and devotion, expressing the enduring female traditions of the nun. Louisa does not question her choice of the metaphoric rosary. But the narrative voice does question. What is a woman's "birthright"? In the Judeo-Christian myth of Jacob and Esau, to which Freeman here alludes, the choice of a domestic product, a bowl of soup ("pottage"), signaled the relinquishment of a birthright, a patriarchal heritage. The domestic metaphor of "a mess of pottage" has become a Western cultural code for a choice of triviality and immediate gratification over the complexities of full humanity. Is Freeman yet again reinscribing this code—or is she suggesting that it may signify differently? In "A New England Nun," she demonstrates that, to a Louisa Ellis, pottage can taste "so delicious." Has Louisa chosen out of the true imperatives of her best self or because the requirements of waiting, her "woman's portion,"[9] became inviolably habitual? A prevailing pattern in Freeman's stories, as in the previous three discussed here, is for a woman to break out of a domestic confinement by some enlarging, expanding strategy. Louisa Ellis has instead broken *in,* to secure and perfect her solitary domestic art. Freeman tells Louisa's story in a manner that conveys its powerful beauties and attractions.[10] But she ends it by setting Louisa against a picture of the equally compelling world she has *not* chosen, the "fervid," fecund, ambiguously noisy world of "men and birds and bees" which is the domain of Lily Dyer.

Leah Blatt Glasser has observed, with other recent readers of Freeman, that this writer struggled "throughout her life" with a division "between rebellion and submission, self-fulfillment and acceptability [which] became the central focus of her work" (232). Such doubleness is expressed in the ending of "A New England Nun." Having written a story that widens the range of domestic plots for women, Freeman pulls back from the full weight of its implications with a conclusion that suggests a more critical view of Louisa's choice. The fulcrum of this paragraph is in two words. The first is *birthright*—an especially weighty term in a period of debate about suffrage. Are marriage, active heterosexuality, and participation in the various rhythms of the world outside her domestic domain a heritage that Louisa must claim to live fully? The second crucial word is *if.* "'If Louisa Ellis had sold her birthright. . . .'" The nature and implications of Louisa's female birthright are framed by that word as an inquiry. Louisa presents herself as a statement, artfully fulfilled. But Freeman's final comments on her character frame Louisa's life as a subtle question.

Another version of Louisa's plot is essayed in "A Poetess," also one of Freeman's finest stories. None is closer to Mary Wilkins's own situation, as she wrote her first books, living in the New England world that was her most frequent subject. As she became more generally known and accepted in the wider, male-dominated culture of books and magazines, which printed first her poems and then her stories, the writer's relation to her own town grew tenuous. No story by a realist examines the problematic relation between a woman writer and her place and her art, or the double pull nature and gendered culture exert on her, more directly and powerfully than "A Poetess."

The artist of the title is Betsey Dole, who was "born with the wantin' to write poetry" (*Nun* 154–55). Betsey has created an individualistic, intensely aesthetic ménage where she keeps house according to her own priorities. The house is full of an other-worldly "green light," with a rich profusion of flowers, grasses, shells, and gourds. Betsey's companion is a singing canary, and her well-tended garden yields an abundance of ornamental plants, but few vegetables (although she is dependent on the garden for food). When she is at work on a poem, mealtimes come and go—for Betsey's poetry is the central impulse of her life, and she has shaped her life by that impulse.

A more prosaic visitor, Mrs. Caxton, notes that a garden and a life like Betsey's could never sustain *her;* she asserts, "I never set up for a butterfly, an' I want something else to live on" (143). Like the other villagers, she sees a poetess as an inexplicably different sort of person. Yet Mrs. Caxton *needs* a poet's art; she has come to order a memorial poem for her little boy, recently dead. Happy for the commission (although she has no thought of monetary payment and has never received any), Betsey bends to her work: "Betsey . . . bending over her portfolio looked like the very genius of gentle, old-fashioned sentimental poetry. It seemed as if one, given the promise of herself and the room, could easily deduce what she would write, and read without seeing those lines wherein flowers rhymed with bowers, home with beyond the tomb, and heaven with even" (146–47). Like Louisa Ellis, Betsey seems in perfect communion with her environment (which is her creation) and with her image. Barbara H. Solomon says that, in this passage, Freeman "wants us to be certain . . . that indeed Betsey writes dreadful, sentimental verses" (25). But, in fact, the language here is carefully qualified. Betsey *"looked like"* the genius of a particular type of poetry; *"it seemed as if"* one could look at the poet and predict the poetry. Although we may have our suspicions about the nature of Betsey's verse, Freeman will not confirm or deny them and thus enable her readers to dismiss or define Betsey Dole. We must take this protagonist as her author does, as serious and credible artist.

For Betsey, her success is achieved when she meets her patron's specified need (Mrs. Caxton listed the topics she wished the poem to cover) *and* exercises her own powers of empathy. She says to herself, as she concludes her draft, "I guess I can enter into her feelin's considerable. . . . There! I've wrote sixteen verses . . . an' I guess I've got everything in" (147–48). Betsey's poetry is an instrument of communion, by which the values of her house-hold are joined to the community that surrounds it. Writing her poems, Betsey naturally achieves the communion that characters like Jane Muzzy and Hetty Fifield won through climactic effort. Despite her poverty, Betsey is portrayed in the first half of this story as a successful woman.

In the second half of the story, Betsey's success is destroyed. Mrs. Caxton, pleased with Betsey's poem, has copies of it set in print—to the delight of Betsey, whose work has never been printed before. Now the product of Betsey's harmonious world finds its way into patriarchal culture. And Mrs. Caxton reports indignantly the reaction of that culture's local arbiter: *"Sarah Rogers says that the minister told her Ida that the poetry you wrote was jest as poor as it could be, an' it was in dreadful bad taste to have it printed an' sent round that way.* What do you think of that?" (153)

Betsey is literally frozen with horror; her flowerlike face is now "a pale wedge of ice," and she is described as an executioner's victim, standing as rigidly "as if she were bound to a stake" (153–54). She never questions the minister's sentence. He comes from outside the village, bringing the judgment of a wider and presumably more discerning world; he has even published poems himself, in a magazine. His words, repeated and reinforced by local women, represent the late nineteenth-century alliance of ministers and women which, as Ann Douglas says, ruled the cultural life of New England and enforced rigid canons of "good taste." Devout Betsey Dole cannot challenge the most potent authority in her village.

So the force of her degraded will is channeled into a passionate protest, against her own existence. She says, "I'd like to know if it's fair. . . . Had I ought to have been born with the wantin' to write poetry if I couldn't write—had I? . . . Would it be fair if that canary-bird there, that ain't never done anything but sing, should turn out not to be singin'? Would it, I'd like to know? S'pose them sweet-peas shouldn't be smellin' the right way? I ain't been dealt with as fair as they have" (154–55). Betsey rails against "unfairness," and her sense of what *is* fair comes from nature. A sweet pea smells "right" and a canary sings genuinely because they are living out their own natures—as Betsey herself formerly was. Centered in her household, she had created a world of harmony and communion where she bloomed as naturally as a flower. But when her verse finds its way into the more complex and contradictory, male-dominated culture of "taste" and magazines, Betsey is shattered by a judgment she will not deny.

In a domestic ritual, which amounts to self-immolation, Betsey burns at her hearth every scrap of poetry she has written, and, with a silver spoon, ladles the ashes into a prized sugar bowl. Everything Betsey does now illustrates the deep split within her. She destroys her poems, yet she honors them with ceremony. She acquiesces, yet she protests. And while her body and her intelligence still live, her spirit, which was in the poems, is dead. Throughout her ordeal, the canary continues to trill, and the description emphasizes the natural unity of *his* song and self: "It was as if the golden down on his throat bubbled" (155). Such unity is no longer available to Betsey. So—although she is only fifty—she begins immediately to decline and die.

When the minister (unaware of his part in Betsey's decline) makes a last pastoral call, she has two requests: that the sugar bowl be buried with her body and that he memorialize her with a poem: "I never wrote none that was—good . . . but I've been thinkin'—that mebbee my—dyin' was goin' to make me—a good subject for—poetry, if I never wrote none. If you would jest write a few lines" (159). Thus Betsey completes her self-destruction by resigning her identity as a poetess: "I never wrote none," she says. At the same time, she preserves a version of herself. Her body and her spirit (in the sugarbowl) will be reunited, in her coffin. And if she cannot be the *maker* of poetry, she will become its subject. Virginia Woolf observed that, although the names of few women poets have survived, women as *subjects* "have burnt like beacons in all the works of all the poets from the beginning of time" (44–45). Betsey can gain access to the world of printed, legitimized poetry only by her patriarchally sanctioned death, not by her female life. Thus she conscripts the bewildered minister, insuring that poetry and its traditional subjects will continue, through him, and insuring herself a place in that poetry, through her death. Memorializing her, the minister will continue her art. But the poetess, Betsey Dole's true self, is dead. The story ends with the canary's triumphant song.

Louisa Ellis triumphed through her discovery of multiple female possibility, which allowed her to retain her domestic art. Betsey Dole can triumph only by obliterating the home plot that she was living so artfully in the first half of this story. Because she believes the minister's formulations, she must destroy her life as a poetess and assume a woman's more traditional late nineteenth-century place, as consumer of culture and as patroness, muse, and subject of male art. The horror of "A Poetess" is the immolation of Betsey's text, in a world of "taste" implemented by print culture. Cremated, that text is concealed in a domestic artifact, the sugarbowl. In the world of the story, there is no place for such art, except in a grave. The surviving artists, minister and canary, are both male. The canary survives because he is securely placed in nature; his song *is* his self. The minister survives because he is securely placed in culture. Such status was unavailable to a village woman artist. None of the saving forces that preserved the protagonists of other stories—female sympathy and domestic art—can rescue Betsey Dole.

Betsey's story dramatizes the dilemma of the woman artist with commitments to a female, domestic tradition in the accelerating, patriarchal capitalism of late nineteenth-century America. The subsequent decline of Freeman's own once-considerable reputation, as she tried to compete in the early twentieth-century marketplace, indicates how historically prescient "A Poetess" proved to be. In this later writing, including novels, plays, film scripts, and children's fiction, Freeman almost inevitably returned to the short story for her best work. Although the "old women" certainly do not disappear from this fiction, most of the more original later stories have young female protagonists, usually middle or upper class, who are often embroiled in more conventional courtship plots, which Freeman underplayed in her earlier volumes. These stories are often longer, more complexly plotted. Donovan has identified a pervasive Lacanian plot here: daughters, drawn toward new opportunities (such as formal education) and "an experience of male-dominated heterosexuality," must turn their backs on the nineteenth-century female Arcadia of women's culture, where their mothers (or other female elders) remain ("Silence or Capitulation" 43–48).

One of the most bizarre and surprising of such tales, a story that has received no recent critical attention, is "Silence," first published in *Harper's* in 1892. Longer and more densely populated than earlier stories, it reflects 1890s enthusiasm for historical fiction; it is a fictionalized account of the Deerfield Massacre. The view of this legendary catastrophe is entirely a female one, with a domestic setting. Young Silence Hoit, a New England Cassandra, has a vision of disaster; she says, "I have seen blotches of blood everywhere all day. The enemy will be upon us" (*Silence* 3). Deerfield is in domestic order; "there was an odor of boiling meal in the air; the housewives were preparing supper" (3). Silence, who is engaged to David Walcutt, beseeches his aunt to protect him, and the older woman scoffs at her fears: "There will be no war-screech to-night, nor tomorrow night, nor the night after that. The Lord will preserve His people that trust in Him. To-day I have set a web of linen in the loom, and I have candles ready to dip to-morrow, and the day after that I have a quilting. I look not for Indians. If they come I will set them to work" (8).

To such women, bustling housekeepers, the rhythm of domestic life supersedes all else; it is a shield as powerful as their "trust" in a patriarchal god. The widowed aunt with whom Silence lives is annoyed when her niece calls her to the window to see another bloody omen; she says, "Get you away from the window and to your work. . . . Here I have left my knitting for nothing, and I just about setting the heel. You'd best keep to your spinning instead of spying out the window at your own nightmares, and gadding about the town after David Walcutt. Pretty doings for a modest maid" (12). The older women will admit no threat that cannot be put in its place by their faculty. But Silence, in the throes of the first passion of her life, intuits the fragility of the order around Deerfield hearths. She is right, of course; the massacre will occur. But her aunt is correct, as well—for Silence's premonitions *are* nightmare manifestations of her inner life. The "blotches of blood" she sees connote passion and danger. For a "modest maid," contemplating her coming marriage, such imagery may suggest menstruation, first inter-course, and childbirth. A housekeeper, whether she is cooking, nursing, doing laundry, or attending to her personal hygiene, is accustomed to dealing with blood (housekeeping manuals invariably include receipts for removing bloodstains). But young Silence, living in her single aunt's female household and anticipating her married life with David, has not yet integrated domestic order with the constant incursions of blood. She both needs the domestic hearth's protection and rails against the ordered round that it exacts from her.

Within a few hours, Silence's premonitions are confirmed. Her aunt's house becomes a fort, and the dearest household treasures—pewter, silver—are melted into bullets to fend off attacking Indians. Finally the Indians are routed, but as a parting thrust, they torch the house, and it goes up in flame. Outside, the survivors find many of their townspeople scalped and dead or disappeared, taken captives. David's aunt, despite her domestic assurances, is dead, with her little girl.

The range of the surviving women's responses is wide and astonishing. A single woman snatches up a scalped baby from the snow and cares for it, claiming it is alive. Silence's aunt, after all her housewifely propriety, shrieks at the Indians in a "rage as mad as theirs. Her speech . . . was almost inarticulate . . . a mad frenzy; her tongue stuttered over abusive epithets. . . . It was like the solo of a fury" (17). A few hours later, as her house burns, she regains her domestic priorities, rescuing her feather bed and looking glass from the flames. The aunt, who normally devotes her faculty to the communal welfare, suddenly erupts in an angry, inspired *solo,* as opposed to the ensemble of female culture in which her life is deeply implicated. For her and all the story's women, Freeman implies both the necessity and the cost of their commitment to housekeeping. The massacre reveals the furies beneath the competent, modest demeanor of even the most reserved and housebound women. And although she does not scream or cry, no one is more affected than Silence. Unflinchingly, she turns over every corpse, looking for David. Finally she hears that he is among the captives, taken to Canada.

Freeman shows the women resuming their domestic rituals after the disaster, piecing their civilization back together with determination and dignity. Dealing with bloody aftermath, they prepare the bodies for burial. Although David's aunt is dead, the tasks she had planned must be done, by other women. In the dead woman's house,

[they] were hard at work. They were baking in the great brick oven, spinning, even dipping poor Goodwife Sheldon's candles.

"Bind up your hair, like an honest maid, and go to spinning," said [Silence's aunt] Eunice. . . . "We that be spared have to work, and not sit down and trot our hearts on our knees. There is scarce a yard of linen left in Deerfield, to say naught of woolen cloth. Bind up your hair!"

And Silence bound up her hair, and sat down by her wheel meekly, and yet with a certain dignity. (40)

In a household of women, Silence does her tasks assiduously, but as if by rote. Her eyes are vacant, and at intervals she gets up abruptly to go outdoors and to call out, north toward Canada, "David! David! David Walcutt!"

When the "plot" of the massacre first emerged from her own unconscious, Silence tried to avert it and to protect David from the attacking furies. She turned to the strongest power she knew, a competent housekeeper, begging David's aunt to keep him in the house. The housekeeper, despite her faculty, could protect neither David nor herself. At last, David manages to escape, returns to Deerfield, and embraces Silence. But she will not recognize him. Instead she looks toward Canada, still calling his name. This goes on for weeks. Like Martha Patch, Silence is in the grip of compulsion she cannot break. Like an automaton, she spins dutifully all day, stopping only to call out, imperiously, David's name. To recognize him would be to allow yet another incursion of chance into the protection of routine, making her again subject to horror, like that of the massacre. For Silence, the present, arousing fact of her lover and a life of dangerous individual passion cannot be integrated with the hypnotic repetitions of domestic routine. The young woman is caught between two overpowering commitments.

Silence is rescued by the most knowing woman in the story, old homeless Goody Crane, who approaches David with a plan. He is dubious, for the woman is suspected of witchcraft. "'I'll try no witchcraft but my own wits,' said Goody Crane. . . . 'None but I can cure her. I tell ye, come out here tonight when the moon is an hour high; and mind ye wear a white sheep's fleece over your shoulders. I'll harm her not so much with my witch-work as ye'll do with your love, for all your prating'" (50). Then Goody Crane informs Silence that David will arrive from Canada that night, in a white sheep's fleece. The girl too fears witchcraft, but at the appointed hour she goes out to recognize her fiancé at last. Doing so, she claims her full self, as a loving, feeling, choosing woman. As the story ends, she and David are placed in a timeless natural order, in which the village is only part of a harmonious larger design: "The trees arched like arbors with the weight of the wild grapes . . . Deerfield village and the whole valley lay in the moonlight like a landscape of silver. The lovers stood in each other's arms, motionless, and seemingly fixed as the New England flora around them, as if they too might reappear hundreds of spring-times hence, with their loves as fairly in blossom" (54). This concluding scene is consciously artful; the language presents nature in civilizing terms (trees are *arbor*like; it is "a *landscape* of silver"). The scene resolves the rending conflict of nature and culture in Silence's psyche, where blotches of blood opposed the spinning wheel.

In the last sentence, Freeman also implies the continuing pertinence of Silence's situation, suggesting she might reappear hundreds of years later, in the present. In this colonial setting, Freeman has examined, in a period of colonial revival, antecedents of the nineteenth-century ideal of a female Arcadia, implying that, especially for heterosexual women, working out commitments to domestic, female culture has always been problematic. Silence, with her signifying name, resembles many of Freeman's turn-of-the-century women. For her, domestic ritual is the way women silence the furies within themselves. It is the only kind of control a woman can exert over insistent eventualities, and although it may be interrupted—by such incursions as the massacre and individuals' deaths—it cannot be stopped. When one woman dies, others step in to bake and spin; to keep civilization going. To do so, they must suppress rebellious impulses within themselves, as Silence did. Although the culmination she yearned toward presented itself, with David's return, she was unable to grasp it, to confirm her personal plot, and to leave the sheltering household of spinning women. She required the aid of a woman from outside the domestic circle, Goody Crane, who knew how to live by her "own wits." Only such a woman can fully exercise her intelligence, risking acts that go beyond the communal rituals of nurture and preservation sanctioned by housekeeping. In Deerfield, a woman's *wits* are the generating force of *wit*chcraft. Goody Crane reminds the housekeepers of what they are prone to suppress: that while they may be committed to an ongoing domestic enterprise, they are also mortal women. On the morning after the massacre, in the kitchen of David's dead aunt, she says, "Who stirred the porridge this morning? I trow [dead] Goody Sheldon's hands be too still and too cold, though they have stirred well in their day. Hath she dipped her candles yet? Hath she begun her weaving?" (31) Only a woman who will speak such hard wisdom can break through to Silence.

Joining her lover, Silence also reflects the Victorian American norms of gendered culture described by Smith-Rosenberg. Silence is living a typical pattern; during a young woman's engagement, the domestic training she had received since childhood intensified, becoming "more systematized, almost ritualistic" (16). In this story, as in the others by Freeman I have discussed, men are not important characters; Smith-Rosenberg finds that this was a common Victorian situation, especially "in times of sickness, sorrow, or trouble [such as the massacre]. Entire days, even weeks, might be spent almost exclusively with other women" (10). For a young woman, such immersion in female culture could make the prospect of marriage especially disorienting: "with marriage both women and men had to adjust to life with a person who was, in essence, a member of an alien group" (28). Goody

Crane offers Silence a scenario in which she can control the forces of accident and contingency by *choosing* to meet and recognize David at a given hour and place. But she also makes the alien man, who is even more alien as a returned captive, more acceptable by associating him with symbols validated by female culture. Most obvious of these symbols is the full moon. The sheep's fleece too would be familiar to the domestic Silence; in the story's first scene she has "been spinning all day . . . shreds of wool still clung to her indigo petticoat" (1), and she reappears again and again at the spinning wheel, symbolic of women's culture and the independent female spinster. Although the sheepskin David wears is a result of slaughter, here there is no blood, but an emblem of snowy innocence, in contrast to the first scene between the two, when Silence hallucinated a bloody spot on David's (patriarchal?) coat.

Goody Crane's intelligent intervention has at last allowed Silence to accomplish the integration of her male lover into the vocabulary of female culture. The old woman's "witch-work" is a profound understanding of human psychology. The timeless picture of the embracing lovers, the work of art that ends the story, is in fact the creation of an unseen, shaping artist-woman, Goody Crane. No longer tied to her spinning wheel, Silence is now part of a continuum of nature and time in which domestic ritual is one part of a larger whole. For a woman to see in such large terms is almost heresy, "witch-work." Yet Deerfield has always sheltered Goody Crane, and the women are dimly attracted to her: "In the midst of their nervous terror it was often a sore temptation to consult old Goody Crane, since she was held to have occult knowledge" (43). This is the same "occult knowledge" Jewett found (*or* portrayed) in Mrs. Todd: the knowledge of how to live as an un-muffled individual within the oldest traditions of women's culture. Women who have such knowledge are often figures of power and terror—sibyls, furies—and like Goody Crane and Mrs. Todd, they are also compelling models for the woman artist. Compared with Betsey Dole, there is nothing self-effacing or suicidal about such creative women. But it is telling that, while Jewett projected a contemporary countrywoman in Mrs. Todd, Free-man looked more than two hundred years into the past for the shaping intelligence of a Goody Crane. In Freeman's stories, especially those of the eighties and nineties, acts of housekeeping *signify* with stunning urgency. But, unlike Jewett, Freeman does not evoke on the page the character of a contemporary woman artist who wields a domestic vocabulary with the assurance that was, in fact, Freeman's own.

The combat of the domestic plot and the courtship plot implicit in "Silence" is nowhere more explicitly evident than in another later story,

"The Willow-Ware." The 1907 story is set in the present in a household of genteel wealth and privilege, where two elderly single aunts live with their devoted woman servant and their eighteen-year-old niece, Adeline. Adeline's description opens the story: "Adeline Weaver sat under the green trellis of the south door of the old Weaver mansion, and sewed her seam of fine linen. She did not like to sew but her aunts . . . would have turned faint with horror had she suggested the possibility of ready-made garments. All the ladies of the Weaver family had always made their own underwear. . . . There was a tradition that no women of the family ever screamed. If protest they had against pain or fear or injustice they kept it locked in their own breasts. This young Adeline was a true Weaver" (*Fair Lavinia* 145–46). Here domestic ritual has been made partially optional by the industrial revolution; Adeline thinks that she would much prefer to "have machine-worked handkerchiefs. . . . than sit and sew as I do" (154). But Adeline, "a true Weaver" whose name evokes one of the oldest female occupations, is trained by her relatives (all female) in a cyclical culture of domestic repetition. Repetition becomes tradition and tradition demands filial piety, and so Adeline Weaver is trained and taught. The most crippling of these traditions is repression, the prohibition against screaming. For Adeline too, the problem is *silence*.

Driven by frustration, she looks for ways to protest without screaming. She persuades the servant to try a new cake recipe, which fails and provokes a reproof from her aunts. "Adeline had acquiesced sweetly, but she had eaten the cake failure, soggy as it was, with a sort of fierce animal relish. At least it was something different" (153). Such small alterations in routine are major heresies in the Weaver household, with its elaborate, often soundless language. When Adeline is late for tea, for the first time in her life, her aunts only say, in chorus, " 'My dear.' . . . but there was a world of meaning in the two words" (160). And Adeline's demure demeanor conceals a "surge" of passionate meanings. "She felt a hysterical delight that . . . she had successfully invaded the monotony of things, and yet she was conscious of remorse and grief—that she had disturbed her aunts. She loved her aunts. . . . And yet she had that delight in rebellion against that which she loved" (161).

The weekly ritual that most infuriates Adeline is the visit of the minister, an old beau of an aunt, for a weekly "company" tea, with the same dishes, the same menu, the same insipid music, which Adeline must obediently play. On one such day, Adeline commits her first effective protest: she packs up the entire set of company china, "the willow-ware," and hides it under the summerhouse floor. The aunts do not suspect her. And the girl is amazed at the magnitude of her act, which "was to her consciousness a deed of the

nature of sacrilege. . . . She was frightened as she had never been frightened, she was wretched as she had never been wretched, and yet she was
conscious of a mad exhilaration which was entrancing" (165).

That very day, another plot presents itself. The minister brings his
handsome, eligible young nephew to tea. The young man and Adeline draw
apart to speak a common language of sexual attraction and impatience with
the established Weaver domestic order. They kiss and fall in love. He
proposes immediately—in the summerhouse. And Adeline is caught between two plots: "She remembered the blue china under the very floor on
which they stood. How could she tell him? And yet she could not marry him
unless she did tell" (172). For a month, she spurns the young man, Elias
Farwell. The courtship plot is completed because of *his* persistence; watching Adeline's face, he perceives that her resistance is connected to the
vanished willow-ware. Prodded, Adeline breaks her silence and says what
had seemed unsayable: "Every day was like every other, and I was tired of it."
Elias empathizes: "I should have smashed the willow-ware if I had to live
the way you do with your dear old aunts." And even more incredibly, in
Adeline's view, he claims to comprehend her situation:

> "You understand?" faltered Adeline.
> "I think you can never do anything which I shall not be able to understand,"
> said Elias Farwell. (181)

This is the last dialogue between the lovers that the story records. In the
next paragraph, the plot has been abruptly ordered, and the domestic and
matrimonial fronts are joined: the willow-ware mysteriously reappears in
the china closet, the engagement is announced, to aunts' and uncle's approval, and tea is served, in willow-ware. On one level, this tale ends with
beatific resolution. The exclusive tension between male and female culture
has been emphasized by many of Freeman's stories: the selectmen evict
Hetty Fifield, the minister damns Betsey Dole, and Joe Dagget, in Louisa
Ellis's parlor, feels hopelessly alien, "as if surrounded by a hedge of lace" (6).
But now that tension dissipates, with Elias's near-magical assertion of
understanding. Elias has effected the plot's climax: he "lays siege" to Adeline and finally demolishes "the obstacle to his wooing." He knows how to
complete a linear campaign to achieve an end. His action is based on the
premise that the domestic plot, or the strict version of it that has prevailed in
the aunts' airless house, is unlivable. Adeline has been entirely surrounded
and educated by women; in her aunts' household, even courtship has been
transformed from a finite course of action to a cycle of repetition, as the
elderly aunt and Elias's uncle exchange romantic glances and luxuriate in

innuendo, year after year. Adeline does not even know how to rebel effectively; her defiant gestures propose modest revisions (adjusting the menu,
changing the chinaware) instead of sweeping alterations, and they are
executed in domestic language. Elias would have smashed the family por-
celain, he says. Adeline hid it, but she did not break a piece. Thus, at the
story's end, tea can be served again in the former style. In other words,
despite the romantic and sexual accord of Adeline and Elias, there are
differences between them, determined by the gendered educations they
have received, which may make Elias's declaration of universal understanding seem both foolish and ominous, although there is nothing either ironic
or ominous about Elias's presentation in this story. His declaration denies
the present pertinence of gendered culture; for him it is a relic as dispensable
as the willow-ware, to be relegated to the "old people." At best, this
declaration points toward the early twentieth-century ideal of companionate marriage, described by Phyllis Palmer as "the idea that sexuality, even
without children, justified marriage, [and] joined men and women in durable social bonds" (37). But Elias's declaration is more probably based in male
hegemony; speaking from the center of the dominant culture, he typically
cannot acknowledge the priorities of the "wild zone" of female culture,
described by Ardener, in which Adeline has spent her life.

In some ways, the story argues the decline of traditional women's culture.
Some of the rituals that Adeline has been taught to observe are rendered
pointless by an industrial culture. And there seems to be no possibility that
the aunts' rituals could be meaningful and expressive for Adeline. At least
that is the girl's view of her situation: "The tragedy of a tight leash upon
growth forced itself upon her consciousness. The holiest force in the world,
that of the growth of youth, was being restrained. . . . 'It is cruel,' she said to
herself—'cruel.' Again she heard the clink of silver. She smelled the bread
toasting. . . . the choice green tea. . . . She looked at the little gold watch
which had been her [dead] mother's. . . . It was almost tea time" (155). As
the story ends, the "force" of youth has been released. Elias and Adeline will
leave the village and marry. Will they live in a utopia of companionate
accord, where everything is accomplished as easily, invisibly, and effectively
as the replacement of the willow-ware? Or will their separate gendered pasts
continue to assert themselves, especially when (and if) Adeline is established as housekeeper in her own right? The story will not acknowledge
these questions: Adeline and Elias are borne forward on the trajectory
of their courtship, an accomplished plot. The Aristotelean plot, with its
emphasis on climax, is analogous to sexual intercourse, as is implied by
Nancy K. Miller's discussion of the linear "heroine's plot," usually deter-

mined by a sexual event. Such a foregrounding of women's heterosexual experience obscures (among other matters) the repetitive domestic traditions of women's culture, as we have seen.

In the last paragraphs of "The Willow-ware," Freeman returns to the characters who are still living home plots; the Weaver aunts, who are going nowhere. The mystery of the willow-ware's disappearance and reappearance has its real importance for them, who have unknowingly suffered the cramp of routine. The story ends: "They probably had not realized it . . . but the monotony of their lives had told upon them as well as their niece. They had become wearily stagnated. Now all was changed. . . . they seemed to acquire an afterbloom in their old age. . . . It was all due to [the mystery of] the willow-ware. . . . Right or wrong, they had gotten a jolt towards happiness out of their ruts of life, which had been wearing their very souls bare of youth and hope" (182–83). Here the language suggests the press of domestic ritual even for its most conservative devotées. Their "very souls" have been endangered. But they are saved, brought again to bloom (or "afterbloom"), not by the marriage, although it has their approval. Instead, it is Adeline's rebellious gesture that has rejuvenated them; it provides a small adjustment in routine, a sense that variation is possible—"who could tell if the willow-ware would be on its accustomed shelves when the china-closet door was opened or not?" (182). The change itself becomes ritual—a subject of discussion that recurs as often as the serving of tea. The last sentence of the story makes it very clear that "ruts" are opposed to "happiness." Adeline's plot was completed when she turned her back on the "ruts" where she had grown to maturity. But for the old people, the ruts remain and always will; the uncle still comes for weekly tea with the aunts. Small adjustments of perspective bring that routine new savor, although to an observer, it would appear that nothing has changed; it is still the same tea, still the same willow-ware.

As noted earlier, one of the initial problems of this story is silence. The Weavers' household has been a small domain of women. As Nina Auerbach observes, both male and female communities live by codes, but male codes tend to be "explicit, formulated," while for women, a code is "a whispered and a fleeting thing, more a buried language than a rallying cry" (9). For Mrs. Todd and the narrator in Jewett's book and for the more successful of Freeman's domestic protagonists, such as Hetty Fifield, such a code of repetition and innuendo can become a rich language. But for the Weavers it is an alphabet with too few syllables, which cannot express what they most need to say. Adeline's theft was an effort to extend that language, but she could not complete her act and effect her escape until Elias, fluent in "explicit" male codes, pushed her to confess her act to a man and to enter the world of words, breaking with the Weaver women and eventually, through marriage, relinquishing the *name* Weaver. The disappearance and reappearance of the willow-ware (presumably effected by the lovers' collaboration) also brings a new dimension to the old people's language, which flows back into the larger community, for the minister-uncle "wrote new sermons under this strange influence. He went home in those days from the Weaver mansion feeling an odd mental strengthening after a discussion about the willow-ware" (183). Here it is the male minister, traditional patriarchal voice of the New England village, who broadcasts the dilemmas of domestic life in words. This story provides no models for female authorship.

"The Willow-ware" illustrates Freeman's own problems with authorship at the beginning of the twentieth century, with two decades of trenchant domestic fiction behind her. On one level, it is a courtship tale; on another level, it is a tale about the continuation and extension of a domestic code; on yet another level, it is a fable of male-female collaboration in a world where the female domain of domestic ritual is essentially obsolete. On none of these levels is the story entirely successful. Freeman never locates a consistent tone for the narration; it skids from facetiousness to moral exhortation. The theft of the willow-ware, on which the story turns, is a brilliant stroke; it shows how originally Freeman could still exploit the vocabulary of housekeeping. But in this genteel world, ritualized housekeeping seems an option and a luxury, not the necessity that empowered Freeman's earlier plots. The perfected romance of Adeline and Elias is little more than a charmingly elaborated theory. "Silence," anchored in the past, is more compelling. Silence Hoit and the colonial women *must* weave; in a devastated frontier village, in freezing winter, cloth—like other domestic products—is a matter of life and death. By contrast, Adeline Weaver's hand-stitched underwear seems an effete and archaic fetish. It is Adeline's loyalty to her aunts that keeps her stitching—and that loyalty is the real problem and subject of the story, although Freeman's ending will not acknowledge it.

In much of her fiction after the first two books of her finest stories, Freeman returned to the combat between plots that is dramatized in "The Willow-ware." The courtship plot, sequential, is a version of Miller's "heroine's plot," a plot of completion. The domestic plot, within which Freeman effected so many variations, is a plot of continuation. In most women's lives, versions of these two plots have been interwoven; that interweaving was a primary interest for Freeman, and the longer fiction to which she increasingly devoted herself after 1891 was a way to pursue it more complexly. Her best novels, *Pembroke* and *The Shoulders of Atlas*, are such projects. But

Freeman's genius is largely found in her short fiction. With domestic metaphors, Jewett was able to expand the plot of continuation, so that it contained smaller episodes of completion, such as William's marriage and the narrator's departure, which found their meaning within that larger, controlling repetitive rhythm. But Freeman's plots, clearly articulated, both enact a sequence and question it. Domestic life, although repetitive by nature, is of course sequential too. Every evening, step by step, dinner is prepared, eaten, and the table cleared. Dinner is completed, over—but tomorrow night, it must be served again. Freeman's plots, with their repetitions of character and situation, of which Freeman was so aware, can evoke the same rhythm. *Completing* Jane Muzzy's story in *A Humble Romance and Other Stories,* we turn the page to encounter—and continue with—Martha Patch. Freeman's best books inscribe a culture where, story after story, women are working, with plot their tool, to excavate meaning. Their job is housekeeping.

Eric Sundquist writes (quoting William Dean Howells) that the attempt "to escape 'the paralysis of tradition' is . . . the typifying American gesture" ("The Country" 9). In that sense, Freeman is a typically American writer. Martha Patch, bent over her patchwork; Silence Hoit, who cannot acknowledge her lover; and the Weaver women, who suppress screams—all are afflicted with paralysis. For women, the paralyzing tradition is likely to be domestic ritual. In another sense, "the paralysis of tradition" is a patriarchal formulation; for many traditional American women, domestic culture has provided both enabling continuity and validation. What is peculiarly American in Freeman's late nineteenth-century stories is the way her plots enact the complex interplay between the impulse to escape for a more expansive, less prescriptive "territory," as in so many works of the male canon, and the need for a continuing relationship with women's domestic culture. In the Freeman stories I have discussed, none of the women protagonists, except Adeline Weaver, leaves the community where she has always lived (although male mobility is a frequent feature of these stories). In the world of fixity and routine where the women remain, what can *escape* mean and be? Again and again, Freeman's American stories enact that question. Every repetition and variation of plot adds weight to the question, and every apparently minor matter, whether patchwork or willow-ware, takes on major weight, so that the reader of Freeman's stories finds herself inside a domestic aesthetic. A careless comment on an unpublished poem becomes, for Betsey Dole, a matter of life and death; household goods are transformed, at the hearth, into bullets that save the Deerfield settlers. From inside these stories, the central issue of Freeman's plots becomes apparent. Basically, that issue is always survival.

Ozzie J. Mayers, in an ambitious recent essay, suggests that the domestic act of sewing, a commonplace of women's culture, is a resonant metaphor for rootedness. He writes, "I sense we need . . . stories about surviving within American civilization, not only ones," as in the traditional canon, "about escaping it" (664). A very positive reading of "A New England Nun" is a linchpin of Mayers's argument. But, read en masse, Freeman's dozens of housekeeping stories provide a more complex view of the costs of survival for American women. In their repetitions, they are an analogue for the dangers, satisfactions, and perils of domestic life, and their stakes are very high. In these stories, with such shaping characters as Louisa Ellis, Goody Crane, and Betsey Dole, women's art must start in the house, with an understanding of domestic ritual.

4

Willa Cather

Repudiating Home Plots

JEWETT's and Freeman's first books, *Deephaven* and *A Humble Romance*, were both deeply marked by their unequivocal commitment to domestic ritual as a central subject and concern. But as Willa Cather began her career, at the turn of the century, she seemed determined to evade their preoccupation with domestic subjects. When she published her first book of fiction, *The Troll Garden*, in 1905, she had not yet, at age thirty-two, found American women writers to admire or emulate.[1] The best story from that first book, "A Wagner Matinee," shows that domestic ritual was a weighted subject for young Willa Cather, both verboten and inescapable.

"A Wagner Matinee" recounts a Boston visit by "Aunt Georgianna," a former Boston music teacher who married at thirty and moved to a Nebraska homestead, where she stayed for thirty years, until this brief return. The narrator is her nephew, Clark, who spent part of his childhood on the bleak homestead and now lives comfortably in Boston. The story is suffused with Clark's horror of prairie domestic life and what he thinks it has done to his aunt. Georgianna is misshapen, toothless; her hands, which once served art, have "been stretched and twisted into mere tentacles to hold and lift and knead with" (*Troll Garden* 99). In Clark's eyes, she has become subhuman, a piece of domestic machinery to perform tasks, which the twentieth century would invent appliances to accomplish. The mere mention of her name is a powerful threat to Clark; it opened "before my feet a gulf of recollection so wide and deep that . . . I felt suddenly a stranger to all the present conditions of my existence. . . . I became, in short, the gangling farmer-boy, scourged with chilblains and bashfulness, my hands cracked and sore from the corn husking" (94). Aunt Georgianna evokes the immediate threat of the abyss, a fall back into a world that predates civilization: "the flat world of the ancients; to the east, a cornfield . . . to the west, a corrall" (99). His aunt arrived there as the result of a classic (female) courtship plot, which Clark regards with contempt as an "inexplicable infatuation" for a "handsome country boy" (95). Clark, by contrast, is living out a classic male plot of *rising in the world*. He is unimpeded by domestic responsibilities; in his apartment house, a capable landlady makes all the arrangements for Georgianna's lodging and care. Clark has put the raw farmhouse behind him for a comfortably eclectic Eastern city life, which gives him entree to the civilized art of his own time. He takes his aunt to a Wagner concert, to hear music "which had kindled the [civilized] world since she left it" (99).[2] He sees the fashionably dressed matinee audience as a bright shimmer of "all the colors that an impressionist finds in a sunlit landscape." But his aunt, he thinks, can no longer see or hear new art—the colors that evoke then-current impressionist painting to Clark, she must regard as dead matter: "so many daubs of tube-paint" (98).

Clark's panic incapacitates him to see his aunt coherently. There is something of embarrassed condescension in his response to the bent, train-sick figure in unfashionable country clothes. When Georgianna speaks for the first time, it is to voice her worry about the "weakling calf" she is nursing and the mackerel she left in her cellar, as if domestic chores now form her only, deprived vocabulary. But this is also the woman who, as Clark lovingly remembers, taught him Latin grammar, Greek mythology, Shakespeare, and music, in Nebraska. Clark does not know what to make of his aunt. He can imagine her life only as a painfully "long struggle" between her perceiving artist-self and the numbing routine of her domestic prairie life. He doubts she will comprehend the music: "Indeed, for her own sake, I could only wish her taste for such things quite dead" (97). If her "taste for such things" is dead, Georgianna is totally a rural housewife, which means to Clark that she is no longer human, merely a piece of work equipment.

Clark both desires and fears to enter his aunt's mind and experience the realities of her life. The dangers of that life, he thinks, are to the spirit and to the hands; thus the story is full of hand imagery. Clark anxiously begins to remember Nebraska: "[I] felt the knuckles of my thumb tentatively, as though they were raw again. I sat again beside her parlor organ, fumbling the scales with my stiff, red hands, while she, beside me, made canvas mittens for the huskers" (94). Farm life uses and threatens the hands, so that they fumble even the most rudimentary foundations of art, scales. Aunt Georgianna combats that debilitative process as much as possible, making mittens to protect the workers' hands—although the domestic task keeps her from the keyboard. But there is only so much she can do; the limits of Georgianna's housekeeping powers are everywhere apparent. Even the things she worries about in Boston—a sickly calf and a "kit of mackerel"— are likely to die or spoil in her absence. Clark can never perceive his aunt's housekeeping as rising to the realm of the aesthetic, epitomized for him by Wagner and by sensory evocations of impressionist painting. Instead, his memories of Nebraska are obsessively repetitive images of the "tall, naked house on the prairie, black and grim," with dank dishcloths drying on the dwarf trees by the kitchen door (99). The artful order that was a mark of achieved domestic ritual in Freeman's New England stories is invisible in Clark's Nebraska (significantly, he is a homesick New England boy).

When his aunt does respond powerfully to the music, Clark is "perplexed"; he trains on her all the instruments of analysis and analogy he has been educated to use, trying to "gauge" how much of her "musical comprehension" has been "dissolved in soapsuds, or worked into bread, or milked into the bottom of a pail" (110–101). In this view, housekeeping is the thief of art, and the artist's gifts are leached away into the byproducts of domestic life: food, drink, and cleaning solution. But Clark is confronted with evidence that his aunt's musical comprehension is undissolved. For the Aunt Georgianna who can hear Wagner's music with perception that matches—and perhaps exceeds—his own, Clark turns to a different vocabulary of *male* power and worldly daring; now she is like Keats's "stout Cortez" or an Egyptian pharoah, "granite Rameses in a museum" (98–99). Thus he co-opts his aunt into a culture dominated by men.

But, as the concert draws to an end, Clark must also abandon his male vocabulary, along with the pretense of measuring his aunt's responses with any tools of description or analysis. He says, "The deluge of sound poured on and on; I never knew what she found in the shining current. . . . From the trembling of her face I could well believe that before the last numbers, she had been carried out where the myriad graves are, into the grey, nameless burying grounds of the sea, or into some world of death vaster yet, where, from the beginning of the world, hope has lain down with hope and dream with dream, and, renouncing, slept" (101). Georgianna, attuned to the music, is in a world Clark cannot know. His best and most intuitive attempt to imagine that world eschews particularities of gender and of culture; he evokes a world as vast as the reaches of a collective unconscious.

The music ends and audience and musicians leave. When the rich world of the populated stage is gone, the hall seems to Clark "empty as a winter cornfield" (101). For him, the prairie is the very image of desolation, a place abandoned by art. He finally speaks to his aunt, returning to the quotidian "living level" (101). She cries, "pleadingly," "I don't want to go, Clark, I don't want to go!" (101). To this ambiguous cry, Clark has a specific response. "I understood. For her, just outside the door of the concert hall, lay the black pond with the cattle-tracked bluffs; the tall, unpainted house, with weather-curled boards; naked as a tower; the crook-backed ash seedlings where the dish-cloths hung to dry; the gaunt, moulting turkeys picking up refuse about the kitchen door" (101).

All we know of Georgianna's response is that she has been deeply moved by the concert and does not yet want to leave the site of that powerful experience. She has known for many years the cost of being separated from music. But we learn nothing of her feelings about her domestic life, her six children, her husband—whom Clark despises, but who did manage to buy his wife a parlor organ after fifteen years of marriage. The story, woven of Clark's intense prairie memories and his close observation of his aunt at the concert, evokes nothing of the rhythm of her life as *she* perceives it. Instead, it is dominated by Clark's recollection of his Nebraska life as an unending task—"ploughing forever and ever . . . as in a treadmill, one might walk from daylight to dusk without perceiving a shadow of change" (98). Repetition and apparent lack of variation, typical of housework, are Clark's particular horror, epitomized in the treadmill image, which suggests a plot without climax or conclusion.

This story's best critics emphasize Clark's empathy with his aunt[3] and Clark himself finally asserts that he "understood" Aunt Georgianna. But we cannot be sure that he does understand. The world of the music, for him, is complexly sensuous, erotic, and emotional, speaking through "the beloved shapes of the instruments, the patches of yellow light thrown by the green shaded lamps on the smooth, varnished bellies of the 'cellos and the bass viols" (98). The world Clark evokes in contrast to that of art is the final bleakly desolate picture, which he *says* his aunt sees. In fact the vision is his own. It is a vision of bad housekeeping. Even the "cattle-tracked" bluffs are messy and despoiled. There is no rich variety of color, only black; the shapes, as Rosowski notes (*Voyage* 28), suggest deformed humanity, as did Clark's initial description of his aunt. This housekeeping is distasteful partly because it is not discreetly invisible; the dishcloths are in plain view. The common farm housekeeper's habit of tossing refuse out the back kitchen door and the free-ranging poultry, typical of many farm households (and recalling the ménage of Jewett's Mrs. Bonny) are here repugnant. It is as if the "wild zone" of women's domestic life is making unwelcome intrusions on Clark's male consciousness. The house itself seems a grim, assertively phallic mark on the horizon. Dark and "naked as a tower," it is another expression of Clark's jealous hostility to the homesteader whom Georgianna inexplicably married. The ugly images of dark house and "black pond," with their gendered implications, suggest Clark's efforts to repudiate the entrapments of family romance.

"A Wagner Matinee" is one of Willa Cather's finest stories. And much of its power comes from the violent intensity of Clark's response when his aunt reappears in his life. In Boston, Clark is living out his own plot, and its goals seem to be escape from the prairie and access to the rich world of art. He imagines domestic work, with its dulling repetitions, as the enemy of that access. Hearing the battling themes of the Tannhäuser overture, with Georgianna beside him, he has a newly "overwhelming sense of the waste and wear we are so powerless to combat" (98). It is Georgianna's presence and his sense of her life that lead Clark to his most profound perceptions. As artist and housekeeper, she has faced the "waste and wear" that Clark would like to escape. When Georgianna speaks, in Boston, about her concern for her ailing calf, she refers to it as "'old Maggie's calf, you know, Clark' . . . evidently having forgotten how long I had been away" (97). The minor misunderstanding underlines major differences between Clark's and Georgianna's sense of time and priority. The calf's care is only a dehumanizing task to Clark; to his aunt it is an obligation with a history, compelling and complex: a domestic ritual. In Clark's plot, the prairie is antagonist, and he thinks in blunt oppositions. Directly outside the symphony hall stands the prairie farmhouse. Finally, Clark must see his aunt's dilemma in the vocabulary of his own memories. Thus the story can have no middle distance—and no place for Georgianna's consciousness.

Nothing in *The Troll Garden* is more persistently problematic for Cather's work to come than this story's questions about what to make of a woman with affinity for art who has committed her energies to a life of housekeeping. And nothing in the story entirely accounts for the intensity of Clark's response to Aunt Georgianna. That response goes beyond the "reverential affection" (96) and the compassion he professes for her. Although Clark's gender would seem to protect him from permanent imprisonment in a prairie kitchen, he perceives his aunt's situation as a direct threat to him in ways that would seem more plausible if he were a young woman, not a young man.

As James Woodress has pointed out, Clark resembles Cather's later, autobiographical young male narrators (*Literary Life* 171). In 1911, when Elizabeth Shepley Sergeant first read the story and wrote of her enthusiasm for it to her friend Willa Cather, Cather replied "bluntly" that she had "outgrown" the story. Seven years after the original publication, she thought that "the starvation of a girl avid for a richer environment seemed to stick out, to deform, to make the picture one-sided." When Cather wrote that response she was visiting Sarah Orne Jewett's surviving sister, writing from her mentor's "very desk." There, the "harsh mood" of "A Wagner Matinee" (and the other two Western stories of *The Troll Garden*) seemed antithetical to the aura of artful domestic order—"the composed and quiet atmosphere of the old Jewett house" (67).

Willa Cather, 1873–1947, was born a few years after the Civil War ended and died two years after World War II ended. Her long career overlapped those of both Sarah Orne Jewett and Eudora Welty. No other writer in this study, and indeed few American writers, ranges so far in time and space— fourteenth to twentieth centuries; Albuquerque to Avignon. As a small girl, she sampled life in the nineteenth-century female Arcadia, sewing patchwork in a Virginia farmhouse governed by omnicompetent housekeepers. She died in a Park Avenue apartment, where she lived with another professional woman.

Throughout her writing life, Cather was engaged with the problem of domestic ritual. That subject, which Stowe, Jewett, and Freeman had assumed as a significant part of their donnée as American women writers, was often troubling excess baggage for young Willa Cather. Yet it was baggage she could never entirely abandon, for it was essentially a part of herself. "A Wagner Matinee" is an early symptom of that lifelong engagement. First published in *Everybody's Magazine* in 1904, the story provoked protests from Nebraska readers, including some of Cather's old friends. *The Nebraska State Journal* described the "wretched figure" of Georgianna as an affront to local pride. And Cather's family was reproachful, for they assumed (probably correctly) that Georgianna was based on Willa Cather's favorite aunt, Franc Cather. They took the portrayal as insulting and "not nice." "Cather wrote a friend that the whole affair had been the nearest she had ever come to personal disgrace. She seemed to have done something horrid without realizing it" (Woodress, *Literary Life* 177–78).

On every level, "A Wagner Matinee" signaled danger to Willa Cather. It threatened estrangement from the approval and support of family and friends and from the orderly, supportive female world of "Miss Jewett," so important to her "emerging voice" (O'Brien). Written during the years when Cather was coming to terms with her lesbian identity, the story is much marked by fear of heterosexual marriage and of the domestic routine in which marriage is likely to involve a woman. Clark's sympathy and empathy are entirely for his aunt, not for his aesthetically repugnant uncle. Yet Clark's very empathy for Georgianna estranges him from the everyday domestic rhythms of her life, which he cannot understand or evoke. In Clark's mind, the kingdom of art (where composers and musicians are all male) must recognize domestic ritual as its deadening foe. Problems of subject, gender, geography, and point of view converge in this telling early story. After the *Troll Garden* version of 1905 (itself altered from the 1904 magazine version), it was reprinted twice, in 1921 (*Youth and the Bright Medusa*) and in 1938 (*The Novels and Stories of Willa Cather*); each time Cather made further revisions, most in the portrait of Georgianna. Her physical appearance is much softened and her final outcry is muffled; the violent tears become "a sad little smile," and she says mildly, "I don't want to go, Clark. I suppose we must" (169).[4] But in all the versions of the story, the dishcloths still hang on the stunted trees and the black house still rears from the flat horizon. The succeeding versions of the story map Cather's continuing, modulating concern with her art's relation to domestic ritual. As much as any other issue in Willa Cather's writing life, this one marked her work from beginning to end.

It was in Nebraska, where the Cather family moved when she was nine, that Willa Cather came to feel the pinch and pull of domestic ritual most complexly. There, as the eldest of six children, she watched her mother, her maternal grandmother, and the woman servant who traveled with them from Virginia as they set up housekeeping in a new country. When she talked about this period of her life, Cather emphasized her own resistance to confinement, claiming that she spent hours outdoors, riding her pony across fields, evading housekeeping and school. She soon made friends with immigrant women on nearby farms. In 1913 she told an interviewer, "I have never found any intellectual excitement any more intense than I used to feel when I spent a morning with one of those old women at her baking or butter making. . . . as if I had actually got inside another person's skin. If one begins that early, it is the story of the man-eating tiger all over again—no other adventure ever carries one quite so far" (*Willie Cather in Person* 10–11). In those kitchens, Cather touched something as unforgettable and dangerous as the "man-eating tiger." Intertwined with baking and butter making, she found an intellectual and spiritual communion that nourished her first roots, as writer, and she sensed the power of a long tradition of female culture, expressed in housekeeping.

When the family moved into town, young Cather began to realize what might lie ahead for her, as a female in Red Cloud, Nebraska, and she took steps to sever herself from a conventionally feminine domestic life. She clipped her hair very short, wore a boy's clothes, and professed what seemed to Red Cloud a boy's ambitions: to become "William Cather, M.D.," or, failing that, an undertaker. In a friend's memory book she wrote decidedly, at age sixteen, that "real misery" was that ornamental domestic occupation, "Doing Fancy Work." For young Cather, conventional female trappings seemed the foe of what she professed to admire most in a man: "An Origonal [sic] Mind" (Bennett 113).

In the small Cather house in Red Cloud, Willa Cather must have first apprehended the mystery of family life of which she wrote in her 1925 essay on Katherine Mansfield: "even in harmonious families there is this double life; the group life, which is the one we can observe in our neighbor's household, and underneath, another—secret and passionate and intense—which is the real life that stamps the faces and gives character to the voices of our friends. Always in his mind each member of these social units is escaping, running away . . ." (*Not Under* 136). For Cather, the most crucial encounters often occurred when "an original mind" wrestled with double loyalties to the life of the household, the stuff of home plots, and the impulse to run away, expressed in many canonical male escape plots. She spoke with her 1913 interviewer about the "poor" early stories she tried to write about Nebraska people, such as the old women—stories that failed because "it is always hard to write about things that are near your heart, from a kind of instinct of self-protection you distort and disguise them." And she went on to suggest that it was Sarah Orne Jewett's advice that freed her to take possession of her own truest materials. The older writer, whom Cather met in the last year of her life, told her, "You can't do it in anybody else's way—you will have to make a way of your own. If the way happens to be new, don't let that frighten you" (*In Person* 11).[5]

"A Wagner Matinee," with its minimal plot, takes its shape from Clark's efforts to locate the meaning Georgianna's life has for his own. It is the most experimental of the stories in *The Troll Garden*, the one that most seems to be written in Cather's "own" way, exemplifying what she told another writer in 1906: "that a feeling could be a story just as much as an incident" (Woodress, *Literary Life* 189). In the last and longest of the early stories, "The Bohemian Girl" (1912), we find Willa Cather, fresh from extended forays as an editor and a Jamesian, returning with new vigor to the Nebraska domestic materials she approached with such oblique intensity in "A Wagner Matinee."[6]

"The Bohemian Girl" is purposefully not a "one-sided" story. Nils Ericson returns to the prairie, where he grew up, from Norway where he has established a life in the land his father left. One of the most successful scenes of this vigorous story is the often-quoted description of the old pioneer women of the farm community, setting out a festive supper for a barn dance. It emphasizes the women's energy, variety, and their "pleased, prosperous air":

> There was a great chattering from the stall where Johanna Vavrika exhibited to the admiring women her platters heaped with fried chicken, her roasts of beef, boiled tongues, and baked hams with cloves stuck in the crisp brown fat and garnished with tansy and parsley. . . . They were a fine company of old women, and a Dutch painter would have loved to find them there together, where the sun made bright patches on the floor. . . . [Nils] fell into amazement when he thought of the Herculean labors those fifteen pairs of hands had performed: of the cows they had milked, the butter they had made, the gardens they had planted, the children and the grandchildren they had tended, the brooms they had worn out, the mountains of food they had cooked. It made him dizzy. (*Collected Short Fiction* 28–29)

As O'Brien has noted (398), Clark's view of domestic life in "A Wagner Matinee," as a cruel routine that brutalized his aunt, is reversed by Nils's romantic view of these grandmother-housekeepers. Heroic and tireless as Hercules, these women have made domesticity a medium for triumph, and their instruments have been their own capable hands. Nils looks on "as they sat chattering in four languages, their fingers never lagging behind their tongues" (28–29). These women's constant, fluent housework is a language as telling as their multilingual talk. Collectively, they seem to have defied time and age; "among all these grandmothers there were more brown heads than white" (29). Here it is the brooms that wear out, not the housekeepers who wield them. This group portrait features rich variety of color and golden light, which were totally absent from Clark's prairie memories; Nils's view of the old women is determinedly celebratory—and thus it, too, holds domestic life at a distance, in order to make it a subject for art.

Although the splendid description of the old women is the most frequently discussed passage in "The Bohemian Girl," in fact the story's view of domestic life is more complex than this passage indicates. Nils is aware of the brutalizing as well as the nurturing potential of the old women's domestic energy; perhaps it is that double potential that makes him "a little dizzy." His own widowed mother, of whom he is very proud *and* very wary, is significantly not included in the group portrait. She is "a regular pile driver" (18), jealously running her own house and farm and driving about in the latest contraption, one of the country's first automobiles. A neighbor describes her: "She does beat all! Nearly seventy, and never lets another soul touch that car. Puts it into commission herself every morning. . . . I never stop work for a drink o' water that I don't hear her a-churnin' up the road. I reckon her darters-in-law never sets down easy nowadays. Never know when she'll pop in" (6). With only one child left at home and her wheat land cultivated by a tenant, Mrs. Ericson's formidable domestic energy, allied with the machine age, has become a force to terrorize the neighborhood, especially her daughters-in-law. Instead of making butter for a large family, she is now "a churnin' up the road" to *buy* "meat for supper" (4), transforming the acts and vocabulary of domestic life. Mrs. Ericson seems to have one foot in the world of nineteenth-century domestic faculty and the other in the late nineteenth-/early twentieth-century culture of scientific housekeeping, allied with consumerism and determined to take full advantage of scientific and mechanical advances. (Enid Royce, Claude Wheeler's "modern" wife in *One of Ours,* is a bitter portrait of such a housekeeper.) "The Bohemian Girl" ends with an ambiguous image of Mrs. Ericson as she greets her youngest son, returned to the farm from a failed attempt to run away, as Nils had been able to do. With her capable hand, she gives the boy an unaccustomed and oddly mechanical caress: "Her hand went out from her suddenly and rested on his head. Her fingers twined themselves in his soft, pale hair" (41). With her competent domestic hands, Mrs. Ericson tethers her last child to the life she has made in the farmhouse, telling him, "I always meant to leave you the home farm" (42). Throughout this story, as in "A Wagner Matinee," images of female hands signal Cather's concern with uses and abuses of domestic culture.

Although his own adult distance, prosperity, and security have enabled Nils to see the pioneer farm women with admiring nostalgia, his memories of the housekeeping he grew up with are nearly as grim as Clark's; he tells his mother, "you were working yourselves to death and the houses were mostly a mess, full of babies and washing and flies" (19). The appeal of the nearby Bohemian saloon seems to have been primarily that of felicitous domestic life: "It was the one jolly house in this country," with music, "good stories," and "a big supper . . . herrings and pickles and poppy-seed bread, and lots of cakes and preserves. . . . I can see [Clara's father] cutting bread, at the head of the table, now" (19). Nils's point of view dominates the story, and his mind is still full of these exaggerated pictures of domestic life. They are like a pair of matched prints, enshrined in his memory: domestic ritual in his own home as hellish mess; domestic ritual with the Vavrikas (where he had all the illusions of a boy inebriated by music, wine, and love) as artful, welcoming paradise.

The sternest critic of these picture is a woman: Nils's former lover, Bohemian Clara, who has lovelessly married his bullying older brother.

Clara is a pianist who spurns housekeeping; she refuses to furnish the big house her husband has built and consigns her domestic chores to a capable aunt. Intermarriage has put Clara in special jeopardy of self-loss; her Norwegian-American husband cannot comprehend art, values housekeeping only as a means of filling his belly, and sees Clara's ethnicity only as a means of capturing "the Bohemian vote" in local elections. Wooing Clara away from his brother, Nils touches her deepest fears when he warns that she is in danger of losing "your race, everything that makes you yourself. . . . your love of life, your capacity for delight" (35). As a young married woman, Clara stands at the edge of a life of housekeeping. Of all this story's many characters, she is in the most complex and vulnerable situation. Although she loves Nils and eventually does elope with him, even his entreaties are troubling, for with him, she must leave the prairie, to which she has powerful ties: "The ground seemed to hold her as if by roots. . . . she felt as if her soul had built itself a nest there on that horizon" (37). Mary Dearborn suggests that intermarriage, such as Clara's, was a crucial issue of fiction about immigrant women, "central to definitions of ethnic female identity" and raising "complex social and economic problems" (132–33).

For Clara, many of these issues converge in her intense attitudes to housekeeping. By contrast, Nils is confident that he has solved the problems of his own heritage as immigrant son by the ploys of distance and mobility. Thus he can appreciate the artful domestic spectacle of the "fine old bunch of dames" (33) at the barn dance. Clara cannot; she responds to Nils's effusions with "a hard enigmatical smile" (29). Nils claims that she will no longer "detest" the old housekeepers when she has eloped with him and looks "back on them from Stockholm or Budapest. Freedom settles all that," he asserts (33), offering her the traditional strategies of American male culture. But, for an immigrant daughter, the solution is not so simple. And Clara's situation is further complicated by the fact that her impulses as an artist, like those of Freeman's Betsey Dole, are often expressed domestically. She loves the generous Bohemian household of her father, the saloonkeeper, and continues to help with his housekeeping, and for the Ericson barn dance, she contributes both her music and artful decorations contrived from the local vegetation. Even her expression of her ties to Nebraska is domestic: a "nest" on the horizon. Yet she resists, with angry rigor, the obliteration which she thinks threatens a housekeeper. Although Nils, not Clara, is the tale's central character, Cather significantly spotlighted Clara in her title. The future of such a woman, artist and housekeeper, Bohemian's daughter and Norwegian's wife, is the most unsettling enigma proposed by this rich, transitional story.

Clara's marriage was made by her single, domestic aunt, who tends to the cooking and cleaning with classic faculty, "concealing from every one Clara's domestic infelicities" (14), while Clara sleeps or plays her piano. She offers Clara a repertoire of strategies; for example, when Clara deplores her husband's appetite for sweets, "her aunt chuckled knowingly. 'Bait a bear with honey,' as we say in the old country" (15). Clara has small patience with such manipulative domestic tactics; Nils reflects on her differences from such traditional housekeepers, thinking, "she'd never be like them, not if she lived here [Nebraska] a hundred years" (29). Marrying Clara, he must put his own domestic pictures, romantic set pieces, behind him. The story does not portray their marriage; we only get reports that the two have returned to Nils's home in Norway, have traveled widely, and are happy. As critics have noted, this is one of the few successful heterosexual marriages in Cather's fiction; it seems to propose a new marital plot of shared mobility and nonrestrictive housekeeping. But that plot is only dimly projected; the final scene of the story, and its substantive interest, remain on the prairie farms, where Mrs. Ericson and the other old housekeepers rule. As Nils and Clara ride toward the train that will bear them away, "the great still land stretched untroubled under the azure night. Two shadows had passed" (38). Such language suggests that the lovers' plot, which will climax when they catch the train, lacks substance, compared to the cyclical story of the land. Clara's dilemma, as artist, housekeeper, and immigrant woman, would become an enduring concern of Cather's fiction. But her escape into a utopian, cosmopolitan marriage was not a direction Cather would pursue; instead, her richest work returns to the constraints and possibilities of domesticating the new territory of North America.

"A Wagner Matinee" and "The Bohemian Girl," although they share this prototypical Cather concern, are very different stories—the first is a private meditation; the second has a complex plot presented through omniscient narration. But both initiate narrative strategies to which Cather returned again and again, as she tried to write about domestic ritual without getting caught in its trap. One is the male point of view (to be repeated in *My Ántonia, One of Ours, A Lost Lady,* and *The Professor's House*), which takes advantage of a male character's relative mobility and his propensity to see domestic ritual from outside and thus to romanticize it, pro or con. Another is the double plot, which plays a housekeeper's story against that of a character who is not centrally involved in domestic ritual: Georgianna against Clark, Nils against his mother, Alexandra against Marie, Ántonia against Jim. Usually the housekeeper's tale is filtered through her opposite, as we must perceive Georgianna through Clark. And third, there is the recurrent search for a kingdom of art that is not antithetical to domestic life. Jim Burden objectifies Ántonia into the housekeeper-goddess of such a kingdom. Theo Kronborg excavates it in the ancient cliff city; Claude Wheeler finds it in the pleasures of French cuisine and music, which he locates in France; Niel Herbert glimpses it in the exquisite charm of Mrs. Forrester's dinner parties, and Nils Ericson creates it in his mind's eye, transforming a group of "old dames" into a Dutch masterpiece. Cather replays these three strategies throughout her first great prairie novels. But these books never take the vantage point that was usual for Freeman and frequent for Jewett: a housekeeper's view of housekeeping.

Such strategies allowed Cather to keep her distance from the ritualistic rhythms of women's domestic lives. In *O Pioneers!, My Ántonia,* and (to a lesser extent) *The Song of the Lark,* she concentrated instead on the clash and blending of cultures that accompanies the settling of a new territory. Yet Cather was well aware that no culture could survive without rituals to transmit it. In her essay on Thomas Mann, she wrote of rituals' importance even in periods of human decline and insensibility: "The rite and the form can be continued even in the sluggish generations when the significance is lost" (*Not Under* 106). Again and again, housekeeping was the medium in which a culture was preserved, whether in Mrs. Shimerda's featherbeds and dried mushrooms, Ántonia's *kolaches,* or Mrs. Rosen's salad dressing.

But in Cather's earlier fiction, authoritative adult women who are fully identified with the powers of domestic ritual, such as Grandmother Burden and Mrs. Shimerda of *My Ántonia,* or Mrs. Ericson of "The Bohemian Girl," are likely to appear narrow, limited, or grasping—or else their domestic competence is romanticized, as in Nils's portrait of the old farm women. In the early prairie novels, Cather created scenes that express a generous and attractive *ideal* of what ritual can be, if freed from the constraints that often typify domestic life. Such scenes include the French Catholic fair in *O Pioneers!* and the Spanish dance in *The Song of the Lark;* they offer a rich, fluid mix, which allows both immediacy and memory, definition and expansion, preservation and change, order and fecundity. The most telling of such scenes is the most domestic—it occurs in the best of the early novels, *My Ántonia,* when Jim Burden and his grandparents celebrate a snowbound Nebraska "Country Christmas."

A little cedar tree is brought into the house and decorated, as was the custom in the Burdens's Virginia home, a custom with European origins and Christian and pre-Christian roots. The decorations are provided by both men and women; they combine the products of an American farm kitchen (cookies, popcorn, candles) with elaborate Austrian paper ornaments sent by a hired man's mother, representing various nativity figures and a "lace-trimmed bleeding heart." Hung with these splendors, "our tree became the talking tree of the fairy tale; legends and stories nestled like birds in its branches. Grandmother said it reminded her of the tree of knowledge." Beneath the tree is a replication of the pioneers' present world, centered by an object for private self-contemplation, brought out of darkness into the center of this family ritual: "we put sheets of cotton wool under it for a snow-field, and Jake's pocket-mirror for a frozen lake" (83). The Christmas tree was treasured in Jim's memory and became part of his narrative because it amalgamated the past and present heritage of the people around it, in a rare domestic occasion of mutual love, respect, and celebration. As a transcendent symbol of all that a child would like to believe of the world, the Christmas tree is the center of a prelapsarian domestic ritual. It makes the farmhouse seem a small, enclosed Eden. Even Mr. Shimerda, Ántonia's father, whose customs, housekeeping, and religion are alien to the elder Burdens, is welcomed to the celebration, and he kneels reverently before the shining tree. The adult Jim Burden spells out all the details of this scene lovingly, in almost excessively symbolic detail.

But Jim also records, less emphatically, the scene's nearly immediate fall into dissolution. The tree itself is symbolically ephemeral. Within a month, Mr. Shimerda will commit suicide. The reliable hired men, "like brothers" to Jim, will soon disappear. Jim himself will move back East in a few years, and his grandparents will die (as his parents had, the year before the Christmas tree). The essence of housekeeping, as we have seen, is continuation and repetition, and one of ritual's deepest and most ambivalent satisfactions is the participants' belief that the observance will outlive them, preserving their values into the future. Thus it is surprising that Jim Burden's account of the years to come never mentions another Christmas celebration. After his fall into fuller awareness of temporality, complexity, and loss, Jim will not idealize another indoor, domestic occasion; he comes to hate the flimsiness and meanness of small town Nebraska housekeeping.

The Christmas tree is typical of the "liminal" stage of ritual, described by anthropologist Victor Turner, which is characterized by "release from normal constraints" into the "domain of . . . 'uncommon sense'" (68). Later scenes in *My Ántonia* will also embody elements of the liminal ideal, scenes such as the summer dancing tent and the prairie picnic, when Jim and the hired girls witness the plow against the sun. But, like the Christmas celebration that was followed by Shimerda's suicide, each of these outdoor scenes is countered by an abrupt dispersal and a scene that taints its festive aura. The picnic, for example, is followed by Jim's near-rape by a man who thinks he is

Ántonia, for which Jim blames Ántonia; he goes off to college "hating" her. This unreasoning anger shows Jim's panic when his precarious sense of order and propriety is threatened, particularly in matters of sex and gender. He seems to intuit that, in such equalizing liminal rituals, he has come close to an inclusive ideal of androgyny, and that, particularly in his experiences with Ántonia, he is approaching an apprehension of what it might be like to be a woman.

In later chapters, Jim never mentions any such ritualized group occasions. The hired girls, much as he likes them, have frightened him with their disruptively energetic, sexual, and unconventional lives. Although Nebraska still engages his emotions and his imagination as no other place ever will, he cannot risk all that full participation there would mean. Yet, what Jim finally almost deifies in Ántonia, when he returns to visit her at the book's end, recalls the beauties of the Christmas tree. Jim's own life is split in several ways—most obviously, between East and West. His solution, a job that keeps him constantly traveling in the West for an Eastern firm, only moves him over the surface of the land. But his most powerful images of Ántonia in her middle age are of deeply *rooted* growth. For Jim, Ántonia has herself become the amalgamating symbol the Christmas tree was, possessing "that something which fires the imagination, could still stop one's breath for a moment by a look or a gesture that somehow revealed the meaning in common things" (353). As much as he has heroicized Ántonia, Jim still betrays his fear of her ménage; he insists on sleeping outdoors, in the barn, with her boys.

During Jim's visit, Ántonia's children insist that he tour her well-stocked "fruit cave." From the Nebraska soil, she has preserved the fruit to make Bohemian *kolaches*—a fact of which her bilingual children are very proud. As the children rush out of the cave, the earth itself seems to be identified with Ántonia's womb. The fruit cave is a hole not unlike the stifling dugout in which the Shimerdas spent their first year in America. But Ántonia's will and energy have redeemed the past; the earlier "cave" was a place of failure and death, while this one is full of regenerate life, children who resemble Ántonia's parents and siblings. To Jim, they are "a veritable explosion of life out of the dark cave into the sunlight. It made me dizzy for a moment" (339). In his mind, Ántonia's fecundity and her housekeeping, both epitomized by the fruit cave, are inseparable.

For Jim Burden, art is the means of coming to terms with all that his prairie years meant to him. Ántonia epitomizes this meaning, and his portrayal of her is weighted with myth and symbol, as was the tree of knowledge. However omnivorously domestic *she* may be, the circumstances in which Jim perceives her are determinedly undomestic. He thinks of her on moving trains, and, when alone, runs through the "woodcuts" of her with which his memory is furnished. For this narrator, art requires a separation from domestic ritual.

As he contemplates his mythologized Ántonia, Jim almost believes that he has triumphed over time and change and is himself Ántonia's child, one of "Cuzak's Boys." This triumph can occur only inside his mind; he has replaced the shared satisfactions of the Christmas tree ritual with the private satisfactions of ordering and control, as accomplished by an artist. But Jim's triumph is brief and his control is fragile. So the language of the fruit cave passage also implies danger, especially with the word "explosion," and Jim, like Nils, is uneasy, made "dizzy" by the engulfing imagery of Ántonia's triumphant housekeeping. He leaves the Cuzaks abruptly, at the novel's end. His last sentence, while ostensibly cementing the link between Jim and "his" Ántonia, actually emphasizes loss and all that they cannot share in the present: "Whatever we had missed, we possessed together the precious, the incommunicable past" (372).

Blanche Gelfant, in a valuable essay, has reminded us "to look at *My Ántonia* . . . not only for its beauty of art and for its affirmation of history, but also, and instructively, for its negations and evasions" (163). Jim's insistence on making Ántonia into a figure of transcendent art is one such evasion. As Susan J. Rosowski has noted, the straightforward, compassionate tale of Ántonia's first pregnancy, told to Jim by old Widow Steavens, "provides a woman's account of a woman's experience and, with it, a significant change in tone toward Ántonia, reminding us of how much has been left out of Jim's view of her" (*Voyage* 90). But Jim's own final account of Ántonia again blurs the outlines of her individuality and suppresses much of the particularly and potential conflict of her life, to make of her that overpowering symbol. In these last pages, Jim Burden and Willa Cather seem coconspirators in the mythologizing of Ántonia. And that mythologizing indicates that they have given up on the liminal ideal of ritual that the Christmas tree represented. It suggests both a dead end and a turning point in Willa Cather's handling of domestic ritual.

In "A Wagner Matinee" and "The Bohemian Girl," with their central male characters, Cather had begun to ponder the relation of housekeeping and art. Aunt Georgianna, as a musician, had access to the kingdom of art, but her choice of prairie housekeeping blocked and blurred that access, in Clark's eyes. The story, fueled by Clark's curiosity and anxiety about his aunt's situation, brings her to an anguished cry against a second separation from the world of art she has just rejoined. It is Clark who concludes that the dreaded opposite of that world must be prairie domestic life; the final image of the black house exists in his mind. And thus, in Clark's version, the story must end in tragic impasse.

"The Bohemian Girl" provides a more expansive and various view. Domestic ritual seems to Nils a likely subject for art; he masses the old women, "fifteen pairs of hands," and celebrates them collectively. But individual women provide more problematic views of housekeeping, as with Clara's antidomesticity and her aunt's officious skill. Most problematic is Nils's mother. She has greedy faculty (she refuses to let anyone help her tend her kitchen fire) which eagerly co-opts the developments of contemporary invention and science, such as the automobile. The story is set near the turn of the century, the era in which housekeeping was renamed "domestic science." Helen Campbell, author of *Household Economics* (1896), claimed that the repetitive rhythms of traditional housekeeping had prevented progress by women: "Man saw a better way, used and perfected it. Women saw only the day's work" (quoted in Shapiro 175). Careening over the soft prairie roads in her new car, attending to her home fires and driving into town for mail and meat, Mrs. Ericson seems larger than life, a comic/heroic, horrifying/exhilarating version of the housekeeper who will not be confined by housekeeping. As she makes plans for dividing up her estate, which she controls, she sees much further than the day's housework. Indeed, her neighbors suspect she will outlive all her heirs!

For young Willa Cather, a vision that encompassed only the day's work was horrifying; the treadmill was Clark's image for it. She celebrated domesticity only when it managed to get beyond the limits of dailiness; improvising, inventing, overcoming, and imagining in ways that popular culture was more likely to sanction in men (who "saw a better way"). In *O Pioneers!* (1913), Alexandra Bergson has that kind of imagination. On a prairie farmstead, she grew up observing how her mother used domestic ritual as a fortress. In her kitchen, Mrs. Bergson transformed the fruit of the often hostile land. Any plant that was even marginally edible was pickled or preserved and stashed away: "She had never quite forgiven John Bergson [her husband] for bringing her to the end of the earth; but now that she was there, she wanted to be let alone to reconstruct her old life in so far as that was possible. She could still take some comfort in the world if she had bacon in the cave, glass jars on the shelves, and sheets in the press. She disapproved of all her neighbors because of their slovenly housekeeping" (30). Mrs. Bergson's obsessive housekeeping is a protection against the exigencies of change; the new country is admitted to her domain only if it can be processed with salt, sugar, spice, or vinegar and contained in a preserving jar.

But Alexandra, the daughter, responds to the land not defensively, but with open "love and yearning" (65), and she transforms the new country into an expanding, prosperous farm. Housekeeping is not her métier, as it was her mother's, although her house is pleasant and well run by well-directed servants. The sense of artful order, which Mrs. Bergson expressed through the jars in her fruit cave, Alexandra expresses in her fertile fields. They show "the order and fine arrangement manifest all over the great farm; in the fencing and hedging, in the windbreaks and sheds, in the symmetrical pasture ponds. . . . There is even a white row of beehives in the orchard, under the walnut trees. You feel that, properly, Alexandra's house is the big out-of-doors, and that it is in the soil that she expresses herself best" (84). Here the skills of housekeeping are translated to a larger medium, acted out through the cycle of the prairie seasons.

In *O Pioneers!*, the young woman character who has the most affinity for housekeeping is Marie Shabata; as Carl Linstrum divines, she is "the best" the region has to offer, with her passionate enthusiasms and fine responsiveness. Marie does and admires intricate needlework and can make twelve kinds of "fancy bread." But such exquisite faculty is no protection for her; she is murdered by her surly husband when he finds her with her lover, Alexandra's brother. The problematic combination of Marie's headlong erotic passion and her happy domestic faculty is a central enigma of this book; only when Alexandra acknowledges it, after the murder, does she begin to lose her obdurate innocence. Alexandra herself, in contrast to Marie, is enduringly heroic because she finds an endeavor that matches the dimensions of her imagination. Her love will be consummated, not ended, by her death, as the novel's last words suggest: "Fortunate country, that is one day to receive hearts like Alexandra's into its bosom, to give them out again in the yellow wheat, in the rustling corn, in the shining eyes of youth!" (309). Such an artful apotheosis is possible for Alexandra because she turned her back on the confines of housekeeping.

In *The Song of the Lark* (1915), Thea Kronborg is also separated from housekeeping, by the fact of her musical gifts, which differentiate her from her siblings. From Thea's childhood, her mother recognizes that this child's first priority must be her daily hours of practice, at the piano. But, with her voracious co-opting impulse, Thea is able to incorporate domestic ritual as a source of her art. The singular solitude of her future as opera singer is figured in the spaces that Thea finds most meaningful. For her, the essential plot is to get herself born—a sequential plot with a predictable climax—and then to get herself *re*born, again and again; eventually, this plot is reflected in the multiple roles she sings. Her teacher Harsanyi intuits Thea's plot; he tells her, "Every artist makes himself born. It is very much harder than the other time, and longer. Your mother did not bring anything into the world to play piano. That you must bring into the world yourself" (175–76). In the process of bringing herself into the world, Thea is attracted to small, enclosed womblike spaces. The childhood acquisition of a room of her own, where she could hear the emerging "voice within herself," was "one of the most important things that ever happened to her" (58). Later, she inhabits hotel rooms and especially values her private bath. In the famous interlude in Panther Canyon, she moves between her bathing pool and her "little house" in the cliff village, where she lies in a small room she has lined with blankets. There, outside "the stream of meaningless activity and undirected effort," she finds a newly coherent sense of her powers, intellectual, emotional, and sensual: "her power to think seemed converted into a power of sustained sensation" (300). In their domestic spaces, Thea feels attuned to the "ancient people" who built the village.

For these pueblo women, domestic ritual had as its center the precious water, which they carried to their high houses in pottery they made. "The stupid women carried water," Thea thinks; "the cleverer ones made the vessels to hold it. Their pottery was their most direct appeal to water, the envelope and sheath of the precious element itself" (303). For these "cleverer" women, art and domestic necessity were one, and as she inhabits their world, Thea imagines she catches the spirit of their housekeeping. Her simplest acts, such as her bath, take on "ceremonial gravity. The atmosphere of the canyon was ritualistic" (304). Thea's great moment of revelation, which becomes a permanent resource of her art as singer, comes from a flash of identification with the ancient women's domestic art: "The stream and the broken pottery: what was any art but an effort to make a sheath, a mould in which to imprison for a moment the shining, elusive element which is life itself,—life hurrying past us and running away, too strong to stop, too sweet to lose? The Indian women had held it in the jars. . . . In singing, one made a vessel of one's throat and nostrils and held it on one's breath, caught the stream in a scale of natural intervals" (304).

Thea's own private life of hotels and restaurants and other people's drawing rooms is antidomestic; she displays no interest in *being* a housekeeper. But as her sense of the Indian women's housework shows, an essential awareness of domestic rhythms informs her art. One of her first great parts is Fricka of the Ring cycle, a housewife, and her Fricka restores dignity and power to domestic life; she is a veritable Hestia. Hearing Thea in the role, a friend thinks, "Fricka had been a jealous spouse to him for so long that he had forgotten she meant wisdom before she meant domestic order, and that, in any event, she was always a goddess" (447). Finally, as the novel recedes further and further from her in its last, magisterial section, Thea is a housekeeper of imagination. Even the old family house in the Colorado town where she grew up has become an inner space, and Thea remembers every shabby detail. She says, "That's the house I rest in when I'm tired. All the old furniture and the worn spots in the carpet—it rests my mind to go over them" (458).

When Thea left Moonstone for good, as a teenager, she had behind her "a rich romantic past"—the "foundation" of her art. A part of that foundation was the beginnings of her domestic intuition; another part was her experience with artful liminal occasions of inclusion, where the "creative, spontaneous, and playful elements" Victor Turner describes could unfold (Ross and Ross 26). Her music lessons in the Kohlers' felicitous German house and garden and the romantic, expansive Mexican dances are such occasions, which help to propel Thea into a world of art far more generous than anything else Moonstone has to offer. But such occasions are also shadowed, as was the Burdens' Christmas tree, by darker human realities; both Professor Wunsch, Thea's first music teacher, and her Mexican friend, Spanish Johnny, are alcoholic wanders, capable of hair-trigger violence, and they are the hearts of these liminal celebrations.

Thus, both Thea and Alexandra, like Willa Cather, make domestic ritual a source for their art, but they eschew housekeeping. In a talk with her friend Elizabeth Sergeant, in 1913, when these characters were incubating in her imagination, Cather spoke about such exclusions and inclusions. Sergeant asked,

> Is it the fate of the creative writer . . . to use the stuff of intense personal experience for art only? . . . Could one let all private and personal experience be burned in the fires of *art?*
>
> Then Willa got up and wandered around the room. To be free, to work at her table—that *was* all in all. What could be more beautiful, if you had it in you, than to be the wife of a farmer and raise a big family in Nebraska? There were fates and fates but one could not live them all. (115–16)

In the early novels, we see Cather wrestling with the implications of this passage. Especially for someone who believed that "to be free . . . *was* all in all," the realization that one could not *live* all the fates one could imagine was bound to be galling. Alexandra and (especially) Thea, neither of whom is a farm wife and mother, are heroic partly because they invent ways to live multiple lives. And the liminal rituals, like the Christmas tree of *My Ántonia,* are occasions when boundaries are stretched and lives are shared,

even for participants whose lives are normally circumscribed and circum-
spect, such as Grandfather and Grandmother Burden. It is significant that
Ántonia is not included in the Christmas tree ritual. Later, it is always her
complexities that complicate and sometimes spoil things for Jim, as when he
is mistaken for her in an attempted rape. She is reinstated in Jim's life only
when aging and menopausal physical change have desexualized her and
made her safe in his eyes.

Cather's handling of Ántonia, through the surrogate of her male narrator, epitomizes her difficulties in dealing with women's lives and women's
culture at this stage of her career. As Deborah G. Lambert has observed,
Jim's point of view will not allow us to perceive Ántonia as the sort of
omnivorous hero that Thea and Alexandra were (676–90). When they were
children together, both Jim and Ántonia were storytellers. They exchanged
tales; they invented, translated, and preserved them mutually, as with the
story of Peter and Pavel. And both have remained storytellers; Ántonia
regales her children with tales and Jim works over the manuscript which "is"
the novel. But Jim has retreated from liminality to convention, from orality
to the silently written word. And although his last view of Ántonia venerates
her life of housekeeping, she is not viewed as an artist, and his last chapter
does not include *her* tales. Instead, she is, for Jim, the mother lode: "a rich
mine of life," always able "to leave images in the mind that did not fade"
(352–53). He sees Ántonia as raw material. The art is his own; the images are
in *his* mind. Although domestic art is typically unsigned and ephemeral,
preserving process and not product, Jim possessively and patriarchally labels
his first manuscript "*My* Ántonia," adopting a phrase first used by Ántonia's
father. "That seemed to satisfy him," the narrator says ("Introduction,"
unpaged, emphasis mine).

As his title suggests, Jim Burden's art is finally a way to distance himself
from Ántonia. Like Aunt Georgianna, the middle-aged Ántonia is "a
battered woman" (353) in the male narrator's eyes, and Jim, like Clark,
refuses us access to the quotidian domestic rhythms of her life. During his
last visit, Jim would like to edit retrospectively Ántonia's life to make it a
rural idyll more appropriate to his art; he tells her, "You ought never to have
gone to town, Tony." But she replies eagerly. "Oh, I'm glad I went! I'd never
have known anything about cooking or housekeeping if I hadn't. I learned
nice ways at the Harlings' [where she worked as a domestic hired girl for a
woman of formidable faculty], and I've been able to bring my children up so
much better" (343). This interchange hints that Ántonia's story of her own
life is far different from anything Jim chooses to imagine. She speaks for
growth and joyous multiplicity; she also speaks for housekeeping. Although

Jim presents Ántonia as a fixed mother figure, stationary like a cave or a mine, Ántonia's own story seems to have all the "creative, spontaneous, and playful elements" that characterize liminality. According to Mary Ellen Ross and Cheryl Lynn Ross, these elements have their psychological roots in the period of human development most dominated by female influence: the child's initial pre-oedipal union with the mother (26–27). As Jim works on his narrative, taking possession of written language and thus of art, he must, if one follows Lacan, move away from a preverbal union with the mother. And thus, as he tells Ántonia's story, he must suppress it.

None of Cather's novels is more compellingly or mysteriously beautiful than *My Ántonia*. By her title, Cather makes a housekeeping woman the *center* of a fiction for the first time. Thus the book embodies Cather's sense that housekeeping/art/home/escape are conjoined, at the true center of her own work. But at the same time, the choice of Jim's point of view, ostensibly male and clearly nondomestic, controls Ántonia's presentation and distorts our sense of her life. As Jim perceives it, he cannot "see" Ántonia and thus be an artist unless he exiles himself from domestic life. Much of the novel's beauty grows from an exile's homesickness.

It was Jim's grandmother who called their Christmas tree a "tree of knowledge"; Jim appropriated her phrase. But he never fully comprehends the language in which the tree's wisdom was inscribed, a language that would be far more comprehensible to a housekeeping woman. Even as an adult, Jim has achieved none of the skills that created the tree—cooking, candle-making, tree-cutting. He does not enter the cycles of domestic ritual, to perceive it as a woman probably would, for he never takes any responsibility for its continuance. Nor does his narrative show any interest in how Ántonia *learned* the housekeeping that he romanticizes. In more than one way, Jim Burden turns his back on the tree of knowledge.

Cather's original introduction to *My Ántonia* portrays the beginnings of Jim's manuscript in a contest between him and a female narrator, who says, "I was ready . . . to make an agreement with him [Jim]; I would set down on paper all that I remembered of Ántonia if he would do the same. We might, in this way, get a picture of her" (*Early Novels* 711). Eagerly and "with some pride," Jim turns up at his friend's apartment with his manuscript, "My Ántonia." He says, "Now, what about yours?" The woman writer confesses that she has only taken a few notes; her role in the enterprise is simply and minimally to provide an introductory frame for Jim's narrative. She says, "My own story was never written" (714).

Viewed in this context, *My Ántonia* becomes the triumph of the written male story, finding its way into print with facilitating female support. Both

Jim and the woman narrator are, of course, autobiographical artist-figures. Having written his last word, enjoying the exhilaration of completion, Jim Burden says to his female fellow artist, "Read it as soon as you can . . . but don't let it influence your own story" (714). Such advice is impossible to follow. In Willa Cather's fiction before 1920, domestic ritual is often a battleground, claimed or spurned by competing, collaborating male and female voices. When she revised the introduction to *My Ántonia* in 1926, Cather obscured the gender of the woman narrator and deleted several passages, including the words "My own story was never written." For by then, another story was underway. It was a story of domestic ritual, and it too was her own.

5

Willa Cather and Women's Culture

"Now I Know"

IN 1922, Willa Cather published her most straightforward statement about the novelist's art, "The Novel Demeublé," in which she renounced the "mere verisimilitude" of realism and advocated a stripped, simplified style (*Not Under* 48). This is how the essay ends: "How wonderful it would be if we could throw all the furniture out the window; and along with it, all the meaningless reiterations concerning physical sensations, all the tiresome old patterns, and leave the room as bare as the stage of a Greek theatre, or as that house into which the glory of Pentecost descended; leave the scene bare for the play of emotions, great and little. . . . The elder Dumas enunciated a great principle when he said that to make a drama, a man needed one passion, and four walls" (51).

To discuss art, Cather has chosen the vocabulary of housekeeping—her title itself assumes that the two endeavors share a common language. And her metaphors are as mixed as ever. She begins with the exhilaration of a violent repudiation of housekeeping, throwing the furniture out the window, with other "meaningless" matters. Yet the locus of inspiration, where language can flower with all the "glory of Pentecost," is also a *house*. The line from Dumas *père*, which Cather paraphrased more than once, takes the "four walls" of a house or room as an essential premise. Cather's fiction, too, often gets its energy from the tension between those walls and a human passion that batters against them—from inside or from out.

In the twenties, a brilliantly productive decade for her, Cather explored a series of relationships between passion and four walls. She felt more and more estranged from the possibilities of contemporary America, as indicated by her famous remark that "the world broke in two in 1922 or thereabouts" (*Not Under* v), and thus she was more inclined to portray those possibilities negatively. Yet the critical and popular successes of the prairie novels and the Pulitzer Prize for *One of Ours* confirmed her confidence and independence. And with the continuation and establishment of central, lifelong relationships with women, she lost much of her earlier fear of being trapped in a traditional, heterosexual woman's life for which she was unsuited.

Domestic ritual is variously important to the novels of the twenties. In *A Lost Lady*, Niel Herbert is mesmerized by Mrs. Forrester's elegant, imperious housekeeping and appalled when she will not put housekeeping above all, preferring "life on any terms." *The Professor's House* catches a man in the process of changing his mind about housekeeping, which becomes a metaphor for values that Cather feared were irrevocably altered by the twenties. In *My Mortal Enemy*, an equivocal young woman contemplates an older woman who has turned her back on a series of diminishing houses, to choose a determinedly antidomestic death. And at the very end of the decade, *Death Comes for the Archbishop* presents the least conflicted version of housekeeping in Cather's fiction thus far. For the French bishop and priest in the new world, domestic ritual—particularly cooking—is a medium by which to express the continuity of a civilization. Their housekeeping is perfectly attuned with their Catholic mission and is quite untouched by the danger and duplicity it could have for women. None of the book's central characters is a woman. In fact, none of the twenties novels, despite their incisive experiments with form and point of view, enters the consciousness of a housekeeping woman.

In 1931, with *Shadows on the Rock*, Willa Cather finally made a full entry into the life of housekeeping, as practiced by traditional women, and such housekeeping became a central concern of the last, great decade of her writing life. *Shadows on the Rock* is the book in which Cather moved furthest afield in time and space: to Quebec, in 1697–98. This subtle and undervalued tenth novel has at its center a twelve-year-old female protagonist, Cécile Auclair, who "makes the ménage" for her widowed father. In this faraway setting, Willa Cather conducts her first full exploration of a world into which she was born: the parish of conventional women.

This fact may be a reason for the relative lack of critical interest in *Shadows on the Rock.* James Woodress, for example, has disparaged this novel as "an old woman's book" (*Life and Art* 237), and Granville Hicks dismissed its events as "trivial" (146). Yet, for a female child, the events of Cécile's life are full of significance. When Willa Cather chose child protagonists for her earlier books, they tended to be extraordinary children, such as Thea Kronborg or Jim Burden, both incipient artists. Their stories were invested with the glamour of their special gifts, and they were always somewhat at odds with the conventional cultures in which they found themselves. But with this novel Cather has attempted something more difficult. Cécile, while lively and intelligent and kind, is not an unusual child, and she has been in many ways the perfect medium for the rules of French bourgeois order with which her dying mother imprinted her. Following these rules, Madame Auclair put her life at the service of a culture. Thus her memory and her beliefs are preserved as the culture's rituals continue. All this is set in motion by Madame's instructions to her daughter, only eight years old:

> During the last winter of her illness she lay much of the time on her red sofa, that had come so far out to this rock in the wilderness. . . . she could hear Cécile moving softly about in the kitchen, putting more wood into the iron stove, washing the casseroles. Then she would think fearfully of how much she was entrusting to that little shingled head; something so precious, so intangible; a feeling about life that had come down to her through so many centuries and that she had brought with her across the wastes of obliterating, brutal ocean. The sense of "our way"—that was what she longed to leave with her daughter. She wanted to believe that when she herself was lying in this rude Canadian earth, life would go on almost unchanged in this room with its dear (and, to her, beautiful) objects; that the proprieties would be observed, all the little shades of feeling which make the common fine. (*Shadows* 25–26)

The "sense of 'our way,'" which Madame Auclair wishes to transmit to her daughter, assures a stability and a continuity that are fixed by women in a round of repetitive household behavior: the laundry, the cleaning, the entertaining. It makes culture portable; thus an immigrant family can remain quintessentially French even in a North American wilderness. In such details, as small as a recipe, civilization is continued, Cather wrote in a published letter about this novel. Her comments on the book also confirm that she is not entirely approving of the "narrow but definite" culture it evokes. Nevertheless, this culture expresses "something new to me," she says, "a kind of feeling about life and human fate that I could not accept, wholly, but which I could not but admire" (*Willa Cather on Writing* 15). In *Shadows on the Rock*, no detail is too small for attention; the book is full of menus, timetables, household hints, and recipes. We even learn exactly how Cécile disposes of her kitchen garbage.[1]

Cécile has not been a favorite protagonist among Cather's readers. Critics have either found her saintly (Rosowski argues persuasively that the book may be read as an account of the education of the Virgin [*Voyage* 175–88]) or priggish; for Woodress, the girl "has no reality at all" (*Literary Life* 430).

Cather's comments on the book anticipated such difficulties, especially for American readers; she said, "It's very hard for an American to catch that rhythm—it's so unlike us" (*Willa Cather on Writing* 17). Yet Cécile's situation is in many ways the very story that young Willa Cather so determinedly turned her back on, in Red Cloud. In a frontier settlement, as she enters adolescence, a female child takes up a domestic plot, a choice made by most women in Cather's time, as well as Cécile's.

Cécile, who was removed from the convent school at eight so she could nurse her dying mother, loves stories, and the novel is crammed with them. As she acts out the domestic motions taught by her mother, the girl hears a whole repertoire of tales: wilderness tortures and adventures, politics, hierarchy and corruption back in France, legends of Canadian saints. When the mother superior completes such a saint's story and begins to append its moral,

> Cécile caught her hand and cried coaxingly,
> "*N'expliquez pas, chere Mère, je vous en supplie!*"
> Mother Juschereau laughed and shook her finger.
> "You always say that, little naughty! *N'expliquez pas!* But it is the explanation of these stories that applies them to our needs."
> "Yes, dear Mother. But there comes my father. Tell me the explanation some other day." (39)

Conventionally devout as she is, Cécile loves the stories for their own sake. They extend the life of a housebound only child, who has no playmates of her own age and sex and does most of the work of a grown woman. Her cry against explanations is a cry for the play of imagination. Cécile does not want the tales, a major delight of her life, to become another everyday remedy, "applied to our needs."

At twelve, Cécile is on the edge of a change and a choice. Other women recognize her changed situation, though her fond father would prefer not to; for the first time, the annual package from her French aunts contains a woman's clothes and jewelry. Eager as she is, the girl shares her father's dread of change. The first three of the novel's six books establish the beauties, satisfactions, and limitations of continuation and order, which have been won with difficulty in a new colony in a new world. *Shadows on the Rock* is beautifully and subtly constructed. Time is simultaneously marked by natural events, by events that indicate the colonists' relations with France, by religious events, and by domestic events, superintended by women, which are linked to the others but also supply a steady rhythm of their own. To Cécile's father, nothing means more than this basic domestic rhythm. His dinner is "the most important event of the day" and "the thing that kept him a civilized man and a Frenchman" (16–17).

Cécile's mother provided for both her husband's and her child's continuous participation in French civilization, "our way," through her domestic indoctrination of the girl. The domestic plot, with all its household caveats and corollaries, was her legacy to her husband and daughter, as well as her own stake in immortality. And she presented it in a hypnotic tone of prediction: "*You will* perhaps find it fatiguing to do all these things alone, over and over. But in time *you will* come to love your duties, as I do. *You will* see that your father's whole happiness depends on order and regularity, and *you will* come to feel a pride in it" (124, emphasis mine).

Much of the life of the town is geared toward the perpetuation of such "order and regularity." For example, Christmas is celebrated by all the villagers in French style, and Cécile will not even make such a small innovation as adding an "untraditional" Canadian beaver to the French crèche without the approval of an older woman, a friend of her mother's. The little walled town of Quebec is replicated in the altar of Cécile's favorite church there, which represents a walled feudal castle, and the girl believes that heaven itself "looked exactly like this . . . this altar was a reproduction of it, made in France by people who knew" (64). As Cécile lies in bed recovering from a cold, she is calmed and comforted, as her dying mother was, by her sense that the rituals of domestic life are continuing, all around her: "All these things seemed to her like layers and layers of shelter, with this one flickering, shadowy room at the core" (158).

As she acts out her mother's conditioning, Cécile is deeply implicated in a domestic plot; as her mother predicted, her deepest feelings make her an agent of its continuation. One of the book's most rapturous passages is Cécile's realization of such feelings, as she heads toward home with the little boy (a prostitute's son) whom she has befriended: "A feeling came over her that there would never be anything better in the world for her than this; to be pulling Jacques on her sled, with the tender, burning sky before her, and on each side . . . the kindly lights from neighbors' houses. If the Count should go back with the ships next summer, and her father with him . . . would not her heart break for just this? For this rock and this winter, this feeling of being in one's own place, for the soft content of pulling Jacques up Holy Family Hill into paler and paler levels of blue air, like a diver coming up from the deep sea" (104).

This Cécile is much more than a torpid little prig. She is finely responsive both to the natural world and to the compelling supports of civilization in the surrounding town; for her, both shed beautiful light. As she willingly pulls a little boy toward her father's house, she is a glad servant of male needs. Yet Cécile is also aware of another kind of plot, which threatens her own—a plot of change and journeys enacted through a male hierarchy: if the king recalls Count Frontenac to France, her father will accompany his patron. Cécile, a girl, will have no voice in the decision and no choice but to obey it. The language of the sledding passage takes much of its intensity from Cécile's emerging double awareness. As she becomes more actively conscious of the satisfactions of her domestic life, she also becomes more conscious of its fragility. The passage ends with an image of a *rising* Cécile—both returning to her father's house and emerging, diverlike, into another element, the air she was born to breathe. Is that native air a life of domestic ritual—or is it something else?

In the novel's first three books, the "layers of shelter" are counterpointed by the wilderness stories told at the Auclair hearth, to which Cécile attends raptly. They both make the fireside more precious, by dramatizing its alternatives, and suggest ways to escape from the confinement that is shelter. Their plots, unlike the domestic cycles within which Cécile lives, are far-reaching and linear. And the stories are fraught with the danger of such plots—that of going too far. One such tale is the mysterious unfinished legend of Robert Cavelier de La Salle. The shoemaker says of him, "that foot will not come back. . . . It went too far. . . . farther than any other in New France" (82–83). Such stories are hard to reconcile with the round of domestic ritual. A woodsman muses, "It's a funny thing. . . . A man sits here by the warm fire, where he can hear the bell ring for mass every morning and smell bread baked fresh every day, and all that happened out there in the woods seems like a dream" (145).

The Canadian tales that fascinate Cécile are usually of men in the wilderness or of venturesome nuns, the only women who manage to alter the domestic plot. No one—not even Cécile herself—imagines that she has a vocation for a nun's life. Yet the story that enchants her most is a nun's tale—the story of Jeanne Le Ber. A beautiful, charming, pampered Montreal heiress, Jeanne—at Cécile's age, twelve—began to withdraw into asceticism, wearing "a little haircloth shirt" under the "gay dresses" which were her father's gift. At seventeen, she took a vow of chastity, and soon after, despite her family's wishes, her ample dowry financed a chapel for the Sisters of the Congregation of the Blessed Virgin. Behind the altar, she had a three-story cell constructed for herself, "from which she would never come forth alive" (134). There she lives, a young woman still, seeing only her confessor, executing exquisite embroidery, and spurning the comfort and solace domestic life can offer, even in Quebec. Not even her dying mother's pleas can bring her out of her cell. Like Louisa Ellis or Joanna Todd, she lives there a life that is both a rejection and an exaltation of domesticity. As a girl she knelt at her window and stared at the spark of a perpetually burning lamp in a nearby church. "She used to whisper, 'I will be that lamp; that shall be my life'" (131).

Instead of tending the male-given lamp in patient housewifery, Jeanne chose to *become* that symbolic object. Thus, for her, art, religion, and housekeeping are one. Choosing such a life, she rejected the filial piety by which Cécile lives and which is highly regarded in Catholic Canada, especially devoted to the holy *family*. Jeanne Le Ber pierced the "layers of shelter" to find her own inclination and then, with an artist's surety, she shaped her life by that inclination. By her withdrawal, she paradoxically gave herself to the very community she left. Tales of her domestic/spiritual adventures—such as the miraculous appearance of two angels who repaired her spinning wheel—find their way into the remotest Canadian parishes, to be recounted at hearths. They are "an incomparable gift. In the long evenings, when the family had told over their tales of Indian massacres and lost hunters and the almost human intelligence of the beaver, someone would speak the name of Jeanne Le Ber, and it again gave out fragrance" (137).

When Cécile hears the latest tale of the recluse nun, she savors it privately, alone in bed. Later she will repeat the story again and again, with "loving exaggeration" (136). It becomes her possession, her creation—a gift by which Jeanne confirms her own artistry and conveys it to every receptive hearer. Such a gift, ravishing as "a blooming rose-tree," does what art can do: it affirms and extends the regenerative powers of imaginative life, even in the coldest world. The fireside ritual of storytelling brings the rich possibilities of art into Cécile's contracted winter world. Through those possibilities, she rises into awareness.

The book's rhythm changes suddenly in Book 4, "Pierre Charron." Suddenly a favorite friend sweeps into Cécile's world, on the balmy first day of June. She begs for a story of his adventures: "have you been to the great falls? . . . you will tell me about the big beaver towns?" (171). This time he does better than that—he takes her onto the river, in her first, initiatory overnight journey, an adventure of discovery. Pierre, a daring young woodsman, has contrived a double plot for himself: he lives promiscuously in the woods, circumspectly in his mother's town, Montreal, saying, "Very well, religion for the fireside, freedom for the woods" (173). But such a plot will not serve Cécile.

With Pierre, she visits a miller's family on the nearby Île d'Orléans.

Outdoors, surrounded by wildflowers, Cécile revels in a natural "paradise" much like the archetypal "green world" of women's novels, described by Annis Pratt, which most typically appears "about to be left behind as one backs into the enclosure" (*Archetypal Patterns* 22). But Cécile cannot be happy on the island because the housekeeping there offends her. Dirty linen and coarse food violate the standards with which she was indoctrinated by her mother. Newly, she realizes "how her mother had always made everything at home beautiful" (192). That beauty was so thoroughly prescribed and finely calibrated that Cécile and her father, years after the mother's death, cannot bring themselves even to move her sofa across the room; to do so "would quite destroy the harmony" (106). Cécile's discomfort on the island, her inability to tumble into a grimy bed with four friendly, grubby little girls, has seemed particularly unattractive to this novel's critics; Woodress calls her behavior "intolerable" (*Literary Life* 430). In fact, the scene movingly conveys the irrevocable power of Cécile's domestic conditioning.

Back in her mother's kitchen, now her own workplace, Cécile experiences the ambivalent epiphany toward which her island journey has led:

> She put on her apron and made a survey of the supplies in the cellar and kitchen. . . . She was accustomed to think that she did all these things so carefully to please her father, and to carry out her mother's wishes. Now she realized that she did them for herself, quite as much. . . . These coppers, big and little, these brooms and clouts and brushes, were tools; and with them one made, not shoes or cabinet-work, but life itself. One made a climate within a climate; one made the days . . . one made life.
>
> Suddenly her father came into the kitchen. "Cécile, why did you not call me to make the fire? And do you need a fire so early?"
>
> "I must have hot water, Papa. It is no trouble to make a fire." She wiped her hands and threw her arms about him. "Oh, Father, I think our house is so beautiful!" (197–98)

As a young adult male, Pierre Charron can comfortably inhabit two worlds. But Cécile, at the onset of female puberty, must choose. And she chooses— not the flowery Edenic island—but the beauty of the domestic enclosure, "our house." Her choice insures the continuity of a culture, although it will almost certainly cost some of the complex potential of Cécile's selfhood.

However, this passage also shows Cécile rejecting her role as domestic puppet. Fully conscious of her domestic powers for the first time, she takes possession of her kitchen with a measure of Jeanne Le Ber's certainty. Assembling her pans and brushes, she distinguishes them from male tools and tasks. What she makes is far less permanent; it is simply "a good dinner," a typical product of female culture, in that it is not meant "to survive eternally." As Marcus says, such a culture survives "in passing on the technique of its making" ("Still Practice" 85). But in Cécile's mind her domestic work has enduring importance. Her medium is time itself, and as a practitioner of domestic culture, she can shape time, creating "a climate within a climate."

With this aim, Cécile kindles a fire. The act signifies her emergence from childhood; now she is qualified to ignite the most dangerous element, with all its ambiguous symbolism. It also signifies her emergence as Hestia, the goddess who tends the hearth fire and validates domestic life. The passage is suffused with Cécile's extended awareness, her first exhilarated sense of the extent and possibilities of her powers, as an adult woman. As she executes her housework with confident energy, Cécile seems newly capable of art. Taking the firemaking upon herself, she reacts against male supervision of her life. For Cécile, this moment in her kitchen is a radiant epiphany.

Cécile's new awareness of her domestic plot aligns her with both her mother and Jeanne Le Ber. And, as we see in the novel's two brief concluding books, it puts her at odds with plots contrived by men. She begins to resent the male decisions that will determine her fate. Cécile's father is busy with plans for their return to France, where Cécile will live under the rule of her commanding aunt; he neglects to provide the ingredients for Cécile's cooking. Just as she is newly conscious of her own domestic vocation, Cécile feels robbed of it, "almost as if she no longer had a home" (229). Her home has lost its security because the plot of domestic *continuation* is threatened. Sometimes Cécile longs to regain that secure plot; she "often wished she could follow the squirrels into their holes and hide away with them for the winter" (229). But at other times, as the exigencies of her own domestic future are made plain to her, she rebelliously wishes that she too could claim a male plot, telling little Jacques, "I wish you and I could go very far up the river in Pierre Charron's canoe, and then off into the forests to the Huron country, and find the very places where the martyrs died. I would rather go out there than—anywhere" (234). With a boy-companion, navigating a man's boat in the territory of male culture, she could put the home plot behind her.

Cécile is "rescued" from the dreaded return to France by the death of a man, Frontenac, a titanic event that dominates the novel's last chapter, as the count's final illness even further upsets the routine in the Auclair household. When his patron is dead, Cécile's father is immobilized. And Cécile must realize how much her childhood well-being has depended on the framework of the count's protection. Even the most basic materials of her kitchen— "sugar and salt and wine" (260)—have come from his storehouses. As her father grieves, Cécile takes the place of a dying woman; wrapped in her mother's shawl, she lies on the sofa where Madame Auclair spent the days of her illness.

At this point, to end the novel, Pierre Charron knocks on the door. Immediately the domestic clock begins to tick again; Cécile and her father revive and conspire to put a creditable dinner on the table. And the protector's role is assumed by Pierre. For Cécile, he provides the structure her housekeeping needs, like a "strong roof . . . over her and the shop and all her mother's things" (265). Falling asleep with Pierre's comforting presence in the house, she renounces her fantasies of wilderness adventures. Instead, "her last thoughts before she sank into forgetfulness" are of his "authority . . . power . . . knowledge, and . . . passion. His daring and his pride seemed to her even more splendid than Count Frontenac's" (268). The novel proper ends with this restoration of Cécile's domestic security; she is back in her house, with Pierre on guard. The language conveys the depth of her restored well-being. But it also suggests—countering her former "rise" into new self-knowledge—that this well-being may be a kind of fall. For now Cécile sinks—"into forgetfulness." It is Pierre, a man, to whom she accords the attributes of an artist; he has the authority, power, knowledge, and passion that would enable him to inscribe his story.

The novel's epilogue, set fifteen years later, is a conversation between the bishop and Cécile's father. From it, we learn that Cécile and Pierre are married and "well established" in "a commodious house" (278), with four sons. Many readers have been dissatisfied with this ending. For John Randall, for example, it expresses an impulse "to eliminate all conflict" which mars Cather's late fiction (253). (Overt conflict is, of course, the generating force of traditional male plot; Randall may be responding to Cather's domestic aesthetic as expressed in the plotting of this novel.) Having been brought to a complex sense of Cécile's situation, we are abruptly hauled away, with only the most perfunctory facts about her adult life. This novel, with its submerged impasse, may seem to represent one of those "deadlocks in women's fiction that many feminist critics deplore" (Pratt, *Archetypal Patterns* 24).

Most readings of *Shadows on the Rock* have concentrated not on Cécile, but on other (usually male) characters, and certainly the book contains a gallery of tellingly sketched figures, particularly the two bishops and Frontenac, whose lives indicate Quebec's complex ties to male, European hierarchies.[2] But, despite the interest of these others, virtually everything about the novel's shape draws our primary interest to Cécile, who is clearly the protagonist. The conflicts we share most intimately and most sustainedly are hers. She is capable of passion; her response to place is suffused with it. But—partly because she is female—she is not permitted full volition. Her most decisive choice is to leave the island and to return home early, but she must effect that choice by appealing to Pierre to take her back. If she looks about her for models of decisive women, she sees only women who live somehow under the authority of a man, as even the sociable nuns do. Cécile's own decisive mother, who determined that the Auclairs would move to Canada, had urged the move because the count, their patron, was immigrating, at the behest of the ultimate male power, the king. Now Madame Auclair is dead; if her values are to survive, it will be through her daughter. Except for the inimitable Jeanne Le Ber, there are no solitary females in this world. So Cécile needs a man: Pierre.

Pierre, of course, needs her as well. Lone fur traders and woodsmen (as histories of North America tell us) did not have a very successful record of imprinting civilization on a wilderness. Pierre must enlist a domestic woman. His first choice was Jeanne Le Ber, and her refusal of his proposal and of the marital domestic plot was a disappointment he can never comprehend. He refuses to recognize the validity of her choice, saying "now she is no better than dead. Worse" (178). Yet Jeanne is very much alive, literally and in Cécile's imagination. As she moves toward her marriage—to a man Jeanne rejected and instructed to marry someone else—Cécile is the heir not only of her mother but also of the recluse nun. It has become increasingly apparent that she shares Jeanne's ardent, artful, passionate nature, as well as her mother's fidelity to housekeeping. Entering her adult life, Cécile too assumes a double female heritage—as Jewett's narrator carried with her both Mrs. Todd's domestic provisions and Joanna Todd's pin, emblem of a solitary woman. But in the epilogue, we hear of her only as a figure in a male story; the apothecary and the bishop exchange news of her marriage and her father speaks of her in language that suggests, already, a distant facilitating figure in a male legend: "she is bringing up four little boys, the Canadians of the future" (278). Yet, from her father's thoughts, we get a hint that the adult Cécile retains her alert intuition: "She would be quicker than anyone to sense the transformation in their old neighbor" (279).

Shadows on the Rock is a romance of domestic ritual. Its true plot is not Cécile's courtship but her discovery of her love for housekeeping—and then her attempts to defend her housekeeping against forces that would shatter it, some of which are within herself. The book represents, far more than *My Ántonia* or any earlier novel, a dense and sustained attempt to portray the rituals of a local culture, without becoming mired in "mere verisimilitude,"[3] and an attempt to examine the stages and levels of a spirited female child's immersion in that culture. Ántonia Shimerda Cuzak must have received some domestic indoctrination, some training in "our way," from her mother, so hostilely portrayed in that novel, or from other knowing immigrant women. Where did Ántonia learn to make the *kolaches* of which her children are so proud? *My Ántonia* cannot answer such questions; it does not even encourage us to ask them. Through Jim Burden's point of view, we cannot enter Ántonia's domestic plot.

But in *Shadows on the Rock* we see Cécile acquiring a complex language and becoming a practitioner and perpetuator of domestic ritual, claiming housekeeping as her medium. She could be the ancestor of one of those immigrant women young Willa Cather met in 1880s Nebraska, plying their domestic skills in the new land. This 1931 novel confronts issues and events of women's lives that Cather had skirted in her earlier work; it immerses us in the creation and maintenance of a ritualized female life.

That subject required a new kind of storytelling from Willa Cather, with some of the qualities that Donovan says might characterize an aesthetic rooted in traditional women's experience. Such experience is "nonprogressive, repetitive, and static," and thus at odds with the Aristotelean, "progressive" plot patterns, which have dominated fiction by men ("Toward" 100). Cather structured her novel to suggest the shape of Cécile's female experience as the girl herself perceives it. These very qualities have led some readers to find the book boring, uninflected. Yet, for Cécile's story, the satisfactions of closure and completion are inappropriate.

Willa Cather herself thought of the book as a stylistic "experiment." Her description of her method in *Shadows on the Rock* suggests an attempt to capture something rarely caught in language—something partly determined by her unusual choice of setting and time, but also, I contend, by the rhythms of traditional female experience. "It is hard to state that feeling in language," she wrote of the novel; "it was more like an old song, incomplete but uncorrupted, than like a legend. The text was mainly anacoluthon, so to speak" (*Willa Cather on Writing* 15). Anacoluthon is a construction involving a *break* in grammatical sequence—or a story that is not fully linear, not structurally complete. This language suggests an attempt to get in touch with an early source, a "feeling" that almost predates language. Much of Cather's own first, passionate energy had gone into efforts to separate herself from that early domestic language. Writing *Shadows on the Rock*, in her late fifties, at the time of her father's death and her mother's long final illness, Cather reclaimed a traditional language of complexity, beauty, and specificity. Yet her text *is* characterized by anacoluthon. At the end, Cécile almost disappears into its structural gaps. In the epilogue, although nominally accorded the "happily ever after" of a prosperous, fertile marriage, she has receded, for us, into oblivion; we hear of her only in men's conversation, as wife and mother of males. But we cannot dismiss her story as trite and stereotypical, for the book has also forced us to respect the deep satisfaction Cécile finds in performing the rituals of a traditional woman's life.

By the book's end, this lively ordinary girl has become as remote as the mysterious Jeanne Le Ber, and she reminds us that such a retreat into storied privacy, unreachable via official culture, was in fact the usual state of affairs for a woman in North America. Reading *Shadows on the Rock*, we experience the simultaneous process of self-discovery and self-loss through which a girl cloaks herself in the traditional life that her culture offers to women. Willa Cather has returned, in the fullness of her intellectual powers, to that early stimulus of the immigrant women, juggling culture and selfhood, old world and new home, as they plied their housekeeping skills. In *Shadows on the Rock* and after, she sought ways to acknowledge and scrutinize the most deeply, ambivalently traditional women's plot: domestic ritual. And her fiction—as the thirties show—would never be the same.

Cather had long known how to insulate a story of special significance and danger, wrapping it in layers of distance, filtering it through multiple languages and narrators. In *My Ántonia*, for example, this is how she handles the incendiary tale of Pavel and Peter, in which a bride—an incipient housekeeper and mother—is thrown to the wolves to preserve a male freedom, which becomes exile. In *Shadows on the Rock*, she employs similar layering, aided by the novel's remote setting. But, at the same time she was writing her historical romance of housekeeping, Cather was working on three long stories of her own times, published in 1932 as *Obscure Destinies*. "Neighbour Rosicky" is set openly in early twentieth-century Nebraska, where farm households are newly equipped with telephones and Ford cars. The other two stories—"Old Mrs. Harris" and "Two Friends"— are set in Colorado and Kansas towns during the years of Cather's adolescence, towns that are obviously based on Red Cloud. Here, writing in the period of her parents' final illnesses and deaths, Willa Cather at last deals with the years of her Western childhood, as David Stouck has suggested ("Willa Cather's Last" 43).

In two of these fine stories, housekeeping is somehow held at bay. "Neighbour Rosicky" recounts the last few weeks of a Bohemian farmer's life, as he plots ways to insure that his sons will continue his gentle and harmonious life on the land. The greatest threat to that continuance is Rosicky's first daughter-in-law, Polly, a "town girl" who has begun to panic at the farm's isolation, the endless round of housework, and her new pregnancy. Before he dies, Rosicky negotiates a loving truce with Polly. First he takes over her housework to give her an evening's respite. Then, when overtaken by an attack of angina, he gives her an opportunity to nurse him through it and to realize that her nursing—and other domestic tasks—can be deeply satisfying acts of communion and care. The story provides an admiring view of Rosicky's marriage to a warmhearted, capable countrywoman and of their felicitous household. But it does not really acknowledge the inevitable tensions of that household. For example, the uneasy relationship of Polly and her mother-in-law, which is more problematic than that with her father-in-law, is not broached; not a word is exchanged by the two rival housekeepers. And while Rosicky is always planning for "his boys," there is no word of his wishes for his one daughter, the youngest child. The story's moving and idyllic final sentence is an observation by someone outside the family, Doctor Ed: "Rosicky's life seemed to him complete and beautiful" (71). From the moment of Rosicky's death, Cather does not allow us to see into his household, where housekeeping and hierarchy must be thrown into change and perhaps disarray by his absence. The story retains its remarkable calm and valedictory beauty by keeping its distance from housekeeping.

The final story of *Obscure Destinies*, "Two Friends," is an account of a small town male friendship and its dissolution, as observed by a child, whose gender is never indicated, but who is presumably based on Willa Cather. The story takes place in an entirely undomestic world, where no woman has a speaking part; it is set in stores, banks, and on the sidewalks where the two friends sit to talk each evening. The determining force that destroys the men's friendship is an 1896 political event, William Jennings Bryan's "Cross of Gold" speech at the Democratic national convention, a male event. Especially if we think of the narrator as female,[4] "Two Friends" becomes a meditation on a precious alternative world—"something delightful . . . one of the truths we want to keep" (230)—a world outside the female confines of housekeeping.

As several critics have observed, the book's title comes from Gray's "Elegy Written in a Country Churchyard."[5] The lives in this book are obscure in the sense that they are not famous or extraordinary—and also in the sense that they are not easily read. The most obscure destinies are found in the book's middle story, its buried heart: "Old Mrs. Harris." Within a family very similar to her own—Southerners transplanted in the West— Cather scrutinizes three generations of women in a cramped little house. In "Old Mrs. Harris," she draws back a curtain from matters that were veiled in the other two stories. This story gives obscurity a voice and a language. It offers the fullest realization of the book's title, and as Cather knew, it is the finest story in the collection (Woodress, *Literary Life* 441). I agree with several others[6] that it is the best story she ever wrote.

To live out a *destiny* is to lead a determined life, to be—to some extent— unfree. In Skyline, Colorado, the women of the Templeton-Harris family, in different stages and positions, are variously confined. Victoria Templeton, a stylish and willful Southern belle, rules the parlor and flirts more or less effectively with husband, neighbors, and children, but her marriage and the responsibilities of childbearing—she seems always to be either pregnant or nursing a baby—limit her mobility. She is freed from kitchen duties and from most of the drudgery of child care by her mother, Mrs. Harris, who oversees the kitchen, according to Southern custom, with the help of Mandy, the "bound girl" who accompanied them from Tennessee.[7] Mrs. Harris has more duties and less freedom than her daughter. Her bedroom is a communal passageway and her "bed," a narrow rickety lounge, is furniture for common use. She is tacitly prohibited from having friends or possessions of her own. Yet maintaining the ongoing ritual of housekeeping, in a hierarchal style better suited to a large Southern household than to a cramped cottage in a Western town, means everything to Mrs. Harris. Her personal dignity, which is powerful and considerable, is dependent on maintaining her place in the housekeeping order into which she was born.

Willa Cather does not gloss over the hardness or the meanness of Mrs. Harris's life, as she rises early to serve two separate breakfasts to the children and their parents. Once she was matriarch of her family house in Tennessee, which was sold to finance her son-in-law's Western venture. But now her daughter does not even accord her a shelf for her few toilet articles; Mrs. Harris must carry her comb in her pocket. Yet her domestic duties legitimize her in the eyes of her family, and in her own eyes. They give her, like Cécile Auclair, a part in a plot of continuance which is more important than any single individual life. Although the children may take her for granted, they also love her and consider her essential to their lives. Some mornings, alone,

> Mrs. Harris felt a little low. . . . She would hang up her towel with a sigh and go into the kitchen, feeling that it was hard to make a start. But the moment she heard the children running down the uncarpeted back stairs, she forgot to be low. Indeed, she ceased to be an individual, an old woman with aching feet; she became part of a group, became a relationship. She was drunk up in their freshness when they burst in upon her, telling her about their dreams, explaining their troubles with buttons and shoelaces and underwear shrunk too small. . . .

suddenly the morning seemed as important to her as it did to the children, and the mornings ahead stretched out sunshiny, important. (136–37)

Housekeeping is Mrs. Harris's entrée into a group life. And the trivial breakfast conversation is a rich ritual that gives her access to the complex life of her tribe, where matters as ordinary as shrunken laundry mix with the archetypal mysteries of dreams and human growth. From such mornings, she gains a place in a future that will outlive her.

Mrs. Harris opposes her daughter only on a few matters, which she considers very important. One such occasion occurs when the tomcat, a cherished pet, dies and Victoria sends for the trash man to haul his body away. Indignant, Mrs. Harris does not quietly bury the cat herself. Instead, she summons her twin grandsons and instructs them: "You git up early in the morning. . . . and you dig a little grave for Blue Boy, an' bury him right" (145). For the grandmother, what matters is not only that the proper rituals, which honor the dignity of life in the conventions of her culture, be performed, but that they be *continued.* So she imprints the children with her own values, through the medium of ritual.

The most obscure destiny in "Old Mrs. Harris" is that of Mandy, the "bound girl" of unspecified age, whose servitude will not even allow her to claim the dignity of the word "woman." Mandy's private life and history are never indicated; she seldom speaks and is mentioned only in connection with her tasks. Her only opportunity to widen her life is through an increase in her domestic duties; when Mrs. Harris is too ill to work, Mandy "felt very important taking Mrs. Harris's place, giving the children their dinner, and carrying a plate of milk toast to Mrs. Templeton" (180–81). Victoria thinks of her as "stupid," but Mandy's intuition suggests otherwise. It is only she who apprehends that Mrs. Harris is ill, and she is first to guess that Victoria is again pregnant. When she relays that news to Mrs. Harris, the old woman hushes her and Mandy replies, "Oh yes'm, I won't say nothin'. I never do" (177).

Mandy is bereft of spoken language; except for Mrs. Harris, no one in the Templeton family is heard to speak to her except in minimal requests for information and service. Yet Mandy performs one of the story's most eloquent acts. At the end of the day, she offers to massage Mrs. Harris's tired, swollen feet. To the older woman, this is "the greatest solace of the day; it was something that Mandy gave, who had nothing else to give. . . . The kitchen was quiet and full of shadow, with only the light from an old lantern. Neither spoke. Mrs. Harris dozed from comfort, and Mandy herself was half asleep, as she performed one of the oldest rites of compassion" (93). The kitchen is an evocative setting for this domestic scene, in which one silent woman offers her care to another, in an act of self-abasement with religious as well as domestic resonance. The half-conscious state of Mandy and Mrs. Harris suggests that this act comes from the deepest levels of humanity. Later, when Mrs. Harris has become mortally ill, Mandy directs the children to sit with her. Albert, one of the twins, gladly takes on the job. He tidies the room, devises a makeshift table, and brings a tumbler of water to "make the room a little nicer," properly "like a sickroom" (181–83). As Rosowski says, the boy's efforts are "an expression of the most tender, thoughtful love" (*Voyage* 199), and they indicate Mrs. Harris's and Mandy's success as housekeepers. They have taught the child that housekeeping is a language for his deepest feelings.

Neither Victoria nor her oldest child and only daughter, Vickie, can use that language to express their love for Mrs. Harris. Both younger women are at crucial moments in their own lives, and housekeeping seems a threat and a trap to them. Victoria has just learned of her fifth pregnancy and she sees the house and her family responsibilities as galling restraints. "She was sick of it all; sick of dragging this chain of life that never let her rest and periodically knotted and overpowered her; made her ill and hideous for months, and then dropped another baby in her arms. . . . Why must she be for ever shut up in a little cluttered house with children and fresh babies and an old woman and a stupid bound girl and a husband who wasn't very successful? . . . life hadn't used her right" (178).

Victoria, with her ironic name, still believes in the myth of her personal freedom, and she would like to be released from the "chain of life," which uses her body and distorts her selfhood. Yet she obviously loves and enjoys her family, and they never doubt that she cares for them. It is her mother who gets the least acknowledged affection from Victoria. With Vickie ready for college, Victoria must be disconcertingly aware that her status will soon change, that she will soon assume the housekeeping role of Mrs. Harris. The family finances are too pinched to buy more household help. Mrs. Harris's death, at the story's end, is likely to change Victoria's life more than anyone else's, drawing her into the kitchen. At last, when Mandy finds the old woman unconscious, "Victoria, and even Vickie, were startled out of their intense self-absorption. Mrs. Harris was hastily . . . laid in Victoria's bed, put into one of Victoria's best nightgowns" (189), and a doctor is called. But it is too late for such attentions; Mrs. Harris never regains consciousness. Victoria is not yet fluent in the housekeeper's language of care.

Vickie has spent the last year studying intensely for a college scholarship and has won it. When her grandmother inconveniently dies, she is caught up in her preparations to go away. In the anxious weeks of waiting for the results of her examinations, "she never asked herself . . . what she would do if she didn't get the scholarship. There was no alternative. If she didn't get it, then everything was over" (154). There *is* an alternative, of course. Without a scholarship, Vickie would stay in Skyline and probably take up housekeeping. That is an intolerable possibility to her. Vickie doesn't dislike her home, but she stays indoors there as little as possible. Instead, she roams the town, trying out her father's office, the Roadmaster's hammock, the Rosen's quiet parlor. Vickie hardly knows why or what she wishes so passionately to learn at the university, but she does tell her neighbor Mrs. Rosen that she desires *languages;* in the multilingual Rosen library, Vickie says, "What I want is to pick up any of these books and just read them" (108). The language of domestic care, proffered by Mrs. Harris and Mandy, is the one language that does not interest Vickie; indeed, it seems a threat to all the other texts she desires. She never knows that her grandmother (who also loves reading)[8] arranged for the loan that will make it possible for her to go to the university, and in her defensive self-absorption, she brushes off the old woman's caretaking caresses—they are executed in a language too loaded with danger and feeling for Vickie now to acknowledge.

Next door to the Templetons live the Rosens, well-to-do and cultivated European Jews. Middle-aged Mrs. Rosen, energetic and intelligent, is a housekeeper of exquisite faculty. Everything about her suggests her domestic skills, from her delicate clear soups to her polished kitchen floor. Even her body is an object for her housekeeping care—tight corsets mould her ample waist, and her lustrous braids are "wound flat at the back of her head, like a braided rug" (76). Mrs. Harris realizes "that their neighbour had a superior cultivation which made everything she did an exercise of skill. She knew well enough that their own ways of cooking and cleaning were primitive beside Mrs. Rosen's" (135).

Despite such differences, Mrs. Rosen values and needs the Templeton's friendship. One reason is the children; Mrs. Rosen's childlessness is a grief to her. Another and apparently deeper reason is Grandma Harris; Mrs. Rosen pursues her friendship, courting her with gifts, "funny little pats and arch pleasantries" (188). The story begins with Mrs. Rosen spying on the Templeton house, approaching Mrs. Harris with almost military strategies and forcing her to eat and evaluate an elaborate "symmetrically plaited coffeecake" (76). It is understood among the Templetons that such dainties, and all visitors that come to the house, are to be for Victoria. Mrs. Rosen's attentions are an attempt to subvert the Templeton household hierarchy, which she thinks devalues Mrs. Harris. Mrs. Harris has an innate dignity that draws the younger woman's respect: a "kind of nobility . . . something absolute" (81). Mrs. Rosen imagines that her attentions can break through to the "real grandmother" but, as ever, she finds that "the real grandmother was on her guard" (83). Mrs. Rosen, despite her faculty, does not yet comprehend that "the real grandmother" is bound up with the traditions of her own household. The delicate coffeecake is an instrument of aggression against a rival domestic order. (Later Mrs. Harris signals her own domestic prowess by proudly sending a traditional Southern cake, "a white coconut," to a Methodist social.)

Mrs. Rosen defends her own housekeeping as a subtle language, quite as expressive and necessary as the several others she and her husband speak and write. Over her dishwashing, she discusses *Wilhelm Meister* with Vickie, to whom the Rosen house is "the nearest thing to an art gallery and a museum" that she has experienced (103). And Mrs. Rosen, while she looks down her nose at the Templetons' more casual family housekeeping, feels a responsibility for the girl's future that goes beyond any ties of family or ethnicity. When Vickie hears that she has won her scholarship, she takes the news first to Mrs. Rosen's kitchen: "Mrs. Rosen had been cutting noodles. She took Vickie's face in two hot, plump hands that were still floury, and looked at her intently. 'Is dat true, Vickie? No mistake? I am delighted—and surprised. . . . Den you will *be* something. . . .' she squeezed the girl's round, good-natured cheeks, as if she could mould them into something definite then and there" (156). For Mrs. Rosen, cooking, sculpture, and nurturing are a seamless creative act, and her ambiguous medium is human life itself. When her kindly husband congratulates Vickie, he does so with words, inscribing a maxim in her "first French lesson." Both the Rosens are multilingual, something Vickie much admires. But Vickie knows one language Mrs. Rosen does not—Latin, the traditional language of patriarchal scholarship. As the girl moves closer to a coeducational university, grasping the new options that the twentieth century offers to women, Mrs. Rosen, however supportive, makes strong claims for her own language. She calls Vickie and Mr. Rosen from the French text to their salad: "'Luncheon is served,' she said in the crisp tone that put people in their places. 'And Miss Vickie, you are to eat your tomatoes with an oil dressing, as we do. If you are going off into the world, it is quite time that you learn to like things that are everywhere accepted'" (158–60). Quite as much as the bit of Michelet that Mr. Rosen inscribes in French, Mrs. Rosen's recipe for salad dressing is civilizing equipment that Vickie will need when she goes off into the world. Cather herself suggested, in a 1931 comment on *Shadows on the Rock,* that "a new society begins in the salad dressing more than with the destruction of

Indian villages" (*Willa Cather on Writing* 16). In "Old Mrs. Harris," house-keeping is not the foe of art. It is itself a medium, a language. The salad dressing bespeaks Mrs. Rosen's hopes for Vickie's future life.

But Mrs. Rosen must be disabused of the belief that hers is the only domestic language. The Templeton household puzzles her; "their feelings were so much finer than their way of living" (110), their housekeeping. In "Old Mrs. Harris," every household has its private language, and not to honor that language is to be an insensitive busybody, like the Templetons' meddling neighbor, Mrs. Jackson, who passes judgments on everyone's housekeeping and is the meanest person in this story. Domestic ritual implies a family language of feeling, slightly different in every household—in a late story, "The Best Years," Cather wrote of it as an unspoken "covenant," "a solemn loyalty" that binds children to a house and a mother: "a consciousness they shared . . . it gave them a family complexion" (*Old Beauty* 104–05). The Templeton children, even Vickie, have such a cove-nant, and the housekeeping within which it is expressed must always be something of a mystery to an outsider, even a close neighbor like Mrs. Rosen.

And yet, as we have seen, there is another domestic language, one that flows from woman to woman, from generation to generation, regardless of genetic kinship. Mrs. Rosen, consummate housekeeper, is intensely con-scious of that language, especially where Vickie is concerned; she itches to *instruct* the girl. For her, as for the New England housekeepers of Stowe, Jewett, and (sometimes) Freeman, faculty carries with it the obligation to teach, to provide the means of its own continuance. And Vickie's obvious admiration makes Mrs. Rosen feel even more bound in a "chain of respon-sibility" (108) for her. For Victoria, the continuing chain is her fertility. Mrs. Harris imagines herself bound too; like other old women, she is "tied to the chariot of young life, and had to go where it went" (97). But Victoria's and Mrs. Harris's ties are to their own family. Mrs. Rosen perceives a female, domestic "chain of responsibility" that reaches beyond kinship—as did the relationship of Jewett's narrator and Mrs. Todd—or of Mrs. Harris and Mandy.

It is Vickie's needs that finally forge Mrs. Rosen's link to Mrs. Harris, a tie that the younger woman has longed for, as signaled in the fact that she calls the old woman "Grandma," as if they were related by blood. When Mrs. Harris learns that there is no Templeton money available to supple-ment Vickie's scholarship, she asks Mrs. Rosen, with difficulty, to speak to Mr. Rosen about a loan. Gladly, Mrs. Rosen makes the arrangement. In their mutual care for the girl's future, the two kinds of domestic care are joined: that of family and that of unrelated women. And Mrs. Harris and Mrs. Rosen's alliance for Vickie is especially unselfish because Vickie has not chosen a domestic future. Their care will provide her with the basis for a life that will almost certainly be more expansive than either of theirs. This alliance has deep, sacramental importance for both older women. As they conclude their agreement,

> Mrs. Harris's red-brown eyes slowly filled with tears—Mrs. Rosen had never seen that happen before. But she simply said, with quiet dignity: "Thank you, ma'am. I wouldn't have turned to nobody else."
> "That means I am an old friend already, doesn't it, Grandma? And that's what I want to be. . . ." She lightly kissed the back of the purple-veined hand she had been holding, and ran home. . . . Grandma sat looking down at her hand. How easy it was for these foreigners to say what they felt! (170)

Mrs. Rosen is dear to Grandma Harris too; as she is dying, some of the old woman's last thoughts are of her friend. The "admiration" of Mrs. Rosen has given her something the women of her own family could not offer. Yet, however much Mrs. Rosen means to Mrs. Harris, she also remains a "foreigner." Part of this story's greatness is its recognition of the differences that do *not* melt, even in the warmest accord.

Like the other stories of *Obscure Destinies*, "Old Mrs. Harris" is written with consummate subtlety and assurance. Nothing is artificially heightened; the story is never cluttered with excess furniture and it eschews Aristotelean plot. The omniscient narration moves seamlessly from the members of the Templeton family to Mrs. Rosen, and back. The story is a complexly resonant meditation on domestic life. Instead of distancing or denying the nuances of housekeeping through male narration, as in "A Wagner Matinee," Cather has here evoked a fictional world in which the smallest domestic matters signify. For example, when Mrs. Harris wakes up cold, she wraps herself in "her little comforter," a soft, torn sweater hidden under her mattress, which Mrs. Rosen gave her, ostensibly to use in her darning. It warms her as the heavy "old home-made quilts, with weight but little warmth" (94) cannot. Such an apparently trivial matter speaks eloquently of Mrs. Harris's needs, and of the ways her neighbor's watchful care nurtures her personally as family and Southern tradition (suggested by the weighty quilts) cannot.

Stouck has suggested that *Shadows on the Rock* and all Cather's following fictions "are subtle, intelligent, and artfully contrived, but the vision which underlies them is one which questions the old urge to expression through art' (*Imagination* 206). I would propose instead that in her late fiction,

Cather extended her definition of art, so that it included a domestic aesthetic instead of (as in "A Wagner Matinee") opposing it. Only such an aesthetic, and a story like "Old Mrs. Harris," could give equally unsentimental weight, dignity, and scrutiny to lives as apparently different as those of Vicky, Victoria, Mrs. Rosen, and Mrs. Harris. Here Cather can give the ultimate respect to housekeeping—through *attention*, not veneration. Unlike *Shadows on the Rock*, this is in no sense a romance of housekeeping or of family life. The scrutiny is too intense for romance.

For example, in Mrs. Harris's memories of her more comfortable life in Tennessee, we glimpse a matriarchal female Arcadia where old women in Mrs. Harris's position received support from a network of female supporters. There, "the hills were full of solitary old women" who, for board and a "little present" (181), willingly provided household services whenever needed. But Cather does not present that Tennessee past as entirely Arcadian; she indicates its tinges of exploitation, describing it as "a feudal society, where there were plenty of landless people glad to render service to the more fortunate." By contrast, Skyline is "a snappy little Western democracy" (133)—and democracy can be cruelly intolerant of anyone (like the Templetons) who does not quite fit its norms. Such language dispels any haze of domestic—or antidomestic—nostalgia.

"Old Mrs. Harris" ends, as does "Neighbour Rosicky," with the most inevitable of human events: the death of an elder. In this story, unlike Rosicky's, Willa Cather encourages us to think not of a "complete and beautiful" finished life, like a perfectly finished work of art, but of a continuum of women's lives, into which Mrs. Harris is forever woven. This is the story's last paragraph:

> Thus Mrs. Harris slipped out of the Templetons' story; but Victoria and Vickie had still to go on, to follow the long road that leads through things unguessed at and unforeseeable. When they are old, they will think a great deal about her, and remember things they never noticed; and their lot will be more or less like hers. They will regret that they heeded her so little; but they, too, will look into the eager, unseeing eyes of young people and feel themselves alone. They will say to themselves: "I was heartless, because I was young and strong and wanted things so much. But now I know." (190)

This passage resounds with sibylline wisdom, predicting for Victoria and Vickie an unwritten understanding "they *will*" achieve—but not yet. It is shaped by Mrs. Harris's values. For her, continuance was the important thing, and housekeeping was her way of insuring it. Her last hope was to die without upsetting that domestic order. Thus Cather does not allow her death to be an ending; Mrs. Harris "slips out" with a death that is an unobtrusive pause instead of a dramatic climax, and the *story* goes on, although this particular piece of writing may stop. This kind of fiction is shaped by domestic occurrences and by the natural accruing of age and wisdom. It is also informed by the French maxim which Mr. Rosen inscribed for Vickie: "Le but n'est rien; le chemin, c'est tout" (158). Here, the story is the thing that continues and matters, leading through what cannot yet be known or told. The source of Mr. Rosen's line is not a writer of fiction, a contriver of plots, but Michelet, a historian. In "Old Mrs. Harris," as deeply, rigorously autobiographical as anything she ever wrote, Willa Cather has achieved a story which is marked by a historian's perspective: it perceives both time and understanding as a continuum, always proceeding, in ways that obviate the idea of an ending. In its attention to the ordinary, everyday stuff of women's lives, this story does what Flaubert directed in the line that Jewett cherished: "Écrire la vie ordinaire comme on écrit l'histoire."

Also like Jewett, Cather here achieves a fiction that moves, through the medium of meditation, both backward and forward in time. Mrs. Harris's story is ended in one sense; she is dead. But, like the fetus in Victoria's womb, her story is also waiting to be born. It will be renewed in the consciousnesses of Victoria and Vickie, who will someday "think a great deal about her."

As Mrs. Harris is dying and Vickie and Victoria are confronting their own crises, Mr. Templeton retreats from his fraught household to spend the night at a tenant's farmhouse and to enjoy the pleasures of good housekeeping as an unimplicated male recipient, anticipating that his hostess will "open her best preserves for him . . . kill a chicken" and decorate his room with flowers (179–80). Similarly, when Mrs. Rosen is out of town, her husband is glad to take his meals at the local hotel. Through such details, Cather emphasizes the vast differences in men's and women's stories of housekeeping. Both Mr. Templeton and Mr. Rosen are sympathetic characters, with real affection and respect for Mrs. Harris. And it is the twin boys, of her family members, who are kindest and closest to her while she is dying. But none of these males is mentioned in the crucial last paragraph; its subject is women and how they repeat each other's destinies. Although they seem so different in temperament and character, and although Vickie, heading for the university, seems to be entering a life as extraordinary and as far from conventional femininity as Willa Cather's own, the implication is that daughter and granddaughter will have a "lot" similar to that of Mrs. Harris. To grow old is to achieve that realization, to have an understanding that reaches backward and forward, and thus to be able to say, "now I know."

Such continuation is a powerful and ambivalent force, pervading female lives; it seems inevitable that Cather would choose domestic ritual as the medium of this story.

Robert J. Nelson sees the last paragraph of "Old Mrs. Harris" as a "dissonant final note," which "will, with rare exception, mark Cather's fiction in the last decade and a half of her life" (152). I don't perceive the note as dissonant. Instead I see it as bearing all the weight of craft, experience, and vision that Willa Cather had achieved in fifty-nine years of life—of all that she had learned about women and stories. That last paragraph distills the quality that drew Mrs. Rosen to Mrs. Harris; it expresses a "nobility . . . something absolute."

In her last novel, *Sapphira and the Slave Girl*, begun in 1937 and published in 1940, Cather turned again to her own history, returning to the Virginia of her earliest memories and to tales of family and local history, which she had heard as a small child. Here the mix is more complex than in any other Cather novel: autobiography, history, and fiction are inextricably interwoven. And despite her failing health in her sixties, Cather found herself inundated with memory material. Still honoring the ideal of the novel démeublé, she wrote and then discarded "exactly six pounds" of additional manuscript (Woodress, *Literary Life* 481).

As a young woman, Cather had romanticized her Southern male past. A photograph from her teen years shows her in a Union army cap, from which she had removed the G.A.R. insignia, replacing it with her own initials (Bennett 76–77). She adopted the middle name "Sibert" in tribute to an uncle who died in the Confederate army and wrote in "The Namesake," through a male persona, that his "proud blood . . . must . . . burn and bite alway" in her veins (*April Twilights* 26). However, what actually seems to have burned most persistently in Willa Cather's consciousness was the heritage of nineteenth-century Southern female relationships, which dominated her early childhood. As a young critic, she had railed against *Uncle Tom's Cabin* as a *Northern* woman's failed attempt to write about the South, "one of the warmest, richest civilizations the world has ever known" (*Kingdom* 276). Such comments indicate that Cather's defensive affection for her birthplace was still intact in 1894. But her Southern heritage did not become a significant part of her fiction until the thirties, with "Old Mrs. Harris." Finally, it dominates her last major work, which is her first, disturbing, Virginia novel: *Sapphira and the Slave Girl*.

Cather found few nineteenth-century American women writers to admire, most notably Jewett, and she never expressed any admiration for Stowe, although she must have heard her praised by Jewett and by Annie

Fields. Nevertheless, in *Sapphira,* Cather took on many concerns of *Uncle Tom's Cabin* and of nineteenth-century American women's culture.[9] As much as Jewett, Stowe is the foremother of this book. The two plots are similar; a woman slave's escape, by underground railroad, is central to both. In conclusion, both escapees, Eliza and Nancy, are reunited with their mothers, Cassy and Till. Both books exalt domestic life and see slavery's most insidious evil in the destruction of families, an important tenet of black and white nineteenth-century ideology. In both books, the most effective opposition to slavery comes from women, who are disenfranchised, and both present versions of a matriarchal domestic utopia. In addition, both books are particularly interested in the relation between women's domestic power and their political powerlessness. Cather had already indicated her interest in these matters in the motif of the "bound" or "chained" woman, which she wove into "Old Mrs. Harris." In *Sapphira,* she was drawn, like Stowe, to a central problem and enigma of Southern American history: the relationship of women and slavery.

The novel has at its center the plot of a white woman, Sapphira Dodderidge Colbert, to dispose of her young slave, Nancy. When Sapphira decides to sell Nancy, she is stopped by the veto of her husband, the miller Henry Colbert, who disapproves of slavery and is especially fond of Nancy. Sapphira can make no overt response to Henry's veto; as a married woman, she cannot dispose of property alone. As her husband turns away, her "small mouth twisted mockingly. 'Then we must find some other way,' she said softly to herself" (9). Sapphira's covert "other way" is to invite Henry's nephew, the rake Martin Colbert, for an extended visit and to facilitate his rape of Nancy. Her husband can do little to deflect this plot, although he longs to protect Nancy. The effective antagonist to Sapphira's plot is her grown daughter, Rachel Blake. Rachel devises a counterplot to effect Nancy's escape by underground railroad. At the novel's center, then, is the conjunction of Sapphira's enormous power and her humiliating helplessness, as woman. Historian Deborah Gray White reminds us that slave women were forced to learn covert ways to seize a measure of power, thus "slave women" came to understand "the value of silence and secrecy." Sapphira, although a slaveholder, has come to the same understanding. For, as White says, "women, like slaves and servants, deliberately dissemble their objective reality. . . . they hide their real sentiments and turn toward him [the master] a changeless smile or an enigmatic impassivity" (24).

Recent scholarship by historians, such as White, Jacqueline Jones, and Elizabeth Fox-Genovese, reminds us of the complexity of slave and white women's antebellum relationships and cautions against oversimplified opposition or equation of the oppressions suffered by black and white women. Cather's 1940 novel is remarkably sensitive to such complexity. To be a Southern-born woman, as Cather was,[10] is, almost inevitably, to be connected with a history of slavery and with the sort of dissembling that White describes and Sapphira practices. It is to be the descendant of women who exercised the ultimate control over other women's lives—as mistresses, housekeepers, mothers—and who yet were (overtly) powerless themselves. Cather might have fantasized that such matters could be put behind her, just as, at the end of *Shadows on the Rock,* the pioneer apothecary imagines that his grandsons will grow up, in Canada, untouched by the historical cruelties of old France. That novel ends with his wish, which Cather shared, that one could turn one's back on the ugliness and abuse of one's history but retain the enhancing, nurturing qualities of one's hereditary culture, which, for Cather, was often epitomized in domestic life. As she wrote her last novel, Willa Cather had to acknowledge that such fantasies of selective escape were impossible. In this novel of Virginia in the 1850s, domestic ritual is the very fabric of life, and that fabric is interwoven inextricably with family and with slavery. The novel is full of close and affectionate observation of Virginia domestic life, rendered with a homesick child's attention to detail. But every detail is weighted with complicity. For example, Nancy is pleased to be complimented on her domestic skill as an expert ironer. Yet the ruffles that she irons so proudly belong to her mistress, who has just beaten her with a hairbrush. Rachel witnesses this household scene and sympathizes with Nancy. To act on that female sympathy, she must betray her mother.

In *Shadows on the Rock,* Cather introduced us to a self-perpetuating, cyclical domestic plot, as we caw Cécile becoming her mother. "Old Mrs. Harris" spotlighted a cycle of female connections, an unending story. In *Sapphira,* the actual and symbolic exigencies of slavery give a special urgency to the work of traditional plot, which presents the completion of an action. To alter her own—or another woman's—situation, a woman must formulate a plot, probably secretly, since overt female power is taboo. Sapphira was once a willful, mobile woman who arranged her life as a man might, riding about the countryside; again and again she is described with a male word, "masterful." (The fact that no corresponding female term is available is itself evidence of the taboos that suppress female power.) And, significantly, in the South "master" also implies the power of the male slave owner. Sapphira's powers, by contrast, are constrained; now she is aging and immobilized by dropsy. The description emphasizes her volume and pallor, as in her "very plump white hands" and feet (6), swollen with edema. She is like a grotesque image of the white mistress, paralyzed by her own weight. When she becomes jealous of her husband's regard for Nancy and begins to suspect (wrongly) their sexual alliance, Sapphira plots to change a situation that has become intolerable to her. And when Henry refuses to allow her a male prerogative—sale of her property—she uses her domestic authority to execute a plot that would make Martin her willing, impregnating puppet. Nancy is placed where she will be vulnerable to Martin's advances by Sapphira's housekeeping machinations. Nancy's bed is moved to the hall-way, where she is unprotected from rape, and she is sent on errands that will put her in Martin's path.

Such a plot is as appalling as slavery itself, and it pushes Rachel to protest, through her own plot for Nancy, which will get her out of slavery and out of Sapphira's house. Rachel too must act in secret. But unlike her mother, she reaches toward a network of support that is not solely female or domestic; in arranging Nancy's escape, she is abetted by men and women, black and white. Yet even when Nancy is safely away and Rachel's plot is accomplished, she is not certain that she has acted rightly. She thinks about her mother: "It's hard for a body to know what to do, sometimes. . . . I hate to mortify her. . . . Maybe I ought to have thought and waited" (247). To *think* and *wait* would be to choose the version of the home plot that values continuance above all else. In form and in theme, *Sapphira* provides both a rejection and an enactment of that plot.

For as long as she can remember, Rachel Blake has been at odds with her mother's household. She grew up as a lonely stranger there, without "a single confidante" (138). Her marriage to a congressman was warm and happy and she flaunted her separation from her mother by an unforgivable omission: she never invited the sociable Sapphira to the capital for a visit. In Washington, Rachel threw herself into domesticity, instructed by a freed slave woman. Her triumphant city dinners, for men only, were feats of domestic magic, which she accomplished in a cramped basement kitchen, in slavelike (though willing) confinement. Cather presents this as a period of growth for Rachel, through the most traditional of female plots: marriage, domesticity, and motherhood. But, ominously, there is always "something of the devotée in Rachel" (141). When her son and husband died of cholera, she locked herself into a contracted female world of despair; the ex-slave tended her daughters, and Rachel hid in her shuttered room. Her husband, fond as he was, did not keep up his insurance payments; Rachel's immersion in traditional domestic concerns left her helpless, and she had to return to Virginia and the support of her parents.

Rachel has always been her father's favorite daughter and the two share antislavery sentiments. But the daughter is effective where her father cannot be, because he is tied to conventional female plots. Much as he dislikes Martin Colbert, Henry cannot override the "Virginia hospitality" of his wife's household; he tells her, "If you take pleasure in his company, I shan't say anything" (199). He is unable to speak, as well, when Rachel tries to discuss Nancy's predicament with him, and he hushes her emphatically, saying, "You and me can't talk about such things. It ain't right. . . . I can't be a party to make away with your mother's property" (277). His violent protest comes in the midst of Rachel's frank account of Nancy's nightly terror of rape. This is a female story Henry cannot bear to hear. Nancy tends to his bedroom at the mill, and he cherishes her because she uses housekeeping as an expressive, loving language. Henry comprehends "how much love and delicate feeling Nancy put into making his bare room as he liked it" (67). Yet Nancy has the care of Henry's room because she is his wife's slave, a fact he is bound to respect.

Henry Colbert's nights are spent reading, searching his Bible and his Bunyan for clues to the meaning of slavery. In *Pilgrim's Progress,* he has found a plot for Nancy that pleases him; he sees her as "Mercy, Christiana's sweet companion" (67), a perpetually chaste, gentle domestic handmaiden. When he hears that Rachel plans to send Nancy to Montreal, he concocts a rape-plot of his own: "A pretty girl like her, she'd be enticed into one of them houses, like as not" (226). Henry is a decent man attempting moral rigor. But as the honorable husband of a slaveholding Southern woman, he is himself enslaved—and he is further bound by his inability to improvise a plot worthy of an independent woman. Rachel is amazed by her father's ineffectuality; she says, " 'Why don't you do something to save her?' He made no reply." With Henry hamstrung and silenced, Rachel declares her plot: "I'm a-going to get Nancy away from here and on the road to freedom." Henry replies, "If only it were possible, Rachel—." And she replies, "Well it is possible" (225). In this novel, facing the alternative of slavery, Rachel and Nancy must take matters into their own, female hands. They are unlike Cécile and (usually) Mrs. Harris, who wait for men to decide their fates.

On the night of her escape, Nancy has second thoughts and is paralyzed by homesickness and dread; she pleads to Rachel, "take me home! . . . Let me go back" (236–37). Nancy had earlier been driven to contemplate suicide by Sapphira and Martin's tormenting; for her, suicide was the classic and only way a slave woman could take her plot into her own hands. It was Rachel who first imagined a life of freedom for Nancy. But the home-girl in Nancy, the part of her that loves housekeeping and "home folks" (including her mother and the master, Henry) protests and quails. Rachel insists that she follow through and go away with the underground railroad people who come for her. As the two women part, Nancy is silently inert, as if drugged. It is Rachel, like Madame Auclair, who exerts her will over the future by predicting a plot. She says, with certainty, "Good-bye, Nancy! We shall meet again" (239). In her epilogue, Cather will celebrate the power and prescience of Rachel's plot.

Nancy puts her life in Rachel's hands and mind because there is no one else who can help her. Her mother, the only parent Nancy has ever known, is Sapphira's housekeeper and her most valued, loyal slave. Although Till loves Nancy, her only child, she is so deeply implicated in the domestic plot of Sapphira's ongoing household that Nancy cannot even imagine telling Till of her fears. Like Rachel, Nancy has grown up without a confidante—with no one who can hear her whole story.

Reasons for this silence begin in Nancy's mother's history, in the crucial event of Till's childhood: she watched her mother burn to death, when her dress caught fire as she dressed for a slaves' party. At the sight, the child Till was "struck dumb" (70). The white English housekeeper, Mrs. Matchem, adopted the orphan girl and taught her a new language: perfected house-keeping. Till had seen how utterly expendable and perishable a slave woman could be. If mother, the center of a child's world, could expire as quickly as rags could burn, what could have meaning and substance? Serious, capable Mrs. Matchem "impressed upon" the traumatized child "that there was all the difference in the world between doing things exactly and doing them somehow-or-other. The little black girl would stand looking up at the tall Devonshire woman, taking these precepts devoutly to heart" (71). Matchem's lesson is essentially that of Madame Auclair: that domestic order gives our lives beauty, security, and meaning, and is central to civilization. And Till is a pupil at least as willing and apt as Cécile Auclair. But the civilization she preserves, as an accomplished housekeeper, conceives of Till as a piece of property; she is herself one of the household objects she puts in order.

Some of Cather's perceptive recent readers have been particularly disturbed by her portrayal of Till. Minrose C. Gwin claims that "it is difficult to take Till seriously as a black woman," because of her treatment of Nancy (140). Marilyn Arnold says that "Till is so well trained that she would even sacrifice her daughter" to the slavery-based system within which she lives ("Bondage" 332). Rachel Blake, herself both daughter and mother of daughters, also speculates about Till's silence with Nancy and thinks she understands the reason: "In Till's mind, her first duty was to her mistress. . . . Anything that made trouble between her and the mistress would wreck the order of the household" (219). For Till, the continuing "order of the household" must come first.

Nancy and Till are reunited, twenty-five years after Nancy's escape, in the epilogue of *Sapphira*, as Eliza and Cassy, daughter and mother, are reunited at the climax of *Uncle Tom's Cabin*. Both of Stowe's women are successful mothers, in the terms of her novel; they have defied slavery and executed spectacular maternal escapes. Everything about Stowe's plotting and characterization underlines the rightness of that reunion. By contrast, Till's critics suggest that she is a failed mother—and thus she may not quite seem to have earned her reunion with Nancy. The reunion is presented through a witness, five-year-old Willa Cather, and even the excited child (already complexly socialized) is slightly dissatisfied, especially with the *language* of this reunited mother and daughter. First, Nancy's speech seems "not exactly 'hearty' . . . enough for the occasion." And the embrace of the two women is disconcertingly silent; "neither spoke a word" (282–84). Till's first and only passionate outburst comes hours later, and it is a comment on her daughter's speech, delivered with "idolatrous pride." She says, "Nancy, darlin', you talks just like Mrs. Matchem. . . . I loves to hear you" (286).

Till has believed that her life has dignity and meaning because of the housekeeping language she learned from Mrs. Matchem. But Mrs. Matchem, a servant herself, never taught Till a speakable, liberating vocabulary of *feeling;* when Matchem learned that she and her protégée were to be separated forever by Till's sale to Sapphira, she merely "looked down her long nose and compressed her lips" (72). Thus it is understandable that Till cannot talk with her daughter about some of the most pressing feelings of their lives. She does not even tell Nancy who her white father was, and the girl never asks. Till is a complex, intelligent woman who does not permit herself full access to her own inner life. Even when Cather is writing from inside Till's point of view, she does so with great circumspection, as if acknowledging that some privacies of a black woman's life may not be accessible to a white woman's imagination. Of Till's arranged marriage to a "capon man," Cather says only, "How much it hurt her pride no one ever knew; perhaps she did not know herself" (72).

According to Deborah Gray White, the daughter's adolescence was a particularly stressful period for a slave mother, because then she became even more intensely aware of her limited capacity to care for her child.[11] "In the long run . . . a mother could do little but hope that her daughter made it through adolescence and young womanhood unscathed by sexual abuse" (95–96). Till is Cather's most compelling and controversial example of this painful ineffectuality. Nevertheless, she does what she can; she teaches

Nancy her domestic arts, and the girl loves "all her mother's ways" (62). The most intimate and touching scene between them occurs early in the book, as they clean Sapphira's house together. Till tries to tell her nubile daughter, who has become the victim of her mistress's sexual jealousy, how to get back in Sapphira's good graces. She urges the only plot she knows, domestic servitude.

> "make a nice eggnog . . . carry it to the mistress. . . . on the small silvah salvah, with a white napkin and some cold biscuit. . . . smile, an' look happy to serve her, an' she'll smile back."
> Nancy shook her head. Her slender hands dropped limp at her side. "No she won't, Mudder," very low. (44–45)

Such recipes can no longer keep Till's daughter safe. Nancy knows that and is silenced by the fact. As Rachel is appalled by her mother's power, Nancy is appalled by her mother's powerlessness.

So Nancy must turn to Rachel for protection. And Rachel can be an effective protector partly because she is not boxed into a domestic system. When Nancy is afraid to go into the woods alone, Rachel accompanies her, even though her bread is ready to bake. To Rachel, Nancy can voice her suicidal fears, and Rachel, abandoning the falsely cheerful language she uses with her mother's slaves, can ask Nancy a formerly unspeakable question: "I think I can get you away. Would you go?" (218) Cather never lets us know whether Nancy told her mother of her plans to escape. But we learn that, when Till meets Rachel for the first time after Nancy's flight, her demeanor and language are changed; she greets Rachel "with such warmth as she seldom betrayed and called her by her given name." On hearing that Nancy is bound for Canada, Till says, suppressing tears, "If she's up there with the English folks, she'll have some chance" (248–49).

Such details, the only fugitive bits of knowledge we can glean about Till's inner life, suggest a woman trying to fulfill a complex set of loyalties. Despite her devotion to Sapphira's household, Till seems to rejoice in Nancy's "chance" for a new life. In Canada, Nancy follows in her mother's footsteps; she becomes a professional housekeeper. Thus, when Till hears Mrs. Matchem's accents in her daughter's voice, it is as if Nancy has become the English housekeeper's descendant. The unsafe, combustible slave mother—Nancy's maternal grandmother—is supplanted, and in her place is the only reliable maternal figure Till has ever known. Till's inner and outer life have been buffeted by the cruel upheavals that were fact for most American blacks before 1860. Born a slave and freed at Sapphira's death, she began as a piece of property and ended as independent woman. The only constant in those years is her artful housekeeping. To see and hear Nancy's success vindicates Till's domestic plot; it lets her feel that she *is* a good mother. But in another sense, when tiny Till looks up to her tall "English" daughter, she has become a child again, in the charge of Matchem, who trained her to be a capable woman and thus a valuable slave. As mother, child, and slave, Till regards her daughter with abjectly "idolatrous pride."

Of Nancy's adult life in Canada, we know only what bits of information an observant five-year-old could assemble; she is wife and mother, prosperous, with a stable, apparently satisfying position. She carries herself with surety and pride. And although she has adopted the precise accents of Canadian English, abandoning the easy Virginia talk, she has not lost her touch with Virginia housekeeping. When she visits with Willa's family, during her stay with Till, she "used to bring a small carpetbag, with her sewing and a fresh apron, and insisted upon helping Mrs. Blake and Moses' Sally in whatever housework was under way. She begged to be allowed to roast the coffee. 'The smell of it is sweeter than roses to me, Mrs. Blake,' she said laughing. 'Up there the coffee is always poor. . . . As soon as it's browned, I'll grind a little and make us all a cup, by your leave'" (286). In the epilogue, Nancy appears a self-possessed woman who takes pride in the life she has made and in her housekeeping skills, but also as a woman who is still, in some ways, homesick for the place she had to leave. And she still speaks the Virginia language of domestic servitude; even to her friend Rachel she says, "by your leave."

In fact, with the youthful Nancy, Cather returned to a protagonist very much like Cécile Auclair. As a girl, Nancy has an affinity for domestic ritual; more than anyone on the plantation, she seems to employ it as a language of feeling, as Cécile did. She too has a rapturous response to her homeplace. Even after a night of terror, she wakes to survey, with passionate joy, the plantation world in which she has grown up: "Oh, this was a beautiful place! Nancy didn't believe there was a lovelier spot in the world. . . . she loved everybody in those vine-covered [slave] cabins, everybody. . . . After all, they were home folks. . . . Was it possible that she might have lost all this happiness last night . . . ? But it was still hers; the home folks and the home place and the precious feeling of belonging here. Maybe that fright back there in the dark hall had been just a bad dream. Out here it didn't seem true" (197).

Nancy yearns to live a plantation version of the domestic romance. Like Cécile, she has been trained by her mother to fastidiousness, and she shrinks from "ugly sights and ugly words" (43). Her tender housekeeping in the master's mill room is an effort to make her own "climate within a climate," an impervious environment of love and order. But she is caught between that compelling fantasy and a world of truths that she is loath to admit, the terrors of a slave woman trapped in a dark hall.[12] Nancy is made especially vulnerable by her budding sexuality—a force that Cather confronts much more openly here than she did in Cécile's tale. One morning, Nancy "plays truant" and climbs a tree to pick blackheart cherries. This is not a house-keeper's task; Nancy is pleasing herself, and she eats the sweetest fruit out of hand, enjoying the touch of the sun and dew on her body. Perched in the cherry tree, Nancy feels carefree: "no troubles followed a body up there; nothing but the foolish, dreamy, nigger side of her nature climbed the tree with her. She knew she had left half her work undone. . . . The leaves over her head laughed softly in the wind; maybe they knew she had run away" (178).

To enjoy her sensuous/sensual nature, Nancy must renounce her domes-tic responsibilities, allowing the "foolish, dreamy nigger side of her" to hold sway—and giving in to the myth of the "shiftless" black, which Mrs. Matchem taught Till and Till taught Nancy to resist. Here, Cather's charged and disturbing racial language suggests that, to enjoy her free and imaginative ("dreamy") black self, she must put housekeeping behind her. Thus, when the distracting Martin Colbert appears, looking for Nancy, he does not seem "wicked" to her from the vantage point of the cherry tree— only "jolly" and flirtatious, and Nancy "laughed a soft darky laugh and dropped a bunch of cherries down to him" (179). He responds by seizing Nancy's legs and holding them around his face. When she asks him to release her, he delays, saying, "pretty soon.—This is just nice.—Something smells sweet—like May apples." And Nancy, unable to move, is terrified; her carefree sensual adventure has become a trap. "Everything had changed, and she couldn't collect her wits" (181). She is back in the contracted world of the dark hall, without control or volition, only an object to be moved about and taken. She screams for help, to Till's husband and another black man, who rescue her, all the while placating Martin.

Soon after this scene, Nancy tells Rachel that she is planning suicide. Rachel offers her counterplot. And the novel never again enters Nancy's point of view. The details of her escape are filtered through Rachel's obser-vation and through omniscient narration. Nancy has been brought to a terrible impasse—her sexuality, her love for her mother, her self-respect, her longing for security and continuity, and her love of place and housekeeping are all at war, and the inner and outer combat are so intense that the only solution Nancy can imagine is self-annihilation.

Nancy's escape is financed by Henry Colbert; he leaves a roll of money where Rachel can steal it from his coat pocket, making her the active aggressor in the plot against the continuance of slavery. As Henry hears Rachel take the money, "he lay still and prayed earnestly, for his daughter and for Nancy." Now he must give up whatever plots he might have harbored for the slave woman—including his probable unconscious wish to become her lover himself.[13] Using the biblical language of his most trusted stories, Henry tries to imagine for Nancy an honorable plot, one that would let her become fully human. As he prays, he recognizes that he is thinking not just of Nancy, but of his daughter as well. Peter Brooks argues that plot is an "engagement with human memory and desire . . . a form of thinking" (319). Along such lines, Henry strains to think a new story, a break from slavery, to be enacted by women. "He would never again hear that light footstep [Nancy's] outside his door. She would go up out of Egypt to a better land. Maybe she would be like the morning star, this child; the last star of night. . . . She was to go out from the dark lethargy of the cared-for and irresponsible; to make her own way in this world where nobody is altogether free, and the best that can happen to you is to walk your own way and be responsible to God only" (228).

As Nancy departs to "walk her own way" in Canada, she clings to what she knows best, domestic routine. She carries three pairs of Sapphira's silk stocking to darn, planning to "send 'em back by stage, or somehow" (232). This intention, more than anything else, causes Rachel to falter. For even she, with her "freedom" and wider experience, cannot imagine the life in Canada of a former slave girl. "She thought how vague . . . was this 'there' that Nancy spoke of—*there* was Canada, wasn't it? Mrs. Blake herself had never been farther north than Baltimore. She had always thought of Boston as very, very far north. And Montreal was away, away longer off than Boston. And Nancy spoke of sending things back by stage! For a moment she felt her courage sink" (232). Rachel steps into the kitchen "to get command of herself"; when she rejoins Nancy, she straightens the chair tidies and assures the girl that she will do the darning herself. In the extremity of departure, both women fix on housework and domestic chores to reassure them of security and continuance. The illusion, at least, that the routines of housework can proceed unbroken sustains the two, as they act out a very different kind of plot.

Nancy, the loving daughter of a dutiful housekeeper-slave, would like to believe that she can run away to a life of her own while still doing her duties as slave girl. Thus it is no wonder that, when Nancy shapes a life of her own in Canada, housekeeping is its center, the profession that affords her mastery and security. When Nancy returns for her epilogue visit, much of what

Rachel and Till are eager to learn of her life has to do with housekeeping—
"about her husband and children, how they had a cottage to themselves at
the end of the park, and how the work was divided between the men and the
maids" (285). Housekeeping keeps Nancy connected with the "home folks."
It is a keystone of both her plots.

Sapphira and the Slave Girl, like Shadows on the Rock, teems with stories,
and most are tales of Virginia women. Most of them are well known to
Nancy, as they were to young Willa Cather, and they are a complex heritage;
they incorporate, as well as figures based on Cather's own female ancestors,
black slave women and white mountain women. For example, a stunning
"inset story" is devoted to Nancy's great-grandmother, Jezebel, a powerful,
spirited African who impressed her captors and owners with her "lively
curiosity" and her sexual, creative energies. At the time of the novel's events,
Jezebel is dying, at ninety-five; she has been a valued cog in the plantation
housekeeping. When Sapphira, on a proprietary visit, reads a psalm to the
old woman and counsels resignation, Jezebel acquiesces weakly: "Yes'm, I'se
resigned." But in fact she is taking her death into her own hands by refusing
food—a form of suicide. When Sapphira tries to tempt her by offering
whatever delicacy she desires, Jezebel replies very differently, with "a flash of
grim humour. 'No'm, I cain't think of nuthin' I could relish, lessen maybe it
was a l'il pickaninny's hand.'" Nancy, standing by, is shocked; she says,
"Oh, she's a-wanderin' agin! . . . She's out of her haid!" Schooled in well-
mannered servitude, the girl is terrified by her voracious kinswoman and by
the energy that still crackles behind her acquiescent facade. Sapphira is
unperturbed, however; she tells Nancy coldly, "I know your granny through
and through. She is no more out of her head than I am" (89). There is a link
between the two older women, mistress and slave, antagonists and domestic
collaborators. Their energy resists bondage, and the younger women whom
they might be expected to nurture may be endangered by them. To Nancy, it
may seem that such old women really do devour their young.

As she surveys the plantation women, Nancy may note how they use
housekeeping to solidify their power. Old Jezebel pronounces fatelike judgments on the slave men through her sewing: "She meted out justice by
giving a slack boy a rough seat in his britches, and a likely boy a smooth seat"
(96–97). Till flies into action the minute Sapphira leaves the house, seizing
the opportunity to clean her mistress's room and to exert her own authority.
And Sapphira, now housebound, has become even more addicted to absolute household authority. One of her main allies and adversaries is her
excellent cook, Lizzie, another nemesis of Nancy's a high-handed woman
who takes all the liberties her domestic skills have earned for her. When

Jezebel finally dies, Sapphira and Lizzie clash over the arrangements for the funeral. For Sapphira, such matters are a means of displaying her propriety to the neighbors; she commands, "Lizzie, I expect you to do me credit this time. I won't have any skimping for the watchers, as there was when Manuel died. . . . You put disgrace on me" (99). And she proceeds to dictate the menu for the occasion, directing Lizzie to follow Rachel's further instructions.

Lizzie agrees. "Yes Mam! I sho'ly will put my bes' foot for'ard fo' ole Aunt Jezebel an' all de yeahs she carry. But dat triflin' li'l Manuel wa'nt no 'count nohow" (100). The cook makes it clear that she is agreeing because Sapphira's largesse expresses *Lizzie's* values: respect for a deserving black woman, Jezebel; it is not simply testimony to the mistress's ego. Sapphira ends the engagement with Lizzie by playing her trump card; she threatens to sell Bluebell, Lizzie's lazy, useless daughter, whom Sapphira keeps only to placate the powerful cook. Both women use their daughters, Rachel and Bluebell, as pawns in their battle. The scene, and many like it, shows that housekeeping, even as it executes the basic rituals of living, can be a code in which the most subtle and deadly wars are waged. *Shadows on the Rock* emphasized its importance as a language of continuance and nurturing. But like any complex language, housekeeping both shapes and expresses the impulses of the women who speak through it. The defiant egotism of Lizzie and Sapphira and their unspeakable rage against their limitations are often acted out in housekeeping. Sapphira never gave it up; she was mistress of her household until the day she died. And it is significant that Lizzie—although she was freed by Henry with all Sapphira's surviving slaves—refused to leave the plantation kitchen where she ruled; she and Bluebell were forcibly ejected by Henry, who despised their imperious housekeeping as much as he loved Nancy's romantic ministrations.

As Nancy takes up her adult life as free woman, she is potentially an heir to all these women and to their language—as were all daughters of the nineteenth century, including Willa Cather. *Sapphira* is the novel in which Cather most fully acknowledges the complexity of that inheritance, and her own connections to Nancy's story. Cather told friends that the return of Nancy was the "greatest event" of her Virginia childhood (O'Brien 44), and she focused her epilogue on the moment where Nancy's story met her own. There, two kinds of female plots converge. In the Cather kitchen, Willa's favorite room, the plot of domestic continuance proceeds; Till and Rachel compete and conspire in cooking, sewing, and storytelling, while the child Willa sits by, working at one of the first household tasks most nineteenth-century girls were taught, patchwork.[14] Nancy has enacted the daughters' plot of discovery and liberation, a plot more easily accessible to men. Yet, by her choice of profession, she seems to suggest that a woman can—and perhaps *must*—claim both these plots.

Young Willa has been schooled to think of Nancy as an archetypal figure, heroine of a story and song the child has heard again and again. To a little girl, Nancy's tale must have seemed the most desirable of stories: it posits that a girl could set out on a voyage of self-discovery and find, at its end, the loving mother she left behind. The women conspire so that Willa can witness the climax of that plot, the mother-daughter reunion of Nancy and Till, the convergence of the two plots. It is the story they want this child to know—a utopian tale.

In *Uncle Tom's Cabin*, Stowe presented a domestic utopia in her picture of the Quaker household, a free-state oasis. There, such everyday domestic chores as the preparation of breakfast demonstrate the working of an ideal community, egalitarian, but ruled by the righteous authority of a Quaker matriarch. To this white woman, the escaped slave Eliza is naturally and inevitably addressed as "daughter" and is welcomed on equal terms at the family table. In many ways, the epilogue of *Sapphira* functions as a similarly utopian scene. Abolition is accomplished and Nancy returns as an honored, storied guest. The house is ordered by female domestic authority; little Willa is whisked about by a vigorously ministering mother and, as in Stowe's scene, a benignly antipatriarchal father is nearby. The radiant kitchen is ruled by Rachel and "Aunt Till," and the child sits with them, drinking up their talk as she sews her patchwork. Through her Quaker household, Stowe would like to persuade her readers that domestic ritual can be the medium and model for an ideal life. Perhaps Willa's mother, grandmother, and "Aunt Till" would like to impress the same lesson on this child, through the medium of Nancy's "happy ending." According to Eugenie Lambert Hamner, it is Willa who "concludes" the story of the older women (347).

But in another sense, *Sapphira* does not conclude. Although the older women may conspire to provide young Willa with a satisfying, wish-fulfilling conclusion, as the child sits listening, soaking up the lore and ambiance of her family, she also picks up other clues about mothers and daughters. "Aunt Till," however welcoming she now seems, did not help Nancy escape; that help came from Rachel, who thus opposed her own mother. Now that defiant Rachel is Willa's comfortable grandmother, who seems very different from her own energetic daughter, Willa's mother. The completed plot of Nancy's departure and return is counterpointed by a cycle of troubling questions about what mothers and daughters can and cannot be to each other. Those questions recur with every generation and thus the "concluding" epilogue sends us both backward and forward—into the novel and into Cather's own work, history, and life.

With such a multiple perspective, it becomes impossible to see this complex scene as utopian. The heritage of slavery lingers; Nancy and Till are not invited to eat at their white hosts' table, and even young Willa thinks of "our Nancy" in a vocabulary of possession that implies a family history of slavery. The tales of Sapphira's last days, which Willa hears from faithful Till, indicate the degree to which Till is still enslaved. Till's words end the novel, as she repeats her white surrogate mother's opinion of her white mistress: "Mrs. Matchem . . . never got over it that Miss Sapphy didn't buy in Chestnut Hill [her family home] and live like a lady, 'stead a' . . . comin' out here where nobody was anybody much" (295). This is the covert language of a dutiful slave and daughter, who does not even express her own judgment directly. And it is language that must seem perversely meaningless to the child. How can this be a place where "*nobody*" is "*anybody much*"? It is Willa's home, the center of her life; the world she knows and will never forget. Till provides the little girl with a richly observed "complete picture" of her Colbert ancestors—and then denies the validity of their human world, including the observer herself, the slave Till. It is significant that, although the epilogue is narrated in the first person, the child takes no speaking part. "While they talked," Cather says, "I looked and listened" (284).

In many ways, the truly utopian scene in *Sapphira* occurs earlier in the book, in the months after Nancy's departure, when Rachel's young daughters fall ill with diptheria. Rachel and the minister are nursing the children; she prepares a chicken broth for him and leaves it to cool on the kitchen table. The minister sees "a white figure," the child Mary, enter the kitchen and drink the bowl of broth. Diptheria patients are forbidden to eat, so the minister knows he should intervene, but he cannot; "there was something solemn in what he saw . . . like a Communion service" (259). Later, the doctor tells him that the nourishing broth was "the child's chance" (264); by taking it, she saved her own life.

This scene has a powerfully sacramental quality; Rosowski notes that the child's act "signals a reassertion of the sacred" (*Voyage* 242). To the witnessing minister, the archetypal scene has the "mysterious significance" of dream (259). Sleepwalking, Mary is acting out of her deepest unconscious self—claiming her life, finding the nourishment she needs. That nourishment is available because her mother is a good housekeeper; even in the upheaval of her daughters' sickness, Rachel has provided for her household by the time-consuming chore of simmering stock. But Mary must find the soup and drink it herself, becoming the central actor in her own plot. Although she acts alone, Mary is abetted by her mother's domestic care, by the intuitive sympathy of the observing minister (who is also her schoolteacher), and by the novelist herself, who is simultaneously the creator and the daughter of this character. Such a continuum of support, collaboration, and independence suggests what the relation of mother, daughter, and community might be, in a true domestic utopia. And it is a matter of life and death; Rachel's other daughter, who cannot feed herself, dies.

Willa Cather's career is marked throughout by an effort to get at—and away from—the truths of housekeeping, and by a sense that domestic ritual can be dangerous to art. Various efforts to distance, incorporate, and defuse domestic ritual mark her work before *Death Comes for the Archbishop*, as we have seen. But her work from the thirties is distinguished by a new and weighty sense that "now I know" about housekeeping. Now that subject is of interest as an inevitable portion of every North American woman's potential heritage, and its cycles mark her finest late work: *Shadows on the Rock*, "Old Mrs. Harris," and *Sapphira and the Slave Girl*.

The distinct formal differences of these three fictions show that Cather was, in her fifties and sixties, still deeply engaged with fictional experiment. In *Shadows on the Rock*, she embraced domestic ritual as subject by creating a historical romance of housekeeping. "Old Mrs. Harris," with its contrapuntal female lives, transforms women into a chorus, which will successively grow into understanding of each other's lives. Younger women, propelled by salutary hubris, plot ways out of that cycle—so the story takes on the weight and classic inevitability of household tragedy. And *Sapphira and the Slave Girl*, her last novel, reaches toward a new form, in which history, fiction, and autobiography are one, as if Willa Cather had come to realize that she would need all three strains for a tale of housekeeping.

Readers persistently find this late book disconcerting, partly because of the frustrating reticences, many of which seem to be built into the mother-daughter relationships. The novel offers no word of dialogue between Rachel and her daughters, between Lizzie and Bluebell, between Jezebel and (granddaughter) Till, or between Willa Cather and her own mother. Although Nancy and Till are glad to be reunited, we do not hear them talk except about twenty-five years of news and matters of housekeeping. Rachel and Sapphira were also reunited, reconciled by the death of Rachel's daughter and Sapphira's impending death. Both recognized the strength of their mother-daughter bond. But there remained between them "a certain formality . . . a reserve on both sides" (293). The pull between that reserve and that undeniable bond, replayed again and again between mother and daughter, is perhaps the deepest source of this book's peculiarly silent tension. As we have seen, this is partly a tension between two kinds of female plots: the mothers' plot of slavery and continuance, the daughters' plot of liberation. After Nancy's escape, when Till learns she is in Montreal, she says that there, at least, her daughter will have "a chance." Thea Kronborg was comforted too, when she heard her teacher pronounce that, as an artist, she must get *herself* born; his words "seemed to give her a chance." Perhaps such a chance is the most any woman can wish for her daughter—and for herself. It is what Till hoped Nancy would find in Canada, what Thea strained to discover through her art, and what Mary swallows, with her mother's broth.

In *Shadows on the Rock*, we may sometimes feel that Cather's silences, especially about Cécile's adult life as housekeeper, are an evasion of complex truths. But in *Sapphira and the Slave Girl*, the silences between mothers and daughters are instead an expression of difficult truths and questions. A mother is twice committed to continuance, because she has borne a child and because she (probably) keeps house. With such commitments, what can a mother *say*, to help her daughter survive, unenslaved? How can she find the plot that is her chance?

That was Willa Cather's past and present question, as she turned at last to her Virginia memories. Like the sleepwalking Mary, Cather found waiting for her, in the family kitchen,[15] the sustaining meal prepared by her mother and grandmother (both now dead). And as the artist explored that material, she claimed another part of her heritage as American woman writer, learning to approach the materials of Stowe and other nineteenth-century American women writers in ways entirely her own.

To the end of her career, Cather went on experimenting with the problem that preoccupies her protagonists in *Sapphira* and elsewhere: what can it mean to imagine, and to live, a female story? That question must be in Cécile's mind, as she ponders the tales of Jeanne le Ber. When Mrs. Harris is dying, and her little grandson lovingly reads to her, she tunes out his "boy's book" and repeats "a passage from the second part of *Pilgrim's Progress*, . . . where Christiana and her band come to the Arbour on the Hill of Difficulty: 'Then said Mercy, how sweet is rest to them that labour'" (183–84). The old woman finds sustenance in the tale of a weary *female* pilgrim; it is Mercy's words that speak deeply to her condition, as dying housekeeper. And when Henry Colbert, a loving father, tries to think of his daughter's and Nancy's future, he strains to imagine a new story, in which a woman could abandon "dark lethargy . . . to make her own way in the world" (128). Throughout her last novel, Cather scrutinizes women as they plot their lives in the language of housekeeping. None of her books required a more profound effort of memory and imagination. With her epilogue, she blurs and extends the boundaries of postmodern fiction to come. Nancy, the nineteenth-century slave girl, as she wrests a life out of bondage and housekeeping, may seem to us peculiarly contemporary. Her plot says, "I can't go on. I'll go on."

6

Welty's Beginnings

Housekeeping and the Other Way to Live

> When I was young enough to still spend a long time buttoning my
> shoes in the morning, I'd listen toward the hall: Daddy upstairs was
> shaving in the bathroom and Mother downstairs was frying the ba-
> con. They would begin whistling back and forth to each other up and
> down the stairwell. My father would whistle his phrase, my mother
> would try to whistle, then hum hers back. It was their duet. I drew
> my buttonhook in and out and listened to it—I knew it was "The
> Merry Widow." . . . They kept it running between them, up and
> down the stairs where I was now just about ready to run clattering
> down and show them my shoes. (*Beginnings* unpaged)

*E*UDORA WELTY´S most recent book, *One Writer's Begin-
nings* (1984), is a meditation on the origins of her life as an artist. At its
beginning, in the place of an epigraph, she has set this luminous paragraph,
a concise domestic idyll. In this scene, as in the celebrated Quaker household of *Uncle Tom's Cabin,* Mother rules the kitchen, while Father, nearby,
shaves off his patriarchal beard. In precisely parallel clauses, the two parents
are given equal billing in a "duet" that expresses the perfectly harmonious
and felicitous art of their lives. In another room their daughter is learning a
wanderer's task, buttoning the shoes in which she will leave the house. In a
moment she will add her noise to their duet, "clattering down" to display her
buttoned shoes.

Eudora Welty was born, in 1909, into a genteel middle-class family in
Jackson, Mississippi. She has lived most of her adult life there, in her
parents' house. Speaking and writing, Welty has again and again emphasized her life's felicities: "I have been truly lucky all my life" (*Conversations*
339–40). Much of that lucky felicity is expressed in the paragraph from *One
Writer's Beginnings,* and it is held in a framework of utopian domestic ritual.
This is a daily household scene, repeated again and again, with a cooking,
kitchen-placed mother sounding her notes in the dancing tune. But even

this tiny drama implies tensions, as well. The tune itself, "The Merry Widow," suggests a woman who is wresting her infectious pleasure from the death of a man. The child listens (and the adult remembers) with delight, but she does not join in to make the duet a trio. Instead, when she runs, she sets up a clatter of competing sound. Her parents' domestic confirmation is necessary—she must "show them [her] shoes"—but those shoes will carry her out and away.

Eudora Welty's fiction is one of the richest achievements of twentieth-century American literature. And even its smallest fragments, like this emblematic paragraph, are marked by Welty's attention to products and processes of traditional culture *and* her simultaneous interest in the exuberant wanderers who will wear their new shoes into a slippery world much wider than Hestia's realm. The genesis of these concerns is suggested by her reminiscences of childhood trips to the neighborhood store for her housebound mother, proudly described as "a thrifty homemaker, wife, and mother of three, [who] also did all her own cooking." On her way back home, taking the "dangerous" underground route through the storm sewer, young Eudora imagined herself another journeying daughter: "down there in the wet dark by myself, I could be Persephone entering into my six-month sojourn underground—though I didn't suppose Persephone had to crawl, hanging onto a loaf of bread, and come out through the teeth of an iron grating. Mother Ceres would indeed be wondering where she could find me, and mad when she knew. 'Now am I going to have to start marching to the Little Store for *myself?*'" (*Eye* 326, 332). The necessity and delicious terror of this daughter's separation from her fruitful, housebound mother are combined with a heavy sense that her mother's myth, with the loaf of bread, is in her hands. If she fails in her mission, domestic ritual will be disrupted, and her mother will be displaced, forced to "march" into the antidomestic world of journeys and transactions—a world that the daughter herself finds powerfully seductive. Every time this girl is sent to the grocery store, she reenacts a process that is both an escape from the jealous maternal Demeter and a return to the mother's womb, "down there in the wet dark." Climbing out the sewer's toothy grating, she emerges from a perilous vagina dentata, ready to run home with her loaf of bread. These cycles of daughterly birth, return, and rebirth become a powerful motif of Welty's fiction, and, as here, as the daughter enacts them, she both perpetuates and repudiates her mother's housekeeping.

Eudora Welty grew up in the era of "scientific housekeeping," which flourished in the teens and twenties. Yet she describes her childhood as untouched by it (although the fact that her mother sometimes *bought* bread tells another story). Perpetuating the domestic myth of omnicompetent mothers, she wrote, "For the generation bringing my generation up, everything made in the kitchen started from scratch. . . . They grated from whole nutmegs, they ground coffee from the beans, went to work on whole coconuts with the hatchet." Fundamentals and fine points of housekeeping were passed on to daughters ritualistically: "Mayonnaise had a *mystique*. Little girls were initiated into it by being allowed to stand at the kitchen table and help make it, for making mayonnaise takes three hands" (*Eye* 323). The woman who had not received a complete education in the techniques of housekeeping would find herself cut off from the nourishment of her past, unable to use her mother's recipes. Welty emphasizes her own difficulties in *reading* her domestic heritage, admitting that her late mother's recipes "don't do me as much good as they might because she never included directions." Recipes were traditionally "imparted—there was something oracular in the transaction," and Mrs. Welty typically reasoned that "any cook worth her salt would know, given a list of ingredients, what to do with them" (*Eye* 324–25).

A girl growing up in Welty's Jackson world of the 1910s and 1920s, then, had two charges: she must *go out*, to keep her mother cooking at the hearth, purchasing ingredients that an earlier housekeeper might have made herself or done without. And she must *stay in*, to learn the skills that would preserve the female traditions of domestic ritual. The weight of those charges is a powerful strain in Eudora Welty's fiction, from beginning to end. Her work is an important contribution to that "dialogue between realism and modernism" described by Joanna Frye, which helped women fiction writers to seize on a concept of "plot based on process rather than product, plot as possible interpretive schema for lived experience rather than the entrapment of a falsifying code" (40).

We can see Welty beginning these projects with women, myth, domestic ritual, and plot in her first published story: "Death of a Travelling Salesman" (1936). The traveling shoe salesman, R. J. Bowman, acts out imperatives of dominant American male culture: money and perpetual motion. In the black hats he "always" wears, he imagines that he resembles a traditional male combatant, a bullfighter. Even his voice is "inflected for selling shoes" (*Collected Stories* 123) and he is furnished with standard equipment: cash, car, and sample cases.

But Bowman has fallen ill and somehow slipped out of linear male-oriented time. During the illness, "nothing had happened except in his head and his body—an almost inaudible life of heartbeats and dreams that came back, a life of fever and privacy, a delicate life which had left him weak" (123). In other words, in a (lunar) month dominated by the rhythms of his body and a woman nurse's ritualistic care, Bowman has slipped into traditional "women's time," as described by Julia Kristeva: time governed by "cycles, gestation, the eternal recurrence of a biological rhythm which conforms to that of nature and imposes a temporality . . . whose regularity and unison with what is experienced as extrasubjective time, cosmic time, occasion vertiginous visions and unnameable *jouissance.*" Such "almost inaudible" experience has "been left mute by culture in the past" and is at odds with predominantly male ideas about "time as project, teleology, linear and prospective unfolding; time as departure, progression, and arrival—in other words, the time of history" (16, 19, 17).

To R. J. Bowman, with his huntsman's, salesman's name, entry into the archaic, unstoried realm of women's time seems a sign of weakness and disease; he has bought his way out, reasserting "the time of history" and the power of money. Buying the nurse "a really expensive bracelet" and paying the doctor, "he had proved his recovery" (119). The story, told exclusively from Bowman's point of view, chronicles his first day back on schedule, on the road. He has set himself a goal: "to reach Beulah by dark" (120). The goal reflects his practiced purposiveness; Beulah is a known place on his usual route. But it also indicates other priorities: as critics have noted, Beulah evokes the peaceful, restful Beulah Land of *Pilgrim's Progress.* It is also, especially in the South, a woman's name.

Physically weak and disoriented, Bowman enters another version of Beulah Land. To do so, he must give up his male version of time. On the road, there are already signs that he is doing so; his competitive, contestant's images of time are inoperative. "The time did not seem to clear the noon hurdle." Bowman's "record was broken, and he had begun even to question it" (119). Instead, images of a female past assail him; he recalls "his dead grandmother . . . a comfortable soul" and her soft feather bed (119). When the linear road runs out and Bowman drives his car onto the edge of a ravine, he gets out, lets the car sink into the crevice (which suggests the entry to a womb), and sets out "with almost childlike willingness" to an archetypal construction: "the house, back on the hill" (121).

One of Welty's early essays on the craft of fiction, "Looking at Short Stories," begins with a discussion of plot, based on the standard male definition provided by E. M. Forster. It is plot, she says, that transforms narrative to art, for it propels readers from merely "asking What next? to asking Why? The word which, of course, opened up everything, or as much of everything as the writer is able to handle" (*Eye* 85–86). She mentions two archetypal plots—"Life *versus* death" and "the errand of search"—and illustrates them in six stories, five by men.

But in "Death of a Travelling Salesman," Welty does something more complex than her essay's formulations. She shows us a character who sets himself a plot to enact: he must certify himself a healthy man by traveling to Beulah. He thinks he can accomplish that goal by following a map. But Bowman's unconscious proposes another plot, a journey back into mythic female time, urged on by his newly demanding heart (which begins to thump erratically, prefiguring a heart attack). As the two projects fight to dominate his consciousness, Bowman's plot becomes, literally, the human plot shared by both genders: "Life *versus* death."

At the primitive shotgun house, Bowman is met by a housekeeper cleaning a lamp, "a big woman" with "a dark passage behind her" (121). When he follows her into the dim, womblike house, she sets aside her half-cleaned lamp and points him to a chair; they await the return of the absent man, Sonny. Bowman, in his practiced salesman's manner, makes abortive efforts at conversation; she volunteers no words. He asserts his mastery of chronology: "Bowman, who automatically judged a woman's age on sight, set her age at fifty" (121). But again he is reminded, by a glimpsed quilt, of his dead grandmother and her "girlhood painting of Rome burning" (123)—a woman's vision of the extinction of male-dominated history. Sitting with the woman, Bowman has entered the thick atmosphere of domestic ritual. The woman is enacting what Rabuzzi calls "the traditional Hestian pattern . . . of being in the home . . . *waiting*" (143). This mode of being "stands at the opposite end of the spectrum from action. It may imply rootedness of a positive as well as a negative sort. As such it is a condition essential for growth" (151). The woman in Welty's story gives herself entirely to her waiting, visibly "feeling how right she was." To Bowman, it seems that his very senses are held in her sure hands: "he held his eyes stiffly wide . . . as though she held the cord they were strung on" (123).

Sonny arrives, a big man in a Confederate coat; with his mule, he retrieves Bowman's car. Then the woman sends him out to "borry fire" to kindle at the hearth. Nothing in this self-sustaining house is touched by the twentieth century; the house is outside historical change. Thus the matches and the money that Bowman offers are rejected. When Sonny returns with a burning stick, the woman cooks and lights the lamp.

> the whole room turned golden-yellow like some sort of flower, and the walls smelled of it and seemed to tremble with the quiet rushing of the fire and the waving of the burning lampwick in its funnel of light.
>
> The woman moved among the iron pots. With the tongs she dropped hot coals on top of the iron lids. They made a set of soft vibrations, like the sound of a bell far away. (127)

To Bowman, this is not just the clatter of everyday housekeeping; the resonant imagery combines nature (flower/fire), household (funnel, pans), and the compelling sounds (bell) of worship. Waiting with the woman, he has wanted to reach for her, speak to her, invite her into his clamoring heart. But his life has taught him no language in which to broach such communion—a communion that she can evoke through her most ordinary acts of housekeeping. The woman and Sonny seem to share an unspoken secret, Bowman thinks; they "cherished something here that he could not see, they withheld some ancient promise of food and warmth and light. Between them they had a conspiracy. . . . it was not fair" (126). Although he shares their fire and food, Bowman cannot really enter the rituals that construct their shelter.

When the woman smiles and says, "You all can eat now," he suddenly sees. As she serves the meal, she appears regenerate before him, not Sonny's mother but his pregnant wife: "She was young, still young. He could think of no number of years for her. . . . she was young. Her teeth were shining and her eyes glowed." Between her and Sonny there is no arcane mystery, only "something private." "A marriage, a fruitful marriage. That simple thing. Anyone could have had that" (128–29). Bowman has found his way into a place beyond all his calculations, where continuance and communion (spiritual and erotic) are contained and expressed in the rituals of a simple shelter, in the most basic acts of housekeeping. Everything he knows of time and language seems irrelevant in such a world, where the "old" woman is suddenly, fruitfully young. When she and her husband have gone to bed, Bowman lies sleepless, and his body longs to share the woman's time. As if he too is pregnant, "emotion swelled patiently within him, and he wished that the child were his" (129).

At such a thought, Bowman must abandon the house. Sick as he is, he struggles up and leaves, "almost ostentatiously" thrusting all his money under the lamp base, countering her emblem with his. Outside, ravenous for destinations, he runs for his car, which is waiting "like a boat." But he collapses and dies of a heart attack. Reclaiming his practical, pragmatic male persona, hurling himself back into historical time and away from the rituals of archaic women's time, Bowman has fatally betrayed his own heart.

Welty wrote in *One Writer's Beginnings* that "writing 'Death of a Travelling Salesman' opened my eyes" (87). In many ways, R. J. Bowman's vision is like Welty's own. Welty links her first intimations of herself as artist with childhood travel, train trips with her father. From her berth, she "dreamed over what I could see as it passed, as well as over what I couldn't. Part of the dream was what lay beyond. . . . A house back at its distance of night showing a light from an open doorway. . . . For now . . . I was proceeding in fantasy" (75). Welty's "first good story," "Death of a Travelling Salesman," took her into the world that the train passed, "toward what was at the center of it, to a cabin back in the red clay hills." Coming to herself and to her powers as artist, young Welty was drawn to a mortal collision between the rituals of a house, enacted by an archetypal woman, and the traveling vision of a twentieth-century man. Now she had truly begun her life's work. "Story writing, once I was truly in its grip, took me and shook me awake" (87). In her first extraordinary book of stories, *A Curtain of Green* (1941), she replayed notes sounded by female predecessors. Jewett in *The Country of the Pointed Firs*, for example, also launched a "modern" protagonist into a domestic network that seemed both alluring and alien to her; like Bowman, she was initially robbed of her certainty and her language by unspeakable powers of that world. Jewett's narrator made accommodations and extensions—and finally, art—that admitted her, at least partially, to Mrs. Todd's world. Her response finds it way into language. But Welty's protagonist fails, finally— his last thoughts are an attempt to suppress language and feeling:

> He felt as if all this had happened before. He covered his heart with both hands to keep anyone from hearing the noise it made.
> But nobody heard it. (130)

Jewett might suggest that this death of communication is partially caused by Bowman's gender; she had advised Willa Cather that "when a woman writes in the man's character—it must always, I believe, be something of a masquerade" (*Letters* 246). Jewett's best work was executed in the exploratory female first person described by Frye. Cather's experiments with point of view, male and female, broached questions of housekeeping more variously, as myth, ritual, and practice in male and female lives. Welty, drawing as well on the resources of a modernist legacy (especially Faulkner, Woolf, Bowen, and Joyce), ranges even further.

Hélène Cixous, hypothesizing a utopian future in which women will claim the full resources of writing and woman will "put herself into the text," argues against phallocentric women's art. "We are in no way obliged to deposit our lives in their banks of lack, to consider the constitution of the subject in terms of a dream manglingly restaged, to reinstate again and again the religion of the father. Because we don't want that" (245, 255). In Welty's first great story, the *lack* is most obviously Bowman's, and the story clearly indicates that all the resources of male-oriented twentieth-century culture, in which he sells merchandise to women consumers, are not sufficient to sustain the protagonist's life. The woman, by contrast, seems to Bowman to believe fully in the value, meaning, and absolute sufficiency of her household tasks, in their continuity and the continuity of life, indicated by her pregnancy. As Rabuzzi says, "it is not *what* is done but *how* it is done that makes housekeeping chores rituals." A woman cleaning a lamp, cooking supper, may thus be perceived—and perceive herself—as "ritually returning as a priestess to the time of origins, the primordial time in which the gods and goddesses originally created order out of chaos" (96–97).

Bowman, yearning toward the woman, would redress his own lack by entering her "primordial" world, which would require him to give up his system of symbols, most notably his ideas of time. According to Rabuzzi, a ritualistic housekeeper, experiencing her home as "sacred space," may perceive "her home as a bodily extension of herself" (99). Bowman wishes to invite the woman inside *his* symbolic body (thus taking on a feminine role), where he imagines a rich and beautiful natural world: "a deep lake. . . . a warm spring day. . . . Come and stand in my heart, whoever you are, and a whole river would cover your feet and rise higher and take your knees in whirlpools, and draw you down to itself, your whole body, your heart too" (125). Such feelings are echoed in his later wish that the woman's child "were his." Bowman, in his disorientation and growing need, experiencing his own lacks for the first and last time, invests the backwoods woman with layers of mythological meaning, and he labors toward a new (for him) level of expression in a language that perceives the body as a multiplicitous world. That language recalls the work of French feminist critics such as Luce Irigaray and Cixous. Cixous urges her women readers to claim language: "Write! Writing is for you, you are for you; your body is yours, take it" (246).

This exhortation is a reminder of what the woman in Welty's story lacks. She is without mobility (never in the story does she leave her hearth), without the monetary and technological resources of the twentieth century, which could transform her housekeeping. She lacks access to historical time, and she lacks words; she speaks little, and of the three characters, only she is never referred to by name. The men both have fragmentary names. Bowman's is formal and official, suitable for business, and emphasizing the last name. *Bowman,* a *man's* name which was his father's, describes an archaic male occupation and thus is triply male. The personal specificity of his first two names is suppressed by initials. Sonny, by contrast, has no last name; his first name (one borne by many Southern men) indicates that he is someone's child. It evokes the intimate world of early childhood, probably dominated by Mother. Neither character's name is a complete reflection of a twentieth-century man's selfhood. But the woman is identified only by the one sure fact Bowman could at once perceive accurately about her: her gender. In this story, she bears the fullest weight of "primordial" meaning. Must the cost of such meaning, for a housekeeping woman, be her name? Is this absence or presence, (self) possession or *lack?*

These questions persistently emerge when one explores the lore and literature of domestic ritual and the realm of "women's time." In this story, published when she was twenty-seven, young Eudora Welty found a way to pursue such questions beyond her glimpse of a glowing house from a moving train. But the story expresses the vision of a male traveler, drawn toward the mythology of women's culture and then so threatened by the depth and implications of that impulse that he dies in an abortive escape attempt. What could the woman tell him, had she a voice and a language that Bowman could comprehend? What would she say of her life? How would she name herself?

Such questions are a subtext of Welty's earlier stories, with their abundance and exhilaration, their range of voices. In "Clytie," the title character inhabits a gothic household, doing the housework for her abusive family. Over the years, she has lost a vision of an unnamed, longed-for face, a face for which she is always searching. At last, drawing rainwater for her paralyzed father's shave, she finds the face waiting in the rain barrel. Recognizing it as her own visage, marked by age and suffering, Clytie drowns herself in the barrel. As a household drudge, she has lost or spoiled all the possibilities of her selfhood.

In "Old Mr. Marblehall," a man fantasizes—as Bowman did—about another life, a way to "kill time" and its relentless repetitions. So he creates an alternative to his sedate, orderly domestic life: another house, wife, and son, all very much like the ones he left behind. His only relief from such self-replicating tedium is a blaze of inexplicably magnificent imagery: "Otherwise he dreams that he is a great blazing butterfly stitching up a net; which doesn't make sense" (*Collected Stories* 97). No matter that he dreams of flight and calls himself Mr. Bird; Mr. Marblehall is always Marblehall, named by the enduring house, which is his orderly tomb.

In "A Piece of News," a young housekeeper much like the woman Bowman meets comes home from an afternoon of lovemaking with a passing salesman, bearing a sample of coffee he gave her. Looking at the newspaper wrapping, she finds a sentence about herself: "Mrs. Ruby Fisher had the misfortune to be shot in the leg by her husband last week" (*Collected Stories* 13). Ruby's world has been defined by her housekeeping, her eroticism, and her moonshiner husband, who sometimes provokes her to an adventure with a passing man. Seeing "her" name in a Tennessee paper brings another dimension of possibility into Ruby's world, a dimension both titillating and dangerous. The outside world of the literate twentieth century, a world of multiplicity where there is more than one Ruby Fisher, is more threatening to her husband than his wife's occasional unfaithfulness, which he seems to tolerate. When she shows him the paper, he says, "A newspaper! . . . Where'd you get that? Hussy" (16). Dalliance with the world of print and names is the truly incendiary act for the housekeeper Ruby Fisher: the story's ending suggests that, for this passionate, inarticulate young woman, nothing will ever again be quite the same.[1]

Such stories from *A Curtain of Green* hypothesize variously about the mysteries of domestic ritual suggested by "Death of a Travelling Salesman," evoking a complex vocabulary of lack and loss. Perhaps the most striking counterpart to Welty's first story is "Flowers for Marjorie." Marjorie resembles the salesman's woman; she is a pregnant young Mississippian, confident of time. She tells her husband, Howard, "Those things always happen when they're supposed to. Nothing can stop me from having the baby, that's sure" (*Collected Stories* 100). Howard and Marjorie have been transplanted to Depression New York. There her certainties and assurances seem to Howard as compelling as the woman was to Bowman; he thinks "in wonder: let it be the way she says" (100). Marjorie is secure in their rented room, surrounded by the cooking utensils they have moved from place to place. But Howard, even with his face buried in his wife's "sheltering body" with its "cloverlike" smell, cannot drown out clock time, historical time, money time. Hopelessly unemployed, he swings his empty purse "like a little pendulum," and he screams, "You may not know it but you're the only thing left in the world that hasn't stopped" (100–101).

Marjorie's response is a nurturing housekeeper's inevitable question, "'Have you had anything to eat?' . . . He was astonished at her; he hated her, then. Inquiring out of her safety into his hunger and weakness!" (101) With her kitchen knife, Howard fatally stabs Marjorie. Then he washes his hands and throws the clock out the window. Even dead, Marjorie maintains "perfect balance" seated by the window. As her hair softly blows in the spring breeze, she seems to become a domestic artifact. "There was blood everywhere, her lap was like a bowl" (102).

Howard returns to the city and a run of luck; a stranger gives him a dime; a slot machine overflows with nickels for him. At Radio City he is presented with a bouquet of roses and the key to the city; "a woman marched up to him and said, 'You are the ten millionth person to enter Radio City, and you will broadcast over a nationwide . . . network tonight at six o'clock" (104). With Marjorie dead, Howard has immediate entrée into historical time; he has wandered through a turnstile into the twentieth century. But behind him waits murdered women's time, the body of Marjorie. He runs back to her with the luxuriant roses and finds her body still at the window, waiting. Defying her laws of time, Howard *has* stopped her "from having the baby." Realizing her death, "Howard knew for a fact that everything had stopped. It was just as he had feared, just as he had dreamed. He had had a dream to come true" (105).

Pretty Marjorie, described repeatedly as "soft" and "round," is a product of traditional women's culture. But how can she continue, in New York, in the 1930s? For Howard, "it was hard to remember, in this city of dark, nervous, loud-spoken women, that in Victory, Mississippi, all girls were like Marjorie—and that Marjorie was in turn like his home. . . . Or was she?" (99). His despairing murder is an act of horrific liberation, a dream come true. But with Marjorie dead, he discovers that nothing has meaning; all time is spoiled. Howard leads a policeman to Marjorie's body, dropping the Radio City roses on the pavement. Behind him, "the little girls ran up stealthily and put them in their hair" (106). This last haunting image subtly suggests that Marjorie's story is a problematic female inheritance, even in modern New York.

Both "Flowers for Marjorie" and "Death of a Travelling Salesman" are plotted to emphasize male lack, in the face of a powerfully present domestic woman, who may seem an atavistic or archaic figure. The plots climax with male response: Howard commits murder; Bowman virtually commits suicide. Such plots have no way to get *inside* domestic ritual, which remains radiant, exasperating, and impervious to the march of historical time.

Other stories come at housekeeping from different angles. For example, "Clytie" co-opts the quest plot for a housekeeping woman, in a tale as emphatically heightened as one of Freeman's domestic melodramas. "Why I Live at the P.O."—the only dramatic monologue of Welty's first book— presents two grown sisters battling for control, in a contest of lies and housekeeping. And many of the most interesting of these stories, such as "Old Mr. Marblehall" and "A Piece of News," take forms that seem to have little to do with usual conventions of plot. Mr. Marblehall's meditation on his two domestic lives is the story of a man who has been unable to break out of a domestic rhythm; he imagines a *son* who will discover his bigamy and effect the startling climax his father cannot achieve. And "A Piece of News" reflects the inarticulate life of house, body, and weather that Ruby Fisher lives, utterly without self-consciousness. The story is shaped by her delicate movements, as when, serving supper, she makes of her tasks a teasing erotic vocabulary: "Ruby was going through the preparations for the meal gently. She stood almost on tiptoe in her bare, warm feet. Once as she knelt at the safe, getting out the biscuits, she saw Clyde looking at her and she smiled and bent her head tenderly. There was some way she began to move her arms that was mysteriously sweet and yet abrupt and tentative, a delicate and vulnerable manner, as though her breasts gave her pain. She made many unnecessary trips back and forth across the floor, circling Clyde where he sat, in his steamy silence, a knife and fork in his fists" (15). How can fiction respond to something as subtle and wordless as Ruby Fisher putting a meal on the table? The question is made doubly complex by the fact that Welty's story presents *print*, specifically a story about a Ruby Fisher, as the element that opposes the present equilibrium of her life. It is a question that suggests some of Welty's own problems as young woman artist, discovering much of her material embedded in silent traditions of women's culture.

A Curtain of Green offers two central characters who are clearly models of the artist. For the autobiographical young girl of "A Memory," art is a matter of framing and exclusion. The child manipulates her frames—and finally gives up consciousness—to protect her vision from the ugly and the inexplicable, from anything that threatens an adolescent's dream of love. This girl's vision is determinedly undomestic, for she cannot bear to think of the boy she loves in a domestic setting she cannot control and might not approve; "It was unbearable to think that his house might be slovenly and unpainted. . . . I speculated endlessly on the dangers of his home" (76). This girl, with her timidities and squeamishness, is a model of an artist's impulse that cannot complete itself.

In fact, Welty's most triumphantly uncompromising artist-character appears in her first book of stories. He is Powerhouse, in the story of that name, a consummate black jazz musician. Powerhouse has vast powers of invention and improvisation, and the story follows him through an evening on the road. Surrounded by his troupe of traveling jazzmen, he fantasizes an archetypal story about a woman who is his opposite: a stay-at-home woman, his mysterious wife Gypsy, lonely, suicidal, and perhaps promiscuous.

For the young Welty, then, the powers and energies of the artist seem profoundly antidomestic. But two slightly later essays, "Ida M'Toy" (1942) and "A Pageant of Birds" (1943), suggest other models for the artist. Ida M'Toy, an elderly black midwife and seller of used clothing in Jackson, is described in terms as expansive and extravagant as those of "Powerhouse"; she is radiant as a skyrocket, and she has elevated traditional female domestic tasks—nursing people, clothing people, growing flowers—to the realm of art. Ida is seer and sibyl; her voice is "filled with invocation" and "she is inspired" (*Eye* 337). Eudora Welty responds to this personage with an acolyte's delight and wonder, grasping for terms that might capture Ida

M'Toy: "I used to think she must be, a little, the cross between a transcendentalist and a witch" (345). Like Jewett's narrator, bedazzled by Mrs. Todd, Welty mixes language with traditional literary-philosophical allusions with the specifically female mysteries of witchcraft—and acknowledges the inadequacy of all these terms to the phenomenon of Ida M'Toy. The used clothing business, which "could be grubby enough . . . in her handling . . . has become an affair of imagination and, to my notion, an expression of a whole attitude of life as integrated as an art or a philosophy" (340). Ida, grown old and reclusive, has achieved a synthesis of life and art as compelling as that of Cather's Jeanne Le Ber; Welty concludes, "I think she lives today the way she would rather be living, directly in symbols" (348).

In "A Pageant of Birds," Welty celebrates another black Jackson woman, Maude Thompson, who invented and organized an original church pageant of women, featuring "birds" in home-sewn costumes, in a bower of home-grown flowers, tapping women's traditional domestic tasks into a unique blaze of vision and imagination. Maude Thompson, like Ida M'Toy, seems to have some unique artist-priestess's closeness to the mysteries of death and life. Welty concludes, "Every time I would be getting on a train, I would see her in the station. She would be putting on a coffin, usually, or receiving one, in a church capacity. She would always tell me how the Pageant was doing. . . . 'This is going to be one of those things going to grow,' said Maude Thompson" (*Eye* 320).

These essays suggest that Eudora Welty is beginning to think of ways by which the world of domestic ritual feeds into the world of art, and about the kinds of female imagination that might effect such a fusion. Such questions continue to inform her second volume of stories, *The Wide Net* (1943). The title story features an expansive male quest-ritual, invoked by another pregnant, secretive (if playful) domestic priestess, whose point of view is unrevealed. But in two of this volume's finest stories, Welty switches to the viewpoint of a housekeeping woman. "Livvie," another story of extraordinary luminosity, contemplates a very young woman in her very old husband's house. At sixteen Livvie agreed to marry Solomon, honoring the power of patriarchy; "she said 'Yes, sir,' since he was an old man" (*Collected Stories* 228). Instead of a cyclical continuum of domestic rites, Solomon's house is absolutely isolated, built at the end of an untraveled road. Living there, Livvie has not seen her mother since her wedding day, years ago. Although Solomon is "good to" Livvie, "he kept her in the house. She had not thought that she could not get back" (228). Solomon's house is his final address; as Livvie tends him, he is dying of old age. The household arrangements, with their careful geometry,[2] reflect his sense of order and propriety, as do the much-discussed decorative bottle trees. The house, Solomon's "great monumental pyramid" (237–38), is literally a dead end. Livvie's housekeeping there is far from the exuberant expression of an Ida M'Toy; instead, it is a careful round of self-suppression: "Livvie knew she made a nice girl to wait on anybody. . . . She could keep from singing when she ironed . . . sit by a bed and fan away the flies . . . so still she could not hear herself breathe" (230). Watching Solomon sleep, Livvie scans the "beautiful" quilt, "'Trip Around the World,' which had twenty-one different colors, four hundred and forty pieces, and a thousand yards of thread, and that was what Solomon's mother made in her life and old age" (229). Is such meticulous domestic geometry, stitched to cover a sleeping man, what must become of a woman's life and time? The story's action, on the first day of spring, explores Livvie's unvoiced question.

On that day, the quiet order of Solomon's house is broken by two incursions; suddenly, the dead end is enlivened by plot. First comes Miss Baby Marie, a cosmetics saleswoman, enticing Livvie with the sweet smell and intense color of her first lipstick. For Livvie, the lipstick smells of chinaberry flowers, carrying her back home, where she envisions "her mama holding up her heavy apron . . . loaded with ripe figs . . . her papa holding a fish-pole over the pond . . . the little clear fishes swimming up to the brim" (234). In this sensuously remembered world of fecundity and motion, Livvie's parents are part of a continuum that refutes the stasis of Solomon's house. But the lipstick's promises of erotic escape and gratification cannot belong to Livvie, for she has no money. She tells Miss Baby Marie, "My husband, he keep the *money* . . . I wouldn't ever ask him for anything" (234). Livvie offers female, household coin: "Would you take eggs, lady?" But Baby Marie, in her little car, is after the male medium, cash; she says, "I have plenty of eggs" (235).

Then Livvie meets a field hand, the embodiment of male mobility and modernity. His *name* is Cash. In fine, gaudy clothes, he says, "I been to Natchez. . . . *I* taken a trip, I ready for Easter!" Livvie wonders, "How was it possible to look so fine before the harvest? Cash must have stolen the money, stolen it from Solomon" (236). He has subverted the feudal order, rooted in patriarchy and the seasons; *cash* means theft or credit, and immediate gratification. When he reaches for Livvie, she willingly kisses him.

Back in the house, they find Solomon dying, still clutching his treasured silver watch. He speaks, as Vande Kieft says, "with beautiful candor and dignity" (50), as he renounces his own hard-won position as a black patriarch, the "respect" he has "built up" through his life. Solomon has embodied old values of patriarchal culture: protection, prevention, and control. Marrying him, Livvie pledged to make her housekeeping an expression of his values. Solomon recognizes Cash as inevitable: "was no prevention," he says. In his last words, he breaks the rod of his power: "God forgive Solomon for carrying away too young girl for wife and keeping her away from her people and from all the young people would clamor for her back" (238–39). Then he hands her his silver watch. Livvie drops the watch as Cash seizes her, and she relaxes in his arms. But the watch still ticks, its sound countered by a bird's song. And Livvie herself is quiescent in Cash's embrace, "unprotesting as a bird on a nest" (239).

From the moment of Cash's appearance, Livvie has been wordless. She has only cried out Solomon's name, and wept steadily through his dying. As Solomon's heir, she now possesses his timepiece and his house. With Cash, she is also transformed into a sensuously, erotically eager woman, in an image that comes from nature but that is also domestic and maternal: the nesting bird. If Livvie is to spurn Solomon's patriarchal vision, which he himself finally saw as a violation, will she turn to Cash, allying herself with his values of immediacy, as expressed in his sexual arousal and his bright, cheap city clothes? Like the tempting lipstick, Cash's adornments are for the body, not the house.

When originally published, this story was titled "Livvie's Back." For book publication, Welty changed the title to "Livvie." The first title clearly implies that this young woman has been restored to life by the patriarch's death; the present title is truer to the story's full effect. For Welty's achievement is to evoke the import of Livvie's situation—to suggest what it may mean to live as Livvie. Solomon's house and watch and Livvie's aroused body are now hers, to live in, and the story buzzes with competing claims: patriarchy, propriety, cash, nature, sensuality. Livvie's mother is a powerful presence in the story; when Livvie has one rebellious thought about the constraints Solomon has imposed on her, she judges herself "cruel" and remembers, "her mother . . . had said one time, 'I rather a man be anything, than a woman be mean'" (232). Propelled by her mother's wisdom, which implies that men and women have separate moralities, Livvie turns back to her domestic ritual, painstakingly simmering a broth for Solomon. The matriarchal tradition, as Livvie has learned it, would keep Livvie housed— and yet her memory of her mother, apron full of ripe figs, suggests a much more fruitful model of domestic life than has been possible with Solomon. Eager, quiescent, and newly capable of "dazzling" herself, Livvie stands wordless at the brink of her life. To claim that life, she must choose or invent a language of her own.

"Livvie" is the penultimate story of *The Wide Net;* the last is "At the

Landing." It too shows a young woman cut asunder from patriarchy, at the edge of her life.[3] In "Livvie," the complexity of the protagonist's situation may not be at first apparent because of the elegant clarity with which the story is written and the dualistic opposition of Cash and Solomon. "At The Landing," by contrast, is written in a dreamily allusive, multiplicitous style about which Welty has expressed some reservations, telling an interviewer, "*That* has lots of faults to it; *that's* obscure. I was really trying to express something that I felt in that *place*. . . . It was magical to me. . . . Maybe I got carried away by my own words" (*Conversations* 190). The story seems to be launching itself toward the next major project of Welty's career: a full-scale novel, *Delta Wedding*.

Jenny Lockhart is another young woman who can scarcely speak. She lives in The Landing, a river town where houses are periodically flooded. Jenny's mother died mad, "torn" by a "wild desire" to leave and "get to Natchez" (*Collected Stories* 242). Jenny has grown up in her mother's prison-house, ruled by her benevolently despotic grandfather. Like Solomon's house, Jenny's home is a complexly ordered domestic space. The needle-point chair covers were worked in tiny duplicate stitches by her mother. Everything is hung with dancing prisms and the parlor is decorated with "her mother's two paintings, 'The Bird Fair' and 'The Massacre at Fort Rosalie'" (241), suggesting a heritage of violence and a dream of flight. As a girl, Jenny wanders this museum of mute idols: a domestic fantasy, white and wealthy Mississippi style. But she may not depart or exercise her will in any way. "She never performed any act, even a small one, for herself, she would not touch the prisms. It might seem that nothing began in her own heart" (243).

For a successful housekeeper like Mrs. Blackett of *The Country of the Pointed Firs*, domestic ritual becomes a medium for expressing what is generated in her heart; it becomes a medium of love. Jenny Lockhart, whose last name is her only legacy from her father, must begin by learning to love. The man she turns to is Billy Floyd, a wild fisherman who lives outdoors. Silently gazing and meditating while Billy rides a red horse for her wondering eyes, Jenny begins to know what a complex matter it is, to have a self and to love a self. "She walked in the woods . . . and knew about love, how it would have a different story in the world if it could lose the moral knowledge of a mystery that is in the other heart" (245).

Nearby, in the derelict Lockhart house, lives old Mag Lockhart, a wild, solitary albino who laughs and screams and is a match for Billy Floyd. In the despair of her new knowledge of love, Jenny imagines herself in Mag's well, descending "into the dark passage. But my grandfather, she thought even while she sank so deeply, will call me back. I will have to go back. He will ask me if I have put flowers on my mother's grave" (246). For Jenny, fantasies of death and birth are very close together; in the "dark passage," she has entered the territory of the energetic female survivor, Mag, also her relative. Like the Persephone who inhabited Welty's childhood imagination, Jenny thinks of a double life and a daughter's duty, here to the mother who died in the patriarchal house to which Jenny knows she must return, even from death.

When her grandfather dies, the elaborate house is Jenny's, and there is no one alive to call her back. When the flood comes, she follows Mag, leaving the house to the river. Then Billy Floyd takes her in his boat to "a little place he made that was dry and green and smelled good" (251). There he "violated her," built a fire and cooked meat and fish. Jenny, accustomed to dainty meals in her house, learns from Billy an elemental truth at the heart of domestic ritual: "that what people ate in the world was earth, river, wildness and litheness, fire and ashes. People took the fresh death and the hot fire into their mouths and got their own life" (252). When she shyly tells Billy her wish that they could be together in a "little house" (251), he does not answer. Nor does he speak when she vomits the wild food.

Jenny yearns to put together her new, elemental knowledge, to enact her wishes and her passion in the medium of a "little house." But Billy speaks no such language, and she returns alone to her muddy house, which waits "crouched like a child going backwards to the womb" (253). She suddenly finds herself caught up for the first time in "an ecstasy of cleaning. . . . as if driven. . . . she stretched and dried white curtains and sheets . . . and wiped the dark river from all the prisms, she forgot even love, to clean." This episode suggests the compulsive pull of housekeeping. But it is only tempo-rary; having known "the shock of love," Jenny can take no permanent refuge in the house. She is launched out of, not back into, the womb, and her mother's story is a warning; in "her mother's last room," Jenny "thought of her mother who was kept on guard there, who struggled unwearily and in all loneliness, and it was not a hiding place" (253).

In the town, three fatelike old women predict that Jenny will "follow her mother to her mother's grave," and they trim and stitch their fantasies and theories of Billy Floyd's unknown origins, "as if they could take his life up . . . with their sewing and sew it or snip it on their laps" (254). Their snipping is an ancient domestic metaphor of control, trimming people down to a predictable size that will fit in a house or a history. In her mother, Jenny saw the fruit of such confinement. And what is happening in herself is the very opposite of such cutting and confinement; it is multiplicitous expansion. Now "she herself was more people than there were in The Landing" (256).

So in luminous July, she leaves the town and travels to the river's edge, where fishermen and squatters live. There she asks for Billy Floyd, who is fishing the river. The men put her on an old houseboat and rape her, one after another. Her cries mingle with their "rude" laughter "and somehow both the harsh human sounds could easily have been heard as rejoicing, going out over the river in the dark night." Hearing those sounds from fireside, women slap their sons, "as if they knew that the original smile now crossed Jenny's face. . . . no matter what was done to her." One old woman asks after Jenny. "Is she asleep? Is she in a spell? Or is she dead?" The men reply, "She's waiting for Billy Floyd." The woman, in response, "nodded out to the flowing river, with the firelight following her face and showing its dignity. The younger boys separated and took their turns throwing knives with a dull *pit* at the tree" (258).

If this story is "obscure," as Welty has said, it is so because it carries an almost unbearable freight of meaning. Jenny brings her new awareness of food and fire and passion back to a house that she now has strength and will to make her own. But the history of women in her family and her place— the shutting up and the trimming down—cannot coexist with all she has learned of love. To leave The Landing and to launch her own plot and quest make Jenny a target and a victim and put her in an ancient female posture; like Penelope, she awaits a man's return. Even the boys' phallic knives, the story's last image, suggest repeated, ritualized violation. In one sense, this is a story of a girl of delicate sensibility who may or may not survive a gang rape.

In another, concurrent sense, the story's ending is about the indeterminate language of Jenny's situation and how it might be read. As an individual, she is almost lost ("asleep . . . in a spell . . . dead?"), and her protesting (?) cries *can* be heard as "rejoicing." The men repeat what they think is her, and a very old, female story: "She's waiting for Billy Floyd." The old woman, between the river and the fire, nods the acquiescence that is the source of her ancient "dignity." And the other women imagine on Jenny's face "the original smile"—by which this particular wandering girl becomes Eve and the beginning of all women's stories. The smile for them is a mark of self-possession and self-knowledge, stronger than anything "done to her." It puts them at odds with males, making them "cross" with their sons.

Jenny Lockhart's medium is what Welty has called the medium of art: "her life, her perishable life" (*Eye* 60). She has taken all her possibilities, all her human and female history, to the very edge of the river. Back in town,

Jenny was a story, a family, a house, and a whole round of female, domestic rituals that she could have continued—if she could have forgotten all she knew of and shared with her mother. At the nameless place by the river, Jenny has left the house behind. She seems to have entered the very realm of symbols, elemental with possibilities as old—and as new—as Eve's. She has become the story we make of her, taking us as far as we can know and imagine. With Jenny Lockhart's birth as a questing woman, Eudora Welty stretches the boundaries of abuse and possibility, houses and journeys, horror and love, further than we may choose or bear to go. Welty herself thought she might have been "carried away" in this story. "At The Landing," as ambitious and troubling as anything Welty ever wrote, takes us to the very edge of our wishes and fears for women's stories.

Welty's first full-scale novel, *Delta Wedding* (1946), may at first seem a retreat from the extremity of such stories as "At The Landing" and "Livvie," in which young women are propelled to the brink of danger and possibility, in the process turning their backs on containment, marriage, and house-keeping. In *Writing Beyond the Ending: Narrative Strategies of Twentieth-Century Women Writers,* Rachel Blau DuPlessis writes about problems of composition: "To compose a work is to negotiate with these questions: What stories can be told? How can plots be resolved? What is felt to be narratable by both literary and social conventions? Indeed, these are issues very acute to certain feminist critics and women writers, with their senses of the untold story, the other side of a well-known tale, the elements of women's existence that have never been revealed" (3). In the work between "Death of a Travelling Salesman" and "At The Landing," we see Welty wrestling with the questions DuPlessis states. In her first story, the tellable story was that of a man with a destination and a name. The housekeeping woman was something else; much of her power came from the fact that she would not be accommodated by the language of plot and resolution. In patriarchal Western culture, her situation has seldom been "felt to be narratable." Yet, as I have indicated, Welty's stories keep returning to that woman, whose "untold story" is the "other side" of Bowman's tale. Ul-timately, she probes closer and closer to "the elements of women's existence that have never been revealed," so close in a story like "At The Landing" that our reading must become an act of invention, based on what we believe or wish or fear about women's stories.

In nineteenth-century fiction by and about women, DuPlessis sees "a contradiction between love and quest," with "one main mode of resolution: an ending in which one part of that contradiction, usually quest . . . is set aside or repressed, whether by marriage [as in *Jane Eyre*] or by death [as in

The Awakening]" (3–4). The fictions of domestic ritual that this study examines are obviously part of a different female tradition. Few of these works find resolution in marriage *or* death. More typically, the home plot is somehow shaped by the rhythms of domestic ritual, and the perpetuation of those rhythms, as the adversary or the expression of full female consciousness, becomes the work of plot.

DuPlessis discusses writers who are Eudora Welty's contemporaries. Twentieth-century women writers, she says, have attempted "to solve the contradictions between love and quest and to replace the alternate endings in marriage and death that are their cultural legacy from nineteenth-century life and letters by offering a different set of choices. . . . a complex of narrative acts" that DuPlessis calls "writing beyond the ending" (4). Welty is and is not part of the project DuPlessis describes. "The contradiction between love and quest" *can* be real and deadly in her fiction; it is the cause of R. J. Bowman's death. When Jenny Lockhart heads for the river, she seems to perceive love *as* quest, an equation traditionally male. Then she falls into traditional female patterns, often expressed through a domestic medium: waiting, violation, and indeterminate language.

Forebears such as Jewett, Stowe, and Cather[4] offer Welty a set of contexts, precedents, and problems quite different from the precedents so usefully explored by DuPlessis. The very idea of "the ending" is in many ways antithetical to the repetition and cycles emphasized by domestic ritual. To write "beyond the ending" is to respond, however defiantly, to conventions of patriarchal culture, which have often been expressed in the medium of Aristotelean plot. Domestic ritual, as traditionally enacted by women, is something else, another medium. When co-opted by patriarchy, it can reduce a woman to voiceless effacement, like Livvie, tending Solomon's house. Or it can become a language of preservation, celebration, and art, in which unknown tongues find voice.

Welty's first attempt at longer fiction was her novella, *The Robber Bridegroom* (1942). This book, a sparkling romp through Mississippi folklore and early history, as well as Grimms' fairy tales, draws on the stories that *have* been told and have become cultural markers. It has a quest plot, which ends in marriage for the beautiful heroine, death for her voracious and unacquiescent stepmother; although the conventions of plot are handled with delighting mockery, they *are* observed and they *do* obtain. According to Welty, that book differed from all her other fiction, before or after: "it did not spring from the present-day world, from life I could see around me, from human activities I might run into every day" (*Eye* 300). *Delta Wedding*, the second novel, is another matter. Set in Welty's own lifetime, it presents the most predictable of events. A girl has decided to marry, and her family assembles at home, to prepare for and to enact her wedding. While *The Robber Bridegroom* offered all the ancient satisfactions of conventional plot, readers of *Delta Wedding* have always felt the absence of such satisfactions. An early reviewer, John Cournos, wrote, "Rich though Miss Welty is in the creation of background and characters, she does not seem to have any story to tell" (21).

To Welty's agent, Diarmuid Russell, it had seemed that the author had too *much* story for her usual form; when she sent him "The Delta Cousins," he returned it, suggesting she "go on with it" and write a novel (*Conversations* 180).[5] Expanded, the "unsalable" story (Kreyling, *Eudora Welty's Achievement of Order* 55) became an extraordinarily complicated and ambitious work of fiction. The points of view of seven women are interwoven, circling around complexly dramatized scenes, moments in the observance of a domestic wedding. Welty set the book in 1923, an "uneventful" year—no floods, wars, or other natural and economic disasters—because she wanted "to concentrate on the people without any undue outside influences" (*Conversations* 49–50). Thus she elected to eschew some of the most obvious armatures of plot and she eliminated crises, such as war, in which men might take a more traditionally central part. Welty's near-mythic view of the Delta—a place where she had visited briefly but never lived—was as a matriarchy. "Ever since the Civil War when the men were all gone," she told an interviewer, "the women began to take over everything. . . . I've met families up there where the women just ruled the roost" (*Conversations* 304).

In addition, *Delta Wedding* is the book in which Welty is most influenced by Virginia Woolf, especially by her favorite of Woolf's novels, *To the Lighthouse* (*Conversations* 524–25). Welty told an interviewer that, for her, Woolf was "the one who opened the door. When I first read *To the Lighthouse*, I felt, Heavens, *what is this?* I was so excited by the experience I couldn't sleep or eat. I've read it many times since" (*Conversations* 75). Woolf's great modernist novel brings together housekeeping, art, and female consciousness; as Mrs. Ramsey orchestrates her dinner party, she makes an accomplice of every girl and woman around her, including the undomestic painter, Lily Briscoe, whose art becomes an exploration of Mrs. Ramsey's ambiguous power. Although Welty has often written enthusiastically of her reading experiences, she has described nothing else that struck her with the disorienting force of Woolf's novel: "it just knocked me out" (*Conversations* 325). A passionate reader with a lifelong education in the predictabilities of plot,[6] Welty encountered in *To the Lighthouse* an exhilaratingly unclassifiable work. *To the Lighthouse* takes the ancient acts and mythology of housekeeping, as manipulated by a compelling, dangerous Angel in the House, and refracts them through the consciousness of a contemporary woman artist. Woolf invented a form—with a house at its center—that plays these women against each other, in a context of aggressively patriarchal values.

All these qualities, plus the fluidity of Woolf's style, must have given Eudora Welty some importantly generative cues about how domestic ritual might be at the center of a profoundly serious work of art. Louise Westling has provided a thorough and suggestive discussion of parallels between *To the Lighthouse* and *Delta Wedding;* she says that "only another woman could have helped Welty develop [this] celebration of distinctly feminine fertility and community" (65–93, 68).[7] In Woolf, Welty discovered a woman writer who joined traditions of domestic ritual with modernist experiments in the rendering of consciousness.

Woolf's influence, plus choices of plot, place, and point of view that emphasized female culture, put Welty in position to write her most ambitious exploration of female consciousness. Her novel eliminates the ordering, abstracting force of Lily Briscoe's painterly vision. Instead, Welty puts us in the midst of the female-centered rituals surrounding Dabney Fairchild's Delta wedding. All seven women through whom the novel's point of view is filtered are members of the Fairchild family by birth or marriage; each of them is somehow a member of the wedding. The "great" central house is Shellmound; its mistress is Ellen, who married Battle Fairchild; now she is pregnant with her ninth child. Her second child, Dabney, is the bride; Shelley, just graduated from college, is the oldest, and India is nine. Battle's sister, Tempe, oldest of the women whose points of view are explored, lives on a nearby plantation; Robbie, sister-in-law to Ellen and Tempe, is recently married to George, a Memphis lawyer, the youngest surviving Fairchild of his generation and the family idol. Laura, a nine-year-old cousin, is the daughter of a Fairchild sister, recently dead; she lives in Jackson with her father. These Fairchilds conceive of their family housekeeping in the widest possible sense. The plantation itself seems an extended household, dotted with family houses; even the nearby hamlet is named "Fairchilds," and in the store, any family member can claim anything.

Tempe, both aging belle and overseeing aunt and grandmother, thinks of men, at best, as women's accomplices. Her hierarchal vision of "paradise" is a clearly matriarchal place where "men, sweating under their hats like field hands, chopped out difficulties like the green grass and made room for the ladies to flower out and flourish like cotton" (188). Nothing about her niece's wedding escapes or surprises Tempe; for her, weddings are "an old story" (199). Full of advice, certainty, boasts, and domestic lore, Tempe is her own effective stage manager. Although she cooks only one item for the wedding feast, she talks so much of her task and surrounds it with such drama and ceremony that her brother, when fed one of her fabled cornucopias, says, "You're a genius, Tempe" (185). When a man, like Dabney's fiancé, Troy, proclaims *his* expertise or intuition, Tempe counters him readily, as in this exchange:

> "My nose itches," said Troy in the parlor. "Company's coming."
> "I'll tell you how to make the best mousse in the world," said Aunt Tempe.
> "How?" cried India.
> "Take a pair of Pinckney's [her husband's] old drawers." Aunt Tempe began to describe how she made gelatin. (150)

For Tempe, men are meant to serve the domestic enterprise, greeting her accomplishments with praise, providing the old drawers and other necessary materials for such wonders as "the best mousse in the world."

Westling, who provides the most insightful reading of *Delta Wedding* as a celebration of matriarchal values, sees Tempe as a comic version of the traditional "Southern lady [who] asserted herself by demanding the protective indulgence of her men" (79). Tempe is a one-woman parody of the nineteenth-century tradition of domestic faculty: Mrs. Todd, Sapphira Colbert, and Ántonia all rolled into one, Delta style. Yet she cannot be entirely dismissed as a comic convention. We learn from others that Pinckney of the useful drawers is "a terrible drinker"; Tempe herself never mentions that difficult fact. Her daughter is married to a Yankee whose red hair and crooked teeth mark Tempe's grandchildren. Obviously her domestic theatrics are a way to assert some control over forces that assail her powers. In another way, in the tradition of the belle, Tempe resists the domestic cycles; she shows no prospects of giving up her dancing to become a kitchen crone. Dabney fondly discerns that Aunt Tempe has "never put on her grown-up mind. . . . You never had to grow up if you were spoiled enough. It *was* comforting, if things turned out not to be what you expected" (*Delta Wedding* 185).

Delta Wedding catches the ambivalence of the 1920s—the years of Welty's own adolescence—toward the two most traditional forms women's power has taken: housekeeping and childbearing. The headstrong bride, Dabney, must puzzle out what such tradition might mean for her. Is her Aunt Tempe an idol and/or a joke? A model or a warning? Although Dabney can present herself as a very contemporary young woman, she obviously has not dismissed her girlish, "spoiled" aunt as a mentor; indeed, Aunt Tempe can always find a niece willing to heed her pronouncements, just as India listens raptly to her mousse recipe. As in Stowe, Freeman, and Jewett's nineteenth-century fiction, perpetuation of female culture by transmission to the young is a central issue in this book. This is especially problematic with the oldest Fairchild daughter, Shelley, who is *not* yet a bride.

Shelley is in many ways the most time-marked of the characters; she smokes Fatima cigarettes, wears King Tut sandals (a twenties' fad), and is trying to find the privacy, in the commotion of Shellmound, to read *The Beautiful and the Damned*. With her combination of privileged "spoiling" and nervous hypersensitivity, Shelley resembles women of American modernist fiction, such as Daisy Buchanan and Brett Ashley. While Dabney seems an archetypal figure, propelled by eager passion, Shelley is restlessly individual. She is the only Fairchild who shows any interest in reading and writing, and at a particularly hectic moment in the prewedding week, she closets herself to inscribe her own name on her trunk.

Kreyling calls Shelley "an intellectual," with "the coolness of intellectual inspection" (*Eudora Welty's Achievement of Order* 69). She appears to lack the typical Fairchild qualities—headlong and ardent, Fairchilds are "forever . . . opening doors, discovering things . . . running pell-mell down the stairs to meet people, ready to depart for vague and spontaneous occasions" (*Delta Wedding* 15). The Fairchilds all look alike; there is something collective about them. Shelley, eldest child, is presumably heir to all it can mean to be a Fairchild woman. But she is wary of this inheritance and of her own fertile physicality. Her mother worries that there is "something not quite *warm* about Shelley. . . . Could it have been her fault?" (212) *Warmth* seems to imply a willingness to surrender self, melting in the heat of family occasions. If Shelley lacks warmth, her mother imagines that the failure may be hers: a breakdown of the powers of domestic transmission.

While Dabney typically travels on horseback, a mode of travel with archaic and erotic associations, Shelley frequently drives a car, which allies her with speed and modernity. It is she most especially who puts Fairchild life in a wider context. For example, when a love potion is eaten by the wrong person, Shelley writes in her diary that the mixup is like something "in Shakespeare" (197). More than any other Fairchild woman, she has a sense of the temporality of Shellmound, of the quality that Welty has said is "implicit in the novel: that this was all such a fragile, temporary thing. . . . you're living in a very precarious world without knowing it, always" (*Conversations* 50). The night before the wedding, Shelley is nearly paralyzed by her anxious awareness of this precariousness; a large beetle on the screen, with threatening warlike, phallic horns, makes her "sickeningly afraid of life, life itself, afraid for life" (*Delta Wedding* 197).

The ritualized plantation life aims to nudge Shelley out of this fear—to get her eating cake, going to dances, eroticized (in the wedding party, Shelley alone is dressed in "flesh" color), and married. Shelley's cedar chest, itself a domestic icon, is packed with her graduation presents: hand-sewn lingerie for her marriage. One gown, stitched by unmarried Aunt Primrose, has "every edge picoted, and then embroidered all around with lover's knots: it was transparent" (83). Through the domestic ritual of laborious needle-work, Aunt Primrose and the others express their wish that Shelley will join the insular, woman-ruled plantation world, in the most complete and self-perpetuating way—through marriage (preferably to a Delta boy), mother-hood, and housekeeping.

When the overseer-groom is late for the wedding rehearsal, Shelley, sent to fetch him, blunders into worlds that *Delta Wedding* does not explore but that are always *present* in close and tense relation to the intimately rendered world of women's culture. In the plantation office, Troy is dealing with a dispute between male workers; he shoots the finger of a black man who aims a knife at him. The other black men, all bleeding, complain that the altercation was caused by a young black woman, Pinchy, who is "coming through" into womanhood (195). For Shelley, all this interrogates the myths of male power, so confusingly expressed in her own family, which venerates favorite uncles and believes that "it was the boys and men that defined that family always" (14), yet is clearly governed by women, who "rule the roost" and inherit the property (144–45). Troy's "performance" as overseer suggests to Shelley that all male behavior is merely replication of patriarchal conven-tions: "Suppose the behavior of all men was actually no more than this—imitation of other men. . . . Then all men could not know any too well what they were doing." Running back to the shelter of Shellmound, Shelley identifies more fully than before with the world of women: "Women, she was glad to think, did know a *little* better—though everything they knew they would have to keep to themselves . . . oh, forever!" (196)

Shelley will "never tell anybody" (196) what she saw in Troy's office, but through her, we are powerfully reminded of the male network of work, violence, sexual competition, and racial tension, which surrounds the plan-tation household. What women know "a *little* better" is an unspoken matter—a culture of secrecy and "gnosis," as Rabuzzi says (21)—which finds its expression and its perpetuation in the codes of domestic ritual. For example, when Dabney is sent to visit her maiden aunts to "tell" them of her engagement, she and India are (silently) surprised that aunts Primrose and Jim Allen never quiz her: "They're never going to ask Dabney the questions, India meditated" (48). The girls feel that they are visiting a shrine of female culture.[8] Both aunts are famous, ceremonious cooks. They generate kitchen texts; India finds Jim Allen "in the pantry, writing out in her beautiful script the watermelon-rind-preserve labels" (38). They also preserve the sacred texts of female forbears, with their lore and history; ancestral diaries and cookbooks are read, honored, and *used*. In the aunts' parlor, the two girls speak a language of physicality that the aunts obviously consider "not nice"; the culminating shock is Dabney's intentionally provocative announcement that she hopes to become pregnant immediately. The aunts, like all the Fairchild women, don't disapprove of such wishes; they just don't *speak* them. Instead, they express them through their domestic work and things. They ply their visitors with fresh cake and homemade ice cream, promise Dabney a needlepoint footstool and a cutting of the Seven Sisters rose, and present her with an heirloom nightlight because "it's company. . . . You'll find it a friendly little thing" (46). In their immaculate parlor, things and people are almost indistinguishable, and housekeeping, wreathed in mystique and elevated to a high art, is in danger of becoming a dead language. Daughterless, the aunts must keep that language alive by transmitting their treasure and their skill to the first Shellmound niece who marries.

Troy's mother, too, has domestic designs on Dabney. A Mississippi hill country woman, she expresses her priorities with her wedding gift, a stack of quilts. Troy bears them proudly and exultantly into the Shellmound parlor, boasting, "Look, 'Dove in the Window.' Where's everybody?" (112). Troy is a son well schooled by his mother; her housekeeping skills are a marvel to him, and he can recite all the quilts' names. His expectations for Dabney (who has indicated no aptitude for domesticity) are clear when he directs, "fold them nice, Dabney" (113). With the quilts comes Troy's mother's incantatory wish: "A pretty bride. To Miss Dabney Fairchild. The disappointment not to be sending a dozen or make a bride's quilt in the haste. But send you mine. A long life. Manly sons, loving daughters, God willing" (113).

The note invokes two legendary nineteenth-century domestic traditions: the twelve (or more) quilts with which a bride was expected to start housekeeping and the spectacularly celebratory "bride's quilt." Troy and seventeen-year-old Dabney, marrying with a scant two weeks' notice, have forestalled such rituals of preparation. But Mrs. Flavin has thrown her own emblematic quilts into the breech, to insure domestic continuity and perpetuation of gendered culture by "manly sons, loving daughters," as yet unborn. Dabney, reading the note, fastens on only one point: the reference to her prettiness. Her egotism blocks everything else, for the moment at least. But Dabney's mother and aunts read the language of the gift more comprehensively. Unlike the more genteel needlework Fairchild women practice—needlepoint, embroidery, lacework—the bright quilts speak frankly of the marriage bed and offspring. Their jumping colors, energetic traditional designs, and the openly sexual talk they evoke seem a reproach to effetely preservationist, "ladylike" domesticity, particularly that of the maiden aunts: "Aunt Primrose darted her little hand out, as if the quilt were hot and getting hotter. . . . the pattern shone and the ladies and Dabney all fluttered their eyelids as if the simple thing revolved while they held it" (113).

Through such domestic things as the nightlight and the quilts, *Delta Wedding* conveys all that lies ahead for a young woman entering a marriage, indicating the priorities that will compete for Dabney's loyalties and threaten her imperious egotism. In this novel, as ambitiously as any of her nineteenth-century forebears, Eudora Welty elaborates a complex domestic language. And even though the Fairchild men and Troy Flavin perpetuate a myth of male dominance, they all agree that housekeeping is a vocabulary that expresses their most cherished values. For example, the details of the prewedding entertaining matter immensely to Battle. Peremptorily, he orders refreshments: "You can't drink wine and not eat cake! . . . Look here. What kind of house is this?" When Ellen wearily calls for a cake, and "more plates, those little Dabney plates," Battle jealously demands, "Are those the best?" (183). He knows that plates and cake must speak his passionate concern for his marrying daughter and the honor of the house. But he relies on Ellen (and servants) to bear forth the cake and to establish the nuances of the language: only she can pronounce which plates are the "best."

To get past the reviewers' typical notion that *Delta Wedding* offers no "story," or that it is composed largely of "feminine nonsense" (Oates 54), requires mastery of the code of domestic nuance. If one knows it, then such an ordinary object as Troy's mother's quilt can vibrate with powerful import. And one can say, as Aunt Tempe does of Shellmound, which is an unexceptional country house occupied by an ordinary family, that, "Oh, there's always so much—so *much* happening here!" (190). One of the effects of Welty's narrative is extraordinary profusion. Something as apparently trivial as the transportation of the wedding cake from wagon to table becomes Event. Certain expectations and suspenses can be charted in terms of plot that have conventionally defined "story." Will Dabney's wish to marry, across class lines, in passionate haste, be sanctioned and civilized "in time" for Saturday's wedding? Will Robbie and George reconcile "in time" for the ceremony? Will the wedding trappings arrive from Memphis "in time"? Will Laura emerge from her mourning "in time" to join the wedding party? Such questions indicate how Welty uses the fictional alliance of time and plot in the way she described in "Some Notes on Time in Fiction," as "an instrument of pressure. Any novel's situation must constitute some version of a matter of life and death." The issues of growth and change, permanence and upheaval broached at Shellmound *are* matters of life and death; they express the central fictional questions as Welty formulated them in her essay: "What can a character come to know, of himself and others, by working through a given situation? This is what fiction asks, with an emotional urgency driving it all the way; and can he know it in time?" (*Eye* 166). The wedding date provides a marker of external urgency, which mirrors the internal urgency of each woman. Ellen, for example, carries the timely urgency both of her pregnancy and of her anxiety for her two eldest daughters, one marrying and one not.

As Welty writes, "time is plot's right arm" (165) in this novel. However, she does much to undercut the urgency of plot. The wedding ceremony is not elaborated; flowers, cake, and chicken salad get far more attention than the minister's pronouncements. The wedding itself is not the book's climax; the narrative continues three days longer, until after the newlyweds return, to indicate continuing problems of housekeeping. For example, on the morning after the wedding, Ellen discovers that her garden has been neglected dangerously in the wedding hubbub. She thinks, "What would happen to everything if she were not here to watch it?" (226). One of the most singular achievements of *Delta Wedding* is its sense of the intricate interlocking time involved in housekeeping. While Dabney's wedding finery is stitched, so must be Shelley's traveling clothes. While the cake is beaten, the flowers are wilting. And while all the women vie for private time to occupy the kitchen and prepare their own specialties, finally—at least momentarily—the collective domestic culture triumphs, and all the novel's adult women come together, on the wedding day: "Primrose was making the chicken salad . . . Ellen baking the beaten biscuit with Robbie (swallowed in a Fairchild apron) watching the pans, Tempe rolling out her cornucopias, and Roxie and Pinchy [black servants] squeezing the fruit for the punch all in the kitchen together" (207).

Against the linear sequence of plot, in which events are accomplished "in time," *Delta Wedding* plays a rhythm of circular repetition. Although it is intensified by the excitement of the wedding, this is the basic pulse of domestic life at Shellmound. The round of daily routine, of assembly around the abundant table and dispersal, has a hurtling energy. At the slightest provocation, the young people dance to that rhythm. For example, the arrival of the wedding dresses occasions an ecstatic dance, while a cousin endlessly pounds out "Country Gardens" on the piano. Such moments express the obliterating urgency of collective life and of sexuality. In each case, a girl or woman intuits the *danger* of that rhythm. For example, when the children stampede through the house in pursuit of a bird (omen of death) which has gotten inside, they defend the life of the family and the death of the individual (the female bird is injured in the fray). For Ellen, this is the moment of greatest distress in the novel; her sense of complexity and complicity becomes so great that, for the only time, she loses consciousness and faints.

Ellen's consciousness is the center of Shellmound and of Welty's novel. Without Tempe's preening faculty and Shelley's paralyzing fear, she is the housekeeper as reflective woman, always aware that her role is not a perfect fit. On the night before the wedding, in a scene that alludes to a classic moment of domestic transmission, Ellen entrusts her keys, emblem of a housekeeper's authority, to her eldest daughter, sending Shelley on an errand:

> "Take my keys."
> "Mama, they're the heaviest and most keys in the world."
> "I know it! Some of them are to things I'll never be able to think of or never will see again," said Ellen. (182)

All the complex and wearing tasks and skills of domestic tradition are symbolized by Ellen's weighty keys; she bequeaths them to Shelley accompanied by her doubts about their use and value. It is Ellen who most fully expresses the cyclical aesthetic that is the female governing principle of this novel. Later, riding across the plantation, she thinks: "The repeating fields, the repeating cycles of season and her own life—There was something in the monotony itself that was beautiful, rewarding—perhaps to what was womanly within her. No, she had never had time—much time at all, to contemplate . . . but she knew. . . . one moment was enough for you to know the greatest thing" (240). To be "womanly," Ellen thinks, is to shape a life that reflects these natural rhythms and contains *moments* of awareness that put one in touch with "the greatest things." Welty has structured the novel as a series of such moments, for each of the narrative's central women, set in a generative, protective network of domestic ritual.

That this formulation of "womanly" life comes from Ellen is especially interesting, for her own history does not express a linear mother-to-daughter transmission of domestic surety. For several crucial years of her childhood, Ellen was an abandoned daughter; her mother eloped with a lover. Later, although her mother was present for the ritual occasion of Ellen's first childbirth, both she and the attending male doctor incapacitated themselves in a comedy of errors during Ellen's labor, and Partheny, drawing on old female traditions of midwifery, delivered the child. The collective, continuing force of black and white women's culture, not the valorized mother, has been Ellen's most dependable support. At Dabney's wedding party, she recites the (comic) tale of Shelley's birth to a large audience, including her daughters, as if its implications are a necessary part of the wedding ritual.

When young Laura arrives at Shellmound for the wedding, only a few months after her mother's death, she is greeted by her aunt Ellen, "the mother of them all" (10). At the very threshold, Laura suddenly vomits, as if purging herself of the outside world, before entering the great family house of her mother and her aunt's welcoming embrace. Almost immediately, Laura is hungry again; she bites the lace of Ellen's collar and runs inside to claim a place at the dinner table. She longs for the cooking and rituals of Shellmound, which are set forth daily at the dinner table. Rabuzzi suggests that "every meal can be seen at one level as a sacrifice in which the bountiful mother is symbolically consumed through the food she proffers" (129). Laura's hunger is so intense that she literally bites her aunt's collar. That hunger involves more than just a desire for female nurturing, for she also wants to perform such nurturing herself. As she leaves Ellen's arms, she longs to pat her aunt's hair and soothe *her*.

However carefully Laura has been tended by her responsible father in Jackson, she enters Shellmound empty and voracious. Carving at the head of the table, Uncle Battle sends her a plate of turkey, saying, "How Annie Laurie [Laura's mother] would have loved this very plate! Breast, gizzard, and wing! Pass it, boy" (12). For Battle, Laura's care is a matter of feeding the daughter as her mother was fed, passing her the traditions, provender, and property of the family. But for Ellen, schooled in a domestic culture of which feeding is the central act, Laura's nourishment is a more subtle matter. She responds to Laura's wish to feed, as well as to be fed, and offers her the process as well as the products of domestic ritual. To her the motherless girl seems "skinny" and underfed, suffering from the deficiencies of male care. After dinner, Ellen summons Laura to help her make a cake.

The following passage is one of the extraordinary texts of American women's literature. As Ellen stirs up a traditional Fairchild cake, "Mashula's coconut," as made by a pioneer ancestor, Welty shows how the execution of a recipe can be a tradition, a tribute (to both the past and the future; the cake is being baked for tomorrow's guests), and a way of thinking. It is possible, if the reader has some experience with cooking, to bake a cake according to this passage; Ellen's thoughts, acts, and commands to Laura indicate the ingredients and processes. In terms suggested by Susan J. Leonardi, this recipe is an "embedded discourse" (340) and a rudimentary code by which a particular woman is celebrated and her memory kept alive. (It is notable that food—the plate of turkey—is the only way that Laura's elders can allow themselves to refer to Annie Laurie, for whom they still grieve.) Immortality, for a woman, has often been a matter of attaching her name to a domestic artifact or process that will survive her, such as a recipe. Welty wrote of this in "The Flavor of Jackson": "I daresay any fine recipe in Jackson could be attributed to a local lady, or her mother. . . . I make Mrs. Mosal's White Fruitcake every Christmas, having got it from my mother, who got it from Mrs. Mosal, and I often think that to make a friend's fine recipe is to celebrate her once more, and in that cheeriest, most aromatic of places to celebrate in, the home kitchen" (*Eye* 324).

Next day, when a slice of Ellen's cake is served to Tempe, she will identify it immediately: "Oh, Mashula's coconut!" (107), commemorating her kinswoman, for whom the production of such a rich, delicate cake must have been a strenuous feat, in Mississippi wilderness. Such celebration is a process that Welty has obviously kept alive in her own life as woman and writer.

Presumably, Laura will eat and someday bake Mashula's cake herself, and thus be reminded of how women can survive, as antidote to her mother's sudden, shocking death. As Ellen follows the recipe, she gives Laura occasional instructions. But for the most part she is silent, for what she is making, along with the cake, is her own peace. From her position at the center of her greatest domestic power, in the kitchen, Ellen faces equally formidable forces: sexual passion and individual will, as embodied in George's love for Robbie and Dabney's for Troy. Creaming butter and sugar, "she remembered, as if she vigorously worked the memory up out of the mixture" (25), a family picnic when George undressed Robbie in the river in a dazzling display of triumphant erotic energy, and then deposited Robbie in the aunts' garden, crushing "a bed of their darling sweet peas" (125).

The recipe itself—its alternation of tasks, its combination of contemplation of directions and skilled physical execution—becomes a medium for Ellen's most complex efforts at thought, on the subjects that concern her most. Tradition and change, passion and order, thrashing lovers and tended flowerbeds; all are accommodated. Making Mashula's cake, in the almost hypnotic state of reverie that a recipe can induce, Ellen has found a way to *think* as complexly as her sensibility and her culture will allow. "As Ellen put in the nutmeg and the grated lemon rind she diligently assumed George's happiness. . . . But—adding the milk, the egg whites, the flour, carefully and alternately as Mashula's recipe said—she could be diligent and still not be wholly sure—never wholly. She loved George too dearly herself to seek her knowledge of him through the family attitude, keen and subtle as that was—just as she loved Dabney too much to see her prospect without its risk, now family-deplored, around it, the happiness covered with danger" (26). Is the recipe embedded in the text, or is the text embedded in the recipe? They seem interchangeable here. Making a cake and instructing Laura establish Ellen in a continuum of female culture that enables her to think thoughts that endanger the continuum itself.

As the cake goes into the oven, Dabney appears in the kitchen. The conflicting forces in Ellen's mind are now physical presences in her kitchen. For a minute, Ellen sees radiant Dabney as the adversary to domestic continuity; " 'Smell my cake?' she challenged" her daughter. But Ellen is also subject to the powerful erotic charge of Dabney's beauty; it makes her dizzy, and she wonders, as the cake becomes a metaphor of Dabney's survival as a passionate and traditional woman, "was the cake going to turn out all right? She was always nervous about her cakes" (27).

The scene ends in a crescendo of female voices:

"*Don't* pound your poor finger, Laura."

"I wasn't going to, Aunt Ellen."

"Oh, Mother, am I beautiful—tonight?" Dabney asked urgently, almost painfully, as though she would run if she heard the answer.

Laura laid down the noisy pestle. Her lips parted. Dabney rushed across the kitchen and threw her arms tightly around her mother and clung to her.

Roxie, waiting on the porch, could be heard laughing, two high gentle notes out in the dark.

From an upper window India's voice came out on the soft air, chanting,

Star light,
Star bright,
First star I've seen tonight,
I wish I may, I wish I might,
Have the wish I wish tonight.

For a moment longer they all held still: India was wishing. (27)

In her kitchen, Ellen labors to feed the insistent hungers of motherless Laura and passionate Dabney; her "care" for them and the other family members stirs in her "like the child she carried" (26), suggesting a continuous cycle of need that fills Ellen's consciousness (and body) almost to bursting. Although the scene has been presented through Ellen's point of view, Welty now switches to a wider lens and an outsider's vision, as if some act of enlarging transmission is completed with the cake. Thus, we witness the embrace of mother and daughter. Outside, we hear more female sounds— the laugh from Roxie the cook, turned out of the kitchen where she is customarily ensconced so her white employer can indulge a whim to bake a cake, and India's ritual recitation, directed to the farthest thing she can see: a star. They all honor India's private wish. Indeed this is a scene that tries to honor the wishes and needs of each of the women, who have separate, rending desires, but who are also drawn to the kitchen, perfumed by Mashula's coconut cake.

This great scene, of course, recalls Mrs. Ramsey's dinner party in *To the Lighthouse*, in its richly nuanced mix of private reflection, communal occasion, and domestic care. The final effects of the two scenes are very different, however. Mrs. Ramsey's scene ends with a triumph of female, unspoken language over the male alphabet: "she had triumphed again. She had not said it: yet he knew" (186). An act of oblique communication between man and woman is completed. Welty's scene emphasizes instead the multiplicity of female discourse. Communion here is also wordless and employs domestic ritual as a primary medium, but it is among *women*. Elizabeth Kerr writes of "the notable absence of scenes between the mother and the seventeen-year-old bride" and Ellen's apparent lack of interest in Dabney (136). Dabney realizes that, as soon as she announced her engagement, she "and her mother had gone into shells of mutual contemplation—like two shy young girls meeting in a country of a strange language" (33). What is happening between Ellen and Dabney does not, I think, denote Ellen's disinterest; instead it indicates that, as Dabney approaches a new life of childbearing and housekeeping, she is entering a country where the language is not words, but the "mutual contemplation" that Laura and Ellen share as they make the cake. When Dabney rushes in, she questions her mother in words, but her demeanor makes it apparent that she does not want to be answered in words; it is "as though she would run if she heard the answer" (27). Dabney is still a neophyte at such communication—while practiced Aunt Tempe, by contrast, can telegraph her concern with only "a long look" (113), which Ellen knows just how to read.

With such looks, mutualities, and domestic rituals, Welty indicates the complex meanings within the women's world of *Delta Wedding*, and the uninitiated reader's response may be like Welty's own after first reading Woolf: "*What is this?*" In the earlier stories, Welty stopped short at the boundaries of this world; either her domestic women are seen entirely from outside (like the woman in "Death of a Travelling Salesman") or they are cut off from any communication with other housekeepers (like Livvie, Jenny Lockhart, and Ruby Fisher).[9] Diana Trilling's famous negative review of *Delta Wedding* expressed a common reaction; Trilling concluded that the earlier stories were in touch with "reality" but that *Delta Wedding* was a narcissistic retreat, in which Welty threatened to become "just another if more ingenious dreamer on the Southern past" (678). Obviously, Welty's singular efforts to render the consciousness of a group of largely conventional housekeeping women and girls are here considered a failure because such characters aren't an admissible part of *reality*.

Trilling finds the exclusivity of Shellmound morally repugnant (although the fact that Dabney chose a spouse of a different class, as did George, suggests that the Fairchilds aren't entirely exclusive). As critics have long noted, Welty encourages our awareness of the arbitrariness of Fairchild distinctions, throughout the novel. Her handling of black women characters is a telling example of this. Two powerful black women stalk the boundaries of Shellmound; one is Partheny, Dabney's old nurse, also a conjure woman of repute, who invests her domestic rituals with supernatural import. She bakes love potions into cakes and locates lost objects by divination. The other is Aunt Studney, an oblivious figure who carries a mysterious sack (the children think it is the place babies come from) and speaks only one line: "Ain't studyin' you." Young Pinchy, as she "comes through" into sexual and spiritual maturity, causes commotion in the world around her, much as Dabney is doing. These three black women, who embody domestic faculty, fertility, and the transition into womanhood, parallel the Fairchild women's female powers.[10] But the black women, seen through Fairchild eyes, are blown up to mythic, even supernatural dimensions, and (with one exception) the narrative never enters the consciousness of a black woman character. The parallels and exclusivities of these two sets of women, who occupy the same physical territory, inscribe and interrogate race relations in plantation Mississippi.

The cook Roxie is the most complexly presented of the black characters. She and Ellen, who share a kitchen, are both rivals and collaborators, and their relationship, minimally but suggestively rendered, indicates how domestic culture served as vocabulary for a problematic complex of female relations between white employers and black domestic workers.[11] For example, Roxie makes "belittling" comments to Ellen, and her laughter, from outside, adds an ironic note to the chorale that ends the cake-baking scene. In a single brief paragraph, Welty enters Roxie's point of view as she watches the family's alarm when Ellen faints. Her interior language is conventional, deferent, especially solicitous of "Poor Miss Ellen." When Roxie thinks of the unconscious Ellen, "Wasn't it pitiful to see her so white?" (167), the language suggests that she both sympathizes with Ellen, her domestic collaborator, and considers her weakness and momentary insensibility to be a mark of her whiteness. Such a moment provides a tiny glimpse of all that separates and unites white and black women.

On her way to visit Partheny, who is "in a spell" and has sent for her, Ellen glimpses a girl in the forest and assumes she is black, perhaps Pinchy. But she sees otherwise: "So she was white. A whole mystery of life opened up" (70). Although Fairchilds share space, sympathy, and work intimately with black servants, even the best of them identify full humanity—the "whole mystery of life"—with whiteness. Coming from gentle Ellen, the sentence has shocking import. The wandering white girl, delicately beautiful, is outside the web of domestic protection that surrounds Ellen and her daughters; Ellen thinks of her as "the lost girl," and though she fears for her, she does not attempt to capture her. All she can give the girl is an answer to her one question:

> "Which way is the big road, please ma'am?"
> "That way." Ellen pointed. . . . "Memphis," she said. . . . the name seemed to recede . . . into its legendary form, the old Delta synonym for pleasure, trouble, and shame. (72)

For Ellen, the girl seems to inhabit a realm of myth and legend, fraught with undomesticated danger and possibility, where the "pleasure" of a wandering woman is juxtaposed with "trouble and shame." When she tells George about seeing the girl, he says, "I took her over to the old Argyle gin and slept with her" (79). Ellen learns that the girl was killed by the Memphis train on Dabney's wedding day. A girl making her undomesticated way through the world is likely to become the tool or victim of male plots of desire or destination; even George, "the sweetest man in the Delta," who risked his life to save his mentally retarded niece from a train, can say of the lost girl without apology, "I took her. . . ." Joyce Carol Oates points to the similarity of this girl and Dabney, also Memphis-bound (Ellen thinks) for her honeymoon. "Why does society protect one and exclude the other. . . . Eudora Welty does not answer these questions, nor does she ask them: she causes them to be asked" (120). Although certain domestic moments in *Delta Wedding* are as enchanting as anything in American literature, Welty's constant evocation of such questions keeps this novel from being a nostalgic household romance and makes it a rich, troubling meditation.

Within the novel, no one meditates on Fairchild rituals more intently than two female outsiders, Robbie and Laura. The novel begins with Laura's journey to Fairchilds. On the train, the child is not particularly conscious of being a girl; she has a unisex Buster Brown haircut and sticks her ticket in her hat "in imitation of the drummer across the aisle" (4). But once at Shellmound, Laura is immediately, acutely aware of gender differences, as constructed by housekeeping prerogative; she thinks of her dress "in the suitcase, folded by her father, and for a man to fold anything suddenly nearly killed her" (9). Her adventures there make her more acutely aware of what it must mean to be a girl in the Delta; Aunt Ellen teaches her cake baking and puts her hair up in curls, her boy cousin Roy takes her on a journey of sexual discovery in the great house, Marmion, where Dabney will live,[12] and finally, when a cousin gets chicken pox, Laura is admitted to the wedding party after all, as a flower *girl*.

Laura's most cherished possession, which she carries "suspended" in her suitcase as if in a portable womb, is her doll, her memento of life as her mother's daughter, when female culture existed as the instrument of her instantaneous gratification. At an "inconvenient" moment, with a storm approaching, Laura demanded a new doll, and her mother, as if empowered to grant any wish, smiled and replied, "'Would you like a stocking doll?' And she began to turn things out of her basket, a shower of all kinds of colorful things." In this act of creation, fertility and domestic invention are joined, and the mother pulls out all the stops as she bends to her sewing:

> It was like a race between the creation of the doll and the bursting of the storm. . . . The sewing machine whirred as if it spoke to the whirring outside. "Oh, Mother, hurry!"
>
> "Just enough to stuff him!" She put every scrap in—every bright bit she had, all in one doll. (231–32)

Every step of the process is "like magic to watch" for Laura, and her mother finishes before the first raindrops fall. But her mood has changed, and Laura thinks, "Had she been, after all, tired? Had she wanted to do something else . . . something of her own? She spoke almost grudgingly, as if everything, everything in that whole day's fund of life had gone into the making of the doll" (232). As she remembers the doll's making, Laura is beginning to understand the exhilaration and surety a woman can feel, working full speed at the height of her domestic powers, managing to create something in a contest with the forces of nature. But now Laura also intuits the possible cost of such acts for an individual woman: her mother put all she had saved into the doll, including her time, which she might have wanted for herself. That the whole event was related to something in Annie Laurie's upbringing is suggested by the Fairchild name she gives the doll: "Marmion," the name of the house that will be Laura's maternal inheritance. Just approaching puberty, Laura preserves her doll as a reminder of the loss of her privileged childhood: "she could kiss his fragrant face and know, Never more would she have this, the instant answer to a wish, for her mother was dead" (235).

If Laura were to remain with her Delta family, as they invite her to, she would commit herself to accepting a feminine Fairchild version of her life. Although Laura's father seems nearly effaced in the rhythms of Shellmound, the girl thinks silently, "in the end she would go—go from all this, go back to her father" (237). Life with him offers journeys, linear extension, knowledge of a wider world, which Laura identifies with her paternal heritage. She tells her cousins, " 'My papa has taken me on trips—I know about geography. . . . ' But in the great confines of Shellmound, no one listened" (240). The plantation, both great and confining, will not heed the traveler's voice and wisdom; life at Shellmound is always a round trip.

The other Fairchild outsider is Robbie, recently married to George Fairchild. George is precious to his female relatives because he has managed to live passionately and fully without denying his allegiance to the family or trimming his selfhood to fit a Fairchild pattern. When Dabney and Shelley are trying to invent adult lives for themselves, they both imagine themselves "much like George" (220); none of the Fairchild women offers them such a capacious vision of possibility.

But Robbie is infuriated by her husband's Fairchild loyalties; when he risks his life to save a niece from an oncoming train, it is the last straw, and she leaves him. Robbie resembles the postlapsarian American women Donovan describes in *After the Fall*, in her commitment to a marriage based in an all-consuming heterosexual romantic alliance. Coming from a lower social class, Robbie at first emulates the Fairchild domestic mode, patterning her Memphis apartment after Tempe's parlor. But she turned instead to contemporary popular culture, romantic movies, for precedents of interior decoration. While the Shellmound furniture is a family inheritance, encrusted with legend, Robbie's parlor furniture is matched, anonymous, and shiningly new. Everything is arranged for immediate, sybaritic gratification; Robbie likes to bite the golden tassels on her silky pillows. As the haremlike imagery suggests, she has chosen a patriarchal marriage over the Shellmound version of matriarchy; to her, Fairchild women "always ruled the roost, and Robbie believed . . . that men should rule the roost" (144).

Robbie, who hungers for "veracity" (149), is also a very contemporary young woman. She is married to a returned veteran and is a member of the first generation of American women to vote. She embodies contradictions of the neoconservative "new woman" of the 1920s. In another sense, she attempts to revise gender roles; when she leaves George, she throws pots and pans out the window, wrecks the car, and returns alone on foot, traveling as Fairchild women are forbidden to do. (When George hears this, he says, "I ought to whip you all the way home" [169].) At the novel's end, George talks of returning to the plantation to live. For Robbie, who may be pregnant, a return would necessitate facing down the portrait of the Fairchild great-grandmother: "Once more she and Mary Shannon would be looking at each other in that house. Things almost never happened, almost never could be, for one time only! They went back again . . . started over . . ." (244).

Wherever she is, Robbie's future, as George's wife, will require her to confront Fairchild female culture. As she thinks of repetitions, she seems already to have grasped its central principle, assuming Ellen's "womanly" cyclical vision and perpetuating it into a modernist present. Laura finally shares that vision too; she says, "My secret is . . . I've been in Marmion afore ye. I've seen it all afore. It's all happened afore" (241). The novel's last image is of Laura, standing at the river's edge, facing her family, watching a falling star. " 'I saw it where it fell,' said Laura, bragging and in reassurance. She turned again to them, both arms held out to the radiant night" (247). The family, the river, the stars: all lie before her. Within her, whatever her future, is the knowledge she shares with Fairchild women: "It's all happened afore." Like Jenny Lockhart or Livvie, Laura stands at the far edge of this novel, an almost mythic figure, momentarily magnified and vaunting with bold gestures that characterize Welty's male heroes. Her figure, set against the Fairchild female rhythm, epitomizes the novel. It is only "one moment," but—as Ellen has thought—"One moment was enough to know the greatest thing."

By the rhythms of *Delta Wedding*, Welty evokes Ellen Fairchild's reflection about her life: it is both *monotonous* and *beautiful*. And she evokes, too, the fragility of Shellmound housekeeping: the constant internal stresses and suppressions that women "have to keep to themselves." Elderly Aunt Mac, for example, chafes at such restrictions. A shrewd, capable woman with a talent for managing, she asserts her desire for control over the family business by subjecting it to her domestic authority; she washes and irons the payroll bills for the cotton plantation. Her senile sister, Aunt Shannon, refuses to eat and hides food in her room, imagining marauders and privations like those of Reconstruction times. When Battle tries to reassure her, she mistakes him for his dead brother and says, "My little old boy . . . Oh, you have a great deal to learn. . . . I wish you wouldn't go out in the world unshielded and unprotected as you are. I have a feeling . . . something will happen to you." Although Battle protests, "I'll stay. I'm here," Aunt Shannon replies, "Goodbye, my darling" (238). Aunt Shannon believes that the house is the only safe place, which men (who have "a great deal to learn") insist on leaving—imperiling themselves and shattering the mythical safety of the women who love them. Aunt Shannon and Aunt Mac, whose eccentricity hovers near madness, express intensified versions of attitudes all the Fairchild women share. Shellmound is ringed with madwomen—including the dead brother's defiant wife, who will "have none of" her Fairchild in-laws. Her daughter, retarded Maureen, lives with Battle and Ellen's family and brings an alarming capacity for violence to the children's games and rituals (a capacity implicit in all the children). Laura notes, "Maureen was a circle breaker. . . . she liked to change a circle into 'Crack the Whip'" (73).

Through all these women, *Delta Wedding* expresses the *cost*, as well as the beauties and the strengths, of domestic culture. Ellen, who is mistress of Shellmound and thus deeply implicated in its housekeeping, comprehends this most fully. She understands the felicity of her household as a constant series of narrowly averted disasters, of overlapping contingencies: "The Yellow Dog [local train] had not run down George and Maureen; Robbie had not stayed away too long; Battle had not driven Troy out of the Delta; no one realized Aunt Shannon was out of her mind; even Laura had not yet cried for her mother. For a little while it was a charmed life" (166).

In her next book, *The Golden Apples* (1949), Eudora Welty put many of the constraints of *Delta Wedding* behind her. In this unclassifiable book—a group of seven linked stories, which form a larger narrative but can also stand independently—she claims new freedom to move about in time, space, and gender. *The Golden Apples* may be Welty's best book; it is her own favorite, and she remembers the joy of working on it as "the time when I went through the most intense, sustained writing. . . . These stories were revealing themselves as interrelated. I wasn't quite sure in what way. . . . Halfway through I realized the big connection there, the deep connections. But I was writing without stop, going from one story to the other, a sustained burst. It was writing something as long as a novel but as stories. Also I was very happy writing that book. I loved working on those stories. I love that period" (*Conversations* 326).

Welty's ardent description suggests an artist working at the peak of her powers, someone who has gone beyond rote replication of a recipe and is claiming the authority to recognize a new order as it emerges from her unconscious. As with *The Country of the Pointed Firs,* there is continuing controversy over the form of this book; for example, a fine recent critic, Patricia Yaeger, calls it a novel, although Welty does not.[13] One of the ways in which this book is receptive to domestic culture is in its willingness to discover form in process. Welty's repetition of smaller units (the stories) is reminiscent of the adjustments, juxtapositions, and other aesthetic discoveries and decisions that a seamstress might make assembling the blocks of a quilt. In a 1980 interview, Welty indicated that the process of assembling *The Golden Apples* was still on her mind, more than thirty years later. She wondered about "one story ["Music from Spain"] I wasn't sure belonged. . . . I thought it was all right as a story; I just wasn't sure if its proportion was correct or its placing was correct in the context of *The Golden Apples*" (*Conversations* 285–86).

The Golden Apples, set in the small town of Morgana, Mississippi, has at its center a housekeeping woman, married to a wandering man. They evoke myth, legend, and fairy tale; such allusions pervade the book and have been much discussed by critics. In this archetypal marriage, the wife, Snowdie, is an albino; she *must* stay in the house, for light hurts her pale skin and weak eyes. As a bride, "all in white . . . she was whiter than your dreams" and "as sweet and gentle as you find them." Married, "she stayed home and cooked and kept house" (*Collected Stories* 264–65). Her husband, compelling as Zeus and footloose as Odysseus, is King MacLain, who comes and (mostly) goes, unpredictably, slipping in and out of multiple identities. His sexual prowess and potency are legendary in Morgana. Yet he fears what his wife and other women routinely deal with: the constant responsibilities of housekeeping and child care. When he returns to Snowdie on one occasion, after years of absence, he is greeted by his rambunctious twin sons (whom he has never seen). Dressed in Halloween costumes, roller skates, and the basted pajamas their mother is sewing for them, they so thoroughly frighten their father with their din and energy that he turns tail and runs, for another years-long absence.

Although Welty tries out many point-of-view strategies—first and third persons and various combinations of male and female viewpoints—in these stories, she never enters the consciousness of either King or Snowdie MacLain. Instead, the stories circle around them, meditating the enduring mysteries of their legend and twining it with another central and unplumbed character, Snowdie's lodger, German-born music teacher Miss Eckhart. Miss Eckhart evokes the passionate possibilities of an unclassifiable outsider-artist; in a "studio" hung with engravings of Perseus and Circe, she gives piano lessons to local girls. At the book's center, in its longest and most ambitious story, "June Recital" (the story that Welty called her favorite because writing it gave her the most "personal pleasure" [*Conversations* 285]), is the house that Snowdie and Miss Eckhart, the housekeeper and the artist, share. Their conjunction raises questions and echoes that pervade this endlessly suggestive book.

The Golden Apples is framed by a housekeeping woman, Katie Rainey; the first story, "Shower of Gold," is her monologue, and the last, "The Wanderers," is the story of her death, her funeral, and her daughter. Katie lives, with her husband, son, and daughter, Virgie, at the edge of Morgana and at the outer border of its white middle class; with energy and wit, she has invented a life in which housekeeping and the traditions of women's culture are medium and fulfillment. She crochets, grows and preserves fruit, and keeps cows, selling her butter and vending ice cream "at speakings." When King MacLain, who may have been her lover, asks her what she "would rather have than anything," she asked for—and he provided—"a swivel chair, so I can sit out front and sell crochet and peaches" (443–44). Sewing, gardening, cooking, childrearing—Kate practices all the domestic skills, but unlike Snowdie, the sequestered white queen, she takes those skills outside the house and sells her wares, sitting in her swivel chair facing the road where she can "see Passing." Unlike Snowdie and many of the housekeeping women in American fiction, Katie Rainey has a voice, lively and confident. At the male-dominated evenings of music and politics, "in the soft parts of *Carmen* or before the story in *William Tell*—even during dramatic pauses in the speaking, Mrs. Ice Cream Rainey's voice could be heard quickly calling, 'Ice cream?'" (297). And she advertises in the *Market Bulletin*, the newspaper in which countrywomen broadcast their domestic wares.

Like one of Stowe's omnicompetent New England housekeepers, Kate Rainey is an exemplum of faculty and hardwon pride; her housekeeping language is broadcast and becomes a part of the life of the town. To small children, she is a domestic institution; "they took her for granted like the lady on the Old Dutch Cleanser can" (428). Dying, she catalogs her achievements, as itemized in her *Market Bulletin* advertisement:

> Purple althea cuttings, true box, four colors of cannas for 15¢, moonvine seed by the teaspoonful, green and purple jew. Roses: big white rose, little thorn rose, beauty-red sister rose. . . . [This catalog continues for half a page.]
>
> And when Mama is gone, almost gone now, she meditated, I can tack on to my ad: the quilts. Road to Dublin, Starry Sky, Strange Spider Web, Hands All Around, Double Wedding Ring. Mama's rich in quilts, child. (431)

At the climax of her life, with her last consciousness, Katie Rainey summons up her feats of gardening and housekeeping, in a triumphant catalog of domestic details. The quilt names, evoking traditions of women's art, are the "riches" Katie has to bequeath.

She thinks of her daughter, Virgie, who is with her as she dies, imagining that Virgie is planning to marry. But, in her last thought, she realizes her error: "Mistake. Never Virgie at all. It was me, the bride—with more than they guessed. Why Virgie, go away, it was me" (431). Dying, Katie Rainey claims the central role in her completed life. That life is a feat of domestic invention: in her faculty and in the traditional resources of women's culture, Katie Rainey found the vocabulary of a rich life. Yet even she dies with a dim sense that some part of her went unexpressed, that she could not be fully known and valued in the terms Morgana allowed. Within her, there was "more than they guessed."

Although they share a house, and love, Katie and Virgie Rainey do not share their thoughts; Virgie kneels silently fanning her mother while Katie silently dies. It is the familiar things of her mother's bedroom that bring Virgie to awareness of Katie's death, things such as "the warm and knotty medallions of the familiar [crocheted] counterpane—the overworked, inherited, and personal pattern—from which her mother's black shoes now pointed up." Nearby, "the window was full of pressing flowers and leaves in heavy light, like a jar of figs in syrup held up" (431). Virgie's understanding of her mother is expressed in the way she sees things, as if Katie's housekeeping vision has been transmitted to her daughter, so that the light itself is seen in terms of a domestic product—a jar of preserves—and the bedspread spells out Virgie's sense of her mother's life: "the overworked, inherited, and personal pattern."

What does a daughter do with such an inheritance? How does a housekeeper's daughter claim her own life? Especially if that daughter has the nerve and voracious passion that could make her an artist? Such questions are at the center of *The Golden Apples*, clustering around the piano teacher, Miss Eckhart. She introduces little girls to another vocabulary of practice, discipline, and passion. Headstrong Virgie is her prize pupil, the only girl with "a gift."

At first, Miss Eckhart seems the antithesis of the girls' mothers, domestic virtuosos all; she is clumsy and heavy, does not know or observe the ritual nuances of Morgana life, and has an alien language (German), strange recipes, and an unknown religion (Lutheran). Yet she too is a housekeeper, sharing her apartment with an old, crippled mother. Welty states in her autobiography that, more than with any other of her characters, she feels a

special connection with Miss Eckhart. Despite the lack of outward resem-
blances, Welty says, "Miss Eckhart came from me. . . . What animates me
and possesses me is what drives Miss Eckhart, the love of her art and the
love of giving it, the desire to give it until there is no more left" (*Beginnings*
101).

In interviews, Welty has again and again resisted links between her
gender and her art. She said in 1972, after praising several "great" women
writers, "I'm not interested in any kind of a feminine repartee. I don't care
what sex people are when they write. I just want the result to be a good
book" (*Conversations* 54). But *One Writer's Beginnings*, published in 1984, is a
more complex and telling story of a female, and often feminine, education.[14]
When she identifies herself with Miss Eckhart, she chooses a character who
does not see her music in *opposition* to the domestic culture practiced by
Morgana women, but as something that coexists with domestic ritual.
When Alice Walker asked Welty in 1972 if she regretted not having a
marriage and children, Welty replied that she "would have been glad if it
had come along. . . . It wasn't a matter of choosing one thing in place of the
other. I think the more things the better" (*Conversations* 136). This phrase
also seems to express the aesthetic of *The Golden Apples:* "the more things
the better."

Welty never enters Miss Eckhart's point of view, yet she says that "what
the story 'June Recital' most acutely shows the reader lies in her inner life"
(*Beginnings* 101). The annual recital, remembered raptly by teenaged Cassie
Morrison, one of the participants, was Miss Eckhart's entree into the
domestic culture of Morgana women, and her fullest expression. With the
music at its center, this ritual combines hospitality, sewing, cooking, and
decoration. For example, "Miss Eckhart decided . . . what color each child
should wear, with what color sash and hair ribbon, and sent written word to
the mother. She explained to the children that it was important which color
followed which. 'Think of God's rainbow and its order,' and she would
shake her pencil in abrupt little beats in an arch overhead" (309). To
Miss Eckhart it all matters; in her instructions to her pupils, we cannot
distinguish between dressmaking, metaphysics, and art. The recital ends
in "'Punch and *kuchen!*' . . . the little cakes that Miss Eckhart tirelessly
brought out were sweet, light, and warm" (314). Presiding over all this, Miss
Eckhart to the children's eyes resembles Circe, "on the fourth grade wall
feeding her swine" (314). Like that islanded sorceress, Miss Eckhart's magic
is inseparable from her housekeeping.

Attended only by mothers, daughters, and Virgie Rainey's father, the
recital is very much a female ritual. It is "better than school's being let

out . . . or the opening political fireworks"—both events that include or are dominated by males. "Both dread and delight were to come down on little girls on that special night, when only certain sashes and certain flowers could possibly belong, and with only smart, pretty little girls to carry things out" (311). All the delicious possibilities of discovery and confirmation are epitomized on this night, as well as the pitiless exclusions of class, race, and gender, which are inherent in the occasion. "The recital celebrated June" (311), the moment in the seasonal cycle when fruit begins to form. In a sense, it celebrates puberty, too; the moment when girls begin to claim their full inheritance as women. These possibilities are epitomized by Virgie Rainey, remembered by timid Cassie Morrison on the recital night when she "was most wonderful in her life." She wore "a red sash drawn around under the arms of a starched white swiss dress. She was thirteen. She played the *Fantasia on Beethoven's Ruins of Athens,* and when she finished and got up and made her bow, the red of the sash was all over the front of her waist, she was wet and stained as if she had been stabbed in the heart, and a delicious and enviable sweat ran down from her forehead and cheeks and she licked it with her tongue" (313).

To Cassie, the "wonderful" thing about this moment is that Virgie, at the traditional age for menarche, found a way to make her passion visible and audible, in the full vocabulary of her culture, utilizing everything from organdy to Beethoven to the fluids of her own body, blood and sweat. Yaeger, commenting on this passage in comparison with Welty's description of Miss Eckhart sweating in her dense brown recital dress, says that "images of licking, of violence, of delirium bind child and woman together and reveal the price both must pay for their art. . . . Miss Eckhart loses her pupils and Virgie her inspiration" ("Dialogic Imagination" 966). Yaeger emphasizes the undeniably dark portent of Virgie's "wonderful" moment. Virgie strains to experience as fully, and on as many levels, as humanly possible, sometimes straining beyond human capacity; she is the embodiment of "the more the better." Cassie identifies the danger in Virgie's passion, like being "stabbed in the heart." In this female rite, the blood red on white organdy evokes menstruation, first intercourse, and entry into sexual life, as well. The June recital is a ritual with all the stops pulled out, utilizing the vocabulary of domestic ritual but not confined to it. Virgie Rainey, of the girls, is the one best suited to act out all its expanded meanings; "recital night was Virgie's night" (313).

In contrast to the recital, the sanctioned domestic rituals of *The Golden Apples* often seem constricted. For example, Cassie's mother, coming home from a ladies' Rook party, recites the menu; it includes such items as "a sweet peach pickle with flower petals around it of different-colored cream cheese" and a cream puff swan. Ending her recital, "she sighed abruptly" (328). Yaeger reads this speech as a "parable about the permissible range of feminine creativity" in Morgana ("Dialogic imagination" 965). Restricted to a domestic vocabulary, the hostess (recalling some of the more effete conventions of embroidery, another domestic art)[15] produces a decadently over-elaborate meal, neglecting the primary function of food, to nourish. Welty later described such ostentatious menus in her Jackson cookbook foreword; she says, "Party food drew its praises for how pretty it was . . . or for how much trouble the hostess went to to make it" (*Eye* 322). Party food is a medium by which women solicit confirmation of their domestic artistry from the only audience discerning enough to judge: other housekeeping women. Such menus are a far cry from the substantial fare served by earlier house-keepers such as Mrs. Todd, Ántonia, or Cécile Auclair; even the solitary meals of Freeman's New England nun were satisfying in their substance as well as their art. In *The Golden Apples,* published when she was forty and entering her own full artistic maturity, Welty is impatient with the limits of domestic ritual as sole medium of women's art. "Gay and flighty" Mrs. Morrison, who recites the menu, had wished to be a musician; later, without explanation, she commits suicide, offstage. Compared to the Rook party, Miss Eckhart's recital offers nourishment, passion, discipline, and grace, subsuming domestic ritual in its larger art. In fact, Welty in *One Writer's Beginnings* wrote of the recital as a model for her own art in *The Golden Apples*: "What I had done in connecting all the stories in *The Golden Apples,* and bringing them off as one, was not too unlike the June recital itself" (101).

In one of her earliest critical essays, "The Reading and Writing of Short Stories," also published in 1949, Welty uses a domestic vocabulary to explore the very process of fiction writing: "I think we write stories in the ultimate hope of communication, but so do we make jelly in that hope. . . . We hope somebody will taste our jelly and eat it with even more pleasure than it deserves and ask for another helping—no more can we hope for in writing a story. . . . we do everything out of the energy of some form of love or desire to please. The writing of a story uses the *power* of this love or hope, of course, and not its simple, surface form such as comes out—rather nicely—in jelly-making" (54). Margaret Jones Bolsterli has noted that, in this important and deeply serious passage, Welty's choice of jelly making as metaphor for the art of fiction "is the kind of imagery one might expect from an author whose creative imagination encompasses both art and household tasks" (151). Such language honors housekeeping by admitting it to the arena of public discourse; this essay was published in *Atlantic Monthly* for a mass audience. But the wrenching questions about housekeeping, art, and gender that surface in *The Golden Apples* are present here, too, for Welty insists that jelly making (in which *form* and holding a shape are very important) is a matter of "simple, surface form," which at best can turn out "nicely." Story-writing, Welty's chosen art, goes inside that form; it taps into the original creative impulse. Such distinctions—unlike Welty's earlier veneration of Ida M'Toy, whose art had domestic origins—suggest a woman artist very aware of the danger that the traditions of domestic culture pose, for her art.

Snowdie MacLain is Miss Eckhart's collaborator in the June recital—she lends her dishes, her parlor, and her legitimizing presence. But when Snowdie must move from her house, Miss Eckhart, who has lost her pupils by now, is left homeless; eventually she ends up destitute at the county poorhouse. In "June Recital," she returns to the scene of her recitals. In a sequence of ritualized preparations that both mock and replicate the decorating of her "studio" for the festive recitals, she festoons the same room, and her own piano, with fire-starting streamers, preparing to burn the house down. Bereft of all but her central resources—will and passion—Miss Eckhart turns her powers to destruction. Although she manages to kindle fire, she is stopped before the house is damaged by the bungling male constable, who marches her off to jail and eventually to the state hospital for the insane.

Yeats's "Song of Wandering Aengus" provides the title of *The Golden Apples* and a line that ends "June Recital," waking the sleeping Cassie Morrison: "Because a fire was in my head." In a process explored by Yaeger in her important essay, that line is transferred by Welty from Yeats's male narrator to female consciousness. What does it mean, when a woman carries a fire in her mind?

In Miss Eckhart's case, we see only the external signs of that inner fire—in her thwarted mourning for a man she loved, her survival of a violent rape, her dramatic quarrels with her mother, the power with which she plays a Beethoven sonata, her unstinting efforts to nurture Virgie's musical gifts, and, of course, the recital itself. We cannot know why she returns to burn her old house—is it out of anger at a world that denied her passion? Is it an act of vengeance at sixteen-year-old Virgie, who ended her lessons years before and is, at that very moment, making love with a sailor in an upstairs room of the abandoned house? Or is it an attempt to replicate, once more, the recital evenings when she was closest to triumph? As she weaves newspaper streamers and makes a nest of green boughs in her piano, it becomes apparent that the domestic trappings of her recital were crucially important. The first mark and problem of civilization, according to our mythology of prehistory, was fire: how to use it, how to contain it. Hestia's hearth fire has long been the central emblem of domestic life; "Death of a Travelling Salesman" tapped these archetypal implications. Miss Eckhart, in her last years, has taken fire as her medium; as Welty wrote of Ida M'Toy, Miss Eckhart too seems to live "directly in symbols" (348). When the men find her, practicing her incendiary art, they march her off to lifelong incarceration. "Do you place her?" the constable asks his companion. "Who's this here firebug?" (321). In the hierarchy of Morgana, Miss Eckhart has become that most dangerous creature, a woman who will not restrict her powers to tending and containing the hearth fire. There is no "place" for such a woman, and in the eyes of the men (who are joined by King MacLain), she has lost both name and gender; she is only "this here firebug." Pariah, Miss Eckhart embodies the extraordinary dangers for a Morgana woman who does not confine herself to housekeeping.

As Miss Eckhart is hauled away to jail, she is watched by sixteen-year-old Cassie, from her window next door. Point of view in this story emphasizes gender differences, alternating between Cassie and her venturesome brother, Loch. When Cassie recognizes her old piano teacher, she rushes outside, "running barefooted down the front walk in her petticoat and in full awareness turned toward town, crying, 'You can't take her! Miss Eckhart'" (324). Timid and conventional as she is, Cassie recognizes something in Miss Eckhart that must be saved, and by women; she cries out against the town's legal, official hierarchy, embodied by the two bungling men, protesting their authority: "you can't take her. . . ." For Cassie, this is an act of daring impropriety and exposure. Helpless to prevent Miss Eckhart's arrest, she calls out despairingly for female power: "Oh, Mother!"

Yet, when Miss Eckhart was in her full power a few years earlier, Cassie was unwilling to recognize her range. Once she heard her teacher play Beethoven "with unstilled persistence, insolence, violence" (302). As with her images of Virgie's recital performance, Cassie associates Miss Eckhart's performance with blood: "she had been pricked and the music came like the red blood under the scab of a forgotten fall" (301). The pricking suggests the fairy tale imagery of blood associated with female sexual maturing; it indicates how easily a woman may be opened up to her deepest and most dangerous levels of feeling, symbolized again by a body fluid. And the "forgotten fall" suggests that all the human history of feeling and loss is somehow epitomized in every person; art is a way to tap into it. What Miss Eckhart has to teach her girl pupils is the bottomless complexity of being human: "that there was more than the ear could bear to hear or the eye to see, even for her. The music was too much for Cassie Morrison" (301).

In Cassie's memory, this multiplicitous view of Miss Eckhart is twined with images of Miss Eckhart's life with her mother; their quarrels sometimes spilled into the studio and Cassie remembers one occasion—so unprecedented that she cannot quite believe it—when the mother mocked her daughter and Miss Eckhart slapped her in retaliation. All of this raises unbearable questions for Cassie, questions that circle closer and closer to her own female life: "Should daughters *forgive* mothers (with mothers under their heel)?" (304) The girls refuse Miss Eckhart's offer of *domestic* communion. Housekeeping is always a part of the studio's atmosphere; it smells of Miss Eckhart's cooking. She prepares foods unknown to Morgana: cabbage in wine, pigs' brains. Cassie yearns for a taste, but to partake of Miss Eckhart's cooking would be to claim her as kin, to admit that her world of ardor and doom is the same world of mothers, daughters, and domesticity that she inhabits herself: that the hearth fire and the fire of passion are the same blaze.

That this is the case, however inadmissible to Cassie, is indicated by Snowdie MacLain, the book's most purely domestic woman and Miss Eckhart's only woman friend and truest supporter. Finally, after Miss Eckhart's death at the hospital for the insane, Snowdie buries her in her own cemetery plot. Although the friendship of Miss Eckhart and Snowdie is explicated in none of the stories—they never exchange a word of dialogue—it embodies a powerful truth: the pariah and the domestic woman are profoundly connected. In life and in death, they share territory: a house, a grave, and a plot.

The transmission of that plot from generation to generation, from mother to daughter, has been one of the most persistent problems of domestic fiction, and it is a central subject of *The Golden Apples*. "The most important mother" in Morgana is Miss Lizzie Morgan Stark (her maiden name is the root of the town's name). Among Morgana housekeepers, her word is law, and her law is an arrogant advocacy of generic female power. When she hears of Katie Rainey's death, she directs her black maid: "Only thing I can do for people any more, in joy or sorrow, is send 'em you. . . . Go on down there. Get in the kitchen and clean it up for Miss Virgie, don't pay any attention to her. . . . I know what any old woman owes another old woman" (427). Katie's and Virgie's and the maid's identities are irrelevant to the imperative steamroller of Miss Lizzie's will to control domestic ritual.

Miss Lizzie's monolithic female power is central to the third story, "Moon Lake," rightly called "a female mystery story" (Demmin and Curley 245). A group of pubescent Morgana girls are spending a week camping at nearby Moon Lake. Miss Lizzie, the "camp mother," visits every day, gliding like Juno in her electric car. In the story's central event, the charismatic orphan girl, Easter, falls into the lake and is rescued and at last revived by the Boy Scout lifeguard, Loch Morrison. As Loch performs artificial respiration on a picnic table before all the girls, it is as if he is miming intercourse and acting out the lifegiving powers of male sexuality before the girls' eyes. At this moment, Miss Lizzie arrives and opposes Loch—even though he is saving Easter's life: "He ought to be put out of business . . . get him off her." Miss Lizzie's decisiveness reassures the clustered girls: "it was somehow for this that they had given those yells for Miss Lizzie as Camp Mother. Under her gaze the Boy Scout's actions seemed to lose a good deal of significance. He was reduced almost to a nuisance" (367). Miss Lizzie's power is rooted in domestic order. Even at camp, supposedly outside the constraints of housekeeping, the girls are "always getting ready for Miss Lizzie; the tents even now were straight and the ground picked up and raked for her" (368).

The real hero of "Moon Lake" is Loch, because he saves Easter.[16] But Miss Lizzie's presence encourages the girls to deny that fact and the individual possibilities of passion and heroism. The story ends with Jinny Love Stark, Miss Lizzie's daughter, saying to another girl, after disparaging Loch, "You and I will always be old maids" (374). Then they join the other girls, singing, affirming a collective female culture.

Earlier, Jinny Love, spoiled and selfish as she is, was the only girl to attempt to help Loch; she took a part in the drama of Easter's resurrection, tirelessly fanning her with a towel. But finally she gives up and retreats to her mother's welcoming arms. Miss Lizzie has other plans for the picnic table; she has brought watermelons for the girls, a "treat" to be served for their last camp day. The picnic table has become a stage and the question is what to put on it: the heart-stopping drama of life, death, heroism, and sexuality or the domesticated treat served forth by Miss Lizzie? Jinny Love remains Miss Lizzie's daughter. In the last story she is a mother herself, married to one of the MacLain twins. But she is trivial, self-absorbed, and perpetually childish; at Katie's funeral, she refuses to look at the dead woman and draws attention, instead, to her own new diamond ring. Stunted and thwarted as a feeling individual, Jinny Love is presented as the logical product of her mother's driven housekeeping.

Cassie Morrison, although her sensibility is richer than Jinny Love's, is thwarted too. Deeply conservative, she longs for and loves the predictability of domestic ritual. As a small child, at the speakings, "Cassie would try to stay in sight of her mother, but . . . she always lost her mother" (298). As indicated by her recital of the party menu, Mrs. Morrison views domestic ritual with skepticism, while Cassie longs for devout surety. Cassie has endured her mother's unexpected suicide and at Katie Rainey's funeral her notion of how best to comfort Virgie is to serve as her guide to the ritual of a mother's funeral, rendering it predictable and thus bearable. "Sit by me, Virgie," she says, "This is when it's the worst" (445). Virgie scorned the metronome when they were piano pupils, but Cassie is the metronome's true heir. Following both her mother and Miss Eckhart, she now lives as a companion to her mad father, serving as his caretaker in a corner of the old Morrison house (cut up for boarders), and she is the piano teacher for Morgana. She has invested "all she has" in a stone angel for her mother's grave and has planted hundreds of bulbs in the yard, spelling "Mama's name" in flowers. With these icons, which evoke strict conventions of mourning, Cassie has finally created the mother she longed for: a domestic mama, planted in her place. "June Recital" ends with Cassie's meditation on Virgie and Miss Eckhart as "human beings terribly at large, roaming on the face of the earth" (330). To be "at large" is a terror to Cassie; she recognizes herself as a creature of rituals and enclosures: "she could not see herself do an unknown thing. She was not Loch, she was not Virgie Rainey; she was not her mother. She was Cassie in her room" (316).

After Katie Rainey's funeral, Cassie acknowledges the difference between Virgie and herself. She is "glad" for her old friend, for she will have "a life of [her] own, away" (457). After a brief earlier time "away," following her affair with the young sailor, Virgie returned to Morgana and her parents' house, working as a typist, taking lovers, and, since her mother's stroke, doing the housekeeping. Her mother thinks, on her last day, that it is "a blessed wonder to see the child [over forty] mind" (430).

Katie Rainey is the most creative and least conventional housekeeper of *The Golden Apples*. And Virgie is not without faculty herself; she sews her clothes (and relishes "struggling against a real hard plaid" [430]), cooks, and does not protest when the women of Morgana descend upon her house to prepare for Katie's funeral. As the minister intones the first words of the service, "Virgie rose right up. In the pink china jar on the mantel shelf, someone had placed her mother's old stick—like a peach branch, as though it would flower. . . . Before his eyes and everybody's she marched over, took the stick out of the vase, and carried it away to the hall, where she placed it in the ring on the hatrack. When she was back in her chair, Dr. Williams opened the book and held the service" (446). Like her mother who inserted her cry of "Ice cream!" into the political speaking, Virgie interrupts male discourse. Honoring her mother's house and her things, she puts Katie's stick in its appointed place. But the other women cannot admit that an eccentric single woman can have any domestic skills. Jinny Love urges Virgie to put herself in place and "marry now," with her mother dead. Like Miss Eckhart's, Virgie Rainey's range is a threat to Morgana order. They want everything accounted for; with Katie only a few hours dead, her friends have already gathered to speculate on the disposal of her household goods: the quilts, her mother's embroidery, her recipes. Such things are not trivial; they have been the medium in which much of women's surviving history is inscribed.[17] In *The Country of the Pointed Firs*, for example, a character as substantial as Mrs. Todd is deeply concerned with the disposition of such objects, and in *Delta Wedding*, much of the import of women's culture is indicated by a cherished cake recipe.

Virgie Rainey has no interest in her mother's household goods once the funeral is over; the next day, they are packed or given away, and Virgie is ready to leave Morgana. She takes with her a few practical skills—cooking, sewing, typing, milking—and a way of viewing the world, the domestic vision that allows her to look at a counterpane and see "the overworked, inherited, and personal pattern." Such language pervades *The Golden Apples;* it is often the substance of Welty's metaphors and reveals her own implication in housekeeping and domestic ritual.[18]

Like Miss Eckhart, Virgie Rainey is a character of special import for Welty. She said in a 1981 interview, "Everybody was sort of trapped in their own dream world there [Morgana], or were apprehensive of leaving, of getting outside of it; all but Virgie who really was and is a courageous and fine person. . . . I love Virgie" (*Conversations* 332). Virgie's extraordinary qualities are apparent the night after her mother's death, as she swims ecstatically in the nearby river, inventing a "personal ritual," as Vande Kieft calls it (114), to complement what is happening in the house. In a passage of liminal sensuality, she enacts her birth as a woman, in language that seems a response to Cixous's directive to women writers, nearly thirty years later: "your body is yours, take it" (46). As Virgie enters the river,

> All was one warmth, air, water, and her own body. All seemed one weight, one matter. . . . She began to swim in the river, forcing it gently, as she would wish for gentleness to her body. Her breasts around which she felt the water curving were as sensitive at that moment as the tips of wings must feel to birds, or antennae to insects. She felt the sand, grains as intricate as little cogged wheels, minute shells of old seas, and the many dark ribbons of grass and mud touch her and leave her, like suggestions and withdrawals of some bondage that might have been dear, now dismembering and losing itself. . . . Virgie had reached the point where in the next moment she might turn into something without feeling it shock her. (440)

Here, Virgie has achieved a state where she can perceive herself as a continuum. In womblike fluid, she moves as a grown, breasted woman, touching a history as old as seas and as personal as the bondages of her own recent life. The resources Virgie reveals in this sublime passage show why she cannot live as a passive devotée of Mama's Name.

Luce Irigaray's probing 1981 essay on mother-daughter relationships, "And the One Doesn't Stir Without the Other," describes crippling conventions of mothering, by which the requirements of maternity—most basic of which is feeding—limit both mother and daughter and prevent their experiencing and sharing their full selfhood. In the daughter's voice, Irigaray addresses the mother's lack: "There is no one in whom to remember the dream of yourself. The house, the garden, everywhere is empty of you. You search for yourself everywhere in vain. . . . And this makes you empty yourself even more into my body—to maintain the memory of yourself. . . . [The daughter concludes,] what I wanted from you Mother, was this: that in giving me life, you still remain alive" (65–67).

The Golden Apples anticipates the concerns of Irigaray's essay. Mrs. Morrison, for example, with her belief that she "could have sung" and found fulfillment as a musician, finally found "the house, the garden" empty of her self and committed suicide. In the domestic homage of Mama's name, Cassie is ironically denying her mother's self, by inscribing her name in the language of traditional femininity. As a girl, Cassie already apprehended the terrible, victimizing power daughters and mothers have over each other, as she wondered, "Should daughters *forgive* mothers (with mothers under their heel)?" It is Virgie and Katie Rainey who come closest to the ideal of simultaneous, mutual life expressed by Irigaray's conclusion. Dying, Katie apprehends that she, not Virgie, is the richly endowed hero of her own life, the "bride." Although she "kept everything"—baby clothes, needlework, dishes—with cherishing domestic care, Katie thought of her faculty as something to be circulated in a wider world, the network of women who read the *Market Bulletin;* even her prized quilts she imagines sold after her death, not entrusted to Virgie. Yet, while Kate lives, Virgie is still a child in her mother's mind, and expected to milk the cows and cook supper. In this book, even in the best of circumstances, a daughter's life begins with her mother's death. By her own will and her mother's example, Virgie (whose first name suggests possibilities as yet unfulfilled) has not been effaced by the obliterating weight of women's domestic culture, passed from mother to daughter. As her swim indicates, she is ready to claim her life. And in her, Katie's energy, relish, and courage still live.

The night after the funeral, Virgie is awakened by "an old lady in a

Mother Hubbard and clay boots," saying, "It's you. . . . Child, you don't know me, but I know you and brought you somethin'. . . . My night-blooming cereus throwed a flower tonight, and I couldn't forbear to bring you it. . . . It's for you . . . won't do the dead no good. . . . Look at it enduring the night" (453–54). This old woman seems archaic, a wise crone of fairy tale or legend, materializing out of night as fantastic (and ordinary) as the hill country woman seemed to R. J. Bowman. Having achieved the difficult domestic feat of coaxing a cereus to bloom, she makes the flower an emblem of something she must share with a younger woman, a woman *not* her daughter. The flower is not a tribute to the dead mother or her memory; instead, it honors the daughter and all she must endure and will feel. It represents the oldest kind of female wisdom that a traditional woman has been able to discover in her life. The bloom is "naked, luminous, compli-cated . . . large and pale as a face" (453). As nothing else has, it frightens Virgie; she begins to tremble, and when the woman is gone, she throws the flower away. Then, looking to the river, she envisions the moonlight there: "from the eyes to the moon would be a cone, a long silent horn, of white light. It was a connection visible as the hair is in air, between the self and the moon, to make the self feel the child, a daughter far, far back" (454).

Although Virgie Rainey knows the language of domestic ritual, the sense of female connection and continuity that she feels most powerfully, with resonance that shakes her, is perceived through the cycles of nature (which are the basis of much domestic ritual) and her own body; they put her in touch with that oldest female emblem, the moon—connecting her to a chain of women as "a daughter far, far back." The old woman's gift has provoked, within herself, the cue that makes it possible for Virgie fully to claim her life. As Irigaray's daughter-speaker longed to do, she can live her life without violating her mother's.

On her last morning in Morgana, Virgie drives, her car "abreast" of Cassie, circling the cemetery where both their mothers lie. Cassie turns in her driveway and Virgie drives on; nearly involuntarily, she visits the Mac-Lain cemetery, where Miss Eckhart is buried, and acknowledges that the music teacher, too, is one of "her dead," and that she loves her. As Virgie gropes for images to suggest how and what she will be, where she is going, she calls on the pictures and sounds that filled the Eckhart studio: Perseus, Medusa, Beethoven, Miss Eckhart's own commanding passion. King Mac-Lain, too, who snacked on ham and made faces during Katie's funeral—his defiance sustains Virgie. Poised to depart, she sits in the rain with an old black woman, hearing "through falling rain the running of the horse and bear, the stroke of the leopard, the dragon's crusty slither, the glimmer and the trumpet of the swan" (461). The world is restored with all its original beauty, danger and promise, untamed and undomesticated. Earlier it seemed that the collective sound of the Morgana ladies, bound to their Rook party, was "drowning out something" (280). But now Virgie and her companion, women outside when they should be in, hear the sound beneath the distracting hubbub: "The magical percussion, the world beating in their ears" (461).

In an important and troubling 1981 essay, Myra Jehlen writes about the dangers implicit in Elaine Showalter's urging in *A Literature of Their Own* (and also in subsequent work) that women "begin to create an autonomous literary universe with a 'female tradition' as its 'center.'" Obviously, my own work in this study has been much influenced by Showalter's urging and by my own belief that domestic ritual has long been central to women's culture. However validating and crucial the rites of housekeeping may have been to many strong women, the dark and constricting qualities of those rites are also unavoidably real. Jehlen—in generalizations perhaps too sweeping but compelling nonetheless—warns that Showalter's literature of "women's culture" depicts "not actual independence but action despite dependence—and not a self-defined female culture either, but a sub-culture born out of oppression and either stunted or victorious only at often-fatal cost" (581–82).

Much of the great fiction of domestic ritual by the American women I am discussing acknowledges both Jehlen's and Showalter's views. The commanding figure of Mrs. Todd, plying her housekeeping magic contained in a "low room," the ambivalences of Freeman's New England nun or Cather's Mrs. Harris: such characters and the continuing emphatic responses of women readers to them suggest the strength, the pervasiveness, and the possibilities for repression and expression implicit in women's culture. But no American woman writer has embodied this controversy in her fiction more ambitiously than Eudora Welty. Her first story evoked the mystery and romance of domestic ritual as compellingly as any American fiction ever has, while raising questions about its relation to a male-dominated culture of technology, movement, money, and change. When young women—such as Livvie or Jenny Lockhart or Ruby Fisher—became her protagonists, they registered the perils of self-loss, as well as the confirmations, that were part of housekeeping. And in the expansive experiment of *Delta Wedding*, Welty conjured up a world as it was shaped in the minds of seven women, living within women's culture.

The Golden Apples, which seems a very different book, is in fact a brilliant extension of the same project, for it explores how ideas of gender and gendered culture develop and limit human imagination. At the center of the book, the MacLains—Zeus and the white queen—embody gender myths that fascinate the citizens of Morgana. The stories of the MacLain sons, "The Whole World Knows" and "Music from Spain," and a country girl's meditation on her erotic encounters with King and his sons in "Sir Rabbit," explore male mythology and the possibilities of living as a man. But it is woman's culture, centered in domestic ritual and the mother-daughter bonds, that Welty explores most expansively in this book and that is primary agent of the entrapping qualities Welty cites as inherent in Morgana. As the finest characters in *The Golden Apples* apprehend, one can be fully human only if one somehow manages to transcend categories, rituals, definitions, and forms. Miss Eckhart at her best exemplifies this: as she plays her piano, her face "could have belonged to someone else—not even to a woman necessarily. It was the face a mountain could have" (300). Virgie discovers this same quality as she floats in the river: a fluidity, an openness to infinite transformation. A little girl at Moon Lake thinks exultantly and eagerly of "The orphan! . . . The other way to live. . . . It's only interesting, only worthy, to try for the fiercest secrets. To slip into them all—to change. . . . for a moment into Gertrude, into Mrs. Gruenwald, into Twosie—into a boy. To *have been* an orphan" (361). As the little girl tries to imagine the richest human possibilities, she starts by divesting herself of her parents (and in this story, mothers are the more powerful parents), and then ends with the furthest reach of her imagination—into another gender. Then she returns to the seeming impossibility: "to *have been* an orphan." For the risk and exhilaration of changing form—as pubescent girls do, at least physically—is attended by the possibility of orphaning, of being a child—like the orphans at camp—uncared-for by the "camp mother," unsheltered by domestic ritual and traditions of care.

The very shape of this book, as Welty said, is related to Miss Eckhart's aesthetic; it is inclusive, shifting, allusive. It includes a knowledge of domestic ritual and its transmission, which is as deep and disturbing as Virgie Rainey's ties to the moon. Yet the book also asks a question that has possessed American women in this century, and toward which the thrust of Eudora Welty's best fiction has propelled her: *is* there "another way to live"?

7

Welty and the Dynamo in the House

"Why Keep It Up, Old Woman?"

*I*N 1977, Reynolds Price, always one of Welty's best readers, said of her, "An American writer has at last produced a third act in
her career—an act unimaginably better than its own great predecessors"
("Thanks" 126). In fact, the five writers discussed in this book all had long
and consistently productive careers and did much of their best work after the
age of forty. It is worth speculating about whether the cyclical conventions
of "women's time," as expressed in domestic life, are not a more generative
model for an artist's life than a linear, goal-oriented, more traditionally male
concept of time. All the women writers in this study made productive use of
repetitions and recycling in their work—Freeman with her series of "old
ladies" and Jewett with her transformations of the materials of *Deephaven*
into *The Country of the Pointed Firs*, for examples. In 1972, Welty acknowledged similar repetitions in her own fiction: "In looking back I can see the
pattern. . . . Your mind works that way. Yet they occur to me as new every
time" (*Conversations* 89).

One of the most striking and suggestive patterns in Welty's fiction is that
of the character taken to the very edge of experience, a jumping-off-place of
sheer fall and possibility. To face such a prospect is to turn one's back on
domestic ritual and to forfeit the sense of form and identity that is shaped by
the keeping of houses. Like Virgie Rainey, who feels herself at the edge of
transformation, or Jenny Lockhart, gone so far that she is lost to our
imagining, or R. J. Bowman, clutching his death, or Livvie looking out her
door, these characters—mostly women—are at the border of another way
to live. Can they enter that other life, and can Welty's fiction go with them?
These questions are central to the second half of Welty's career.

The seven stories in Welty's next collection, *The Bride of the Innisfallen*

(1955), were individually published between 1949 and 1954. She described the volume in 1981 as a "book of stories all laid in Europe, but I had to write every one of them from the point of view of the traveler or the outsider" (*Conversations* 329). But in fact, only two of the stories are about European travel; a third is set on Circe's legendary Greek island, and the other four are set in the American South. It is the possibilities of travel that pervade the book, the setting aside of home, ritual, and custom, which must occur when one commits oneself to a journey. "No Place for You, My Love," one of Welty's greatest stories, takes this situation to its ultimate. A nameless man and woman meet in New Orleans, a strange city, slough off the acquaintances who accompany them, and drive together, remaining strangers, to a place they had not known existed, "south of south." They follow a road to its ending, at the Gulf; enter a bar and apprehend some of the complexity and solidity of local life, but do not let themselves be touched by it or by the possibilities of their own relationship. When they dance, briefly and expertly, they are "imperviousness in motion" (478). After a wordless kiss and a fast drive back to the city, they return to their separate particularities: a man appears to be waiting for her in her hotel lobby and he is flooded with memory of his first apprehensions of love. For many readers, this story seems a chronicle of missed opportunities; Kreyling, for example, calls it an "aborted pilgrimage" ending in "retreat" (*Eudora Welty's Achievement of Order* 122). But to me it seems a brief journey into the "other way to live"—a necessary respite from webs of relationship, from all the multiplying cares and vulnerabilities of being inside a place, a house, and a pattern of life.

Repeatedly, the stories in *The Bride of the Innisfallen* take a character to the very edge of extremity. As many of the first readers complained, conventions of plot are less apparent here than in the earlier stories.[1] Welty told an interviewer in 1978, "I've sort of developed new forms for my more recent stories. They're not nearly as compact in one way as they used to be, but they're more compact in another. That is, they have density of another kind than the plot itself. I want there to be a 'felt' form running through that the reader will get" (*Conversations* 261).

Nowhere is this new density more powerfully felt than in Welty's one venture into Civil War fiction, "The Burning." Like "At The Landing," this is also one of the few of her stories about which Welty has expressed grave doubts; she said, "I don't know why I tried to write anything historical" and added, "I think it is the worst story I ever wrote" (*Conversations* 221). Many readers—including me—have nevertheless found "The Burning" a great story. Harold Bloom, for example, claims that its "extraordinary prose rises to an American sublime that is neither grotesque nor ironic" (10). Several perceptive readings of this demanding story exist,[2] but none notes a fact that is stunningly obvious when one reads "The Burning" in the context of women's culture: the story is a paradigm of the most horrific and liberating violations of housekeeping. The first sentence establishes the point-of-view character: a young, obedient slave, Delilah. The second sentence states, "A horse was coming in the house, by the front door" (*Collected Stories* 482). The horse is accompanied by Union soldiers, come to burn Rose Hill, a plantation house on the Vicksburg Road, occupied only by two white sisters and their slaves. The sentence indicates the abrogation of housekeeping by a classic male plot, war. The two white sisters—"mad," Bloom calls them— react differently. Miss Myra casts herself as a heroine in a romance of escape, rescue, and precedence: "Will you take me on the horse? Please take me first," she says (482). Miss Theo, turning to face the incursion, ignores the men, replying only in terms of her household authority:

> "Delilah, what is it you came in your dirty apron to tell me?" . . .
> "Come to tell you we got the eggs away from black broody hen and sure enough, they're addled," said Delilah. (482–83)

Miss Theo insistently defines herself as a housekeeper; no detail escapes her eye. With Delilah, her "immensely passive" (Bloom 7) instrument, she attends to the running of her household in the face of insistent historical fact, male imperatives, which burst into her house.

The men act out their orders and complete their plot: Myra and Delilah are raped, the house is looted, burned, and abandoned, and Miss Theo's will and faculty are ignored. Gathering up Delilah, their only remaining slave, the sisters walk to Jackson, also burned and abandoned, then find a hammock on a nearby plantation. Theo unravels its rope and, with Delilah's assistance, Myra and Theo hang themselves.

The world of the sisters denies color, action, and drama; no wonder that Myra asks the soldiers to carry her away. When the horse bursts into their house, they are sitting in a parlor darkened against July sun, occupied with "white sewing," their backs to the door. Shaped by the "cult of true womanhood" (Welter 21–41), the sisters both disdain men and defer to them. When their brother Benton (now missing in the war) fathered an illegitimate child, Theo impressed him with his fault and his responsibilities: "I told him what he owed a little life! Each little life is a man's fault." The baby, Phinny, was cared for at Rose Hill and kept upstairs; Theo told her brother "he must never dream he was *inflicting* his sisters. That's what we're for" (488).

Myra's frustration at men's absences, incursions, and inflictions is reflected in the fantastic alternate plots she concocts for herself. Even as she "bids" to be the first to hang, she speaks in a "spoiled sweet way" (490) that reflects her "sheltered" upbringing. Over Theo's protests, she insists that Phinny is her child, making up her tale as she goes along. "I had him, dear. It was an officer, no, one of our beaux. . . . And if Phinny *was* mine—" (489). Theo stops her with a blunt fact: the child is black. Theo, the stronger sister, did not invent plots for herself that required male powers, of either rescue or impregnation. She has turned instead to female powers of rigorous house-keeping, running the house and supervising the slaves. Delilah claims that "Miss Theo had eyes in the back of her head" (482) and "was always too powerful for a lady" (491). As she prepares for the hanging, displaying her skill with knots, Theo betrays that she has chafed since childhood against the limits of the plots offered to ladies; "I learned as a child how to tie, from a picture book in Papa's library—not that I ever was called on. . . . I guess I was always something of a tomboy." Having watched her sister die, she says to Delilah, "I've proved . . . what I've always suspicioned: that I'm brave as a lion." Houseless, bereft of her domestic realm, Theo has her first oppor-tunity for self-testing and self-discovery, in terms beyond gender: "brave as a lion." If she were a man, she would surely be an effective officer in the war. But as a woman, unhoused, she concludes that suicide is her only possible plot; as much as possible she manages her own death, dictating its denoue-ment and moral to Delilah: "go, and leave us where you've put us, un-spared. . . . that's the way they'll find us. The sight will be good for them for what they've done" (491).

Of the story's three women, Delilah has the least power. Not even the housework is hers to command; she follows orders. She is the mother of Phinny—but that very fact has been stolen from her and effaced. The house has imposed its shape on her life, and when she is dragged from it and raped, Delilah shrieks, "screaming her loudest for Delilah, who was lost now—carried out of the house, not knowing how to get back" (485). Much of the elliptical, allusive quality, which may make "The Burning," as Bloom calls it, "the most formidable" of Welty's stories (6), is the result of Delilah's point of view. As the story begins, she is unable to do anything but receive impressions, like a photographic plate; she has not been permitted to develop her capacity for moral evaluation. Even her child, confined upstairs, registers in Delilah's mind only through displaced things that must be put in place: "if a cup or a silver spoon or a little string of spools on a blue ribbon came hopping down the steps like a frog, sometimes Delilah was the one to pick it up and run back with it" (483). As a slave, Delilah has been reduced to a housekeeping machine, and any acts that she may commit that do not fit that role, her consciousness cannot acknowledge. Delilah has been lost all her life, lost to the house and her place in it. When she reports to Theo that a black hen has been robbed, in a sense Delilah is telling her own story. Although Theo is dead, Delilah continues to ask her for orders: "What must I do now? Where must I go?" (491). Undirected—and free—for the first time in her life, she returns to Rose Hill, where Phinny was left to burn to death. The sisters allowed this rather than acknowledge the child and the full complexity of the story of their house. Delilah's one act of assertion is to speak of the child's existence; when the sisters claim that no male relatives are left, she says, "Phinney here. He a he" (484). At first, back at Rose Hill, Delilah can see the charred remains of the house only in the terms she knows; when she sees the great Venetian parlor mirror, its surface looks "addled" like the black hen's eggs. Delilah's whole life has been a mirror image inflicted upon her, a reflection of a "young kitchen Negro" and "good obedient slave" (484). Although they ruled Delilah, the sisters too lived in the mirror; only in her unhoused death did Theo find a life of heroism and volition.

Delilah gazes into the scorched mirror at "gold and honey twisted up into houses, trembling. She saw people walking the bridges in early light with hives of houses on their heads, men in dresses, some with red birds; and monkeys in velvet; and ladies with masks laid over their faces looking down from pointed windows. Delilah supposed that was Jackson before Sherman came" (493). She envisions a fantasy world of luxury and houses, suggesting that the houses are the products of men's minds ("hives of houses on their heads"). Ladies are sequestered inside, behind masks. It is a fantasia upon the world where Delilah has spent her life, a world in which not even an image of herself appears.

But then the mirror roils with deeper images: "quivering, leaping to life, fighting, aping old things Delilah had seen done in this world already, sometimes what men had done to Miss Theo and Miss Myra and the peacocks [Theo's pets, strangled by soldiers] and to slaves, and what anybody now could do to anybody. . . . The mirror felled her flat." To Delilah the world of her new freedom is an anarchy of victimization in which the possibilities of brutality are infinite, involving even the most fragile natural creatures: "bees saddled like horses, butterflies harnessed to one another. . . . all this world that was flying, striking, stricken, falling, gilded or blackened, mortally splitting and falling apart, proud turbans unwinding" (493).

For Delilah to succumb to this anarchic vision would mean madness and loss of her human capacities. She is rescued by her memory of Phinny, when she recalls her love for the child. Now the mirror gives back another image. No longer the obedient slave, Delilah "caught the motherly image—head wagging in the flayed forehead of a horse with ears and crest up stiff, the shield and the drum of big swamp birdskins, the horns of deer sharpened to cut and kill with. She showed her teeth. Then she looked in the feathery ashes and found Phinny's bones. She ripped a square from her manifold fullness of skirts and tied up the bones in it" (493). Delilah's new images seem to spring from a collective unconscious; they are primitive images of mastery of natural powers. As a self-validated mother, Delilah has a role, identity, and duties beyond a slave's servitude. Now she is reinventing the world and inventing her own story. It is *not* a story of plantation housekeeping. Instead, Delilah has begun a journey. She carries with her the effects she took from the dead sisters' bodies; although she did not admit it (or anything) to herself, Delilah too has been a looting ex-slave. On her head, like an African woman, she sets the silver "Jubilee cup" they found in the abandoned hammock. If white Myra and Theo have a heir, it is black Delilah; she is the surviving woman, carrying their memory and their goods and the bones of their kin toward a new life.

Delilah follows "the smell of horses and fire, to men," and another story. Carrying "her own black locust stick to drive the snakes" (494), asserting her power over the forces of nature, she now resembles Phoenix Jackson, the heroic former slave who is the ancient, determined protagonist of "A Worn Path" (*A Curtain of Green*). In the original version of this story, Delilah's name was "Florabel": revising, Welty gave her the name of a biblical heroine, a man-vanquishing woman. When she reaches the Big Black River, Delilah—like Virgie Rainey at the same river—wades in. This paragraph ends the story: "Submerged to the waist, to the breast, stretching her throat like a sunflower stalk above the river's opaque skin, she kept on, her treasure stacked on the roof of her head, hands laced upon it. She had forgotten how or when she knew, and she did not know what day this was, but she knew—it would not rain, the river would not rise, until Saturday" (494).

Bloom says that here Delilah marches toward "what is presented ambiguously as her own freedom, or her death, or perhaps both together" (9). I see her as more definitively claiming her life, creating another "way to live." No longer does the house give her form and validity; instead, she *is* the house, her head its roof, and her intelligence, intuition, and fealty to human life—including her otherwise repudiated child—are her shelter and her hope. It is Delilah herself who divined that it would not rain until Saturday; this is the one oracular statement she ventures to make to the sisters. Saving intuition has always been Delilah's own possession; at last, freed from the confinement of mirror and house, she can claim her strength. As she does so, she enters the world of original energy, such as Virgie did, hearing the leopard, the dragon, and "the trumpet of the swan."

Most of the stories in *The Bride of the Innisfallen* have that original energy as their destination. In the title story, for example, a young wife has left her husband because her selfhood has been "nearly destroyed" (517) by the confinement of her marriage, in London. In "Going to Naples," an Italian woman, with her grown daughter, returns to her home city and a reunion with her mother. And in "Kin," another of the Mississippi stories, Dicey, a contemporary young engaged woman from a northern city, whose parents are dead, returns to the Mississippi of her girlhood for a visit with relatives. There she enters the female world of her widowed aunt Ethel and her single cousin Kate. In one sense, that world is a perfect fit; on arrival she goes "straight into Kate's clothes" (545) and is welcomed by friends and family alike, as if she has no life anywhere else. "Everywhere, the yawning, inconvenient, and suddenly familiar rooms were as deep and inviting and compelling as the yawning big roses opening and shattering in one day in the heating gardens. At night, the moths were already pounding against the screens" (539). Dicey sees the houses and rituals of her birthplace in antithetical terms of ease and violence, beauty and bondage; they both beckon and threaten her. This story has the atmosphere of *Delta Wedding* or "June Recital"; it is thick with conversation and domestic, genealogical detail, evoking the riches and dangers of traditional women's culture.

The two young women go on an obligatory visit to the ailing family patriarch, aged Uncle Felix. He is tended by a distant relative, Sister Anne, who has made a life for herself by invading the houses of ailing relatives and nursing them. On the day they arrive, she has stashed the old man in a storeroom and given over the house to an itinerant photographer, who is using it for a studio. Aunt Ethel and the "girls" have nothing but contempt for Sister Anne; she "can't cook and loves to eat" (543), "has no inner resources" (544), and Dicey notes that she dyes her hair and wears clothes long out of fashion. In Albert Devlin's interestingly dark reading of "Kin" as a "relentless tale of 'attrition,'" Sister Anne Fry appears as "an incarnation of the divided modern sensibility. . . . As her name implies, she will probably suffer the eternal agonies reserved for the ahistorical" (159–61). Sister Anne is "modern" in another way important to this study; alone and houseless, she has been obliged to invent a way to survive and to enjoy her life. Exuberant and unapologetic, she manages to enjoy the cousins' visit, sample the cake they bring, have herself photographed, and execute a bit of a flirtation with

the photographer, simultaneously. To Dicey she seems a "tomboy," survey-
ing Uncle Felix and her guests with the alert interest of a "prospector." All
the language of the other women questions the "femininity" and the faculty
of Anne. Yet Aunt Ethel, Kate, and Dicey are all themselves somehow cut
off from the continuity of traditional domestic life as it was once celebrated
at Mingo. Dicey remembers childhood Sunday dinners there: "the old soft
airs of Mingo as I knew them—the interior airs that were always kitchen-
like, of oil-lamps, wood ashes, and that golden scrapement off cake-
papers. . . . In those days . . . I could imagine the Magi riding through,
laden" (563). Her memory is a domestic idyl of housekeeping abundance,
with the rich house the center of life and mystery. It attracts the most
powerful of patriarchs, magi, who bear tributes to a fertile domestic woman.
Now, however, all three women are somehow excluded from the remembered Mingo. Dicey is a northern city dweller; Aunt Ethel is too ill to visit
Mingo, and Kate is stuck in a tedious bank job. Although they do not
acknowledge the close relation, they *are* sisters to Anne Fry.

Uncle Felix, his name itself suggesting the remembered happiness of
Mingo, is a fixture of the women's memories; Dicey sees him in terms of a
patriarchal myth, a constellation: "he looked like the story-book picture of
the Big Bear . . . with star children on his back and more star children
following, in triangle dresses, starting down the Milky Way" (559). But
Dicey begins to suspect that the Mingo myth has been in some respects a
trap for her uncle; seeing the old stereopticon, she recalls that when she was
a little girl, she and Uncle Felix would gaze together at pictures of faraway
cities—one of which is now Dicey's home. Now the old man seems a
prisoner in his own house, at the mercy of Sister Anne's energetic imperatives. When he sees Kate and Dicey he utters one word, a warning: "Hide,"
as if their very selves are in danger, as his is. Then he writes a note with much
difficulty and passes it to Dicey; it says, "River—Daisy—Midnight—
Please" (561). The note suggests a wish for another life: midnight, not the
noon of the Sunday dinners; Daisy, not his wife Beck, and the river, not the
house. Kate, relentlessly proper, refuses to acknowledge the note's meanings. But Dicey is smitten by it.

Before leaving, Kate rediscovers her true sister at Mingo, in the portrait
of her great-grandmother, also executed by an itinerant artist:

> The yellow skirt spread fanlike, straw hat held ribbon-in-hand . . . none of that,
> any more than the forest scene so unlike the Mississippi wilderness (that enor-
> mity she had been carried to as a bride, when the logs of this house were cut, her
> bounded world drop by drop of sweat exposed, where she'd died in the end of
> yellow fever) or the melancholy clouds obscuring the passive figure with the

small, crossed feet—none of it, world or body, was really her. *She* had eaten bear meat, seen Indians, she had married into the wilderness at Mingo, to what unknown feelings. Slaves had died in her arms. She had grown a rose for Aunt Ethel to send back by me. And still those eyes, opaque, all pupil, belonged to Evalina—I knew, because they saw out, as mine did; weren't warned, as mine weren't, and never shut before the end, as mine would not. I, her divided sister, knew who had felt the wildness of the world behind the ladies' view. We were homesick for somewhere that was the same place. (561)

By an act of rapt imagination, Dicey subverts the "ladies view" of order and propriety. Her great-grandmother, she intuits, inhabited a "bounded world" of wilderness housekeeping that the portrait painter almost entirely obliterated with his readymade conventions, much like the blurry romantic backdrop—"the same old thing"—of the itinerant photographer. The things that Dicey shares with her ancestor have been preserved by generations of housekeepers: the rose, carefully nurtured; the old house, the portrait itself. But what she imagines that they share spiritually is a kind of "homesickness" for the full range of human experience, a fullness antithetical to boundaries and "the ladies' view."

By these conclusions, Dicey realizes that kinship involves more than genealogy. Although she and Kate are "double cousins," they do not have kindred imaginations. On the edge of a marriage and an adult life in a place far from Mingo, Dicey locates—or does she invent?—the ancestor she needs in her passionate great-grandmother. Uncle Felix, too, is her true kin, a man with a taste for wandering and river meetings (recalling the legends of King MacLain) confined in an old house and an infirm body. About Sister Anne, at least, Kate and Dicey are in agreement; they jointly conclude that "She's common" (566). Yet Anne Frye—as Carol Manning says, "one of Welty's best talkers and most vivid characters ever" (53)—is, like the great-grandmother Dicey identifies with, also a woman who refuses to shut her eyes on the world. Itinerant herself, she has the wit, interest, and energy to contrive herself a contemporary life in old houses. Sister Anne opposes attrition; she is the alternative to Aunt Ethel, who despite her "niceness" and perfect domestic taste, is a genteel invalid.

As a contemporary young Southern woman, Dicey must salvage—or create—the portions of her female history that will sustain her, which means that she must take a very selective view of domestic ritual. But she is still romantic, conventional, and young enough that she cannot yet claim kinship to all the voracious and "unfeminine" qualities, embodied in Sister Anne, that she may need in her coming life. Leaving Mingo with Kate, Dicey hears sounds that epitomize the life there: "It was hard . . . to tell whether it was a throbbing, a dance, a rattle, or a ringing." The portentous sounds, suggesting death, celebration, and bodily urgency, all indicate the weight of meaning, as yet unacknowledged, which Mingo will have in Dicey's imagination. But for now she is intent on her romance, and finally she casts herself, romantically, as a figure in a man's mind: "I thought of my sweetheart, riding, and wondered if he were writing to me" (566). Dicey has only begun the process that Delilah enacted when she gathered up Phinny's bones and the sisters' goods: the complex process of claiming one's true kin. Significantly, a *man* (not a woman) writing is on her mind.

In many ways, "Circe," which may seem an aberrant story, is the quintessence of *The Bride of the Innisfallen* and of much of Welty's fiction. Odysseus is the prototypical wanderer and perhaps the prototypical protagonist of Western literature. But his adventures are specifically male; no woman can join his voyaging. By framing her story as a monologue in Circe's voice, Welty puts us inside the other story, that of the fixed woman, who defines herself by domestic ritual. (See the introduction of this book for a fuller discussion of "Circe.") To inhabit her immortal self and to exercise her powers, Circe must keep to her island. Her time is very different from Odysseus'; what seems a day to her is a year to him, and time for departure. Circe cannot depart; she is "tied to my island, as Cassiopeia must be to the sticks and stars of her chair" ("Circe" 537). She exults in her faculty, epitomized in her practical magic, which works through cooking, cleaning, and laundry and is powerfully seductive to wandering men. But at moments her endless life seems unbearable, as "on those lonely dull mornings when mist wraps the island and hides every path of the sea, and when my heart is black" (534).

Some of Welty's most formidable housekeepers, also fixed in their rituals, have exulted in the stories of men's mobility. Ellen and Tempe, for example, delight in the goings and comings of George, whom they are not free to emulate, and stay-at-home Katie Rainey says of her rascally hero King MacLain, "I believe he's been to California. . . . I see King in the West, out where it's gold and all that. Everybody to their own visioning" (268). But Circe, also left behind, pregnant, by a venturing man, is embittered and bereft. With her immortal visioning, she can see farther than Kate Rainey's lively imagination; she knows the sailors' fates and their destination, the "bright and indelible and menacing world under which they all must go" (536). Her knowledge, her rituals, and her immortal security are not enough: she longs for a man's mobility and voyages.

Circe's story is the stuff of myth and legend; it embodies the cyclical time of domestic ritual. Other female protagonists in *The Bride of the Innis-*

fallen—Delilah in 1863, Dicey and the immigrant woman of "Going to Naples," visiting their childhood homes; the nameless travelers of "No Place for You, My Love" and the title story—are very much placed in historical time. Although they may be drawn to Circe's realm and her powers, their prototype is, in many ways, Odysseus. The problems of "resistance" which, as Judith Fetterley has pointed out, American fiction has posed for women readers, here take a uniquely compelling form. The contemporary woman reader of "Circe," in the process of identification which Fetterley says is central to our reading of fiction, looks for the "divided sister" with whom she may claim kin. To be modern and to be human is to identify with Odysseus and his story. But to be a housekeeping woman, or the daughter of such women, is to identify with Circe, the islanded witch—even though she is not constructed as human. By giving Circe a voice and acknowledging her story, as Odysseus did not, Welty has placed her dilemma in the center of *The Bride of the Innisfallen* and its travelers' tales. Circe is a woman for whom there is no way to die and no "other way to live."

For the title of this volume, Welty chose the image of a bride, a voiceless young woman who makes a single radiant appearance in the title story. In many ways, the white-clad bride epitomizes the women protagonists of the book's stories, who have traveled, dressed in the regalia of their patriarchal ties, to the borders of new life. Circe, with her rituals and her powers, embodies the strengths and limits of traditional female culture. And her singular story adds an edge and a resonance to every woman's tale.

In the years between *The Bride of the Innisfallen* and her next-published novel, *Losing Battles* (1970), Eudora Welty was perhaps more tied to her house than at any time in her adult life. Her mother underwent eye surgery, became an invalid, and required increasing care; these and other "personal responsibilities" fragmented Welty's writing time, making it impossible for her to work "with any sustainment or any regularity" (*Conversations* 47). Mrs. Welty died in 1966. "The Optimist's Daughter" appeared in *The New Yorker* in 1969; revised, it was published as a novella in 1972. Charlotte Capers, an old friend, asked Welty in a 1973 interview if the book had helped her to "work through" her emotions after her mother's death. Welty replied, "I think it did; although, I did not undertake it for any therapeutic reasons, because I don't believe in that kind of thing. I believe in really trying to comprehend something. Comprehension is more important to me than healing; but, I suppose the by-product of that was being able to understand something better—my own feelings about it. It was helpful to me. But that's not important, really, because the important thing is if the novel itself was able to show these feelings I'm talking about" (*Conversations* 116). *The Opti-*

mist's Daughter is a stripped novella of remarkable purity; Welty has said that "it came to be a kind of essence of what I've been trying" (*Conversations* 198). It is dedicated to C.A.W., the initials of Eudora Welty's mother. (In the dedications of her other books, names—even family names—are fully spelled out.)

In this book, Welty makes her central consciousness the modern woman, living in history, who has been moving toward center stage in her fiction. Laurel McKelva Hand, a small-town Mississippian by birth and genteel upbringing, is a successful artist in Chicago; she was widowed twenty years ago, by World War II. She returns to the south for her father's final illness and his funeral; her mother has been dead for several years and her father has remarried. Laurel seems to have been living on emotional *hold;* now she must confront her past, must identify and claim its value. The language in which this confrontation is broached is provided by the oldest patterns of Laurel's life, those of domestic ritual. The stage is her parents' house, in Mount Salus, Mississippi.

Laurel's father's wife, Fay, is almost a parody of narcissistic modernity. Judge McKelva met her in a hotel, where she was working in a typing pool. In the New Orleans hospital where her husband is recuperating from surgery, she is utterly self-involved; her impatience finally provokes Judge McKelva's fatal heart attack. At Mardi Gras time she says to her dying husband, "What's the good of a Carnival if we don't get to go, hon?" (35). For Fay, rituals—whether Mardi Gras or her husband's funeral—are simply occasions for aggressive personal display. She observes the funeral with ostentatious trappings and histrionics. Fay is about Laurel's age—around forty—and she consciously presents her history to Laurel as a repudiation of Laurel's own story. She responds to Laurel's question about her family: "My family? . . . None of 'em living. That's why I ever left. We may not have had much . . . but we were all so close. Never had any secrets from each other, like some families. Sis was just like my twin. My brothers were all so unselfish! After Papa died, we all gave up everything for Mama, of course. Now that she's gone, I'm glad we did. Oh, I wouldn't have run off and left anybody that needed me. Just to call myself an artist and make a lot of money" (37). This account, largely fabricated, shows Fay's unerring instinct for Laurel's guilts. Despite Laurel's great love for her parents, whose only child she was,[3] her adult life has been spent far from them, in a world unlike theirs. Fay frames her past as an enduring domestic fantasy—the loving family of perfect devotion and accord—and she touches Laurel's sorest spots. In fact, Fay's mother, grandmother, and siblings are alive and show up in full form for the funeral, driving a truck with a bumper sign, "Do Unto Others Before They Do Unto You" (109).

Fay has been received with veiled horror by the older women of Mount Salus, Laurel's parents' contemporaries and friends. They tell Laurel gravely, "Do you know that when he brought her here to your house, she had very little idea of how to separate an egg? . . . 'Frying pan' was the one name she could give you of all the things your mother had in that kitchen, Laurel" (128). To these women, housekeeping is the medium in which women enact their values; continuity, order, fidelity, and filial piety. When Laurel arrives at the house, bringing her father's body home for burial, she finds it filled with evidences of traditional women's care: it is shining clean (although Fay left it in disorder), full of flowers, food, and hospitality. The domestic rituals of the funeral (here as in "The Wanderers") are a language that denies change; the longtime housekeeper, Missouri, says to Laurel with satisfaction, as the postfuneral buffet is served, "Now! . . . The house looking like it used to look!" (114) And Laurel herself is "at her old place at the dinner table" (65). Later, the old housekeepers try to persuade Laurel to stay on in Mount Salus (even though Fay has inherited the house), living on the money her father left her.

Laurel is bombarded by rival stories. Is she the selfish betrayer of an impossible domestic ideal, as Fay described her, or the heir to a domestic tradition that she must perpetuate to honor her mother's memory and skills, as embodied in her well-equipped kitchen? Either story reduces Laurel to an object, a piece that should find its place in a domestic puzzle. Such solutions are not for Fay; she later says to Laurel, contemptuously, "The past isn't a thing to me. I belong to the future, didn't you know that?" (207).

Fay has been the focus of much of the criticism of *The Optimist's Daughter;* some critics find Welty condescending to her on the bases of propriety and social class. When an interviewer asked if she looked "down her nose" at Fay and her family, Welty replied with some indignation, "I don't look down my nose at anyone among my characters. I wouldn't invent somebody in order to look down my nose at them. No, I see the absurd qualities in everybody, and it doesn't matter who they are. I saw the absurd qualities in Judge McKelva, who was of a different order" (*Conversations* 216). But later in the same interview, she used Fay as an illustration of her belief in *evil,* saying, "I do feel there is 'evil' in the world and in people. . . . I recognize its power and value. I do! I thought there was 'evil' in Fay in *The Optimist's Daughter*" (227).

The quality that appears "evil" in Fay is a malaise that does not recognize itself; as Laurel concludes, "Fay was without any powers of passion or imagination in herself and had no way to see it or reach it in the other person. . . . She could no more fight a feeling person than she could love him" (206). Such lack is the potential evil of the modern world, in Welty's eyes; Fay might as well be a tenant of the Waste Land, Mississippi style. Yet, ironically, much of the energy of this book comes from her. Laurel is clearly Fay's "superior" in intelligence, insight, and feeling—not to mention social graces—but her powers of passion are also impaired; they are frozen. If Fay tries to frame herself as a woman without a past, Laurel seems without a present. Her life in Chicago is indicated in the most minimal details, all concerning her work; she can arrange for an absence of some weeks, during her father's illness, with no apparent difficulty, and she has no contact with Chicago friends during this period of intense stress. Although she has achieved success as an artist, with her own studio and important commissions, Laurel's nourishment has been her past: her childhood with her parents and her brief, enchanted marriage in Chicago, ended by Phil's death. She realizes that the past has "been everything and done everything to me, everything for me" (206).

If Laurel is to be anything more than a preservationist, a civilized mourner, she must find a life in the present. The third, last, and longest section of *The Optimist's Daughter* is devoted to that necessary process; it occupies the three days between the funeral and Laurel's final departure from her parents' house. Fay has left for a brief visit with her family, so Laurel is alone.

Mount Salus, as Laurel perceives it, is almost entirely a world of women. Although many men appear at the funeral, only one—her father's law partner, Major Bullock—is fully differentiated, and he is blunderingly ineffective, although well-meaning, and drunk throughout the funeral observances. It is women who keep things going, and when Laurel arrives she is met by two generations of women friends: the surviving members of her mother's garden club and her own six bridesmaids, all of whom still live in Mount Salus. The day after the funeral, the older women push Laurel to begin the process of *comprehending* her father's marriage and the last months of his life. The "ladies" bemoan Fay's style and her domestic deficiencies and probe Judge McKelva's judgment in marrying her; what they cannot forgive is that their old friend did not choose a housekeeping woman for his second wife. Instead of providing traditional nurturing, all Fay did was "sit and eat" herself. "'She had to eat. Had nothing else to do to occupy her hands,' said Mrs. Pease, holding up a perfectly enormous afghan she was knitting" (126). These women measure Fay against their own lives: the afghans they have knitted, the houses they have kept. And Laurel, who has been impassive throughout her father's second marriage, begins to express her feelings for Fay:

> "I hope I never see her again," said Laurel.
> "There, girlie, you got it out," said Miss Tennyson. "She's a trial to us all and nothing else. Why don't you stay on here, and help us with her? . . . Who's going to kill you if you don't draw those pictures? As I was saying to Tish [her daughter, one of the bridesmaids], 'Tish, if Laurel would stay home . . . we could have as tough a bridge foursome as when Becky [Laurel's mother] was playing'" (133–34).

Laurel badly needs a language of honest feeling, and she has just reason for her dislike of Fay, who hastened Judge McKelva's death. The older women recognize her as a potential acolyte in their own female culture; to them middle-aged Laurel is still "girlie." Their language of domestic ritual and tradition is one that both Laurel's parents valued, and she herself defended it to Fay, who objected to the caretaking female visitors who filled the house. Then Laurel explained, "They're exactly the ones he'd have counted on to be here. . . . And I count on them" (66). But after the funeral, Miss Tennyson has made it clear that if Laura were to take that old language, the easy medium of her Mount Salus childhood, as her primary means of expression now, she would be forced to forfeit large portions of her selfhood. Just as Fay goaded Laurel for "calling herself an artist and making a lot of money," the Mount Salus women mock and devalue her Chicago life, "drawing pictures" at the North Pole. Were Laurel to take up her mother's old place in the bridge foursome, she would forfeit much of her individuality and her art.

Laurel's contemporaries, the bridesmaids, now with their own families and houses in Mount Salus, joke and reminisce affectionately about their own and Laurel's parents, in the language of fond accommodation with which they have learned to share their lives with an older generation. Laurel resists this language too; it seems, as the funeral storytelling did, to devalue the individual realities of her parents' lives:

> "Since when have you started laughing at them?" Laurel asked in a trembling voice. "Are they just figures from now on to make a good story?" . . .
> "Polly [Laurel's childhood name]!" Tish grabbed her. "We weren't laughing at them. They weren't funny—no more than. . . . all our fathers and mothers are!" She laughed again, into Laurel's face. "Aren't we grieving? We're grieving *with* you."
> "I know. Of course I know it," said Laurel. (151)

The bridesmaids too efface individuality; they see their dear parents as a generational lump and Laurel's grief as communal. On one level Laurel accedes to the communal culture, which she has "known" since birth. But in another way she protests the "good stories" by which that culture perpetuates itself, fearing that they do not do justice to the complexities and privacies of individual lives. To locate and honor the legacy of her parents' stories, she must begin the truest work of her mourning—alone, in the house.

There, she searches for the deepest springs of her life. For the search, she makes herself a housekeeper. Although she will never see them again, she tends the garden flowers. Inside she straightens and surveys, "studiously" effacing a few drops of nail polish spilled by Fay. On Laurel's last, solitary night, she is startled into atavistic fear by a chimney swift, which has gotten into the house, ancient omen of bad luck and death. The sooty bird is a housekeeper's horror; when Missouri, the longtime housekeeper, hears of it, she say, "Now I got all that wrenching out to do over" (196). Although Laurel acts the part of housekeeper, trying unsuccessfully to maneuver the bird outside, the swift seems to represent some part of her own repressed and endangered self. It drives her into the place she has avoided: her parents' bedroom, where she was born, later Fay and the judge's room, and now Fay's. There, frantic, Laurel finally begins to locate her true language. The house itself vibrates with sound, on the edge of meaning: "Windows and doors alike were singing, buffeted by the storm. The bird touched, tapped, brushed itself against the walls and closed doors, never resting. Laurel thought with longing of the telephone just outside the door" (155). But the telephone, offering access to an outer world, is not the link she needs now. Admitting Fay's "abuse" of her dying father, with a truthfulness she has not before permitted herself, Laurel releases a train of powerful emotions and realizes that it is her *mother* she wishes to tell about Fay—and then is shocked by the thought that she would burden her dead mother with such hurtful knowledge. At this point, the bird becomes an instrument of insistent percussion; Laurel "heard the bird drum itself against the door all its length from top to bottom" (157). The sound drives her into the little room that opens off the bedroom; now it contains her mother's writing desk, filled with a lifetime of papers. Sent by the imperative bird, Laurel has entered a womblike space, pregnant with meanings: a rich repository of female culture and female language.

Among her father's letters to her mother, her mother's gardening diaries and recipes and her college notebooks, with careful diagrams of *Paradise Lost*, Laurel finds a photograph album. In one youthful photograph, Becky wears a blouse about which she told her daughter:

"The most beautiful blouse I ever owned in my life—I made it. Cloth from Mother's own spinning, and dyed a deep, rich American Beauty color with pokeberries. . . . I'll never have anything to wear that to me is as satisfactory as that blouse."

How darling and vain she was when she was young! Laurel thought now. She'd made the blouse—and developed the pictures too, for why couldn't she? And very likely she had made the paste that held them. (162)

As Vande Kieft has written, the blouse's rich color suggests "Becky's genuinely passionate nature" (cf., "the sexy 'foolish' pink" chosen by Fay) (179). It also indicates Becky's omnivorous sense of her own powers, based in—but not limited to—traditional women's skills (sewing, dying, etc.) and executed in collaboration with her mother, who spun the cloth. Becky, who lived on a West Virginia farm with her widowed mother and six younger brothers, made long summer visits "up home" after her Mississippi marriage, taking Laurel with her. Her only child was named for the West Virginia state flower, to mark her with the beauties of that original world. (Fay's contempt for that Edenic world is indicated when she scoffs to Laurel, "What ever made Becky give you a name like that?" [36].) Laurel's earliest memories of childhood visits to the mountains are, according to Welty, almost entirely drawn from her own earliest memories of similar visits (*Conversations* 297–98). Becky's family home seems a mythical place of female prowess; she emphasized to Laurel her brothers' devotion to her mother and to her. Yet Becky's mother died unexpectedly and alone; then Laurel heard her mother "cry uncontrollably" for the first time (168).

Although Becky grew magnificent roses, kept a beautiful house, and "made the best bread in Mount Salus" (200), none of her passion or her faculty could save her mother—or herself. Soon after Laurel's husband's death, Becky died mad, after a rending five-year illness, during which she lost her sight and was confined to her room and her bed. Her last words to Laurel "while she still knew her" were, "You could have saved your mother's life. But you stood by and wouldn't intervene. I despair for you" (177–78). This is the most bottomless grief of Laurel's past. None of her tending now—her careful housekeeping—can save her mother from separation, loss, and death. Nothing can save Laurel from her mother's need and her own mortal incapacity to meet it. What Becky wished was a world restored to wholeness by her own "darling and vain" belief in her omnicompetence, linked to her mother and transmissible to her daughter—as epitomized in the tale of the homemade blouse.

Laurel does not read anything she finds in the old desk but the packet of letters from her grandmother to her mother; it is the story of mother and daughter, which she claims as her inheritance. The childhood horror Laurel associates with her beloved grandmother (especially vivid when she is sharing the house with a bird) is the pigeons the old woman kept; she was repulsed to see them "sticking their beaks down each other's throats, gagging each other, eating out of each other's craws, swallowing down all over again what had been swallowed before. . . . They convinced her [the child Laurel] that they could not escape each other and could not themselves be escaped from. So when the pigeons flew down, she tried to position herself behind her grandmother's skirt, which was long and black, but her grandmother said again, 'They're just hungry, like we are'" (166). Feeding, the basic domestic act that was so large a part of Laurel's mother's and grandmother's lives, is here seen in its most universal form—as an act in which the stuff of life is inevitably shared, in which the very idea of individuality, of sole individual possession, is obliterated. The grandmother does not shelter Laurel from such potential obliteration; instead, she reinforces it: the feeding pigeons are "hungry" *like us.* Reading the letters, Laurel realizes that her grandmother, far from Becky, felt that same sense of painful estrangement that she heard in her last message from her own mother: "Widowed, her health failing, lonely and sometimes bedridden, Grandma wrote . . . as to an exile, without ever allowing herself to put it into so many words. Laurel could hardly believe the bravery and serenity she had put into these short letters. . . . She read on and met her own name on a page. "I will try to send Laurel a cup of sugar for her birthday. Though if I can find a way to do it, I would like to send her one of my pigeons. It would eat from her hand, if she would let it" (180). Through time, the message and the gift at last reach Laurel: the language of generations of maternal love, expressed in domestic care and the pigeons' relentless truth about relationships, now expressed in Laurel's understanding of her mother's death and life. (The letter closely resembles a childhood birthday letter the young Eudora Welty received from her own maternal grandmother, quoted in *One Writer's Beginnings* [56].) Reading her grandmother's letter, she mourns as she has not yet let herself mourn either of her parents. In "a flood of feeling" she "put her head down on the open lid of the desk and wept in grief for love and for the dead. . . . The deepest spring in her heart had uncovered itself, and it began to flow again" (180–81).

Laurel has found the deepest truths of the house—truths that her father, the "optimist," had been unable to sustain. Having admitted her mother's and her grandmother's unbearable, unavoidable stories—all the bravery of their housekeeping and their love, all its necessity and futility—she is ready to claim her other suppressed story, that of her brief, "perfect" marriage. Her young husband appears, with deathless hunger for his own life and story. "He looked at her out of eyes wild with the craving for his unlived life, with mouth open like a funnel's. . . . His voice rose with the wind in the night and went around the house and around the house. It became a roar. 'I wanted it'" (181).

Laurel's truest heritage is not limited to one gender. It is the hungry passion of Becky and Phil, ravening beyond the regret and discretion that have been Laurel's pose. They *wanted it*. If Laurel herself has expressed such hunger—the hunger that, since childhood, has inspired her fear—it must have been in her art, the one part of her that seems to have stayed alive and functioning since Becky's and Phil's deaths. (Even flying to meet her father in a medical emergency, she automatically packed her sketchbook.) The sewing room interlude also offers clues to the sources of that art. As a fabric designer, working with textiles, Laurel evokes some of the oldest domestic activities. As her mother indicates in her proud description of the red blouse, women have often expressed their deepest feelings, as well as practical imperatives, in the creation of fabrics. Laurel intimates that such traditions were suggested to her in her earliest childhood, in the sewing room; she had "sat on this floor and put together the fallen scraps of cloth into stars, flowers, birds, people, or whatever she liked to call them, lining them up, spacing them out, making them into patterns, families, on the sweet-smelling matting, with the shine of firelight, or the summer light, moving over mother and child and what they were both making" (159).

Domestic ritual obviously had much to do with the launching of the artist's imagination. But later, Laurel recalls that her architect husband, Phil Hand, whom she met while attending art school, helped her to mature as an artist. He seemed to her a creator of godlike surety:

> When she watched his right hand go about its work, it looked to her like the Hand of his name.
> She had a certain gift of her own. He taught her, through his example, how to use it. She learned how to work by working beside him. He taught her to draw, to work toward and into her pattern, not to sketch peripheries. (188)

Laurel is also her father's daughter; she shares his emotional timidity and a tendency to hang back on peripheries of pattern and of feeling. What Laurel learned from Phil and Becky had to do with centering, working into the center with all its inexorable truths. Although "Hand" has been her name too, for many years, Laurel is still diffident about herself as an artist, admitting only that she "had a certain gift."

The last pages of *The Optimist's Daughter* show Laurel at last in full possession of that gift, acting from the center of her feeling self. The next morning, she must banish the bird from the house. Again, a housekeeper—Missouri—is her helper. At last, the swift flies free. "In the air, it was nothing but a pair of wings—she saw no body any more, no tail, just a tilting crescent being drawn back into the sky. 'All birds got to fly, even them no-count dirty ones,' said Missouri. 'Now I got all that wrenching out to do over'" (196). Freed from the confining house, with its ambiguous riches, the bird too—like the feeding pigeons—is enacting its essential nature. As Missouri says, "all birds got to fly." In the sky, Laurel sees its shape as an ancient symbol of a single woman: the crescent moon. Missouri (who fittingly bears the name of a border state) speaks one of the most insoluble truths of Welty's fiction. The single bird, which Laurel sees with revulsion and tenderness, is very much like herself; to fly is its nature, and its shape against the sky is a crescent arc, an *open* circle. But a housekeeper's story is a closed circle, an endless cycle of repetitions: "wrenching out" again and again. Laurel and Missouri are not opposites; despite their racial differences, they have as much affinity as any two women in the novella. Welty told an interviewer, "they were . . . big friends and both of them knew it. . . . in these really wrenching experiences that Laurel is going through by herself, Missouri's instincts are perfect" (*Conversations* 225).

The most positively powerful women in Welty's work are women like Miss Eckhart, Katie Rainey, and Ida M'Toy, whose lives aspire to both the female plots indicated by Missouri: housekeeping *and* the "other way to live." Just before she leaves the house, having burned all her mother's papers, Laurel makes her bid for such power. In a kitchen cabinet, she discovers the breadboard her husband had made for her mother, scarred by Fay's careless misuse. The domestic object, made by a man who honored housekeeping and "loved good bread" (201) such as Becky made and who was welcomed by Becky into her kitchen, suddenly becomes the one object of her past that Laurel wants to *possess*. When Fay reappears, she finds Laurel preparing to leave with the breadboard. Fay challenges her:

> "Fine Miss Laurel! . . . If they all could see you now! . . . It's dirty as sin."
> "A coat of grime is something I can get rid of."
> "If all you want to do is rub the skin off your bones."
> "The scars it's got are a different matter. But I'd work."
> "And do what with it when you got through?" Fay said mockingly.
> "Have my try at making bread. Only last night . . . I had my mother's recipe, written in her own hand, right before by eyes."
> "It all tastes alike, don't it?"

"You never tasted my mother's. I could turn out a good loaf too—I'd work at it." (204–05)

Here Laurel seems to believe that housekeeping can be the language of her truest, central self: by honoring her husband's careful craftsmanship and continuing her mother's domestic work, she can express a life of fidelity and passion. For a moment, she expresses the faith in domestic transmission that nineteenth-century housekeepers longed to pass to their daughters. To Fay, the labors Laurel projects are nothing but dirty, pointless drudgery. She is incapable of investing housework with meaning or of performing domestic ritual, and the nuances of traditional women's culture are meaningless to her; to Fay, all bread tastes alike. Another of the "evils" Fay embodies (bearing perhaps an unjust weight of meaning, as few other Welty characters do) is the obliterating, homogenizing modernity of mass culture, in which domestic ritual is lost. When Laurel goes on to speak of Phil and his love for warm, fresh bread, Fay replies scornfully, "What has *he* got to do with it? He's dead, isn't he?" Laurel prepares to attack; she raises the breadboard above Fay's head. For her, it has become "the whole solid past" (205–06).

But she does not strike, and she does not take the breadboard with her. Laurel's story of herself as housekeeper was framed conditionally: "I *would* work . . . I *could* turn out a good loaf." Much as she values the past, she cannot live fully in it. Relinquishing the breadboard and the domestic mythology it signifies is the last step by which Laurel is prepared for her coming life. The waiting bridesmaids no longer seem anachronistic attendants for a middle-aged widow; at the novel's end they are entirely appropriate companions, for as she flies back to Chicago to reclaim her artist's life, Laurel—like Virgie Rainey at the same age—is just entering her full womanhood. Finally Laurel lays the breadboard on Fay's table, "where it belonged." She says, 'I think I can get along without that too.' Memory lived not in initial possession but in the freed hands, pardoned and freed, and in the heart that can empty but fill again, in the patterns restored by dreams" (207–08). Passing Fay, Laurel embraces Missouri and joins her bridesmaids, who are "holding the door open for her and impatiently calling her name" (208).

Reynolds Price, in an admiring essay on the *New Yorker* version of this novella, praises it as "Eudora Welty's strongest, richest work" and speaks of its clarity and "quality of summary" and the language's "stripped iron efficiency" ("Onlooker" 76, 86). These qualities are stunningly present in the final passages I have just quoted. Laurel realizes, finally, what *memory* must mean in her life. She has located its essence, at the core of her self, by stripping away. "The more the better" may have been a fit coda for *The Golden Apples* and Virgie Rainey, but it does not speak for Laurel Hand. This stripped, essential quality in *The Optimist's Daughter* makes the book's ending all the more disturbing for some readers. Patricia Meyer Spacks, for example, sees the "evocative rhetoric of freedom, heart, dreams" as Welty's insistence "that memory solves all problems. . . . If society encourages women finally to retreat within, guarding precious private heritage, it thus fosters a straitened maturity, involving the giving up of external claims. The optimist's daughter seems from this point of view an emblem of despair" (347).

Compared with the vitality of a Virgie Rainey, there *is* something "straitened" about Laurel Hand. One reason for this is that she seems (quite unlike Virgie) to have abdicated both sexuality and sensuality; both her mother's passion and Fay's palpable sexiness[4] frighten Laurel. The part of her artist-self which is still functioning as she mourns in Mount Salus is her capacity for centering, which is expressed in the novel's style. But finally, I differ with Spacks's reading. For I see Laurel facing up to a central decision of most middle-aged women's lives: what will they inherit from their mothers? For Welty herself, that decision must have been very intense. The most significant choice of her life, Welty wrote in answer to a questionnaire, was that she chose "to live at home to do my writing in a familiar world and have never regretted it" (*Conversations* 36). This meant a choice to live almost her entire adult life, until 1966, with her mother, who emerges from *One Writer's Beginnings* as an intense and demanding person "of character." Vande Kieft, speaking of her long acquaintance and friendship with Welty, wrote recently that this writer's "strongest and most admirable piety is the filial one" ("Eudora Welty: Visited" 465). Laurel's choice, as artist and daughter, was externally different from Eudora Welty's but still, acknowledging, mourning, and remembering her mother is her central problem in Mount Salus; as Welty has said, Becky's "influence" on her daughter is "the focal point" of this book: "So much went back to Becky" (*Conversations* 242).

Laurel's most pious possible daughterly response would be to take up housekeeping, following her mother's recipe and baking her bread, with her equipment. She could join the Mount Salus ladies and help to preserve the bridge game, going through the motions and cherishing the past. *That* would be a "straitened maturity," as Spacks says. It would also be a denial of Becky's own example. She too left home and a life with her mother, which she obviously loved. The papers she preserved were not entirely domestic; *Paradise Lost* was kept alongside her recipes. And Becky continued to change throughout her passionate life, finally growing into her own unbearable, tempestuous death (as opposed to Laurel's father, who died in quiet, unacknowledged despair). Laurel's hands are freed now, to take on her own life. And they are "pardoned"; by acknowledging her own passion and speaking it to Fay, Laurel has earned that pardon from herself. In the deepest sense, Laurel is acknowledging the "women's time" of domestic ritual, with its repetitions, cycles, and recurrences (Kristeva 16). Thus the "emptied" heart can "fill again," and patterns may be "restored by dreams." But if this happens for Laurel, if she ever returns to patterns as traditional as her mother's breadbaking, it will be because they are generated in her own unconscious, the world of her dreams. In my reading of this passage, Laurel has become one of Welty's voyaging brides, having internalized at last all that her mother and grandmother could give her, through their domestic culture and their valiant individual lives.

Although we know little of Laurel's work as an artist, we imagine that she may have been hampered by her timidity and her veneration of Phil's godlike male example. Her night in the sewing room has put her in touch with her complex female heritage, and it has restored Phil's passionate, desirous humanity—as well as her own. The book's last paragraph, with haunting echoes of "Because I could not stop for death," launches Laurel into another realm; it is full of acceleration, exhilaration, and speed. "They flashed by the Courthouse, turned at the school, Miss Adele [Laurel's own first grade teacher] was out with her first-graders . . . she waved. So did the children. The last thing Laurel saw, before they whirled into speed, was the twinkling of their hands, the many small and unknown hands, wishing her goodbye" (208). Like Virgie and Delilah, Laurel seems at last to have tapped into cosmic energy; the children's hands twinkle starlike as she whirls into the firmament, on the verge of flight. What is truly Dickinsonian here is the sense of boundless possibility. It is not as immediately apparent as Virgie Rainey's images of primeval bear, leopard, and swan—but in many ways *The Optimist's Daughter* is Welty's mature working-out of how to launch a contemporary woman. For me, it is very far from the "emblem of despair" Spacks describes.

Eudora Welty herself has affinities with Missouri, who tells two female stories: flight and domestic ritual. *The Optimist's Daughter* and her longest book, the novel *Losing Battles*, were written concurrently. Welty worked on the novel over an extended period, perhaps as long as fifteen years. "I didn't write it in a normal way," she told Walter Clemons, "because I had private things at home"—presumably the illnesses and deaths of her mother and two younger brothers (*Conversations* 30). (*Losing Battles* is dedicated to the memory of her brothers.) The novel was an attempt at something new for Welty; she said in 1972, "I wanted to see if I could do something that was new for me: translating every thought and feeling into action and speech. . . . I felt that I'd been writing too much by way of description, of introspection on the part of my characters. I tried to see if I could make everything shown, brought forth, without benefit of the author's telling any more about what was going on inside the characters' minds and hearts" (*Conversations* 77). With everything externalized, matters of plot and pattern become especially important in this long novel, and much of the first critical response concentrated on the formal conventions of *Losing Battles*.[5]

Formally, this book could not be more different from *The Optimist's Daughter*, which is a rigorously *demeublé* book. *Losing Battles* teems with people, voices, and furniture. *The Optimist's Daughter* postulates a modern woman who internalizes domestic ritual, making it a resource of her art and her newly invented life. As Price says, *The Optimist's Daughter* ends with "a complicated sense of joy"—especially in the sense that Laurel has located her own "vision, distance, stamina," along with "the courage of all three" ("Onlooker" 88). In fact, this impression (which I share) is conveyed entirely by the tone of Welty's last paragraphs, not by narrative, the demonstration of storytelling. Laurel is the woman Welty has again and again labored to bring forth—only to eschew the working out of her story. What will Laurel do now in Chicago? Whom and what will she love? How will she invent and remember? We might as well ask these same questions of Jenny Lockhart or of Virgie Rainey or of Delilah—all women who have disentangled themselves from domestic ritual.

Losing Battles, by contrast, is about entanglements—"home ties," as one character says (163). If *The Optimist's Daughter* is the spare story of a woman's going away, *Losing Battles* is (or at first seems) the sprawling tale of a man's homecoming. It is an August Sunday in Depression-poor hill country north Mississippi; in a tiny settlement called Banner, the Beecham-Renfro family is gathering for the ninetieth birthday of their matriarch, Granny Vaughn. Granny's favorite great-grandson, Jack Jordan Renfro, has been sent to the penitentiary because of a brawl with the local storekeeper. Disapproving Judge Moody, who did not understand that the long-standing feud was essentially good-natured play, made an example of Jack and convicted him. Now the gathered family, including Jack's young wife, Gloria, and the baby daughter he has not yet seen, expect him to show up for the reunion in a loyal son's act of fealty, even though his prison term is not over until the next day. Jack does not disappoint them; he manages to escape and appears at his parents and Granny's house, the reunion site, to universal rejoicing. Then someone informs him that the car he helped out of the ditch on his way home belonged to his enemy, Judge Moody. Jack considers himself obligated by family honor to put that car back in the ditch, and he lies in wait for it. But when Judge and Mrs. Moody drive by, Jack and Gloria's baby darts in the path of their car, and the judge swerves to save the child, running his car onto a precipice. Now Jack is indebted to Judge Moody and must undertake the complicated feat of getting the car down. Meanwhile, he invites the Moodys to the reunion. Judge Moody had been heading to visit the aged and legendary local schoolteacher, Julia Mortimer, who dies on the day of the reunion; she was the mentor of Jack's wife, Gloria, who succeeded her as teacher of Banner School. The two rival gatherings—for Granny's birthday and Miss Julia's funeral—honor two different female stories.

Obviously, the reunion sanctions domestic ritual, and it sanctions staying put. Granny Vaughn, who has lived in one house for ninety years, is its logical icon. Taciturn and wizened with age, Granny is beyond our access as a character; she speaks in riddles and dresses and behaves as autocratically as an oracle. Staying in place and keeping a household going is most especially a female duty and triumph; Granny has outlived her preacher husband and her one daughter, and the family would like her to stay fixed in time as well, living on forever, like Circe. Granny in fact tries to claim such a triumph for herself; she says this is her hundredth birthday, not merely her ninetieth.

Granny's one granddaughter, Beulah Beecham Renfro, has also stayed home all her life. She and her husband and five children (plus Gloria and the baby) all live with Granny. A sturdy middle-aged woman, Beulah has the responsibility of executing the reunion. The yearly gathering is her chance to vindicate her domestic life. Her five surviving brothers, their large families, and peripheral friends and kin gather. Beulah is everywhere. For days ahead she has been cooking, laundering, and plotting; even the family's half-wild pig is caught and tied up, to "look sassy" for the great day. Before dawn she takes the delicate birthday cake out of the oven (a triumph of domestic art, it will "cut like cream" [188]). Not content with having prepared ahead, she stirs up a (surely superfluous) batch of gingerbread after the guests have mostly arrived, running from kitchen to porch in a frenetic display of faculty. Her skills, especially cooking, are a means of control as well as of nurturing and art. Beulah oversees, prompts, brags, cooks, offers, withholds, and pitches most of the songs; she is like a superstar athlete, racking up points. The others have brought food, flowers, and gifts to the reunion too; Aunt Beck, for example, contributes an enormous and legendary chicken pie, to which she attributes magical powers to draw Jack home from the pen. But Beulah will not be outdone even at the day's end; as the family departs, she detains them with a last offering. "At some moment during the day she had found time to run out and cut the remainder of her own flowers against their departure. She was ready to load everybody home. Here was the duplication of what they'd come bringing here—milk-and-wine lilies, zinnias, phlox, tuberoses" (352). Why send them home with flowers duplicating those they brought? And why did they bring those flowers, knowing Beulah grew them too? Obviously this is a ritual demonstration, powerfully competitive and related to issues of control.[6] Granny knows well how to play the game; when Beulah's cake is a triumph, she appropriates it. "'I made it in the biggest pan I had,' said Granny. 'If it don't go round, I'll have to stir up another one'" (188). No one worships Granny as Beulah does. Yet, while Granny lives and they share a roof, she is always in danger of obliteration, of having her housekeeping triumphs stolen.

Although the reunion elicits an endless barrage of annual stories, none of them celebrates Beulah. Jack, the family favorite, is still a boy, but his every "triumph" is recounted and inflated by his loving family—led by his mother. On the morning after the reunion, she is up while he still sleeps, having "fried up every morsel I had left over to spread company breakfast" (372). Then she prepares to go watch Jack's efforts to rescue the Moody car, supporting the male mythology: "If my boy's ready to turn in the performance I think he is, it's a mother's place to be there and see it done right!" (373).

In one sense, Beulah Beecham Renfro is the woman R. J. Bowman sought. She is deeply implicated in domestic ritual and she is men's destination; her brothers and sons are drawn back to her bountiful table. And her first name recalls Bowman's quest to Beulah. But, although we have no more access to her inner thoughts than we do to those of the nameless woman in Welty's first story, Beulah's is an enormously more complicated tale. Although Beulah constantly alludes to the mythology of housekeeping, Welty portrays her domestic life as a constant balancing act of reaching and stretching. Welty has said that she set the novel in the Depression because she wanted "to get a year in which I could show people at the rock bottom. . . . I wanted the poorest part of the state . . . I wanted a clear stage to bring on this family, to show them when they had really no props to their lives, had only themselves, plus an indomitable will to live even with losing battles" (*Conversations* 50).

Beulah shows these stresses more clearly than any other character; the task of finding something to "fry up" and serve forth falls squarely on her. The reunion, which occurs every year in a regular cycle, is her tour de force. And she feels its ending with keener pain than the others display; when the day is over and she is getting in bed, her voice is heard, speaking to her husband: "I've got to stand it and I've got to stand it. And you've got to stand it. . . . After they've all gone home, Ralph, and the children's in bed, that's what's left. Standing it" (360). The family is financially strapped; the oldest child has a prison record, and despite her lifelong efforts, Beulah cannot change this story. The best she can do is to stay put, to *stand* and stand it. The immobility of housekeeping is obviously galling her, here.

Despite all Beulah's ostentatious displays of faculty at the reunion, the one story she tells about herself is about domestic failure, a terrible little parable of gendered plots. It has to do with Sam Dale, her youngest brother who was killed in World War I, and the accident that made him sterile. Beulah recounts:

> "Sam Dale's a little fellow sitting up close to the big hearth—still in dresses. I was supposed to be minding him but I don't know and can't ever remember what I was doing instead. Coal flew out of the fire and hit in his lap. Oh, it was a terrible thing! Granny called for some slippery elm for it and I said I'd go, I'd go! And instead of settling for the first elm I could find—instead of settling for the closest-to, I had to send myself farther and farther and farther, hunting for the *best!* For what's good enough to help what I'd done? They thought when I came running back late that I'd dawdled along the way. . . .
>
> Grandpa whipped me himself. . . . They had me to grow up in torment for little Sam Dale." (324)

Even as a small girl, Beulah was expected to use the language of domestic care to safeguard gender conventions. It was up to her to guard Sam Dale's incipient manhood, his sexual potency, so he would not have to live forever "in dresses" which, for a boy, signify immaturity and impotence. The castrating force is the hearth fire itself, a "terrible" force that young Beulah could not control. A motherless child herself, she was entrusted with one of the heaviest responsibilities of domestic life—the protection of a baby. When she stole a few minutes for herself, minutes so verboten that they are still blocked after years of attempts at memory, the fire exerted its original, uncontained force. Then, when Beulah was given a second traditional housekeeper's task—gathering an herbal remedy—she was so eager to excel that she failed again. Beulah's story is a grim account of the education and ceaseless responsibilities of the housekeeper. If she lapses into undomestic privacy, disaster can strike, and if she aims at domestic excellence, disaster may strike again. Beulah's tarrying in the woods may also suggest an unacknowledged desire for another kind of life, a life of wandering and quest, not housekeeping.

Beulah suffers tormenting guilt because she kept Sam Dale from "being a father" and thus excluded him from patriarchal domestic life. When the reunion is debating Gloria's parentage and believes briefly that Sam Dale might have been her father, Beulah is ecstatic. She wants to accept Gloria as "proof, living proof! I didn't do harm to my own, after all. I can die happy!" (268). Beulah's happiness is dependent on the belief that she has kept domestic faith and kept "her own" unharmed at the hearth. But when Granny later reveals that Sam Dale was not Gloria's father but only the prospective husband of her mother, Beulah is robbed—again by her rival Granny—of her brief happiness and returned to the state of guilt and contingency in which she—and all such housekeepers—must live. For who can protect "her own" forever against fire, change, and death? Yet, since girlhood, Beulah has been trained to believe that she *must* try. No wonder she seems near hysteria throughout the reunion day.

One way to read *Losing Battles* is to see Eudora Welty bringing on all the conventions of traditional male and female plots, in a battle royal of stories. Beulah tends home fires and keeps the reunion going; her cyclical and prototypically domestic plot is "standing it," year after year. Jack, fighting, championing, avenging, and repaying, returns like Odysseus on his journey from the pen. His dearest possessions are his truck, his horse, and the school bus he once drove because he was "most popular" boy in Banner School. While Beulah is serving forth her triumphant reunion dinner, he is wrestling with the Moodys' Buick, having an affectionate reunion with his traditional male foe Curly Stovall, and making love with Gloria. Rabuzzi emphasizes that a housekeeper's life is typically characterized by "the amorphousness and circularity of mythic time"; the Beechams' annual veneration and canonization of Granny indicate their allegiance to domestic values, traditionally female. Rabuzzi also observes that traditional men's experience, "by contrast . . . is dominated by characteristics associated with space" (150). Thus means of travel, by which space can be conquered, are often venerated by men's culture. So it is appropriate that the *truck* is central to the male contest between Jack and Curly and that the burgeoning struggle for dominance between Jack and his younger brother Vaughn centers on control of the school bus.

However, the male plots in this novel, epitomized by the car maneuvering into which even Judge Moody is drawn, are transient and trivial; entertaining as they may be, they are what Beulah calls "Man-foolishness. . . . Ever hear of it?" (379). (This assessment is almost the first thing that Gloria and her mother-in-law agree about.) Jack is heroic to his family because he is a home boy; he takes on the home plot and works, running the farm, to perpetuate domestic life. Jack's middle name is Granny's maiden name, and he worships her as a symbol of the family, defying legal strictures to make it home to celebrate her day. When he hears that he and Gloria may be first cousins and may have to move across the state line to keep their marriage legal, he is horrified—not at the possibility of incest (marrying a relative is attractive in this family, which is besotted with itself) but at the prospect of leaving Granny's hearth. He says to the judge, "You want me and Gloria and Lady May to leave all we hold dear and all that holds us dear? Leave Granny and everybody else that's not getting any younger? . . . Why, it would put an end to the reunion" (321). Jack is committed to cyclical endeavors as repetitive as housekeeping and his aims serve the family welfare, history, and honor. With his father disabled from a dynamite accident since before Jack's birth, Jack has all his life felt the force of "home ties," and he tells Gloria, "I'm beholden to the reunion to keep it running on a smooth track today, for Granny's birthday to be worth her living to see. For Mama's chickens not to go wasted, and for all of 'em that's travelled through dust not to go home disappointed" (112). All the male byplay with trucks, cars, and horses is simply diversion, a way of playing at the conventions of voyaging, a distraction from the hard fact that for men, too, life is a matter of *standing it*, from year to year in this place.

Jack's mild father, Ralph Renfro, exemplifies this fact. Although his family were the earliest settlers in this part of Mississippi, he has lost the family business and is in danger of losing the farm, which came from Beulah's maternal ancestors. Just managing to stay in place is a struggle for him. Ralph Renfro's escape is dynamite; he plays with fire and delights in blowing things up. His contribution to the car plot is to blow up a tree that is holding the Buick. Obviously, the phallic dynamite reflects an effort to explode static domestic plots. Yet Ralph's overt and truest loyalties are also domestic; he serves the stability of house and family. While his son Jack is in prison, he sells Jack's dearest possession, the prototypically male truck, to put a new tin roof on Granny's farmhouse. And Jack's horse is sold too, to put food on the table.

Mary Anne Ferguson, in her useful reading of *Losing Battles*, has observed that Welty both uses and transforms the conventions of comedy and epic. Many of these transformations have the effect of emphasizing the communal values of "the reunion" over the imperatives of individual quest—and thus the emphasis also falls on values traditionally associated with domestic life. For example, Ferguson notes that "conspicuous by its absence in *Losing Battles* is the epic motif of the search of the hero for his father, symbolically the search for identity" (312). When the search for identity does surface in *Losing Battles*, it is enacted by a woman, Gloria, whose unknown parentage becomes a subject of the reunion's investigation, and whose mother, at least, is identified in the course of the day.

In the world of Granny's family, for worse or better, traditionally domestic female values prevail. Their male champion, Jack, is a feminized man, like the male hero of another domestic classic, *Uncle Tom's Cabin*, a novel of similarly sprawling scope and ambition. Elizabeth Ammons argues convincingly that Stowe feminized Tom, using him to demonstrate her "belief that a man can live admirably in accord with her nineteenth-century maternal ideal." Tom expresses Stowe's "wish that masculinity be defined along more feminine lines for the reformation of society" ("Heroines" 159–60, 162). Welty is less sanguine than Stowe about the possibilities of social reform, as her title witnesses. But the character of Jack is obviously engrossing and important to her; she has said that she planned to write a short story ending with Jack's return from the pen, but that "the moment he arrived, it became a novel. Because he was somebody. And the story was his" (*Conversations* 46). Jack's eager generosity, his capacity for love, his filial piety (especially directed to women), and his capacity for sticking to repetitive tasks, which offer minimal rewards in terms of money and recognition from a wider world, are all values that domestic women's culture has honored. Aunt Beck pays him a high compliment when she predicts, "Jack's going to make a wonderful little mother" (94). He also has some of the limitations of a domestic perspective; he tends to emphasize moment-to-moment performance and to eschew long-range plans, dealing with each task as it comes along.

In the terms of male plots, aimed at arrival and achievement, *Losing Battles* ends in a rout for Jack. Curly Stovall, Jack's rival, is on the verge of marrying Jack's oldest sister and has finally collected the long-coveted trophy of Jack's shirt tail, and Gloria has allowed Jack's truck to be hauled away to the junk yard, to be disassembled and sold for parts. Yet these traditional humiliations don't much matter, even to Jack, for he manages to get Gloria to Miss Julia Mortimer's funeral, so she can pay her respects to her mentor, and then to return, on the novel's last page, to his mother's hearth, a battered, feminized champion of domestic ritual:

One of his eyes still imperfectly opened [he was punched by Curly and kicked by his baby daughter], and the new lump blossoming on his forehead for his

mother's kiss, Jack raised his voice and sang. All Banner could hear him and
know who he was.

> *"Bringing in the sheaves,*
> *Bringing in the sheaves!*
> *We shall come rejoicing,*
> *Bringing in the sheaves!"* (435–36)

Jack's song tells one of the oldest stories of human civilization, featuring
harvest, the completion of a cycle, and return for the blessing of the
stationary mother, who will bestow her nurturing, confirming kiss.

The real conflict in *Losing Battles* is between female plots. The two poles
are Julia Mortimer and Granny Vaughn; as Ferguson observes, "the tensions
of the women's role are shown by the struggle between the two old women
for the loyalty of the family" (311). Against Granny and her domestic gospel
of staying put, keeping house, and endurance, Julia Mortimer urges a
progressive, inclusive plot of growth, self-improvement, and *rise*. This
achievement-oriented plot is more usually associated with traditional male
culture. Its dark side is exemplified in *Losing Battles* by the Sutpen-like
figure of Herman Dearman (whose prototypical masculinity is emphasized
by the double *man* in his name), an exploitative speculator who came into
Banner about twenty years earlier. He made a killing in timber, brought
black laborers into an all-white region, acquired local property (it was to
Dearman that Ralph Renfro lost the family store), and lived an aggressively
antidomestic life, surrounded by other men. Beulah reports, angrily, "he put
up a sawmill where he found the prettiest trees on earth. Lived with men in
a boxcar and drank liquor. Pretty soon the tallest trees was all gone" (341).
Dearman may have seduced Rachel Sojourner, whom Sam Dale loved, and
fathered Gloria; he was murdered by the oldest Beecham brother, Nathan,
to avenge Sam Dale. Although a black man was blamed and hanged for the
murder, Nathan punished himself for becoming the tool of a plot of male
competition and violence; he cut off his right hand, refused to marry and
start his own family, and lives the life of a wandering evangelist. Attending
the annual reunion is his one gesture of fealty to the home plot; even then,
he refuses home comforts and will not sleep under Granny's roof or eat
Beulah's good cooking.

Julia Mortimer is associated with both these men; Nathan was her star
pupil and Dearman is rumored to have been her lover. Most of her successes
are men, who return for her funeral from faraway places. Many are "big
shots," including priests, politicians, a doctor, a professor, a governor, and
Judge Moody himself. If Jack is feminized by his domestic fealty, Julia

Mortimer is a woman associated with the best traditional male values, pledged to humane achievement and progress. In a youthful photograph, she has exceptional beauty: "the long-focused eye, the tall sweep of black hair laid with a rosebud that looked like a small diploma tied up in its ribbon, the very way the head was held, all said that the prospect was serious" (330). Miss Julia's beauty came from her sense of aim and distances. Banner School was the chosen center of her life as a memorable, passionate, unstinting teacher. Even when she was dying, Miss Julia maintained her belief in educational advance, as she wrote to Judge Moody: "I'm as alive as ever, on the brink of oblivion. . . . Things like this are put in your path to teach you. You can make use of them, they'll bring you one stage, one milestone, further along your road. You can go crawling next along the edge of madness, if that's where you've come to. There's a lesson in it. . . . I haven't spent a lifetime fighting my battle to give up now" (299). This is the determined language of linear progression; it opposed the cycles of domestic ritual.

Julia Mortimer resembles Laurel's mother, Becky, also a schoolteacher. Like Becky, she does not actually appear in the novel. Instead, her story is pieced together at the reunion. As she comes to passionate life through the patchwork of tales, it seems that Julia Mortimer may represent the "other way to live" for a woman in the world of *Losing Battles,* a passionate ambitious alternative to the domestic plot. Her work, teaching, is virtually the only profession open to women in her time and place. Lexie Renfro, Beulah's sister-in-law, took Julia Mortimer as her mentor and aspired to become a teacher; when she failed Latin and could not qualify to teach, she fell back into the traditional domestic occupations of a single woman, working as a seamstress and an uncertified nurse. When Miss Julia is her patient, she becomes Lexie's adversary, and another female battle ensues. Lexie deprives her charge of pencil, paper, visitors, mail, mobility, and food; the doctor claims that Miss Julia died of starvation and neglect. Lexie's tale of Julia Mortimer's last days is the most horrific narrative to emerge from the reunion talk; it shows the rage of a traditionally domestic woman against someone who showed her another way to live, which she was unable to claim for her own. Granny, too, perceives Miss Julia as her most powerful female rival; when the teacher's painful story threatens to usurp the reunion's attention, Granny reclaims that attention by singing and jigging on the table. The youngest Renfro daughter is aghast to see her great-grandmother breaking Baptist law and dancing on a Sunday, but Miss Beulah instructs the child in the preeminent *family* gospel: "You got the brain of a bird? She's got track of what day this is . . . better than anybody here. . . . Her own birthday." Then, when Jack springs forward to catch Granny as she falls, she mistakes him for his long-dead uncle. Granny asserts again that, with the achievement of a long domestic life, *she* controls time, and Beulah passionately backs her up; "'She's all right, Granny's all right,' said Miss Beulah in a desperate voice" (308).

Yet their adversary, Julia Mortimer, is not an antidomestic woman. She knits sweaters, raises flowers, cooks, hauls milk to school to nurture her pupils, raises peach trees, and sends a free seedling to everyone on her mail route. Gloria reports, "She wanted to make everybody grow as satisfying an orchard as hers. . . . She wasn't fooling" (243). For Julia Mortimer—as for Miss Eckhart, another teacher, and for Becky McKelva, with her recipes, flowers, and notes on *Paradise Lost*—domestic skills were a *part* of a life of growth and achievement, which she wanted to share with everyone around her. To her, the strong domestic loyalties of the Beechams were a dangerous kind of self-love, because they shut out new possibilities and valorized limits, including those of gender conventions.

Here too language becomes a central issue. Julia Mortimer advocates a language of openness and expansion, where everything can be brought into the open. Beulah Beecham was once one of her star pupils; her one memory of triumph, which counters the guilt and failure of Sam Dale's accident, is of the occasion when she spelled down the entire Banner School, in a state of such excitement that she wet her pants. But as a housekeeper and a domestic devotée, Beulah now serves a language that usually cannot be spelled or spoken; it is secretive and controlled by managing women. During the debate about Gloria's parentage, for example, Granny brings out a faded, unmailed postcard that was left among Sam Dale's effects when he died. It has been concealed for twenty years between the pages of the Vaughn Bible. Judge Moody, Miss Julia's protegé, scoffs at such unofficial evidence; it would never "stand up in court." But Beulah protests that the card is much better than a legal document; "there's a whole lot more of Sam Dale in that postcard, if you know how it read it" (322). Granny's sacred texts—the postcard, her dead daughter's wedding ring, and a lock of her hair—are cryptic and elliptical; they are preserved with care between the pages of the great patriarchal text, her preacher-husband's Bible, and they yield intimate knowledge that the necessary and efficacious legal documents, enacted by the judge, can never reach. One of these iconic objects, the gold ring, was removed by Beulah's eldest daughter who wanted to show it off in a wider world. But it was seized by Curly Stovall as partial payment for the overdue Renfro grocery bill. Jack's efforts to retrieve it only resulted in the loss of the ring and Jack's prison term.

Intertextuality is in some ways the ideal of *Losing Battles*. In the course of the reunion, *all* the stories, domestic and not, are brought out for the telling; Julia Mortimer, Judge Moody, and Granny all have their tales. But the novel emphasizes the fragility and contingency of all texts. The county courthouse was recently burned by arsonists and the public records are lost; even Judge Moody must admit, "There's no written proof left that any of us at all are alive here tonight" (322). And when Ella Fay took Granny's hidden treasure—the gold circlet, symbol of the precious, unbroken continuity of the family and of domestic ritual—into the public world of school and store, it was irretrievably lost. Ideally, one would not have to choose among the competing texts of *Losing Battles;* Beulah could preserve the talents that made her a champion speller and also develop the insights, spawned in the intimacy of domestic life, that allow her to decipher the nuanced text of Sam Dale's postcard. But such inclusiveness—however much Julia Mortimer might have urged it—is not permitted in the Beecham family and the Banner community. Beulah, now a domestic virtuoso, must speak with contempt of the courts and the schoools, for they are her rivals.

For her last protegée, Julia Mortimer chose Gloria Short from the orphanage and sent her to normal school, hoping to "pass on the torch" of "a teacher's life" (244), giving the girl a flaming emblem of achievement and tradition, which was *not* a hearth fire. As far as we can tell, Julia Mortimer never successfully launched a female protegée; Beulah and Lexie, for examples, both failed her. No wonder that, when she made her last choice, she picked an orphan, Welty's symbol in *The Golden Apples* of "the other way to live." It was perhaps Gloria's lack of a traditional domestic education like Beulah's that made Julia Mortimer hope she could make the girl a teacher.

But Gloria, as her last name suggests, also falls short of Miss Julia's expectations; she falls in love with the most popular boy in her first school, gets pregnant, and marries him. However, she resists the domestic ideal as promulgated by Beulah and Granny and urged by Jack. She refuses the domestic language of Granny's house; Beulah complains again and again that she "just can't read her!" (94). Dressed in her homemade wedding dress to welcome Jack home, Gloria boasts, "Nothing I have on is second-hand!" (264) While Beulah's three daughters wear hand-me-down feed sack dresses, Gloria resists the communal recycling of domestic life. Although the aunts advise otherwise, she is still nursing Lady May, who is old enough to walk and talk, and the baby's first dress is not a hand-me-down from Beulah's youngest, but is cut from Gloria's own schoolteaching dress. Gloria's most characteristic instruction to her daughter is that she "copy" her mother, and no one else. Gloria's domestic care—feeding and clothing her child—is an act of *individual* self-assertion, and she sees the communal traditions of women's culture, epitomized in the home reunion, as a threat that may swallow up her selfhood and her child. She dreads the prospect Jack hopes for: a life of staying put under the family roof. While the reunion cherishes its collective past, Gloria (who has no history and is not eager to identify her parents) recites a future-oriented creed: "I'm one to myself, and nobody's kin, and my own boss, and nobody knows the one I am or where I came from. . . . all that counts in life is the road up ahead" (315). Characteristically individual and independent, Gloria's creed emphasizes a solitary linear quest; she sounds like a prototypical male hero such as Natty Bumppo or Huckleberry Finn. Much of Julia Mortimer's teaching serves such typically male aims and heroes.

Miss Julia tried to prevent Gloria's marriage, believing that Sam Dale was her father and honoring the Mississippi law that prohibits marriage between cousins. In fact, she helped to get the law passed. Intermarriage must have been a special horror for her, for it intensified "home ties," which seemed to Julia Mortimer the foe of education. She feared for Gloria and Jack's children, and warned Gloria that her baby might be "deaf and dumb"—bereft of language, which for Miss Julia was the greatest horror. Lexie reports, "I hid her pencil and she said, 'Now I want to die'" (284). Gloria too values written language; she was the only family member who wrote to Jack in the pen. But she broke with Miss Julia when she married Jack; she never returned to visit her mentor, although she planned to take Lady May, as soon as the child was old enough to talk and to vindicate her mother. At Miss Julia's burial, Gloria cries out, "She changed. I'll never change!" (432). Gloria intends to preserve her individuality, protect her daughter from the encroachments of the Beecham/Renfro household, detach her husband, and stave off change and attrition.

Such aims are particularly maddening to the women of the reunion. When she resists the possibility that she may be a Beecham, Sam Dale's daughter, they wrestle her to the ground in a watermelon fight, forcing her into abasement, humiliation, and self-effacement. "Feeding" Gloria in an act of horrifying domestic aggression, they force her to submit to their symbolically domestic power and eat from their hands. The language of this scene echoes the violence more characteristic of male plots; the cracking melon sounds "like a firecracker," and the women are "ramming the sweet, breaking chunks inside her mouth. . . . 'Come on, sisters, help feed her! Let's cram it down her little red lane. Let's make her say Beecham! *We* did!' came the women's voices" (269). These older women are all Beechams by marriage; when they "said Beecham," they gave up their original names.

Although Miss Beulah and Granny do not participate in the "fight," no one intervenes to rescue Gloria. (She calls for Jack, but he has joined his male friend in the Buick.) To these Beecham women, any female who does not replicate the pattern of their own domestic lives is a threat and must be put in her place, helpless and prone. The little girls, watching, intuit that their time is coming. Finally, Gloria seems to lose consciousness. Then Beulah pulls her up, saying, "Gloria Beecham Renfro [calling Gloria by the name she has denied]. . . . Get up and join your family, for a change. . . . go back in the house and wash that face and get rid of some of that tangly hair, then shake that dress and come out again. . . ." But Gloria resists her mother-in-law's managing care. "'No, thank you, ma'am. . . . I'm standing my ground,' she told everybody" (270–71).

Next, the women undertake to alter Gloria's wedding dress, which she made too large (probably to conceal her pregnancy). Lexie now acts as seamstress, pinning, trimming, prodding, and snipping away Gloria's precious pocket to make a patch. Ferguson sees this scene, after the "rough scrubbing" of the watermelon fight, as demonstrating the women's "wholehearted" love for Gloria (313). I take a less sanguine view of it; again, the older women use their domestic authority and faculty to cut Gloria to their prescribed pattern. Gloria does not bolt and run, but she has almost lost her resistance and her voice. As she sews, Lexie proudly recounts her brutalization of her patient, Julia Mortimer. Listening, Gloria, who loved Miss Julia, is nearly undone. But Lexie sews and talks on, her next remark even more shocking: "'I tied her, that was the upshoot,' said Miss Lexie" (278). The story becomes so horrible that Beulah makes her one intervention in domestic process. She says, "Lexie, you're about to ruin this reunion . . . giving out talk of death and disgrace. . . . Take away her needle, if that's what sewing brings on" (282). Beulah is acknowledging the dangers of domestic authority for the vulnerable individual, especially a woman who aspires to a life outside the reunion circle, as Julia Mortimer did and Gloria does. Feeding and sewing—the very skills that keep the reunion going and are the heart of domestic ritual—have a malevolent potential, which even Beulah must acknowledge and fear.

When an interviewer expressed sympathy for Gloria in the watermelon rout and said it made him feel "squeamish," Eudora Welty replied, "Yes, well, that's the way people are, though. No, I don't think [Gloria is] going to win. . . . She's the most naive soul there; she's not Miss Julia Mortimer at all, by any means. And she totally lacks imagination. How could she have married Jack and thought she was going to change him?" (*Conversations* 49).

In such a comment, Welty acknowledges the power of the reunion and of communal life as expressed through domestic ritual: "That's the way people are." In her perceptive discussion of *Losing Battles* as comic epic, Ferguson emphasizes Welty's "lack of stress on the individual seeking" identity (that classic American plot) in this novel (314). Ironically, the Beecham-Renfro family has a member-by-marriage who bears a name that resounds with epic quest: Uncle Homer Champion. Uncle Homer, who is running for office, is the only family member who skips out on part of the reunion; he also attends (and gets drunk at) Julia Mortimer's wake and he finds her a grave in Banner Cemetery to win votes: "'Getting Miss Julia buried to Banner's credit is worth a heap to me,' said Uncle Homer. 'I can always point to it'" (338). Through Homer Champion, Welty indicates dislike for some of the conventions of male seeking. Her champion, instead, is Jack, who honors the best of female culture in his fealty to the reunion. In a 1980 interview, Welty emphasized Jack's "goodness" and noted that if he has a "bad" quality, it is that "he allows himself to be used by everybody," becoming the tool of the reunion's collective will. Welty concluded, "Yes, I really like Jack. He's a much better person than Gloria" (*Conversations* 306).

Jack's goodness is his capacity for love. Hearing his Aunt Lexie's tale of Julia Mortimer, whom he never met, he concludes, "I reckon I even love her. . . . I heard her story" (361). Gloria saves her love for Jack and their child, but Jack urges her to extend it to others too. Jack has the potential to be one of Welty's exemplary characters who can honor domestic ritual without making it their only story and giving up their lives to its perpetuation. But Jack has fewer resources of nerve, intelligence, and culture than Virgie Rainey, Miss Eckhart, and Laurel Hand—or Julia Mortimer. When Gloria tells him about Miss Julia's wisdom, Jack says, "She sounds like Solomon. Like she ought to have been Solomon. . . . She was way up over our heads, you and me" (432). He has the range to think of a woman in terms of a wise male hero, right out of Grandpa Vaughn's Bible. But he knows, too, that he belongs on a different plane, below Julia Mortimer.

Although she lacks Jack's constant breadth of sympathy and his occasional range of imagination, Gloria is in a position far more difficult than his. He has been nurtured and groomed by the family's myth of his gifts. But she, trying to create a quest-myth for herself, met only opposition from the domestic culture that supported Jack. And, although Jack may imagine a single female schoolteacher as "Solomon," he has no such ideas for his own wife. Instead, he tries to persuade her into a trite scenario of domestic life, more cloying and constricted than anything offered by Alcott or Stowe:

"Wouldn't you like to keep Mama company in the kitchen while I'm ploughing or fence-mending, give her somebody she can talk to? And encourage Ella Fay out of being timid, and talk Elvie out of her crying and wanting to be a teacher? You can give Etoyle ladylike examples of behavior. . . . Honey, won't you change your mind about my family?"

"Not for all the tea in China," she declared. (360)

Jack imagines his adult wife in a secondary domestic position, keeping Beulah company but not sharing her authority, nurturing and cajoling and repudiating her own history by talking Elvie out of her ambition to be a teacher. Gloria's ambitions for a life beyond obliterating domestic conventions are reflected even in her language, which is equally trite—"Not for all the tea in China"—but indicates her longing for a wider world. Of all the people at the reunion, she perhaps has the most to lose under Granny's roof, as well as much to gain. Kreyling notes that she has been "heavily influenced by her teacher Julia Mortimer, the champion of the historical. Gloria's perspective on life is largely that of the historical mind, and her 'peculiarities' stand out sharply in her mythic surroundings" (*Eudora Welty's Achievement of Order* 148). Jack works to persuade his wife into the mythic cycles of traditional domestic culture and women's time.

Ritual often expresses a human impulse to control the uncontrollable. The domestic reunion staged by the Beechams enacts such an impulse. Welty has shaped her book to reflect both the strength of that shaping impulse and its futility. The first of the book's six parts, for example, begins as the reunion day does, with light dawning on the farmhouse. Its logical ending would be what Welty first thought of as her "story's" ending: the much-anticipated arrival of Jack. But in fact, Part 1 goes on until Jack has *departed* again, to capsize the Moodys' car. Thus Welty indicates both the reunion's compelling power, which brought Jack home a fugitive when he could have been legally freed the next day, and the equally powerful forces that draw him away again. The progression of the following five parts continues to reflect these same forces. The entire second part takes place away from the house and chronicles the wrangling over the Moodys' car and Jack and Gloria's efforts to get some time to themselves to make love. Part 3 is dominated by the central event of the reunion, the ritualized dinner and recital of the family history, while Part 4 is dominated by the telling of Julia Mortimer's rival story, ending with Granny's efforts to direct attention back to herself. In Part 5, the guests depart and the house and family subside into dark and sleep. This would be the novel's logical conclusion, countering the initial images of dawn. Part 5 ends with an encounter between Beulah and her granddaughter, Lady May, as a midnight thunderstorm begins:

Hearing what sounded like great treads going over her head, the baby opened her eyes. She put her voice into the fray, and spoke to it the first sentence of her life: "What you huntin', man?"

Miss Beulah ran out onto the porch, snatched up the baby, and ran with her back to her own bed, as if a life had been saved. (368)

Lady May, having met her father and her entire family on the greatest day of her short life, is stimulated into speech: she begins to claim a voice that will allow her to compete in the great family activity, storytelling. Her first sentence is a question about men's stories, which take them outside the house and indicate another way to live. Beulah reacts as if to a terrible portent; the little girl's voice and her venturesome curiosity threaten to remove her from the circle of domestic ritual. As nearly as possible, Lady May is pulled back into the sheltering house and into her grandmother's womb, which is for Beulah the only reliable way to save a life.

But this is not the ending of Welty's novel. She said in 1972, "I had originally planned *Losing Battles* to happen in one day, but you see it goes over the night into the next morning. That is probably a flaw, but I couldn't resolve it. . . . I realized it while I was working because I kept making notes, putting them in another folder saying, 'Next A.M.,' and then I realized that was a whole section. I realized that I could not incorporate everything into the one day, so I had to have a Monday" (*Conversations* 46). In this final section, Beulah serves breakfast, the children set forth for the first day of school, the men disengage the Buick, with help from a "human chain" largely made of women, plus Vaughn's school bus. Then they set off for town and Miss Julia's burial, after which Jack and Gloria return home. This book confirms that the reunion—the self-vindicating, woman-centered tale of domestic ritual—is not entirely self-sufficient; it must coexist with other pressures, other demands, and other tales. It vindicates what Welty's domestic champion, Jack, says to Gloria, as he tries to persuade her to pay her respects to her mentor, Miss Julia: "There's room enough for everything, and time for everybody, if you take your day the way it comes along and try not to be much later than you can help" (362). However generous and practical, Jack's credo also makes him the servant of contingency and of others' needs and demands; in the scheme of his day, there is no place for his individual priorities. By showing us how her characters survive, keeping faith and keeping house in a weekday world unlike the high ritual festivity of Reunion Sunday, Welty has invented a form for her novel that indicates the constant competition and interweaving of its many ongoing, battling stories.

The beautiful and precarious balance of the novel's tensions is indicated at its exact formal midpoint, the end of Part 3. Dinner over, the storytelling reaches an annual crux: the reason for the Beechams' extreme devotion to Granny Vaughn. Their parents were drowned in the act of running away, abandoning the children in the middle of the night. The mother, Granny's daughter, was the perpetrator; she held the reins and drove the wagon. This family's heritage, the suppressed truth about their past, is that their own mother could not bear to stay in the house; she died in search of another way to live. When the storytelling seems mired in betrayal and death, Beulah reasserts control of the proceedings; she summons the children forth, bearing Granny's birthday gifts, tributes to a woman's domestic fealty and endurance. The procession culminates with the major gift, a domestic achievement, the Delectable Mountains quilt pieced by aunts and girl cousins over the past year. (Granny claims this achievement too; she says, "Finished it last night.") Then they sing their reunion song:

> All their voices rose as one. . . .
>
> > *"Gathering home! Gathering home!*
> > *Never to sorrow more, never to roam!*
> > *Gathering home! Gathering home!*
> > *God's children are gathering home."*
>
> As they sang, the tree over them . . . looked bright as a river, and the tables might have been a little train of barges it was carrying with it, moving slowly downstream. . . . nothing at all was unmovable, or empowered to hold the scene still fixed or stake the reunion there. (223)

This is a transcendent moment, as beautiful as anything in this extraordinary book. The fervent song expresses a yearning for external domestic union—"gathering home" for permanent security and fixity. That sense of security and continuance is what the Beechams have traveled "home" to affirm, and the novel's formal order, with this scene and song placed at this centrally emphatic spot, expresses the satisfying weight of the affirmation. But Welty's description expresses a countertruth: fixity is an illusion, for the reunion itself, existing in time, is in perpetual motion, and nothing, not even Granny, is "empowered to hold" it still.

Ultimately, *Losing Battles* is Welty's most challenging fictional world because, within it, everything contains its own opposite and is constantly (as in the very title) in moving process. The Beechams, loving parents, were abandoning travelers. Their children, who arrived in filial piety, gathering to worship Granny, depart at day's end. They cannot stay and thus they too become deserting "murderers" in Granny's eyes. Granny herself, a tough, durable icon, is at last a pathetic old woman, compelled to "beg" the children to stay. The domestic-maternal homage of festival Reunion Sunday subsides to the ordinary routine of Monday—and to the rival rituals for Julia Mortimer. And Monday too will subside to the coming Tuesday—election day, dominated by the male contest between rival candidates, Curly Stovall and Homer Champion. Although Welty's last pages offer classic satisfactions of fictional closure, with the male-female "human chain," Julia's burial, and Jack's triumphant return to his mother, those satisfactions are played out against the constantly moving backdrop of change and opposition. The medium of *Losing Battles* is domestic life; Welty both legitimizes that life as a fictional subject and takes it as the expression of the most complex and challenging human truths. *Losing Battles* is comic in the truest sense; it locates human meaning in the contingencies of social life. Home and family are the context all Welty's characters share. Men and women may grasp at voyages, other kinds of tales. But the constant they all value most highly is "gathering home," there to wrestle with the inexorable oppositions that contain the most necessary truths of their lives.

One more way in which Welty broaches these oppositions is by contrasting the two Renfro sons, Jack and Vaughn. Vaughn, only twelve, has done Jack's chores well while his brother was gone and has won the prize job of school bus driver by excelling at his studies. Besotted with school, he seems yet another (posthumous) male protégé of Julia Mortimer. All Jack's triumphs endanger his younger brother; the family's enthusiastic espousal of Jack's domestic heroism means that Vaughn is fated for neglect and suppression.[7] Vaughn reminds us that within the homogenous ideal of Granny's loving family, which even casts its vote as one (a hundred strong), there is a constant tug of dangerous competition. Beulah's view of the family constellation places Jack squarely at the center; she sees him as Granny's favorite, as he is her own, and thus devalues her younger son: "'Vaughn is not Jack, and never will be,' Miss Beulah confided at the top of her voice" (402).

With *Losing Battles*, Welty "challenged" herself to write an externalized novel, "to express everything in dialogue and not enter inside anybody's mind." But finally, she opposed her own principle. Late on the night of the reunion, Welty enters Vaughn's point of view: "I went inside the little boy's mind—I couldn't resist that" (*Conversations* 271). To claim his thoughts and his selfhood, Vaughn must find a counterworld to the noisy din of family life which threatens to snuff him out, the "huge, soul-defying reunion" (363). In order to locate his silent world, the boy must touch base with his beloved school bus and geography book; with him we perceive one of the individual continents that can be traced, mapped, under the obliterating overlay of family life. When Vaughn returns to the darkened house, wearing his dead grandfather's hat, he passes his grandmother's room:

> Then all of a sudden there came a current of air. A door swung open in Vaughn's face and there was Granny, tiny in her bed in full lamplight. For a moment the black bearskin on the floor by the bed shone red-haired, live enough to spring at him. After the moonlight and the outdoors, the room was as yellow and close as if he and Granny were embedded together in a bar of yellow soap.
> "Take off your hat," Granny's mouth said. "And climb in wi' me."
> He fled out of her dazzled sight. "She didn't know who I was," he told himself, running. And then, "she didn't care!" (366)

The reunion, for Vaughn, has embodied all the enduring, prepossessing qualities of domestic ritual and his own energies have been conscripted to make him the reunion's domestic chore boy, assisting his mother and protecting Granny and the legend of her ongoing housekeeping. (When Granny begins to fall, Beulah screams, "Catch-her-*Vaughn!*" [308].) Opening up Vaughn's mind, at the end of her novel, Welty shows us a primal, actual room, which exists at the center of his consciousness. In this brightly lamplit, intensely domestic, and sexual female place, Vaughn sees himself fixed with Granny in a domestic medium, "embedded" in light as solid as household soap. There, every object gleams with meaning and dangerous life, like the bearskin rug. And when the woman welcomes Vaughn to this shelter, she speaks a sexual invitation that is implicitly incestuous and obliterates all particularities of age, relationship, and identity. Seeing the boy in her dead husband's hat, Granny responds to only one central fact: his gender. Vaughn is so thoroughly alarmed that he runs from the house and from consciousness: bedding down in the barn, he dives headlong into sleep.

For all its rich profusion, *Losing Battles* would be incomplete without this dreamlike scene. The bright room recalls the magical lamplit cabin of Welty's first story, "Death of a Travelling Salesman." In each case, a male, bent on wandering, is sexually and emotionally compelled by a domestic invitation that offers solace and threatens identity. While R. J. Bowman dimly associates his dead grandmother with the backwoods woman, Vaughn's vision is as clearly incisive as dream; his grandmother *is* the beckoning, primal woman. *Losing Battles* has been a domestic panorama, unrolling the elaborate, self-justifying tapestry of housekeeping as woven by women's culture. But through Vaughn, Welty reminds us of the domestic vision with which she began, a construct of male imagination. Vaughn's view affords access to a truth about Granny untouched anywhere else in the novel: a direct view of the commanding, terrifying energy that keeps her alive.

Although Vaughn's vision reveals much that a masculine imagination may make of a woman in a house, Granny's imperative words are her own: "Take off your hat. . . . And climb in wi' me." They suggest that, even at ninety, the germ of Granny's survival is sexual energy. Like Laurel's vision of the dead, hungry Phil, Granny "wanted it," wants it still. Her bright room is the dynamo of the house and the reunion. Welty finally found her access to it through a boy's private vision. This great novel, with the ambitious reach of epic, is completed by Vaughn, whose viewpoint has the startling, dreamlike personal immediacy of lyric. All Welty's questions about how to tell the stories of housekeeping are in some sense answered by the form of *Losing Battles*, which contains its own opposites. Welty, late in her career, pulled out all the stops, producing one of the most capacious and uncompromising domestic texts in American literature. At the heart of the housekeeping, the heart of the myth, is an endlessly, complexly, voraciously *desirous* and ancient woman, whose first house is her body. For Welty, again and again—with characters from Ruby Fisher, Livvie, the Delta bride, Virgie Rainey, Laurel Hand, and even Granny Vaughn—the central problem is discovering the links between domesticity and desire.

Welty's three essays in literary autobiography, published in 1984 as *One Writer's Beginnings*, form her most recent book. In her study of women's autobiographies, *Writing a Woman's Life*, Carolyn G. Heilbrun says that this much-admired book exhibits and encourages dangerous "nostalgia and romanticizing" (13). The opening passage of Welty's book, with which I began my discussion of her career, exemplifies the charm and apparent nostalgia that Heilbrun describes; the romance of familial accord is preserved in domestic ritual. Yet, as we saw, even in that little scene, there is another plot: the child prepares for departure, her noise competes with her parents' waltz, and the tune itself, whatever its domestic uses, is "The Merry Widow."

Heilbrun sees *One Writer's Beginnings* as an illustration of Virginia Woolf's observation that "very few women yet have written truthful autobiographies" (13). Like Heilbrun, I believe that Eudora Welty's fiction is the fullest expression of her genius. But her autobiography expresses a profound and central project of many American women's lives: an effort to find a life-giving individual relationship with women's culture, of which housekeeping has been the most constant expression. As the most contemporary of the writers in this study, Welty must necessarily be the most experimental; in her lifetime, the "givens" by which women once articulated connections to women's culture have become less obviously compulsory and less apparent. Witchlike figures like Jewett's Mrs. Todd or the abetting Goody Crane of

"Silence," Freeman's colonial tale, or even such a quiet household presence as Cather's Mrs. Harris, who assisted at the initiation of younger women, are less and less to be taken for granted in the post–1940 world in which Eudora Welty, like us, lives. Welty's fiction, as I have tried to show, invents brilliant formal strategies by which to contemplate questions about women and housekeeping. For most contemporary women, the most common context of such questions is our ties to our mothers. As Welty has said, her most important life decision was to *work*, as a writer, at *home*, where her mother lived. And her mother is the most enigmatic, uncompromising, and problematic character of *One Writer's Beginnings*. For the last thirty years of her life, the years of her daughter's full maturity when they shared a house, Mrs. Welty suffered from the consequences of her husband's death from leukemia. He died during an attempt to revive him with a transfusion of his wife's blood. Welty writes, "My mother never recovered emotionally. Though she lived for over thirty years more, and suffered other bitter losses, she never stopped blaming herself. She saw this as her failure to save his life" (93).

Like Beulah Beecham Renfro, who agonized throughout her life because she could not protect Sam Dale, Mrs. Welty emerges from her daughter's book as an ardent, ambitious woman committed to taking care and doomed by chance and mortality to fail—even when her medium was her own living blood. Eudora Welty (who, as a young woman witnessed her father's death during the attempted transfusion) lived much of her life alongside this story. The effects of her relationship with her mother occasion the most sternly self-revelatory moments of *One Writer's Beginnings*, moments that reach far beyond nostalgia. For example, she writes of early train trips to New York from Jackson, when she was trying to sell her first stories:

> I knew that even as I was moving farther away from Jackson, my mother was already writing to me at her desk, telling me she missed me but only wanted what was best for me. She would not leave the house till she had my wire, sent from Penn Station the third day from now, that I had arrived safely. . . .
> I knew this was how she must have waited when my father had left on one of his business trips and I thought I could guess how he, the train lover, the trip lover, must have felt too while he remained away. . . . Taking trips tore all of us up inside, for they seemed, each journey away from home, something that might have been less selfishly undertaken, or something that would test us, or something that had better be momentous, to justify such a leap into the dark. The torment and guilt—the torment of having the loved one go, the guilt of being the loved one gone—comes into my fiction as it did and does into my life. And most of all the guilt then was because it was true: I had left to arrive at some future and

secret joy, at what was unknown . . . waiting to be discovered. My joy was connected with writing; that was as much as I knew. (93–94)

To be an artist, for Eudora Welty, has been a way to articulate the intensity of the relationship she expresses so powerfully here. A modern woman, fueled by joy, ambition, and desire, she rides the train and easily identifies with her mobile, mortal father. But always with her is the image, torment, and magnet of the woman in the house: her mother, who both sanctions the daughter's journey and compels her return to the shared female world of housekeeping.

Afterword

No one lives in this room
without confronting the whiteness of the wall
behind the poems, planks of books,
photographs of dead heroines.
Without contemplating last and late
the true nature of poetry. The drive
to connect. The dream of a common language.
    Adrienne Rich
    "Origins and History of Consciousness"

IN THIS BOOK I have looked at five important careers, all—
to some degree—canonical careers. Yet Stowe, Jewett, Freeman, Cather,
and Welty have all been undervalued and underread. Often they have been
most neglected when women's traditional work is at the center of their
fiction. For example, *Shadows on the Rock* is perhaps Cather's least valued
novel; Freeman's "A Tardy Thanksgiving" has seldom—if ever—been reprinted; critics have ignored the importance of housekeeping to Welty's
"The Burning." Since women's housework has been consistently regarded as
either trivial or invisible since the Civil War, the literary traditions of the
home plot have been similarly marginalized.

The work of historian Glenna Matthews is helpful in understanding this
history of reading—or not reading—American women's domestic fiction
after 1870. In *"Just a Housewife": The Rise and Fall of Domesticity in America*,
Matthews chronicles the mainstream political efficacy and influence of the
woman-centered domestic sphere in the antebellum United States. In *Uncle
Tom's Cabin*, for example, Stowe galvanized the resources of such an "epic
vision of domesticity" (56). But after the war and after the decline in the
popularity of the woman-written sentimental domestic novel (which Matthews says was by then "dead, having played itself out sometime in the
1860's" [106]), domestic feminism encountered "a backlash among male
authors [and often the literary establishment] in the late nineteenth century" (89). "What happened in the years after the Civil War was a collision
between antagonistic male and female cultures" (73–74).

The home plot was generated in this period of oppressively separate
spheres. I suggest that it may be read as a complex effort to continue the
traditions of woman-centered domestic culture that had long provided a

sense of continuity and self-worth to American women, and most especially to the mothers of women like Stowe, Jewett, and Freeman, who came of age in the heyday of the omnicompetent woman that Matthews calls "the Republican Mother." Mothers and other female elders have traditionally taught domestic work to girls and young women by imprinting them with processes, work order, and rituals. Like my mother and grandmother, the last thing I do before I leave my kitchen is to wring the dishcloth and hang it to dry. Like them, I make cornbread dressing, seasoned with sage, for the Thanksgiving turkey. I toast the cubes of cornbread in a jellyroll pan, as my mother does. The home plot honors such processes, order, and rituals by perpetuating them, in rhythms very different from men's traditional plots.

I feel silly, writing how I toast the cubes of cornbread. I am writing a book, performing a public act that seems a far cry from my turkey dressing. The writers in this study have honored women's domestic history by making it the shape of art. They offer support and sustenance that I much need, telling me that domestic life is not alien to and hidden from my public life, not a dirty little secret that housekeepers share. The home plot is my name for a complex of narrative strategies examined in this book. What these strategies have in common is an effort to respond to, replicate, continue, interrogate, and extend the repetitive rhythms of domestic life, which emphasize continuance over triumphant climax and often subordinate the vaunted individual to an ongoing, life-preserving, and, for some women, life-threatening process.

When the "successful" nineteenth-century woman writer took up the domestic story of Hestia, it was and was not her own tale. (Mary Kelley effectively dramatized this split in the lives of the "literary domestic" writers she discusses by titling her book *Private Woman, Public Stage.*) As Jewett implies, the sibyl became a tutelary matron for such writers,[1] for she points to the seeming paradox of *texts* that are not printed and perhaps not written. Thus *The Country of the Pointed Firs* is not solely an education in domestic ritual; it is also, and perhaps most importantly, an education in *writing domestic ritual.*

For Jewett, Freeman, and Stowe, making and continuing writing careers in the heyday of American realism, which claimed to foreground contemporary social reality but almost inevitably conceived it in patriarchal terms, writing domestic ritual asserted the full weight, reality, and value of traditional women's lives. At the same time, these women's success as writers *released* them, at least partially, from domestic responsibilities. None of the writers in this study, married or single, could conceive of herself as "just a housewife."

Willa Cather and Eudora Welty, from two different generations of twentieth-century American women writers, have contended throughout their careers with a female domestic heritage, contriving plots that acknowledge its weight and excavate valued female history, while also projecting another way to live. *Writing domestic ritual,* in a sense, expresses a belief in a common language. If housekeeping can be inscribed, if the home plot can appear on the page, then it is acknowledged as continuing fact, problem, and resource of our common life. Such writing may postulate a life in which boundaries between public and private spheres and between male and female spheres become elastic, permeable, or perhaps even nonexistent. Thus, in many of the texts I have discussed, relations between men and domestic language are interrogated: in Stowe's and Cather's male narrators and protagonists, in such characters as William Blackett, Captain Littlepage, Jack Jordan Renfro, and R. J. Bowman.

For men as well as women, these books repeatedly evoke Welty's question: Is there another way to live? *Plot* is crucial to this question and to this study because it is a way of thinking through the patterns in lives. The home plot, as opposed to quest stories and Aristotelean conventions, offers us a way to think about the shapes of many obscured lives, especially those of women. Inscribing housekeeping, thinking about home plots, we bring the attention, validation, and enormous resources of public, prevailing culture to women who have previously been marginalized and effaced by that culture, which did not know how to read—or to see—their lives. The institution of canonical American literature is a history of such effacement; it has traditionally said that domestic ritual is not worth reading.

Writing and living this book, I have joined other domestic scholars who dream of multivocal lives, in which the daily and the domestic voices that speak to and through all of us are heard and are written, in a constant, plural discourse that engages both women and men. Bettina Aptheker, for example, in *Tapestries of Life: Women's Work, Women's Consciousness, and the Meaning of Daily Experience,* names both the dangers and the promise of such a dream: "Sometimes it produces in women an inability to focus anywhere but on their own house, their own culture, their own problems in ways that divide women from each other. Yet the dream of connection, the need for ritual and beauty, the drive to nurture the human spirit continually rekindle these patterns of resistance in women's everyday lives" (228). Matthews ends her book with a similar argument that domesticity be given a place at the center of human concern; she says, "We cannot go back—nor would we want to—to the nineteenth-century home. But we can learn from history, and we can be sustained by the heritage of women and men like

Harriet Beecher Stowe [and others]. . . . It seems to me that the essence of what they have to teach us is as follows: the good society and the good home are inextricably intertwined" (226).

When Marilynne Robinson, in 1981, published her domestic narrative, *Housekeeping,* one of the best American novels of recent decades, she framed it as the tale of two orphaned sisters in a house. One joined her undomestic aunt for the freedom of transience; the other fled to a domestic stronghold, to be adopted by the home economics teacher. The book ends with the transient's palpable and eloquent longing for her lost sister. For they are forever incomplete in their separation. Indeed, many of the most bitter and persistent divisions between American women of the past thirty years have concerned the relation of these two sisters, the sister who valorizes housekeeping and the sister who rejects it. My dream of multivocality is a dream of a world and of languages in which both sisters may find voices in which to acknowledge and value themselves, each other, and their blood kinship.

For a number of complicated and important reasons, women writers have seemed to have a special affinity for the journal form. One of those reasons may be that the journal replicates the daily rhythms of housekeeping; its ongoingness precludes a dominant, completable plot. So perhaps it is not surprising that a very recent American book about domestic ritual, *Reinventing Home: Six Working Women Look at Their Home Lives* (1991), is written as a series of short, journallike meditations. The book has six female authors, one of whom died as the book was being written; their voices are interwoven. It seems both a utopian and a profoundly conservative project. In the editors' prefatory note, the premises on which my book and the fiction I have discussed are founded resound, yet again. "This book," they say, "is about the conviction that a rich domestic life is worth having and therefore worth thinking about. . . . domestic life is a serious matter. . . . This book is about quandaries—because we simply do not know how big a place our homes should hold in our lives" (Abraham et al. 1–2). The pressure that such matters exert is indicated by the fact that these women have written a book collectively, relinquishing the valorization of individual authorship, yet they aggressively define themselves in their title as "Six *Working* Women"—and by that they mean that housework is not their only occupation. None of the six, they want us to know, is "just a housewife." These women imply that writing a book about "home" has made them fear their own triviality, when they assert: "We need to stop feeling silly, if not downright embarrassed, about our interest in all these matters" (3).

This problematic and innovative book, which just appeared at my local feminist bookstore, indicates how thoroughly domestic history, work, and art continue to preoccupy Americans, especially women. In an early chapter, Nancy Eberle (writing soon before her death) describes a rare and deeply comforting experience of domestic ease: "I had my epiphany: this is what it's like to feel at home, at home. This is the way children feel all the time. And very possibly men as well. And this is why the failure of others to share the responsibility for a house is so terrible: because it robs women of this experience" (11). The urgency of Eberle's language conveys the linked importance of housekeeping, home, and gender in her life. In a later piece, "Family Rituals," Mary Beth Danielson recounts her sister Karen's efforts, in the months preceding her death from cancer, to be at the table every night for dinner with her family. Danielson concludes, "That is ritual. That is saying that we are a family no matter what, and we will sit down together, and we will eat this food, and we will look at each other, and we will love each other in the fragility of an ordinary dinner. Within a week of Karen's death, her husband and children were back in their own places for meals. It may not be triumph, but it is survival" (157).

Survival and its costs are a persistent concern of the home plot, by which American women have written domestic ritual. The family dinner is one of the many ordinary, daily domestic traditions that survive largely because of a female history of work, care, and continuance. It is valuable and necessary that women and men recognize that such a history exists and that we think about its worth and its cost. This book has also tried to demonstrate that we have a women's tradition of *writing domestic ritual,* which both inscribes and interrogates women's housekeeping work and art. Such a tradition opposes the confines of essentialism. It implies, instead, that women's traditional lives are worth thinking about, worth writing about, worth reading. It implies that housekeeping may be one of our common human languages, in which we may confront our history and dream our future.

Notes

Introduction

1. Special thanks to my George Washington University colleague Professor Miriam Dow, who helped me trace various versions of Circe's story.

2. For one example, see Annette Kolodny.

3. See especially Mary Ellen Ross and Cheryl Lynn Ross.

4. The strategies Wolff urges for feminist art, those of "engaging with, and destabilizing, the images, ideologies, and systems of representation of patriarchal culture" (82), are pertinent to all the writers in this study.

1. False Starts and False Endings

1. There is continuing disagreement about how to classify Stowe's fiction, particularly *Uncle Tom's Cabin*. For example, Mary Kelley considers Stowe one of the "literary domestics" she discusses. Nina Baym, while she sees Stowe as "the most important American novelist of her day," asserts that "she did not write woman's fiction" as it is defined by Baym in *Woman's Fiction* (232).

2. Sarah Way Sherman provides a pertinent discussion of this letter and of the importance of *The Pearl of Orr's Island* to Jewett (27–45).

3. For an example of this view, see Donovan's comments in *New England Local Color Literature* (67).

4. A third and less interesting book from this period, *Pink and White Tyranny*, shares the New York setting and the concern with contemporary social life. However, Stowe framed this book as a moral fable, specifying in her preface that this is *not* a novel and asking readers "please to call this little sketch a parable and wait for the exposition thereof" (ix–x).

5. Sandra M. Gilbert and Susan Gubar, in *The Madwoman in the Attic*, observe that "when Stowe, in 'My Wife and I,' assumes the persona of an avuncular

patriarch educating females in their domestic duties, we resent the duplicity and compromise involved, as well as Stowe's betrayal of her own sex" (69–70).

6. Baym makes this point in *Woman's Fiction* (12).

7. Robyn Warhol provides an important and pertinent recent discussion of the feminist implications of Stowe's narrative voice.

8. Stowe and her sister, Catharine Beecher, had recently published *The American Woman's Home*, a new manual of domestic economy. According to Kathryn Kish Sklar, Stowe's major contribution to that book was "elaborate designs, ranging from shoe bags to entryways" (263).

9. Rabuzzi explores these qualities of housekeeping (93–139).

10. T. J. Jackson Lears explores this revival in *No Place of Grace* (141–81).

11. It is worth noting that, in a context that takes housework seriously, James's figure of the "canvasser for sewing machines" could be read *not* as an officious meddler but as someone who introduces an important means of revolutionizing a traditional female task, sewing.

12. For example, see Dorothy Berkson, "Millennial Politics and the Feminine Fiction of Harriet Beecher Stowe."

13. Habegger counters Nina Baym's view of "female self-sufficiency," as presented in *Woman's Fiction.*

14. Donovan's *New England Local Color Literature* discusses Stowe, Rose Terry Cooke, Elizabeth Stuart Phelps, Jewett, and Freeman.

15. For a single view of the two generations, see Donovan, *New England Local Color Literature.*

16. On the important Jewett-Fields relationship, see Donovan's chapter on Fields in *New England Local Color Literature;* Judith Roman's "A Closer Look at the Jewett-Fields Relationship"; and Sarah Way Sherman's analysis, the most thorough and recent (69–90 and passim).

17. Donovan provides the most complete description of this phenomenon, in *New England Local Color Literature.* Also see Susan Coultrap-McQuin, *Doing Literary Business,* on the publishing industry within which many nineteenth-century American women writers worked.

18. Donovan has established that this section was probably written in 1873, when Jewett herself was Helen's age, twenty-four (*Sarah Orne Jewett* 35).

19. Sherman discusses this female construction of nature, giving it a somewhat more positive reading (98).

20. For a useful survey of responses to this ending, see Stephen Mailloux (179–91).

2. The Country of the Pointed Firs

1. Debate over the book's form is usefully summarized by Marjorie Pryse, "Introduction to the Norton Edition" (vii–viii).

2. Paul D. Voelker discusses this early humor (239).

3. Jewett wrote, "My father never lost a chance of trying to teach me to observe.

I owe a great deal to his patience with a heedless little girl given far more to dreams than to accuracy" ("Looking Back on Girlhood" 7). The influence of Jewett's mother, who lived much longer than her father and was an important figure in her daughter's life until 1891, received less specific acknowledgment in Jewett's written comments on her career. Sherman has recently begun to explore this crucial relationship (46–64 and passim).

4. I am drawing on Roland Barthes's famous distinction between readerly and writerly texts, elaborated in *S/Z* (45).

5. Marcia McClintock Folsom discusses the power of such "empathetic imagination," although she does not pursue its domestic roots.

6. Pennyroyal is used "to promote the expulsion of the placenta" and "to induce or increase menstrual flow" (Elizabeth Ammons, "Going in Circles" 91). Ammons sees the essential pattern of *The Country of the Pointed Firs* as weblike, with the pennyroyal plot at its literal and thematic center, source of "primal, archetypal female love" (89–90).

7. Strasser emphasizes the pervasiveness of this traditional laundry schedule (104–06).

8. Employing Carol Gilligan's analysis of women's decision processes, Ammons provides an especially interesting and influential view of the book's structure in "Going in Circles."

9. Rabuzzi discusses these repetitive qualities of housework.

10. Pryse provides a fine reading of this story in "Women 'at Sea': Feminist Realism in Sarah Orne Jewett's 'The Foreigner.'"

11. Sherman discusses the importance of silence here (263).

12. This scene resembles a famous photograph of a middle-aged Jewett and the older Annie Fields seated in Fields's complexly furnished sitting room. The two women are not facing and are separated by some distance; Jewett is occupied with a book. The photograph is reproduced in Sherman (figure 9, between 46 and 47).

13. A recent book by historian Nancy M. Theriot, *The Bio-Social Construction of Femininity: Mothers and Daughters in Nineteenth-Century America*, emphasizes the special complexities of mother-daughter relations in the second half of the nineteenth century and corroborates many of Jewett's emphases.

14. Other domestic fiction of this period also experimented with series, sequels, and fictional sequences as a similarly domestic project. Stowe's New York novels, discussed here, are examples, as is another series of enduring popularity, which Jewett read avidly as a young woman: Louisa May Alcott's *Little Women* and the succeeding novels about the March sisters.

3. Freeman's Repetitions

1. Although most of the fiction I discuss here was written before Mary Wilkins's marriage to Dr. Charles Freeman in 1902, I am using her married name because she preferred it and attached it to all her work.

2. Susan Koppelman briefly discusses the importance of such occasional stories in the careers of American women writers and cites Freeman as one of the most "productive" writers of holiday stories (258).

3. On this subject, see the letters and biographical essay in *The Infant Sphinx: Collected Letters of Mary E. Wilkins Freeman*, ed. Brent L. Kendrick.

4. See Showalter, "Piecing and Writing," for a preliminary discussion of the quilting process and its implications for women's writing.

5. Jonathan Holstein hypothesizes that the grid quilt was invented by American women in the nineteenth century, in responses to technological developments (22, 26). However, quilt styles express persistent continuities of women's culture and need not be read solely as a response to patriarchal culture.

6. For two influential discussions of this issue, see Gail Parker and Donovan, *New England Local Color Literature*.

7. For Rich's most complete elaboration of this dream, see especially "Origins and History of Consciousness" (7–9).

8. For discussions of this literature, see Sklar, Strasser, and Shapiro.

9. See Rabuzzi on waiting as a quintessential female occupation (143–53).

10. Sylvia Townsend Warner, for example, recalled how charmed and attracted she was, on a first youthful reading of the story, by the compelling domestic details of Louisa's life: starched aprons, currants in a blue bowl (132).

4. Willa Cather

1. Sharon O'Brien provides a thorough discussion of Cather's responses to women writers in her apprentice years.

2. In the earlier magazine version of the story, Cather emphasized the newness of Wagner's art more specifically: "Wagner had been a sealed book to Americans before the sixties" (*Troll Garden* 167).

3. See especially Susan J. Rosowski (*Voyage* 26–28) and Marilyn Arnold (*Short Fiction* 58–60).

4. Also see Woodress's useful comments on the revisions of this story (*Troll Garden* xxvii–xxviii).

5. Cather wrote at length about the importance of Jewett's influence in the years when she began to do her first mature work, culminating in *O Pioneers!*, which she dedicated to "the memory of Sarah Orne Jewett." For Cather's comments on that relationship, see "Miss Jewett" and "148 Charles Street" in *Not Under Forty* and Cather's preface to her edition of *The Country of the Pointed Firs and Other Stories*. O'Brien provides an extended discussion of this important literary friendship and Jewett's letters to Cather are collected in *Letters of Sarah Orne Jewett*.

6. On the importance of "The Bohemian Girl," see O'Brien (394–400) and Sergeant (76–78).

5. Willa Cather and Women's Culture

1. Woodress reports that Cather wrote to Zoë Akins that the book's knowledge of "French household economics" came from her long-time French cook, Josephine Bourda (*Literary Life* 426).

2. For criticism that pursues these characters and interests, see, for examples, Woodress and Randall. E. K. Brown and Leon Edel's discussion of *Shadows on the Rock* emphasizes Cather's French Canadian historical sources, as does Benjamin George. David Stouck provides a valuable discussion of the novel's form; he presents Cécile as a significant figure but not the central one (*Imagination* 149–64). Recently Rosowski has discussed Cécile as central figure (*Voyage* 175–88). Judith Fryer concentrates on the figure of Jeanne Le Ber (326–42).

3. In "The Novel Démeublé," Cather wrote of "hopeful signs that some of the younger writers are trying to break away from mere verisimilitude . . . to present their scene by suggestion rather than by enumeration" (*Not Under* 48).

4. Both Rosowski (*Voyage* 199–204) and Arnold (*Short Fiction* 152–58) assume the child narrator is female.

5. Arnold provides a particularly suggestive discussion of Cather's use of Thomas Gray's poem (134, 138).

6. For example, Rosowski (*Voyage* 195).

7. These three women are based on Cather's mother, Virginia Boak Cather, her maternal grandmother, Rachel Seibert Boak, and their servant, Marjorie Anderson. See O'Brien for a thorough discussion of these prototypes.

8. See O'Brien on the importance of reading as a link between these two characters and their prototypes, Cather and her maternal grandmother (24–28).

9. Gwin also discusses the relationship of Stowe's and Cather's novels.

10. Critics have traditionally emphasized Cather's Nebraska years more than her Southern background. But it is interesting that Eudora Welty, another Southern-born woman, took for granted the importance of Cather's "Southern origin," compared her with Faulkner, and suggested that Cather's sense of history was shaped by her Virginia birth (*Eye* 45–57).

11. Jacqueline Jones also discusses this issue of responsibility in historical terms; she says that "family responsibilities revealed the limited extent to which black women (and men) could control their own lives" (29).

12. Rosowski discusses the gothic implications of this situation (*Voyage* 236–39).

13. Nelson's reading of *Sapphira and the Slave Girl* is based on the assumption that Henry feels "anguished desire for Nancy" (116).

14. Five was the usual age for a girl to begin her first quilt (Ferrero, Hedges, Silber 16–19).

15. Rosowski surveys the importance of kitchen scenes in Cather's fiction ("Foreword").

6. Welty's Beginnings

1. See Patricia Yeager's suggestive and more thorough discussion of this story in *Honey-mad Women*.

2. Ruth Vande Kieft discusses these arrangements in useful detail (48).

3. Albert J. Devlin suggests similar correspondences between these two stories (66–67, 70–72).

4. Of the four other writers discussed in this book, Welty mentions having read only Cather; she told an interviewer, "I wish I had had the sense to read her sooner" (*Conversations* 324). Her admiration is elaborated in an essay, "The House of Willa Cather" (*Eye* 41–60).

5. In *Eudora Welty's Achievement of Order*, Kreyling discusses relationships between the story manuscript and the completed novel in useful detail (52–76). Kreyling's new book, *Author and Agent: Eudora Welty and Diarmuid Russell*, explores Welty's working relationship with her agent in pertinent detail.

6. Welty discusses her early reading in "A Sweet Devouring" (*Eye* 279–88).

7. Kreyling also suggests a relationship between *Delta Wedding* and Elizabeth Bowen's fiction (*Achievement* 54–64).

8. Both Westling (85) and Peggy Prenshaw ("Woman's World" 48–51) make this point.

9. Carol Manning observes the isolation of these young women (53).

10. Prenshaw notes the parallels of black and white women ("Woman's World" 53).

11. Palmer provides a valuable account of the social context of this relationship.

12. This scene is discussed in useful detail by Westling, who calls it a "dual ritual blessing the old place and symbolically initiating Roy and Laura into puberty" (189).

13. See Kreyling on the various possibilities of this book's form. Kreyling's own discussion of the stories suggests a musical structure and is particularly pertinent here (*Achievement* 77–105).

14. Here and elsewhere, I am using the terms *female, feminist,* and *feminine* as Elaine Showalter defines them in *A Literature of Their Own* (13).

15. On embroidery conventions and their history, see Rozsika Parker, *The Subversive Stitch*.

16. Merrill Maguire Skaggs develops this important point (229–30).

17. For example, Ruth Haislip Roberson writes of the "vitality" of quilts "as a form of history" (xvi).

18. Bolsterli notes Welty's "metaphors drawn from the activity of keeping house" (151).

7. Welty and the Dynamo

1. See Kreyling for a survey of initial response to this book (*Eudora Welty's Achievement of Order* 118–19).

2. For examples, see Albert J. Devlin (125–32, 183–88) and Vande Kieft (128–31), as well as Bloom.

3. "The Only Child" was Welty's working title for the novella.

4. See Kreyling's very useful discussion of Fay's sexual presence (*Eudora Welty's Achievement of Order* 169).

5. See Mary Anne Ferguson's survey of critical assertions about the genre of *Losing Battles*, ranging from folk tale to idyl to opera (305).

6. See Marcel Mauss on the cultural functions of gift-giving.

7. Manning's discussion of *Losing Battles* emphasizes the cruel consequences of Jack's heroism (137–62).

Afterword

1. See Schmidt (87–88). Working from Domenichino's "most famous" portrayal of a sibyl, Schmidt notes that she points to a blank spot on a written (not printed) page, and suggests a view of the sibyl's powers "even more radically revisionary than that of Mary Shelley's parable as interpreted by Gilbert and Gubar [discussed in Chapter 2 of this book]; it argues that the sibylline role is to write new texts, not only to recover and rearrange the fragments of old ones" (88).

Works Cited

Abraham, Laurie, et al. *Reinventing Home: Six Working Women Look at Their Home Lives*. New York: Plume, 1991.

Adams, John. "Structure and Theme in the Novels of Harriet Beecher Stowe." *American Transcendentalist Quarterly* 24 (1974): 50–55.

Alcott, Louisa May. *Little Women*. 1868. Boston: Little, Brown, 1968.

Ammons, Elizabeth, ed. *Critical Essays on Harriet Beecher Stowe*. Boston: G. K. Hall, 1980.

———. "Going in Circles: The Female Geography of Jewett's *The Country of the Pointed Firs*." *Studies in the Literary Imagination* 16 (Fall 1983): 83–93.

———. "Heroines in *Uncle Tom's Cabin*." Ammons, *Critical Essays* 152–65.

Aptheker, Bettina. *Tapestries of Life: Women's Work, Women's Consciousness, and the Meaning of Daily Existence*. Amherst: U of Massachusetts P, 1989.

Ardener, Edwin. "The 'Problem' Revisited." *Perceiving Women*. Ed. Shirley Ardener, New York: John Wiley and Sons, 1975. 19–27.

Arnold, Marilyn. "'Of Human Bondage': Cather's Subnarrative in *Sapphira and the Slave Girl*." *Mississippi Quarterly* 40 (1987): 323–38.

———. *Willa Cather's Short Fiction*. Athens: Ohio UP, 1984.

Auerbach, Nina. *Communities of Women*. Cambridge: Harvard UP, 1978.

Barthes, Roland. *S/Z*. Trans. Richard Miller. London: Jonathan Cape, 1974.

Baym, Nina. "Melodramas of Beset Manhood: How Theories of American Fiction Exclude Women Authors." Showalter, *The New Feminist Criticism* 63–80.

———. *Woman's Fiction*. Ithaca: Cornell UP, 1978.

Becker, Ernest. *The Denial of Death*. New York: Free P, 1973.

Beecher, Catharine E., and Harriet Beecher Stowe. *The American Woman's Home*. 1869. Hartford: Stowe-Day Foundation, 1975.

Bennett, Mildred R. *The World of Willa Cather*. New York: Dodd, Mead, 1951.

Berkson, Dorothy. "Millennial Politics and the Feminine Fiction of Harriet Beecher Stowe." Ammons, *Critical Essays* 244–58.

Bolsterli, Margaret Jones. "Women's Vision: The Worlds of Women in *Delta Wedding, Losing Battles,* and *The Optimist's Daughter.*" Prenshaw 149–56.

Bloom, Harold, ed. *Eudora Welty.* New York: Chelsea House, 1986.

Bossard, James H. S., and Eleanor S. Boll. *Ritual in Family Living: A Contemporary Study.* Philadelphia: U of Pennsylvania P, 1950.

Brooks, Peter. *Reading for the Plot: Design and Intention in Narrative.* 1984. New York: Vintage, 1985.

Brown, E. K., and Leon Edel. *Willa Cather: A Critical Biography.* New York: Knopf, 1953.

Brown, Gillian. "Getting in the Kitchen with Dinah: Domestic Politics in *Uncle Tom's Cabin.*" *American Quarterly* 36 (Fall 1984): 503–23.

Burke, Mrs. L. *The Language of Flowers.* Los Angeles: Price, Stern, Sloan, 1965.

Cary, Richard, ed. *Appreciation of Sarah Orne Jewett.* Waterville, Me.: Colby College P, 1973.

———. Introduction. *Deephaven and Other Stories.* By Sarah Orne Jewett. New Haven: College and University P, 1966.

———. "Jewett to Dresel: 33 Letters." *Colby Library Quarterly* 11 (March 1975): 13–49.

Cather, Willa. *April Twilights (1903).* Ed. Bernice Slote. Lincoln: U of Nebraska P, 1968.

———. *Early Novels and Stories.* New York: Library of America, 1987.

———. *The Kingdom of Art.* Ed. Bernice Slote. Lincoln: U of Nebraska P, 1966.

———. *My Ántonia.* Boston: Houghton Mifflin, 1918.

———. *Not Under Forty.* 1936. New York: Knopf, 1964.

———. *The Novels and Stories of Willa Cather.* Boston: Houghton Mifflin, 1937.

———. *Obscure Destinies.* New York: Knopf, 1932.

———. *The Old Beauty and Others.* 1948. New York: Vintage, 1976.

———. *O Pioneers!* Boston: Houghton Mifflin, 1913.

———. Preface. *The Country of the Pointed Firs and Other Stories.* By Sarah Orne Jewett. Garden City, N.Y.: Doubleday, 1956. Unpaged.

———. *Sapphira and the Slave Girl.* New York: Knopf, 1940.

———. *Shadows on the Rock.* New York: Knopf, 1931.

———. *The Song of the Lark.* 1915. Lincoln: U of Nebraska P, 1978.

———. *The Troll Garden.* Ed. James Woodress. 1905. Lincoln: U of Nebraska P, 1987.

———. *Willa Cather in Person.* Ed. L. Brent Bohlke. Lincoln: U of Nebraska P, 1987.

———. *Willa Cather on Writing.* Ed. Stephen Tennant. New York: Knopf, 1949.

———. *Willa Cather's Collected Short Fiction 1892–1912.* Ed. Virginia Faulkner. Lincoln: U of Nebraska P, 1970.

Cixous, Hélène. "The Laugh of the Medusa." Trans. Keith Cohen and Paula Cohen. *New French Feminisms.* Ed. Elaine Marks and Isabelle de Courtivron. Amherst: U of Massachusetts P, 1980.

Coultrap-McQuin, Susan. *Doing Literary Business: American Women Writers in the Nineteenth Century.* Chapel Hill: U of North Carolina P, 1990.

Cournos, John. Rev. of *Delta Wedding,* by Eudora Welty. *New York Sun* 15 April 1946: 21.

Dearborn, Mary. *Pocahontas's Daughters: Gender and Ethnicity in American Culture.* New York: Oxford UP, 1986.

Demmin, Julia, and Daniel Curley. "Golden Apples and Silver Apples." Prenshaw 242–57.

Devlin, Albert J. *Eudora Welty's Chronicle: A Story of Mississippi Life.* Jackson: U P of Mississippi, 1983.

Donovan, Josephine. *After the Fall: The Demeter-Persephone Myth in Wharton, Cather, and Glasgow.* University Park: Pennsylvania State UP, 1989.

———. *New England Local Color Literature: A Women's Tradition.* New York: Frederick Ungar, 1983.

———. *Sarah Orne Jewett.* New York: Frederick Ungar, 1980.

———. "Silence or Capitulation: Pre-Patriarchal Mothers' Gardens in Jewett and Freeman." *Studies in Short Fiction* 23 (Winter 1986): 43–48.

———. "Toward a Women's Poetics." *Tulsa Studies in Women's Literature* 3 (1984): 99–110.

Douglas, Ann. *The Femininization of American Culture.* 1977. New York: Avon, 1978.

DuPlessis, Rachel Blau. *Writing Beyond the Ending: Narrative Strategies of Twentieth-Century Women Writers.* Bloomington: Indiana UP, 1985.

Eakin, Paul John. "Sarah Orne Jewett and the Meaning of Country Life." *American Literature* 38 (Jan. 1967): 508–31.

Earnest, Ernest. *The American Eve in Fact and Fiction, 1775–1914.* Urbana: U of Illinois P, 1974.

Eliade, Mircea. *The Sacred and the Profane.* Trans. Willard R. Trask. New York: Harcourt, Brace, and World, 1959.

Evans, Augusta J. *St. Elmo.* Laurel, N.Y.: Lightyear P, 1984.

Ferguson, Mary Anne. "*Losing Battles* as a Comic Epic in Prose." Prenshaw 305–24.

Ferrero, Pat, Elaine Hedges, and Julie Silber. *Hearts and Hands: The Influence of Women and Quilts on American Society.* San Francisco: Quilt Digest P, 1987.

Fetterley, Judith, ed. *Provisions.* Bloomington: Indiana UP, 1985.

———. *The Resisting Reader: A Feminist Approach to American Fiction.* Bloomington: Indiana UP, 1978.

Folsom, Marcia McClintock. " 'Tact Is a Kind of Mind-Reading': Empathetic Style in Sarah Orne Jewett's *The Country of the Pointed Firs.*" Nagel 66–78.

Fox-Genovese, Elizabeth. *Within the Plantation Household: Black and White Women of the Old South.* Chapel Hill: U of North Carolina P, 1989.

[Freeman], Mary E. Wilkins. *The Fair Lavinia and Others.* New York: Harper, 1907.

———. *A Humble Romance and Other Stories.* New York: Harper and Brothers, 1887.

————. *The Infant Sphinx: Collected Letters of Mary E. Wilkins Freeman.* Ed. Brent L. Kendrick. Metuchen, N.J.: Scarecrow P, 1985.

————. *A New England Nun and Other Stories.* 1891. Ridgewood, N.J.: Gregg P, 1967.

————. *Silence and Other Stories.* New York: Harper, 1898.

Frye, Joanna. *Living Stories, Telling Lives: Women and the Novel in Contemporary Experience.* Ann Arbor: U of Michigan P, 1986.

Fryer, Judith. *Felicitous Space: The Imaginative Structures of Edith Wharton and Willa Cather.* Chapel Hill: U of North Carolina P, 1986.

Garland, Hamlin. *Hamlin Garland's Diaries.* Ed. Donald Pizer. San Marino: Huntington Library, 1968.

Gelfant, Blanche. "The Forgotten Reaping-Hook: Sex in *My Ántonia.*" Murphy 147–64.

George, Benjamin. "The French-Canadian Connection: Willa Cather as a Canadian Writer." Murphy 269–79.

Gerlach, John. *Toward the End: Closure and Structure in the American Short Story.* University: U of Alabama P, 1985.

Gilbert, Sandra M., and Susan Gubar. *The Madwoman in the Attic: The Woman Writer and the Nineteenth-Century Literary Imagination.* New Haven: Yale UP, 1979.

Gilligan, Carol. *In a Different Voice: Psychological Theory and Women's Development.* Cambridge: Harvard UP, 1982.

Glasser, Leah Blatt. "Mary E. Wilkins Freeman: The Stranger in the Mirror." *Massachusetts Review* 25 (Summer 1984): 323–39.

Gwin, Minrose C. *Black and White Women of the Old South.* Knoxville: U of Tennessee P, 1985.

H.D. [Hilda Doolittle]. *Hermetic Definition.* New York: New Directions, 1972.

Habegger, Alfred. *Gender, Fantasy, and Realism in American Literature.* New York: Columbia UP, 1982.

Hamner, Eugenie Lambert. "The Unknown, Well-Known Child in Cather's Last Novel." *Women's Studies* 11 (1984): 347–57.

Heilbrun, Carolyn G. *Writing a Woman's Life.* New York: Norton, 1988.

Hicks, Granville. "The Case Against Willa Cather." *Willa Cather and Her Critics.* Ed. James Schroeter. Ithaca: Cornell UP, 1967. 139–47.

Hirsch, David. "Subdued Meaning in 'A New England Nun.'" *Studies in Short Fiction* 2 (1965): 124–36.

Holstein, Jonathan. "The American Block Quilt." *The Heart of Pennsylvania: Symposium Papers.* Ed. Jeanette Lasansky. Lewisburg, Pa.: Union County Historical Society, 1986. 16–27.

Howells, William Dean. *A Hazard of New Fortunes.* Ed. David Nordloh et al. Bloomington: Indiana UP, 1976.

————. Rev. of *Deephaven,* by Sarah Orne Jewett. 1877. Nagel 25–26.

Irigaray, Luce. "And the One Doesn't Stir Without the Other." Trans. Hélène Vivienne Wenzel. *Signs* 7 (Autumn 1981): 50–67.

———. "This Sex Which Is Not One." Trans. Claudia Reeder. *New French Feminisms*. Ed. Elaine Marks and Isabelle de Courtivron. Amherst: U of Massachusetts P, 1980. 99–106.

James, Henry. Rev. of *We and Our Neighbors*, by Harriet Beecher Stowe. Ammons, *Critical Essays* 210–11.

Jehlen, Myra. "Archimedes and the Paradox of Feminist Criticism." *Signs* 6 (Summer 1981): 575–601.

Jewett, Sarah Orne. *The Country of the Pointed Firs and Other Stories*. Ed. Mary Ellen Chase. New York: Norton, 1981.

———. *Deephaven.* 1877. Boston: Houghton Mifflin, 1893.

———. *Letters of Sarah Orne Jewett.* Ed. Annie Fields. Boston: Houghton Mifflin, 1911.

———. "Looking Back on Girlhood." *Uncollected Short Fiction of Sarah Orne Jewett.* Ed. Richard Cary. Waterville, Me.: Colby College P, 1971.

———. *Sarah Orne Jewett Letters.* Ed. Richard Cary. Waterville, Me.: Colby College P, 1967.

Jones, Jacqueline. *Labor of Love, Labor of Sorrow: Black Women, Work, and the Family from Slavery to the Present.* New York: Basic, 1985.

Kelley, Mary. *Private Woman, Public Stage: Literary Domesticity in Nineteenth-Century America.* New York: Oxford UP, 1984.

Kerr, Elizabeth. "The World of Eudora Welty's Women." Prenshaw 132–48.

Klapp, Orrin E. *Ritual and Cult: A Sociological Interpretation.* Washington, D.C.: Public Affairs Press, 1951.

Kolodny, Annette. *The Lay of the Land: Metaphor as Experience and History in American Life and Letters.* Chapel Hill: U of North Carolina P, 1975.

Koppelman, Susan. Afterword. *May Your Days Be Merry and Bright: Christmas Stories by Women.* Ed. Susan Koppelman. 1988. New York: New American Library, 1989. 255–59.

Kreyling, Michael. *Author and Agent: Eudora Welty and Diarmuid Russell.* New York: Farrar, Straus, Giroux, 1991.

———. *Eudora Welty's Achievement of Order.* Baton Rouge: Louisiana State UP, 1980.

Kristeva, Julia. "Women's Time." Trans. Alice Jardine. *Signs* 7 (Autumn 1981): 5–25.

Lambert, Deborah G. "The Defeat of a Hero: Autonomy and Sexuality in *My Ántonia.*" *American Literature* 53 (Jan. 1982): 676–90.

Lears, T. J. Jackson. *No Place of Grace: Antimodernism and the Transformation of American Culture 1880–1920.* New York: Pantheon, 1981.

Leitch, Thomas M. *What Stories Are: Narrative Theory and Interpretation.* University Park: Pennsylvania State UP, 1986.

Leonardi, Susan J. "Recipes for Reading: Summer Pasta, Lobster à la Riseholme, and Key Lime Pie." *PMLA* 104 (May 1989): 340–47.

Loyd, Bonnie. "Women, Home, and Status." *Housing and Identity: Cross-Cultural Perspectives*. Ed. James S. Duncan. New York: Holmes and Meier, 1982. 181–97.

Lukacs, John. "The Bourgeois Interior." *American Scholar* 39 (Autumn 1970): 616–30.

Mailloux, Stephen. *Interpretive Conventions: The Reader in the Study of American Fiction*. Ithaca: Cornell UP, 1982.

Manning, Carol. *With Ears Opening Like Morning Glories: Eudora Welty and the Love of Storytelling*. Westport, Ct.: Greenwood, 1985.

Marcus, Jane. "Invincible Mediocrity: The Private Selves of Public Women." *The Private Self: Theory and Practice of Women's Autobiographical Writings*. Ed. Shari Benstock. Chapel Hill: U of North Carolina P, 1988. 115–46.

———. "Still Practice, A/Wrested Alphabet: Toward a Feminist Aesthetic." *Tulsa Studies in Women's Literature* 3 (1984): 79–98.

Matthews, Glenna. *"Just a Housewife": The Rise and Fall of Domesticity in America*. New York: Oxford UP, 1987.

Matthiessen, F. O. *Sarah Orne Jewett*. Boston: Houghton Mifflin, 1929.

Mauss, Marcel. *The Gift*. Trans. Dan Cunnison. New York: Norton, 1967.

Mayers, Ozzie J. "The Power of the Pin: Sewing as an Act of Rootedness in American Literature." *College English* 50 (Oct. 1988): 664–80.

Meese, Elizabeth. *Crossing the Double-Cross: The Practice of Feminist Criticism*. Chapel Hill: U of North Carolina P, 1986.

Miller, J. Hillis. "Narrative." *Critical Terms for Literary Study*. Ed. Frank Lentricchia and Thomas McLaughlin. Chicago: U of Chicago P, 1990. 66–79.

Miller, Nancy K. *The Heroine's Text: Readings in the French and English Novel, 1722–1782*. New York: Columbia UP, 1980.

Moers, Ellen. *Literary Women*. Garden City, N.Y.: Anchor, 1977.

Moore, Carol A. "Aunt Studney's Sack," *Southern Review* 16 (Summer 1980): 591–96.

More, Paul Elmer. *Shelburne Essays, Second Series*. New York: Putnam, 1909.

———. "A Writer of New England." Cary, *Appreciation of Sarah Orne Jewett* 49–51.

Murphy, John J., ed. *Critical Essays on Willa Cather*. Boston: G. K. Hall, 1984.

Nagel, Gwen, ed. *Critical Essays on Sarah Orne Jewett*. Boston: G. K. Hall, 1984.

Nelson, Robert J. *Willa Cather and France: In Search of the Lost Language*. Urbana: U of Illinois P, 1988.

Oates, Joyce Carol. "The Art of Eudora Welty." *Shenandoah* 20 (Spring 1969): 54–55.

O'Brien, Sharon. *Willa Cather: The Emerging Voice*. New York: Oxford, 1987.

Ortner, Sherry B. "Is Female to Male as Nature Is to Culture?" *Feminist Studies* 1 (Fall 1972): 5–31.

Palmer, Phyllis. *Domesticity and Dirt: Housewives and Domestic Servants in the United States 1920–1945*. Philadelphia: Temple UP, 1989.

Parker, Gail. *The Oven Birds: American Women on Womanhood 1820–1920*. Garden City, N.Y.: Anchor, 1972.

Parker, Rozsika. *The Subversive Stitch: Embroidery and the Making of the Feminine*. London: Women's P, 1984.

Pattee, F. L. *A History of American Literature Since 1870*. New York: Century, 1917.

Pratt, Annis. *Archetypal Patterns in Women's Fiction*. Bloomington: Indiana UP, 1981.

————. "The New Feminist Criticism." *College English* 32 (May 1971): 872–78.

Prenshaw, Peggy Whitman, ed. *Eudora Welty: Critical Essays*. Jackson: UP of Mississippi, 1979.

————. "Woman's World, Man's Place." *Eudora Welty: A Form of Thanks*. Ed. Louis J. Dollarhide and Ann J. Abadie. Jackson: UP of Mississippi, 1979. 46–76.

Price, Reynolds. "A Form of Thanks." *Eudora Welty: A Form of Thanks*. Ed. Louis J. Dollarhide and Ann J. Abadie. Jackson: UP of Mississippi, 1979. 128–38.

————. "The Onlooker, Smiling: An Early Reading of *The Optimist's Daughter*." Bloom 75–88.

Pryse, Marjorie. "An Uncloistered 'New England Nun.'" *Studies in Short Fiction* 20 (Fall 1983): 289–95.

————. Introduction. *The Country of the Pointed Firs and Other Stories*. By Sarah Orne Jewett. Ed. Mary Ellen Chase. New York: Norton, 1981.

————. "Women 'at Sea': Feminist Realism in Sarah Orne Jewett's 'The Foreigner.'" Nagel 89–98.

Rabuzzi, Kathryn Allen. *The Sacred and the Feminine: Toward a Theology of Housework*. New York: Seabury, 1982.

Randall, John. *The Landscape and the Looking Glass*. Westport, Ct.: Greenwood, 1960.

Rich, Adrienne. *The Dream of a Common Language: Poems 1974–77*. New York: Norton, 1978.

Roberson, Ruth Haislip, ed. *North Carolina Quilts*. Chapel Hill: U of North Carolina P, 1988.

Roberts, Joan I. "Pictures of Power and Powerlessness: A Personal Synthesis." *Beyond Intellectual Sexism*. Ed. Joan I. Roberts. New York: David McKay, 1976. 14–60.

Robinson, Marilynne. *Housekeeping*. 1981. New York: Bantam, 1982.

Roman, Judith. "A Closer Look at the Jewett-Fields Relationship." Nagel 119–34.

Rosowski, Susan J. Foreword. *Cather's Kitchens: Foodways in Literature and Life*. Ed. Welsch and Welsch. ix–xv.

————. *The Voyage Perilous: Willa Cather's Romanticism*. Lincoln: U of Nebraska P, 1986.

Ross, Mary Ellen, and Cheryl Lynn Ross. "Mothers, Infants and the Psychoanalytical Study of Ritual." *Signs* 9 (Autumn 1983): 26–39.

Rybcyzynski, Witold. *Home: A Short History of an Idea*. New York: Viking, 1986.

Schmidt, Peter. "Sibyls in Welty's Stories." Trouard 78–93.

Sergeant, Elizabeth Shepley. *Willa Cather: A Memoir.* Philadelphia: Lippincott, 1953.

Shapiro, Laura. *Perfection Salad: Women and Cooking at the Turn of the Century.* New York: Farrar, Straus and Giroux, 1986.

Sherman, Sarah Way. *Sarah Orne Jewett: An American Persephone.* Hanover, N.H.: UP of New England, 1989.

Showalter, Elaine. *A Literature of Their Own: British Women Novelists from Brontë to Lessing.* Princeton: Princeton UP, 1977.

———, ed. *The New Feminist Criticism: Women, Literature and Theory.* New York: Pantheon, 1985.

———. "Piecing and Writing." *The Poetics of Gender.* Ed. Nancy K. Miller. New York: Columbia UP, 1986. 222–47.

———. "Toward a Feminist Poetics." Showalter, *The New Feminist Criticism* 125–43.

Skaggs, Merrill Maguire. "Morgana's Apples and Pears." Prenshaw 220–41.

Sklar, Kathryn Kish. *Catharine Beecher: A Study in American Domesticity.* New Haven: Yale UP, 1973.

Smith-Rosenberg, Carroll. "The Female World of Love and Ritual." *Signs* 1 (Autumn 1975): 1–29.

Solomon, Barbara H. Introduction. *Short Fiction of Sarah Orne Jewett and Mary Wilkins Freeman.* Ed. Barbara H. Solomon. New York: New American Library, 1979.

Spacks, Patricia Meyer. *The Female Imagination.* 1975. New York: Avon, 1976.

Stouck, David. *Willa Cather's Imagination.* Lincoln: U of Nebraska P, 1975.

———. "Willa Cather's Last Four Books." *Novel* 7 (Fall 1973): 41–53.

Stowe, Harriet Beecher. *The Minister's Wooing.* 1859. Hartford: Stowe-Day Foundation, 1978.

———. *My Wife and I.* 1871. Boston: Houghton Mifflin, 1876.

———. *The Pearl of Orr's Island.* 1862. Boston: Houghton Mifflin, 1896.

———. *Pink and White Tyranny.* 1871. Boston: Houghton Mifflin, 1898.

———. *Poganuc People.* 1878. Hartford: Stowe-Day Foundation, 1977.

———. *Uncle Tom's Cabin.* 1852. New York: Signet, 1966.

———. *We and Our Neighbors.* 1873. Boston: Houghton Mifflin, 1898.

Strasser, Susan. *Never Done: A History of American Housework.* New York: Pantheon, 1982.

Sundquist, Eric. "The Country of the Blue." *American Realism: New Essays.* Ed. Eric Sundquist. Baltimore: Johns Hopkins UP, 1982. 3–24.

———. *Home as Found: Authority and Genealogy in Nineteenth-Century American Literature.* Baltimore: Johns Hopkins UP, 1979.

Theriot, Nancy M. *The Bio-Social Construction of Femininity: Mothers and Daughters in Nineteenth-Century America.* New York: Greenwood, 1988.

Toth, Susan Allen. "Defiant Light: A Positive View of Mary Wilkins Freeman." *New England Quarterly* 4 (March 1973): 82–93.

Trilling, Diana. Rev. of *Delta Wedding,* by Eudora Welty. *Nation* 11 May 1946: 578.

Trouard, Dawn, ed. *Eudora Welty: The Eye of the Storyteller.* Kent, Oh.: Kent State UP, 1989.

Turner, Victor. "Process, System, and Symbol: A New Anthropological Synthesis." *Daedalus* 1 (Summer 1977): 61–80.

Vande Kieft, Ruth M. *Eudora Welty.* New York: Twayne, 1987.

———. "Eudora Welty: Visited and Revisited." *Mississippi Quarterly* 39 (Fall 1986): 455–79.

Voelker, Paul D. "*The Country of the Pointed Firs:* A Novel by Sarah Orne Jewett." Cary, *Appreciation of Sarah Orne Jewett* 238–48.

Warhol, Robyn R. *Gendered Interventions: Narrative Discourse in the Victorian Novel.* New Brunswick, N.J.: Rutgers UP, 1989.

Warner, Susan. *The Wide, Wide World.* 1850. New York: Feminist P, 1987.

Warner, Sylvia Townsend. "Item: One Empty House." *New Yorker* 26 March 1956: 131–38.

Welsch, Roger L., and Linda K. Welsch. *Cather's Kitchens: Foodways in Literature and Life.* Lincoln: U of Nebraska P, 1987.

Welter, Barbara. *Dimity Convictions: The American Woman in the Nineteenth Century.* Athens: Ohio UP, 1976.

Welty, Eudora. *The Collected Stories of Eudora Welty.* New York: Harcourt Brace Jovanovich, 1980. This volume contains Welty's three previously published collections: *A Curtain of Green; The Wide Net;* and *The Bride of the Innisfallen;* plus two previously uncollected stories.

———. *Conversations with Eudora Welty.* Ed. Peggy Whitman Prenshaw. Jackson: UP of Mississippi, 1989.

———. *Delta Wedding.* 1946. New York: Harcourt Brace Jovanovich, 1974.

———. *The Eye of the Story: Selected Essays and Reviews.* New York: Random House, 1977.

———. *Losing Battles.* New York: Random House, 1970.

———. *One Writer's Beginnings.* Cambridge: Harvard UP, 1984.

———. *The Optimist's Daughter.* 1969. New York: Random House, 1978.

———. "The Reading and Writing of Short Stories." *Atlantic Monthly* Feb. 1949: 54–58; March 1949: 46–49.

Westling, Louise. *Sacred Groves and Ravaged Gardens: The Fiction of Eudora Welty, Carson McCullers, and Flannery O'Connor.* Athens: U of Georgia P, 1985.

White, Deborah Gray. *Ar'n't I a Woman? Female Slaves in the Plantation South.* New York: Norton, 1985.

Wilson, Monica. *Rituals of Kinship Among the Nyakyusa.* London: Oxford UP, 1957.

Wolff, Janet. *Feminine Sentences: Essays on Women and Culture.* Berkeley: U of California P, 1990.

Woodress, James. *Willa Cather: A Literary Life.* Lincoln: U of Nebraska P, 1987.

———. *Willa Cather: Her Life and Art.* New York: Pegasus, 1970.

Woolf, Virginia. *A Room of One's Own.* New York: Harcourt Brace and World, 1929.

———. *To the Lighthouse.* 1927. New York: Harcourt Brace Jovanovich, 1955.

Yaeger, Patricia. "Eudora Welty and the Dialogic Imagination." *PMLA* 99 (1984): 955–73.

———. *Honey-mad Women: Emancipatory Strategies in Women's Writing.* New York: Columbia UP, 1987.

Index